ROBERT J. SPJUT

TRANSACTION RISK

A Legal Guide to Contractual Management Strategies

TORT TRIAL & INSURANCE PRACTICE
AMERICAN BAR ASSOCIATION

Cover design by Nick Panos/ABA Publishing.

Library of Congress Cataloging-in-Publication Data

Names: Spjut, Robert J., author.
Title: Transaction risks : using contractual terms / R. J. Spjut.
Description: Chicago : American Bar Association, 2018. | Includes index.
Identifiers: LCCN 2018028184 | ISBN 9781641051910 (pbk.)
Subjects: LCSH: Impossibility of performance—United States—Language. | Contracts—Economic aspects—United States. | Risk management—Law and legislation—United States.
Classification: LCC KF832 .S68 2018 | DDC 346.7302/2—dc23
LC record available at https://lccn.loc.gov/2018028184

Printed in the United States of America.

22 21 20 19 18 5 4 3 2 1

ISBN: 978-1-64105-191-0

To Francesca, Nadine, and Sue

Contents

PART IV
Third-Party and Uncontrollable Event Risks

About the Author

R. J. Spjut joined Pillsbury Winthrop Shaw Pittman LLP in 1988. During his nearly thirty years of practice there, he concentrated on commercial, international, and project finance transactions. He advised on a number of significant infrastructure projects in Africa, Asia, Australia, Europe, and North and South America and in the energy, telecommunications, and other industries. He was a partner in the firm's San Francisco and Hong Kong offices. He retired at the end of 2017.

Spjut served as cochair of the Uniform Commercial Code Subcommittee of the California State Bar's Business Law Section. He authored numerous articles published in scholarly legal and other journals, trade publications, and books. He also coauthored a guide to secured transactions in California under Revised Article 9 of the Uniform Commercial Code.

Before joining Pillsbury, he taught law at The Queen's University of Belfast, University of Khartoum, University of Kent at Canterbury, University of San Diego School of Law, and St. Thomas University, School of Law.

He received a JD from University of San Francisco School of Law in 1971 and an LLM from London School of Economics and Political Science in 1972. He is admitted to practice in California and Florida.

Acknowledgments

The author gives special thanks to Reagan Simpson and Robert Redemann for suggestions that shaped the writer's research and rough drafts into an intelligible presentation. The author is indebted to Jeff Christie for reading and commenting on an earlier draft and urging his persistence. Tireless encouragement to continue with the work came from the author's wife, Sue; daughters, Francesca and Nadine; and the American Bar Association editorial board, in particular, Reagan Simpson, Robert Redemann, and Sarah Forbes Orwig. Scott Dickerson generously corrected grammatical and other mistakes. All remaining errors are those of the author.

Part I

Overview of Transaction Risk Management

1

The Subjective Perspective

TRANSACTIONS AND CONTRACTS

Black's Law Dictionary offers four definitions of transaction:

- an "[a]ct of transacting or an instance of conducting any business or other dealings; esp[ecially] the formation, performance, or discharge of a contract";
- "something performed or carried out; a business agreement or exchange";
- "any activity involving two or more persons; [and]
- "[a]n agreement that is intended by the parties to prevent or end a dispute and in which they make reciprocal concessions."[1]

Only the first three definitions are relevant here; the last pertains to civil law contracts. A contract, by comparison, is narrowly defined as "[a]n agreement between two or more persons creating obligations that are enforceable or otherwise recognizable at law."[2] Whereas the parties' contract is their legal agreement, their transaction includes

---

1 Black's Law Dictionary 1726 (10th ed. 2014).

2 *Id.* at 388.

activities earlier and later than formation of the contract, including the negotiation and performance of their obligations under such a contract. Transaction has an even broader meaning, including in some more general or vague sense, the carrying on of business, conduct, and exchange, which may or may not relate to any specific contract.

This difference between the two—contract and transaction—is relevant to risk management because a successful outcome of an exchange according to the contract may not be the same as the successful outcome of the exchange the parties envisaged when negotiating the transaction. Simply stated, a successful outcome of a contract is the exchange of the performances to which the parties have legally agreed, no more or less. So long as each party gets what it agreed to receive, the deal is a success. If one party receives what it bargained for and the other does not, the deal is a success for the former but not the latter. Conceived as part of a plan with an objective, success is the satisfactory completion of the tasks to be completed during each phase, on time and on budget, and is the realization of the desired objective. So conceived, a transaction is akin to a project that must be planned and implemented, with the outcome favorable or not. The exchange of performances is the centerpiece of this effort, but its success does not ensure that the transaction will be a success.

EXPECTATION, HOPE, AND ASSUMPTION

Expectation

The starting point for identifying transaction risk is the nebulous, often half-baked subjective expectation and hope of a party, whether or not reduced to terms stated in a contract, that jurists eschew. This is because, by definition, a successful transaction is the realization of the benefits a party expected, hoped, or otherwise desired to realize from an exchange with another party or a series of exchanges with multiple parties, all at a cost and on a schedule also as anticipated. This is an initial definition of a successful transaction; it will be modified later in this chapter. It follows that expectation, hope, and desire form the starting point for articulating the benchmarks of success and failure, even if they vary from the terms of the contract. Also, expectation and hope may be misguided, inasmuch as a party may wrongly believe it needs or does not need something (a topic to which we will return later), but what is important is that a party understands what it expects or hopes will be achieved, what tasks it expects to complete to do so, and how it anticipates contingencies will be addressed.

The textbook case *Frigaliment Importing Co. v. B.N.S. International Sales Corp.*[3] illustrates why a party's expectation, and not the terms of a contract, must be the initial measure of success or failure in a transaction. A trader in New York agreed to sell chickens to a buyer in Switzerland; the contract described these chickens as "US Fresh Frozen Chicken, Grade A, Government Inspected, Eviscerated 2½–3 lbs. and 1½–2 lbs. each, all chickens individually wrapped in [C]ryovac, packed in secured fiber cartons or wooden boxes, suitable for export."[4] The buyer, who expected young birds suitable for broiling and frying, received birds suitable for stewing; it protested and sued the seller for breach. Circuit Judge Henry Friendly, who heard the case, began his decision by saying, "Assuming that both parties were acting in good faith, the case nicely illustrates Holmes' remark 'that the making of a contract depends not on the agreement of two minds in one intention, but on the agreement of two sets of external signs—not on the parties' having meant the same thing but on their having said the same thing.'"[5] He acknowledged that "chicken" as used by the parties was ambiguous and had to be interpreted.[6] He considered and rejected the buyer's argument that chickens one and a half to two pounds must be young, as chickens, like apples, may come in all sizes.[7] He also rejected the buyer's contention that "chicken" meant young chickens in the poultry trade. The evidence of this was insufficient for Judge Friendly, who said the usage had to be proved to be so well-established that the seller's knowledge of it could be inferred, and this proof had not been supplied.[8] The buyer also pointed to the practice of a large poultry supplier that published prices separately for "chickens," which included broiler, fryers, and certain other categories, and "fowl," which included stewing chickens.[9] The seller's expert, who operated an eviscerating plant, said a "chicken" is "everything except a goose, a duck, and a turkey."[10] The buyer in its favor pointed to the prevailing price

---

[3] 190 F. Supp. 116 (S.D.N.Y. 1960).

[4] *Id.* at 117.

[5] *Id.*

[6] *Id.* at 118.

[7] *Id.*

[8] *Id.* at 119.

[9] *Id.*

[10] *Id.* at 119–20.

for broilers at thirty-five cents and thirty-seven cents per pound, when the price for stewing chickens was thirty cents per pound; thirty-three cents per pound was closer to the price of broilers than stewing chickens. Judge Friendly dismissed this evidence: "Plaintiff must have expected defendant to make some profit—certainly it could not have expected defendant deliberately to incur a loss."[11] He juxtaposed the "subjective intentions" or expectations of the parties with the objective meaning of "chicken": "Defendant's subjective intent would not be significant if this did not coincide with an objective meaning of 'chicken.' Here it did coincide with one of the dictionary meanings, with the definition in the Department of Agriculture regulations to which the contract made at least oblique reference, with at least some usage in the trade, with the realities of the market, and with what plaintiff's spokesman had said."[12] Judge Friendly acknowledged how a party's "subjective intention" or understanding or expectation about what it would buy or sell can differ from its "objective intention." Only the latter is relevant in court.[13] Having reviewed all the evidence, the judge concluded the buyer failed to prove "chicken" had the meaning it claimed, and because the buyer had the burden of proof, its claim failed.[14]

If the performances are taken in isolation from the buyer's objectives or desired benefits, it received what it bargained for because the court found that the buyer had not proved that it had bargained for anything more than the stewing chickens it received. So viewed, the transaction was certainly not a failure for the buyer, though this is clearly not the case because the buyer considered what it received to be inferior to what it thought it bargained for. To make sense of this disappointment, the outcome of the transaction must be assessed according to what the buyer expected, not contractually agreed, to receive. What went wrong in the *Frigaliment* transaction occurred when the buyer agreed on the terms with the seller because the buyer either chose the wrong counterparty, which did not share its understanding of what the word "chicken" meant, or chose the wrong words to specify the type of chickens the seller was to deliver. In the latter case, it failed to get the documentation sufficiently precise such that the seller would have no choice but to deliver the expected young birds. So viewed, the terms of the contract, instead of

[11] *Id.* at 120.
[12] *Id.* at 121.
[13] *Id.*
[14] *Id.*

serving as the measure of success, are themselves the outcome of the events that contributed to the ultimate outcome, successful or otherwise. Whether the outcome is successful turns on whether the seller's performance was consistent with the buyer's expectations, which are the benchmark of a successful outcome, not the terms of the contract.

Hope

Expectation is only one measure of success in a transaction, as hope often plays the role expectation occupied in *Frigaliment*, where the buyer presumably anticipated that whatever bird it would receive would be young. Where expectation connotes a level of certainty that an event will occur, hope connotes optimism tinged with well-justified doubt. Routine transactions in which at least one party repeats its performances with different parties generate expectations, not just hopes, about what will be exchanged. *Frigaliment* was probably such a case. In these deals, the party repeating a type of transaction can specify the actions that must be completed and can also forecast with near certainty when they must, and will be, completed, subject to interruption by contingent events. In industries in which a party performs with a high level of predictability, those receiving that performance come to expect it. In others, where the performance is less predictable, they hope for the best. Airlines, for example, publish schedules and endeavor to operate flights accordingly, with the result that passengers expect, albeit skeptically, on-time departures and arrivals, at least on some routes and with some airlines, in the absence of disruptive events outside the carriers' control; passengers on other carriers only hope for the best. In a deal that is novel or relatively novel to a party, it may cast about for comparable deals in its effort to predict how the novel deal might turn out. This is as true for a corporation embarking on a major acquisition as it is for the car and home buyer; while the car or house can be identified with particularity, the buyer may harbor hopes about what intangible benefits, such as status, the purchase will yield. In transactions in which chance plays a critical role, a party can but hope for a successful outcome. A rational lottery ticket buyer does not expect to win; she expects to receive a valid lottery ticket and for the contest to be operated by the rules, and she hopes, albeit faintly, to win. She does not expect to realize the benefits of winning—the lifestyle and whatever she hopes to acquire with the winnings—because she does not expect to win. That faint hope is the key driver to the buyer's purchase of the ticket: lottery ticket buyers often indulge in flights of fancy about what they will do with their winnings, while acknowledging winning is most unlikely. While a rational party will accept a dashed hope better than it will accept a disappointed expectation, because it sanguinely recognizes the uncertainty of the outcome, hope often drives parties into deals as passionately as expectation; the failure to receive what was hoped for nonetheless reflects an adverse outcome. Hope plays a significant role in cutting-edge, experimental, and other major transactions. As such, hope, like expectation, serves as another measure of the outcome of a transaction, whether or not those wishes are manifest in the contract.

Leasco Corporation v. Taussig,[15] in which the parties were seasoned players in mergers and acquisitions, illustrates how hope plays a key role in a major commercial deal. Leasco, started in 1961 by Saul Steinberg, then twenty-two years old, leased small office data-processing equipment, expanded rapidly, and in 1965 went public, raising $750,000 in an initial public offering. It then began buying businesses. During a five-month period ending in September 1968, it acquired 91 percent of the shares, notwithstanding the target's opposition, of Reliance Insurance Companies of Philadelphia, which had been underwriting fire and casualty insurance policies since 1817. Reliance was attractive to Steinberg because, like other insurance companies, it held substantial cash reserves to meet potential insured claims that could be released for other acquisitions. Leasco's equity capital increased from $70 million to $236 million. Leasco's shares were trading at $140, a 5,400 percent increase since its initial public offering in 1965.

In November 1968, Leasco began buying Chemical Bank shares and in January 1969 drafted a tender offer to Chemical Bank's shareholders but decided against releasing it. William Renchard, chairman of Chemical, learned of Leasco's plans and organized a counterattack, first leaking news of Leasco's plans to the press, then devising a plan to have large blocks of Leasco's stock dumped on the market, suggesting to other banks that they not lend money to the acquirer, and having a bill introduced in the U.S. Senate that would make bank acquisitions more difficult. New York Governor Nelson Rockefeller urged the state legislature to enact a similar law applicable to banks in New York. Leasco's shares had dropped to ninety-nine dollars in February, two weeks after Renchard's campaign began, and to seven dollars by May 1969.[16]

---

[15] 473 F.2d 777 (2d Cir. 1972).

[16] Davita Silfen Glasberg, The Power of Collective Purse Strings, ch. 4 (1989), http://publishing.cdlib.org/ucpressebooks/view?docId=ft4x0nb2jj&chunk.id=d0e3625&toc.depth=1&toc.id=d0e3625&brand=ucpress.

Steinberg, in the meantime, acquired Louis Berger, Inc. (Berger) and its subsidiary, Louis Berger Associates, an international civil engineering and consulting firm; after closing the acquisition, Leasco's vice president and general counsel, Frederick Jackson, hired Peter T. Taussig (who had civil engineering and law degrees and had practiced law—primarily concerned with construction contracts—in New York City for several years) as Berger's vice president and counsel.[17] Berger then incorporated McCreary-Koretsky International, Inc. (MKI) to acquire the assets of McCreary-Koretsky Engineers, Inc. (MKE), another civil engineering and consulting firm, based in California, which was facing potential bankruptcy because of a lawsuit by a client and income taxes owed to the federal government. The price agreed to was a percentage of MKI's profits. Taussig reviewed MKE's service contracts, balance sheet, and income statement. This acquisition closed in September 1970, and Taussig became vice president of MKI.[18] In December, Leasco's management decided to sell MKI because it lacked experience in the civil engineering business and disliked the income fluctuations characteristic of the industry.

Taussig offered to buy MKI and met Jackson to discuss price. Taussig estimated MKI's pretax earnings for the year ending September 20, 1971, would be $200,000, Jackson suggested that an appropriate sale price would be ten times that amount, or $2 million; they halved this amount, because under the agreement with MKE, MKI had to pay MKE 50 percent of its profits. In this manner, they landed on a $1 million purchase price. Leasco and Taussig signed the agreement for the sale of MKI in February 1971, with a closing date of April 15, later extended to May 28.

In March, Taussig received MKI's February income statement, reporting a $4,702 loss, which he learned, after traveling to San Francisco, had been caused by a design error on one of MKI's construction projects. This error also resulted in losses for the months of March and April. Taussig indicated to Jackson he might not go through with the purchase and refused to accept MKI's stock at the May 28 closing.

Leasco sued Taussig, who claimed mutual mistake, that a basic assumption of the contract was that the pretax earnings of MKI for the year ending September 30, 1971, would be $200,000, and misrepresentation

---

17 473 F.2d 777, 779.

18 *Id.*

that Leasco misrepresented MKI's financial condition.[19] The district court awarded Leasco $669,000 and Taussig appealed. Circuit Judge William Timbers began by distinguishing Taussig's claims: "The legal concept of 'mistake' is similar to the legal concept of 'misrepresentation' in that, under each, a party to a contract may be relieved from his obligations if he was unaware of certain material facts. 'Mistake,' however, is only such error as is made without representation or deception by the other party to the transaction."[20] He stated the rule that where the mistake is unilateral, the contract is not voidable, but where it is mutual, the contract is voidable. This was not a case of mutual mistake, even if both parties assumed, when calculating the purchase price, that MKI's earnings would be $200,000. "In the instant action, we hold that there was no mutual mistake. . . . Neither party intended to allow rescission of the agreement if, as it turned out, one party got a better bargain than had been anticipated."[21] The court also dismissed the misrepresentation claim and upheld the judgment. Taussig could not have expected that MKI would have $200,000 of pretax earnings. The court concluded he was too sophisticated a buyer to have harbored such a naïve expectation. Judge Timbers said, "Both parties had equal access to information indicating that such a projection would be highly unreliable. Indeed, Taussig probably knew more about the business of MKI than anyone else at Leasco since he originally had investigated it, he served as its vice president, and he was a liaison executive between Leasco and MKI."[22] It was thus inconceivable that Taussig could have considered any projection of MKI's income certain or had an expectation that the business would be profitable. The judge instead pointed to hope: "Both Taussig and Leasco may have hoped, but surely could not have been certain, that MKI would earn $200,000 in fiscal 1971. . . . The civil engineering and consulting business is personalized, highly technical, and extremely risky. . . . Neither party could safely assume that the projected earnings would be realized."[23]

Taussig may have been optimistic or even highly optimistic that the target earnings would be achieved, but he could not have expected this to be so. Jackson offered the number for the purpose of calculating the price of MKI. Like someone who bets on a proven winner in a horse

---

[19] *Id.* at 780.
[20] *Id.* at 781.
[21] *Id.* at 782.
[22] *Id.* at 781.
[23] *Id.*

race, Taussig bet on the target's projections. Moreover, he confused expectation and hope, what he hoped to realize with what he expected to receive from the seller. The deal failed for Taussig because his hopes about the benefits of the deal would not be realized.

Assumptions

The expectation and hope by which a successful transaction outcome is measured include completion of the actions and the occurrence of the events that must take place for a party to realize a desired benefit as well as the realization of those benefits. A party will usually expect its counterparty to perform fully its contractual obligations, and the counterparty's failure to perform as expected will constitute a disappointment. A party may also expect or hope a circumstance material to completion of a task or realization of a benefit exists. It may also expect or hope that events that must occur will occur and events that must not occur will not occur. We noted the lottery ticket buyer hopes, not expects, her numbers will be drawn. The failure of the event to occur as hoped is an unsuccessful outcome, even if the hope was faint. Such expectations and hopes are focused on key events that will yield the desired benefits rather than the benefits themselves. Just as an individual planning a trip might try to identify all the actions and events that might facilitate and impair her journey, a party planning a transaction might identify all the circumstances that must exist at contract formation and events that must occur and must not occur after contract formation for it to realize its desired benefits, on time and on budget, forming expectations and hopes concerning each.

However, all too often the party will have given no thought to such circumstances or events. The existence or nonexistence of such facts or the occurrence or nonoccurrence of such events may be so extraordinary that it is not surprising that the party has given it little or no consideration when planning the transaction and negotiating the contract, let alone addressing it in the contract.[24] This is not always the case, however; the

[24] An example is the cancellation of King Edward VII's coronation procession, due to his illness, in Krell v. Henry, [1903] 2 K.B. 740, [1900-3] All E.R. 20, 72 L.J. (K.B.) 794, 89 L.T. 328, 52 W.R. 246, 19 T.L.R. 711, 12 Digest (Repl.) 435 (Ct. App. 1903), where a renter agreed to rent a room in a flat in Pall Mall to view such procession. The renter refused to pay the agreed rent, the landlord sued, and the court held for the renter. Lord Justice Vaughan Williams described the cancelation of the coronation procession as "an event 'of

circumstances and contingencies may well be within contemplation. The response by the party to such facts when they prove to be different or to such events when they occur is often that the party assumed that such fact did or did not exist or that such an event would or would not occur. A sympathetic court will reformulate the point, saying that an assumption that such a fact existed or did not exist or that such an event would or would not occur was a basis on which the contract was made; in the former, the contract may be rescinded because of a mutual mistake of fact and in the latter because of frustration of contract or impossibility of performance. A statement that an assumption about some existing fact or future event has been made may be, first, an acknowledgment that no thought was given to the fact or event that the party assumed existed or did not exist or would or would not occur. If a party actually recognized that such fact might or might not exist or such an event would or would not occur, it either expected or hoped such fact did or did not exist or would or would not occur. Second, the statement is also one about expectation. An assumption of which a party making it is ignorant is functionally equivalent to an expectation or hope about the existence or nonexistence of the fact or occurrence or nonoccurrence of the assumed event; the party is disappointed when a fact proves to be different than assumed or an event that was assumed would not occur, occurs. What is meant is the party expects or hopes to be treated by others as if, all along, it contemplated that all matters to which it gave no thought would be as they normally are or in some sense were understood to be so, and by implication, such facts would or would not exist and such events would or would not occur.

Whether the law should recognize and somehow allow for such assumptions is not the concern here. Assumptions play a significant role in transactions: they supplement the conscious expectations on which transactions are premised. Just as expectations serve as the benchmarks by which a successful outcome is measured, assumptions about material facts and events serve as additional benchmarks where expectations about such facts and events are absent at contract formation.

Chic Organization, Ltd. v. Motown Record Corporation[25] illustrates how a party makes an assumption about an event, the occurrence or nonoccurrence of which will result in an unsuccessful outcome. Chic and Motown agreed that Chic would produce a record album for Motown

such a character that it cannot reasonably be supposed to have been in the contemplation of the contracting parties when made.'" [1903] 2 K.B. at 797.

[25] 582 F. Supp. 812 (S.D.N.Y. 1984).

with Diana Ross, a famous singer under exclusive contract with Motown. As a bonus, the contract also provided that if the sales of the record exceeded $1 million, then Chic could produce a second record with Ross. Chic produced the record, and its sales exceeded $1 million, but after Chic produced the first record and before Chic exercised its option to produce the second record, Ross's contract with Motown expired and Ross refused to do any further work for Motown.[26] Chic sued Motown for breach of contract, and Motown responded that Ross's decision not to do further work for Motown excused its failure to deliver her collaboration. It is interesting that Motown insisted, when the contract was negotiated, that Chic's two principals sign the contract, thus committing them to personally participate in the production of the record.[27] Chic did not do likewise with Ross, a fact that prompted the trial judge to ask Chic's lawyer who negotiated the contract if Ross's leaving Motown had occurred to him. "Well honestly, Judge," the lawyer answered, "it didn't even occur to me."[28] He elaborated, "She started as a child and like Stevie Wonder and all the other Motown people out of the original Motown and everyone assumed it was going on forever."[29]

His assumption—that Ross would stay indefinitely at Motown—was not as implausible as it seemed, with hindsight. Ross started her singing career as the fourth and final member of the Primettes in 1960, while still in high school. That year Berry Gordy Jr. incorporated Motown, and the following year the Primettes changed its name to the Supremes and signed a contract with Motown. Under contract with Motown, Ross was the Supremes' lead singer during the following decade, became a television show host in 1971, and started her career as an actress in 1972, starring in Motown's first film, a hit biography of Billie Holiday, for which she was nominated for the Academy Award as best actress and received a Golden Globe. Her hits during that period included an album of duets with Marvin Gaye (1975) and "Do You Know Where You're Going To." She costarred with Billy Dee Williams in Motown's film *Mahogany*. In 1978, Ross starred in another Motown film, *The Wiz*, an African American reinterpretation of L. Frank Baum's *The Wonderful Wizard of Oz*.[30]

---

26 *Id.* at 815–16.

27 *Id.* at 816.

28 *Id.* at 817.

29 *Id.*

30 *Diana Ross*, Wikipedia, http://en.wikipedia.org/wiki/Diana_Ross (last visited Apr. 24, 2018).

The judge asked Chic's lawyer again, "Is that what you assumed?"[31] He answered, "Yes."[32] Still, given the importance of the contingency to the transaction and the fact that California law limited personal service contracts to seven years, the judge expressed astonishment at the lawyer's assumption. "Since Ross's presence was so fundamental to the success of the projects contemplated by the Agreement, it is incredible to me that Chic never once inquired as to the terms of Ross's ties to Motown."[33]

Chic clearly expected Motown to make Ross available if the option was exercised but gave no thought to the possibility that she might be able to refuse her collaboration, her contract with Motown having expired; it assumed she would remain under contract with Motown. The assumption went to a contingency, not the performance by Motown of an obligation or the realization of the benefits. That assumption functioned as an expectation or its equivalent: an unstated belief that Ross would remain available to enable Motown to perform.

In *Chic Organization, Ltd.*, the assumption could have been identified and verified. Chic could have asked Motown about the duration of Ross's contract and, upon learning that it was about to expire, could have asked Ross to sign, committing herself to Chic, as Chic's principals had committed themselves to Motown. The hazard—the possibility she might refuse to collaborate because she was not obligated to do so—would have been eliminated. A party in Chic's position must ask itself what due diligence is feasible. If the assumption concerns a condition, the existence or nonexistence of which can be verified, it can decide if it wants to verify it. If the assumption concerns a condition that cannot be verified[34] or the party chooses not to verify it, then the party can decide if it expects or hopes such condition to exist or not exist. What would have been an assumption thus becomes a hope or expectation like others in the transaction, unless confirmed. In the absence of converting an assumption into a hope or expectation, it remains an unstated benchmark for the successful outcome of a transaction.

However, hopes and expectations may differ from assumptions in that the party always has the former in its conscious sights when the contract is

[31] 582 F. Supp. at 817.

[32] *Id.*

[33] *Id.*

[34] *E.g.*, Backus v. MacLaury, 278 A.D. 504, 106 NYS 2d 401 (N.Y. App. 1951), where a bull calf was purchased in an auction for the purpose of breeding a herd on the incorrect assumption it was fertile. The calf was too young for its sterility to be determined.

formed, whereas when a party is unaware of the latter they are discoveries with hindsight. When a party discovers an assumption it made at contract formation is incorrect, it supplements the expectations and hopes it had at that time, effectively setting the bar for a successful outcome by a revised set of expectations or hopes. Using an assumption as a benchmark for success thus involves using revised expectations as the standard.

Revised Expectations

Just as a party may receive exactly what it bargained for in the contract and still be dissatisfied with the outcome because the contract did not correctly state its expectations, hopes, and assumptions, a party might receive exactly what it initially hoped to receive and had successfully stated in the contract but still be dissatisfied because it has modified or abandoned those expectations or added new expectations that were not satisfied. Unlike the case where the party unconsciously assumed the existence of a condition or that a contingency would or would not occur, only to later find the assumption was or has been proven to be incorrect, the party consciously forms an expectation about the performance it will give or receive or the benefit it expects to realize, only to later decide that such expectation should be jettisoned for a fresh one. Whatever the reason—the party discovers a better use of its resources than its investment in the contemplated transaction, one or more additional benefits could have been realized but were not, or a better deal could have been made—the transaction fails or is somewhat less successful measured by the revised expectations. To the extent such potential changes in mind can be surfaced when the transaction is planned, they are relevant to the parties during that phase; either the party's expectations can be modified at that time or future changes can be avoided. To the extent such potential changes cannot be surfaced when the transaction is planned, there is nothing to be done at that time. The risk that such changes in mind may occur exists but is unavoidable, and that is a risk that, despite all the good effort in planning and implementing the transaction, it will still fail or be less successful because the revised expectations are not satisfied.

Cutter Laboratories, Inc. v. Twining[35] is good illustration of this risk. Twining, a cofounder and for thirty-five years an officer of Cutter Laboratories, agreed, in exchange for the company insuring his life for

[35] 221 Cal. App.2d 302, 34 Cal. Rptr. 317 (Cal. App. 1963).

$36,000, to surrender 1,800 of his 3,600 shares of stock in the company for twenty dollars per share upon his death, such shares being endorsed and irrevocably placed in escrow until that time.[36] Two years later, when the company valued its stock, then still privately held, at a price much higher than twenty dollars per share, the company asked Twining if he wanted to rescind, and he declined.[37] Seven years later, again, when the company reclassified and revalued its shares, it asked Twining if he wished to modify the agreement; Twining declined.[38] Four years later, after a further reclassification, split, and public offering of the company's stock, Twining's shares in escrow had a value of more than $800,000.[39] Twining sought rescission, claiming lack of mutuality and frustration of purpose; the court refused him relief. While the value of the shares had increased more than twenty-fold, Twining's estate still stood to realize all the benefits he bargained for and presumably expected: his wife would receive a payment not subject to estate taxes because it would be under a life insurance policy not included in his estate, and it would be a fixed amount, not subject to the economic vagaries that could affect the price of the company's stock. Twining could not point to any assumption he had made about the circumstances in which he sold the stock or contingencies that had increased the stock's value; he could only cite their occurrence and their consequences—the potential occurrence of which were known to him when he sold his stock.[40]

What Twining valued as a worthwhile benefit when he sold his stock he no longer valued when the stock had increased more than twenty-fold; his expectation or hope about the value he should receive for those shares had changed. Because he had been asked when he sold his stock and on subsequent occasions if he wanted to rescind his deal, there seems little more that could have been done when the deal was incubated to have averted his later change in mind.

CONCLUSION

An initial benchmark for a successful transaction for a party is not necessarily the counterparty's performance of its obligations under the contract. It may or may not be. Rather, it is the realization of the

[36] *Id.* at 307.
[37] *Id.* at 308.
[38] *Id.*
[39] *Id.* at 310.
[40] *Id.*

benefit the party expected, hoped, and assumed it would receive. For convenience, this text—instead of speaking of what a party expected, hoped, or assumed—occasionally speaks of what the party anticipated. The counterparty's performance will usually be one component of a successful outcome. The initial benchmark is subject to revision with the benefit of hindsight, and when expectations, hopes, and assumptions later change, the outcome will be judged by the changed perspective.

2

Transaction Risks

RISK, HAZARD, CAUSE, AND OUTCOME

Each risk in a transaction has four aspects, the understanding of which is critical to managing such risk:

- the hazard that creates the potential for harm,
- the cause of the hazard,
- the chance or probability the hazard will result in an adverse transaction outcome, and
- the potential adverse outcomes.

Hazard

Black's Law Dictionary defines a hazard as a "danger or peril; esp., a factor contributing to a peril."[1] It is a peril or threat of a harm or loss. A peril or threat occurs in connection with an action or actions or a realm of activity. For example, a driving hazard is a risk of injury or death while using a road. Specific hazards include poor driving, bad road conditions,

[1] BLACK'S LAW DICTIONARY 834 (10th ed. 2014).

speeding, driving while tired, driving while intoxicated, texting, speaking on a cell phone, and answering emails. The chance of harm or loss while engaged in an activity is the essence of risk.

A hazard is a potential for harm—a condition or circumstance that, when combined with events, develops into an active agency of harm. A hazard is a peril or danger that exists or occurs and could, but will not always, lead to a harm. In *Frigaliment Importing Co.*,[2] the hazard was the ambiguous word "chicken" used to describe the chickens to be sold, which could mean young or old birds. Though the buyer ultimately suffered a loss because the seller delivered old birds that also fit the description, the seller might have shared the buyer's understanding and delivered young birds. In *Leasco Corp.*, the hazard was the error in the unaudited income statement on which Taussig relied. Though he too suffered a loss as a result, that outcome might have been avoided, for example, by linking price to actual net income. In *Chic Organization, Ltd.*, the hazard was the potential that Diana Ross might not collaborate if Chic exercised its option to produce a second record. Though Chic suffered a loss because Ross was not obligated at contract formation to later cooperate, Ross might have renewed her contract with Motown or, notwithstanding the absence of a contract with Motown, cooperated with Chic because of the successful sales of the first record. The lurking of a hazard creates or contributes to the creation of potential for an adverse outcome while not always causing it.

Cause

The cause of a hazard in a transaction will be either

- one or both of the parties to the transaction or
- other causes.

The parties to a transaction can be subdivided into

- those who create or contribute to the creation of a hazard and
- the other party or parties.

[2] 190 F. Supp. 116 (S.D.N.Y. 1960).

Other causes can be subdivided into

- human agents other than the parties to the transaction (or third parties) who control the results of their actions but whose actions cannot be controlled by either party to the transaction, and
- other causes or events beyond the control of specific human agents.

Such other causes can be further subdivided into

- natural forces or forces beyond the control of any specific human agent that creates a hazard to a transaction and
- market forces or actions of human agents, the aggregate effects of which are beyond the control of individual agents that create a hazard to a transaction.

Cause is relevant to transaction risk management because a party can eliminate or reduce the chance of the occurrence of a hazard within its control or the control of third parties whose assistance eliminating the hazard can be controlled. Other causes must be differently managed. In *Frigaliment Importing Co.*, the hazard to the buyer was specifying the chickens to be bought and sold using the ambiguous description of them. The causes of the hazard were the seller's formulation and the buyer's acceptance of that description. The cause of the harm was the seller's delivery of stewing hens, consistent with that description. In *Leasco Corp.*, the hazard to the buyer, we have seen, was an error in the financial statements caused by the accountants at the third-party target who prepared the unaudited income statement. The buyer also contributed to the hazard causing the harm by accepting the error and a price, though calculated as a multiple of net income, not linked to the target's actual income. In *Chic Organization, Ltd.*, the hazard was Ross's right to refuse to collaborate on the second record. The hazard to Chic was caused by the limited term of her contract with Motown. Ross's decision not to renew with Motown and refusal to collaborate on the second record caused the harm. Chic's incorrect assumption that she would remain with Motown did not cause the hazard or the harm but did cause Chic to miss the chance to avoid the hazard. The cause of the hazards in one of the three cases was both parties (*Frigaliment Importing Co.*) and in the other two (*Leasco Corp.* and *Chic Organization, Ltd.*) a third party (the target's accountants and the employment law).

Whether a cause is a proximate, substantial, predominant, or otherwise significant is irrelevant to risk management. In risk management, the focus is on the probable occurrence of a hazard, its likely consequences for a transaction outcome, and how a party can best manage its occurrence and the potential losses that might result. For example, ice on a road is a hazard to the road's users. That the road could have been cleared is relevant to how the risk could have been mitigated and responsibility for the losses allocated.

Rosco Corporation v. Cohen[3] illustrates how questions about blame and liability may be distinguished from those about the causes of transaction hazards and adverse outcomes. Arthur Rosen and Edward Consove incorporated Rosco Corporation in 1946, each owning 50 percent of its shares. When Rosen died in February 1978, his shares were redeemed for $130,000. Consove and his son Gerald decided the latter would take over the corporation. The corporation's books reported assets of $683,503.55 and liabilities of $501,032.98, or a net worth of approximately $180,000. Consove sold his shares back to corporation for $300,000, for which he received a note for the full amount, secured by a security interest in the corporation's assets, thus rendering the corporation insolvent, with a negative net worth of approximately $120,000. Interest accrued under the note at 10 percent per annum, and installments of $600 per week were payable. Gerald became the sole shareholder by purchasing a single share for $3,000.[4] After a fire in 1980, the corporation closed its warehouse and stopped paying Consove, who returned, discovered that his son had been diverting the corporation's funds for his personal use, and took over the corporation's management.[5] Before taking control, he had received on his note $21,600 and, after taking control, just over $10,000. Eventually, the corporation filed for bankruptcy, and the trustee sought to recover these payments and to avoid the security interest as fraudulent transfers. The trustee could avoid them if the corporation "received less than a reasonably equivalent value in exchange for such transfer" and "was insolvent on the date [of such transfer] or became insolvent as a result of such transfer."[6] Because the corporation paid only $130,000 for Rosen's shares a year earlier and Gerald paid only $3,000 for 100 percent of the corporation's shares, by either measure $300,000

---

[3] 701 F.2d 978 (1st Cir. 1983).

[4] *Id.* at 979–80.

[5] *Id.* at 980.

[6] 701 F.2d at 981.

was more than the value of Edward's shares.[7] The court went further, questioning whether Consove's shares had any value to the corporation. The court held that the note rendered the corporation insolvent because it added $300,000 to its liabilities, where the corporation had a net worth of only $180,000. The court summed up the transaction thus: "The substance of the redemption was that the father passed along the ownership interest of Rosco to his son and secured for himself a steady retirement income at his prior salary level, all at the expense of the corporation's creditors."[8]

This is true, but while Consove made the corporation insolvent by taking back a note for more than its net worth, he did not cause the corporation to fail to pay its other creditors. He may have contributed to its failure by taking $31,600 from the corporation's cash. For its failure to happen, his son had to mismanage the business so badly that it became bankrupt, an event that was not inevitable when Consove sold his shares and received the note. Put another way, Consove's planning hazard was forecasting on the basis of insufficient information or faulty analysis of the available information that his son would operate the business profitably, as Rosco and he had done for years. He thus forecasted how his son would perform and the business would continue. Most likely, he formed optimistic assessments about his son's talents and the prospects of the business. In any event, he was the source of this hazard. His documentation hazard was taking a note the corporation's creditors could attack and void as a fraudulent transfer. His legal rights to be paid under the note were not effective against such third parties. He was also the source of this hazard. The implementation hazard was his son's mismanagement of the corporation, an event that ultimately ended with default on the note and bankruptcy.

Risk

Risk is "the uncertainty of a result, happening, or loss; the chance of injury, or loss; esp., the existence and extent of the possibility of harm."[9] The focus here is on the chance of an outcome that deviates from what was anticipated. A risk in a transaction could be defined simply as the chance of an outcome that deviates from that anticipated by the parties.

---

[7] *Id.* at 983.

[8] *Id.* at 984.

[9] Black's Law Dictionary, *supra* note 1, at 1524.

Risk is distinguished from variability or uncertainty.[10] Risk is a quantifiable and statistically measurable chance of an adverse event, while variability is the chance that cannot be so measured, or what is referred to as simple "uncertainty." The key to risk management is to define a hazard with sufficient specificity that the likelihood of its occurrence can be mathematically measured. Examples include catastrophic events, such as hurricanes and earthquakes, which are forecasted; the realization of anticipated value in a merger or acquisition that is predicted based on studies of such transactions; the repayment by a debtor of its obligations that is predicted based on credit scores; the realization of projected revenues by a toll road or train project based on analyses of similar projects of the extent to which such revenues were realized. Statistical measurement, the heart of risk management, quantifies the occurrence of a hazard and thus enables a principal to decide the priority to be given to seeking to avoid or mitigate it.

Reformulating any of the uncertainties dealmakers are likely to encounter in a typical transaction into a statistically measurable hazard is outside the scope of this text, but the following example may help the reader understand how this might be done. Consider the buyer's "mistake of fact" in *Leasco Corp.*, which was that the target was profitable. The hazard—an inaccurate statement of the target's income in the unaudited income statement—occurred during the planning phase. One question is the frequency of such error or the hazard occurring, and a separate question is the likelihood the hazard results in an adverse outcome for the buyer. The latter question asks about the chances that the buyer would agree to pay a fixed price for the business and to calculate that price as a multiple of the net income of the business, would rely upon an unaudited income statement when linking price to income, and would fail to find the error in the income statement before contract formation. A study of mergers and acquisitions of privately held companies in which the financial statements were material to the calculation of the purchase price should also reveal how often such financial statements contained material errors, how often such errors went undiscovered before contract formation, and how often buyers relied upon income statements when agreeing to a price. Those computations would also indicate the frequency that a material error in such financial statements results in adverse outcomes for buyers.

---

[10] Michel Crouhy, Dan Galai, and Robert Mark, The Essentials of Risk Management 9 (2006); Glynis M. Breakwell, The Psychology of Risk 22–25 (2nd ed. 2014).

A study of 400 mergers and acquisitions by Deloitte Consulting LLP,[11] which concluded that 60 percent of all mergers fail, illustrates the point.[12] The study divides the merger and acquisition process into four phases: M&A Strategy, Target Screening, Due Diligence and Transaction Execution, and Integration.[13] During the first two and part of the third phases, the acquirer decides on the benefits—what Deloitte calls "value creation"—it desires to realize from an acquisition and the maximum price it is willing to pay for the target, before bidding. It undertakes extensive legal, financial, and other due diligence on the target to understand fully the legal, financial, operational, regulatory, and other risks to the realization of the anticipated benefits.[14] Deloitte groups the potential benefits or value creation into three: efficiency (which includes economies of scale, economies of cost, and cost controls), market power (which includes assets and capabilities that drive market power, brand reputation, and technical knowledge), and reinvention (which includes changing rules of the competitive game, creating paradigm shift, and redirecting industry).[15] During the first two phases, approach errors occur: selection of the wrong target, selection of a target or proceeding on the basis of insufficient information about it, selection of a target that is too far removed from core competencies of the acquirer (perhaps, again, an incorrectly selected target), radical changes in the environment, failure to develop the expected new product, and overestimation of the market. They account for 18 percent, 18 percent, 12 percent, 8 percent, 28 percent, and 16 percent, respectively, of the mergers that fail from approach errors.[16] Though these approach errors are broad and vague, an overlooked error in an income statement or balance sheet should fall into the insufficient information category. Execution errors occur during the last phase (Integration) and include poor leadership, different culture, poor integration, wrong focus, and unclear leadership.[17]

Deloitte's study does not indicate what percentage of the failed mergers and acquisitions are attributable respectively to approach and

---

[11] DELOITTE CONSULTING LLP, LESSONS LEARNED FROM SUCCESSFUL MERGERS AND ACQUISITIONS FOR CASPA (2008).

[12] *Id.* at 12.

[13] *Id.* at 13.

[14] *Id.* at 16–17.

[15] *Id.* at 15.

[16] *Id.* at 12.

[17] *Id.*

execution errors. If we assume that the failure rate for each phase is about equal, 18 percent of the 30 percent (half of the failed mergers, which is 60 percent of all mergers) or 4.8 percent of all mergers and acquisitions failed because the acquirer proceeded on the basis of insufficient information. It seems unlikely that in all cases the insufficient information was incorrect financial statements, but for the moment we assume it was. Restated as a forecast for future transactions, the Deloitte study would indicate that the probability of an acquirer selecting a target or proceeding with an acquisition or merger on the basis of insufficient information is approximately 4.8 percent, based on the previous assumptions.

The chance of a buyer, like Taussig, assuming the financial information in hand was complete and accurate would be 4.8 percent, assuming the Deloitte study is accurate. If the Deloitte study was refined to separate insufficient information due to incorrect financials and other information shortcomings, the probability would most likely be lower. If the data were refined still further to consider certain factors, such as the acquirer's experience in mergers and acquisitions—because the more seasoned the acquirer, the more attuned it should be to the risk—the probability of an expert like Taussig making the error might be even lower. The chance of an error in the income statement that the acquirer would have in hand would be low, but whether that chance would be so low that it should be ignored is another matter.

Another illustration is the follow-up study on a sponsors' demand forecast for a public–private partnership rail project, a forecast on which the project sponsors, lenders, and government relied when deciding to approve the project and its financing.[18] They projected a number of passengers for each of the first five years, after which the demand would be stable, with a 5 percent probability that such targets would be missed by 15 percent or more. Put another way, the sponsors claimed a 95 percent chance that at least 85 percent of the projected revenue would be received. The projected revenues were not realized. A follow-up study was done, using the methods developed in an earlier study of the accuracy of traffic forecasts for comparable projects. It concluded that actual traffic demand on the projects that were studied was on average 51.4 percent lower than the forecasted demand and 65 percent lower

---

[18] Bent Flyvbjerg, *Quality Control and Due Diligence in Project Management: Getting Decisions Right by Taking the Outside View*, INT'L. J. PROJ MGMT (2012), http://www.sciencedirect.com/science/article/pii/S026378631200138X.

in 25 percent of such projects. It found the forecast for the rail project was likely to be no more or less accurate than other traffic forecasts for comparable projects. According to the study, the chance that the project would realize 85 percent of the projected revenue was approximately 50 percent, in contrast to the forecaster's own estimate of 95 percent. The hazard to the project sponsors and lenders—the occurrence of which was statistically measurable—was that the forecast was based on incorrect data or assumptions, did not include assumptions that should have been included, or did not correctly analyze the data.

Adverse Outcome

All adverse outcomes in transactions fall into three broad groups, according to their impact on the benefits or losses a party anticipated realizing or incurring:

- First, a party might realize no or fewer benefits than or benefits inferior to those anticipated. An example is a reseller of a widget who realizes a profit of $5 instead of the $6 it hoped for. Another example is a widget buyer who hoped for but did not receive a rare widget.
- Second, a party might incur additional costs, where it incurs more costs than anticipated to perform, or greater liability to pay compensation for failing to perform, or to realize the desired benefits. For example, a widget buyer pays $6 instead of the $5 it expected. In another example, a judgment for $10 is awarded against it for breach when it expected any such judgment would not exceed $5.
- Finally, a party might incur delay, for example, where a party realizes the benefits later than anticipated.

The four cases previously described illustrate the adverse outcomes described in the first bullet: in *Frigaliment Importing Co.*, the chickens the buyer received were inferior and had less value than the chickens it expected as a result of a documentation hazard; in *Leasco Corp.*, the target had less value than the buyer anticipated as a result of relying upon incorrect information during transaction planning (calculating the price); in *Chic Organization, Ltd.*, Chic received less value than it expected when Ross did not cooperate with production of a second record as a result of overlooking that possibility during planning; and in *Rosco Corp.* Consove received none of the anticipated value because of planning, documentation, and implementation hazards: he miscalculated the potential for his son to ruin the business; for his shares, he accepted a note the corporation's creditors could attack and void; and his son fatally mismanaged the corporation's business. The correlation of hazard with potential adverse outcome helps to frame the relationship between risk and loss in a transaction.

TRANSACTION RISK MANAGEMENT

Transaction Phases

The life of a contract in contract law starts with formation and ends with discharge. If a breach occurs, one or two additional phases are likely: the exercise of remedies and dispute resolution. In transaction risk management, the life of a transaction starts with conceptualization of an exchange and its potential benefits and ends with benefit realization, or if a dispute occurs, dispute resolution, winding through planning, negotiation, documentation, implementation, and benefit realization. Transaction activities fall into four or five discrete classes or groups, which may coincide with and proceed in separate phases: conceptualization, planning, documentation, implementation, and final outcome, the last of which consists of benefit realization or dispute resolution.[19]

Conceptualization differs from planning in that it is an early-stage vision of a deal, such as an acquisition, a joint venture, a construction project, or a financing; planning is the detailed iteration of that vision. Documentation reduces the plan to one or more contracts, although not all of the plan will necessarily be the subject of contractual terms and conditions, only those that state the commitments that must be fulfilled. Implementation of the transaction, which follows, will include performance of those commitments, but it may include more: whatever additional tasks a party must complete after obligations have been discharged to realize the anticipated benefits. For example, a business acquirer realizes value from a merger or acquisition usually only after the target has been integrated, something that occurs after the deal is closed.

However, transactions do not always follow clearly demarcated steps. Tenders, especially by governmental agencies, may follow such

[19] HELENA HAAPIO & GEORGE J. SIEDEL, A SHORT GUIDE TO CONTRACT RISK 16 (2013).

phases. Deals that are negotiated from their inception do not: as a party negotiates, it also decides what benefits it will realize and what tasks it and the other party will complete; conceptualization, planning, and documentation are combined and proceed concurrently, often in haste. In such cases, a decision about what will go into the contract combines conceptualization, planning, and documentation activities. Still, decisions about what benefits should be realized, tasks should be completed, and conditions and contingencies should be addressed differ from the choice of words used in a contract to describe them, and both such decisions and word choices differ from the actions that fulfill the commitments they create.

Discrete Phase Risks. Each phase has its own risks. A party may have expectations about how long and how much it will cost to plan, negotiate, and document a transaction. Those expectations may be met, exceeded, or disappointed because transaction conceptualization, planning, and documentation may itself take longer or cost more than expected. Sponsors of large infrastructure projects, especially novel project financings, have been reported to bemoan the time and cost required to prepare and negotiate the numerous transaction documents.[20] A party will have expectations about how long and how much it will cost to implement the transaction, that is, for the parties to perform all their obligations and, once such obligations are performed, for it to complete whatever additional actions are required for the benefits to be realized. Those expectations will be met, exceeded, or disappointed, perhaps due to actions and events that occur during the implementation phase. A party, while recognizing the potential for disputes to occur concerning a contract, is unlikely, at contract formation, to envisage any specific dispute thereunder. It will likely form impressions, assumptions, hopes, and expectations when a dispute arises about the possible outcomes and the cost of reaching such results. Those expectations will also be met, exceeded, or disappointed. The successful execution of the first three phases—conceptualization, planning, and documentation—does not ensure successful implementation, though successful implementation should avoid disputes concerning the contract. Each phase will be more or less successful as measured by the party's expectations for that phase, and each phase can and should be managed for the risks that

[20] Michael Klein, Jae So & Ben Shin, *Transaction Costs for Private Infrastructure Projects—Are They Too High?*" Public Policy for the Private Sector No. 95 (1996).

occur during it, though the outcome of the implementation phase marks success or failure for the transaction.

Knock-on Effects. Acts and omissions during planning and documentation contribute to the ultimate outcome of the documentation and implementation phases. When planning a transaction, a party must identify the benefits it anticipates realizing and the tasks that must be completed to receive those benefits; during the documentation phase, it must ensure that those tasks are accurately described in the contract and all necessary rights to receive the completion of those tasks are effective. *Leasco Corp.* illustrates the knock-on effect of misinformation during the planning phase: the error in the income statement formed the basis for the calculation of the price, which was stated in the contract and had to be paid at closing. *Chic Organization, Ltd.* illustrates the knock-on effect of missing a contingency during planning: because Chic missed Ross's potential lack of commitment to Motown to collaborate with Chic, Chic did not ask that the contract require, and the contract did not require, that she collaborate on the second album; and not being so required, she did not collaborate with Chic. *Frigaliment* illustrates the knock-on effect of a decision taken during the documentation phase: the ambiguous description of the chickens created the potential for the seller to deliver stewing chickens. No mistake occurred during planning: each party knew clearly what it expected. Hazards during planning and documentation start a causal chain of necessary but insufficient causes and create the potential for an adverse outcome.

Knock-on Effect on Implementation. The success or failure of a transaction is measured by outcome of the implementation phase, whether the anticipated benefits are realized as, and when and at the cost, anticipated. In a simple exchange between two parties, three activities must be completed for each party's anticipated benefit to be realized:

- One party must complete the task that it is expected and committed to complete to enable the second to eventually realize its desired benefit.
- The second party must complete an additional task to realize its benefit. This task is often completed after the first party has performed and either further contributes to or yields benefit realization.
- The second party must realize its anticipated benefit.

For example, two parties agree to buy and sell a widget, which the buyer expects to resell at a profit. The sale by the seller is the completion of a task for the benefit of the buyer, one that contributes toward the buyer's benefit realization; the buyer's resale of the widget is the task it must complete to realize its benefit; and the buyer's receipt of the anticipated profit is its realization of its desired benefit. The seller's sale to the buyer does not ensure the buyer will realize its profit but is expected to contribute to its doing so. A description of the seller's benefits and tasks would be the mirror image of the buyer's, with a few modifications. This outline—two parties, each having expectations about the benefits it will realize, each having to complete a task that will contribute to the other's benefit realization, each having a commitment to complete such task, and each having to complete a task that will contribute to its own benefit realization—is the transaction model used throughout this text, with a few variations. While few transactions conform to this simple model, it is sufficient to illustrate and systematically catalogue the principal risks that occur in most simple and complex transactions.

Each transaction hazard is ultimately a danger to the successful outcome of one or more of the six implementation activities previously described. The risk of an unsuccessful outcome is best understood by correlating each hazard in a transaction to one or more of those six activities.

- A hazard created during the planning phase can adversely affect a task to be completed or the benefit to be realized during implementation. The hazard in *Leasco Corp.* (the incorrect unaudited income statement) created the potential for the buyer's benefit (value of the business) to be less than anticipated. The hazard in *Chic Organization, Ltd.* (the possibility Ross would not collaborate) endangered Motown's ability to perform for Chic's benefit (making Ross available for collaboration on the second record).
- A hazard created during the documentation phase can also adversely affect a task to be completed or a benefit to be realized during implementation. In *Frigaliment,* the ambiguous description of the chickens created the possibility for the seller to perform a task the buyer did not expect: to deliver old birds. In *Rosco Corp.,* Consove's acceptance of a note that rendered the corporation insolvent during documentation precluded his and its compliance

with the legal formalities that would ensure a commitment binding on the corporation and effective against third parties during implementation, thus exposing benefit realization to impairment by third parties.

- A hazard during implementation—for example, the theft by a third party of an item one party agreed to sell to the other, thus depriving the seller of its ability to perform—can adversely affect a party's completion of a task for the benefit of the other party, the completion of a task for its own benefit, and the realization of a benefit.

Each transaction hazard, whenever it occurs, is best understood in relation to the specific implementation activities it endangers.

Risk Avoidance, Mitigation, and Allocation

Hazards and the losses that can flow from them are managed by eliminating them, or failing that, by mitigating the chances they will occur and the losses that will result if they do occur, and by allocating responsibility for such losses to a party to the transaction or a third party.

For purposes of deciding which risks warrant attention, the probability a hazard exists or will occur can be paired with the potential harm to a transaction: on one end of the scale, an event with low probability is paired with little or no damage, whereas at the other is an event with high probability paired with severe damage. Between are events with low probability and severe damage, high probability and little or no damage, and medium probability and medium damage. A matrix of risks can be constructed relying on intuition about likelihood and potential damage, in the absence of statistical studies of such risks.[21] What is identified as a risk might not be statistically calculable. Add an intuitive judgment of the likelihood of and the damage from its occurrence, tainted by the dealmaker's biases, the risk assessment, even if boxed into a matrix like that previously described, is truly about uncertainties. Still, the matrix highlights the choice for a dealmaker, such as Taussig in *Leasco Corp.* Assuming the probability is comparable to the findings in the Deloitte study and insufficient information is synonymous with incorrect financials, a probability of 4.8 percent is low but not statistically

[21] *E.g.*, HAAPIO & SIEDEL, *supra* note 19, at 138–39.

insignificant, especially when paired against the potential loss, which can be (and was for Taussig) the entire value of the anticipated benefits.

Risk Avoidance. Risk avoidance is one of three objectives of managing transaction risk, the other two being mitigation and allocation. Unlike risk mitigation and allocation, risk avoidance eliminates any chance that a specific hazard will occur at any time during the transaction. As we have seen, the risk in *Leasco Corp.*—that the price was higher than the value of the target, based on its net income—could have been avoided by diligence or linking the price to actual net income; the risk in *Chic Organization, Ltd.*, that Ross might not collaborate on a second record, could have been avoided by having had her commit to Chic to cooperate; and the risk in *Frigaliment* could have been avoided by specifying young birds.

Risk Mitigation. Risk mitigation has two objectives: to reduce the chances that a hazard will occur and to reduce the losses that can result when a hazard occurs and could cause losses. For example, a widget buyer has an expert inspect a widget and confirm it has the expected feature; the chance that the widget will not be as expected is reduced but not eliminated. If the buyer also reserves a portion of the price as compensation for the widget not having the expected features, it mitigates the potential losses that might occur if the widget does not conform. Measures aimed at reducing the chance of a hazard occurring are either prophylactic or deterrent. Prophylactic contractual measures, like rules of the road that prescribe safe driving practices, do not eliminate entirely the occurrence of hazards but rather reduce their frequency and likelihood. A contract that includes such measures establishes a private regulatory regime under which one party is a de facto regulator and the other the regulated subject.

Such regulations may be minimal or substantial. For example, a construction contract that requires the contractor to complete milestones according to a schedule and budget promotes compliance by requiring the contractor to submit periodic reports about how the completed work matches the schedule and budget. Covenants in a loan agreement that require a debtor to keep proper books and records, to timely pay its taxes and other creditors, to collect its bills from its customers, to deposit all its cash receipts in a bank account with the creditor, and to preserve and protect its properties, ensure the debtor, who might not otherwise do so, follows practices that minimize its loss of revenues and reduce its risk of default on its obligations to its creditors. A service contract that identifies the key personnel to provide the agreed services requires that such personnel be made available upon request and that the services to be rendered to the customer be given priority over the service provider's other commitments, which reduces the chance that the services will not be completed by qualified personnel as and when requested or required by the customer as a result of other customers making demands on their time.

Mitigation of damage is remedial, allowing a party to take actions to reduce the potential losses that might flow from an adverse event or even to avert a hazard that portends the imminent occurrence of such event.

Risk Allocation. As previously noted, responsibility for the losses that result from a hazard not avoided during the planning and documentation phases must be allocated, either by express provision in the contract or by the rules applicable in the absence of such provisions, with the result that the party to which responsibility for a risk is allocated becomes the insurer of the losses resulting from the occurrence of the allocated risk, subject to certain limitations. The allocation to or assumption by a party of a risk is of the responsibility for the losses that result when the threatened harm occurs. The allocation of a risk—or more accurately, the responsibility for a risk—does not alter the threat from a hazard; that threat remains, while responsibility for losses is allocated. Such insurance may consist of a party covering its own such losses or covering the other party's losses or both.

Risk allocation is effectively self-insurance in which a party covers its own losses and insurance for the counterparty in which it covers the counterparty's losses. Risk allocation is always a zero-sum game: a party can shed responsibility for a risk only by transferring it to another party. One party's gain in risk allocation is always another party's loss. For example, a risk that a widget may not have the features a widget buyer expects must be allocated to the seller, the buyer, both seller and buyer, or a third party. The risk must always be allocated in a transaction. An allocation of the risk to the seller—the seller assumes responsibility for certain of the losses the buyer might incur if the widget does not have such features—does not change the fact that the hazard exists and is a threat to the buyer, but it relieves the buyer of that responsibility and vice versa. While risk allocation and mitigation may be used separately or in combination, risk avoidance may not be combined with either, for an obvious logical reason. Because risk avoidance eliminates an existing or future hazard, it is the best outcome of transaction risk management.

Part II

Planning and Documentation Risks

3

Oversight and Rejection Risks

OVERSIGHT AND REJECTION

When planning any major, nonroutine transaction, a party should

- identify all benefits that might be realized, both as a result of the transaction and other transactions that might be affected by that transaction, and select and prioritize those it wishes to realize;
- identify and describe all of the tasks that must be completed for the realization of the benefits chosen to be realized, and decide who is expected to complete those tasks;
- identify and describe all the conditions and contingencies that will facilitate and impede completion of such tasks and realization of such benefits; and
- assign to one or both parties legal responsibility for the losses that will occur if such benefits are not realized, such tasks are not completed, such conditions do or do not exist as supposed, and such contingencies do or do not occur.

When successfully completed, such efforts will have avoided the creation of any of the hazards that errors in planning create. The outcome of the planning phase or activities is successful, whether or not the time and cost of completing that phase may have fallen short of expectations.

A failure to successfully complete one or more of the actions described in the preceding bullets will be the result of one or more of the following:

- overlooking a benefit, task, condition, contingency, or responsibility that was—but with hindsight, should not have been—omitted from the plan for the transaction,
- choosing to include or to omit a benefit, task, condition, contingency, or responsibility that, with hindsight, should not have been included or omitted from the plan, and
- misunderstanding what a benefit, task, condition, contingency, or responsibility includes, whether or not it was included or omitted.

The party that stands to lose in the scenarios described in the first two bullets also causes the potential for loss: the party that will suffer any loss is that which overlooks or makes a decision it later regrets about a benefit, task, condition, contingency, or responsibility—what will be referred to as benefit, task, etc., remorse. The party that stands to lose in the scenario described in the third bullet may but will not always be the cause of the loss; the other party and third parties may also be causes. This chapter describes the risks created by oversights and regrettable decisions about benefits, tasks, conditions, contingencies, and responsibility. The following chapter describes the risks created by misunderstandings about the same.

The following cases illustrate benefit oversight and remorse, respectively:

- *Wildmon v. Berwick Universal Pictures*[1]: Paul Yule, who was producing a television program about censorship in the United States—in particular, the battle over public funding of two artists, Andres Serrano and Robert Mapplethorpe—asked Donald Wildmon, who was a prominent figure in promoting censorship of the media and arts in the United States and had campaigned against the public funding of both artists, for an interview. Wildmon replied to Yule, saying, "A contract would also have to be signed, containing a substantial damage clause, forbidding the interview or any part of

[1] 803 F. Supp. 1167 (N.D. Miss. 1992).

the interview being used in any manner other than that stipulated in the contract without my prior written permission."[2] The contract, prepared by Wildmon's attorney, read:

> Mr. Yule agrees specifically to refrain from making the interview available to any other media outlet including any portions that are not used in the television presentation made by Berwick Universal Pictures, London for Channel 4. In addition, Mr. Yule agrees that any material obtained from the interview or derived from this interview shall not form the basis of any other media presentation or [sic] in England, the United States or any other country without written permission from American Family Association.

Yule decided to broadcast the original Channel 4 program in the United States. Wildmon objected. One benefit to each party was control over use of the interview in later productions, and another was control over the original program. If Wildmon's benefits included both, his consent was required for the broadcast in the United States. Otherwise Yule was primarily at liberty to profit from subsequent broadcasts.[3] If the contract stated Wildmon's intent at contract formation, he overlooked control over rebroadcasting of the original program as a benefit. The hazard to Wildmon was his lack of control over repeated broadcastings of the original program. His oversight of the benefit enabled the hazard to occur (assuming he would have insisted upon controlling subsequent broadcasts of the original production).

---

[2] *Id.* at 1170.

[3] *Id.* at 1171. While media releases were commonplace, contracts giving the photographed or interviewed subject a degree of control over the use of the material were not, at least to the point that forms had been published; the Wildmon contract was an attempt to specify the benefit he expected to enjoy. When, after airing the program in Britain, Channel Four sought to distribute it in the United States, Wildmon sued for damages, claiming his consent was required to show the film outside of England. The court held that the quoted language was ambiguous because it could be read "as preventing the distribution of the interview in any form and any manner except for scheduled showings by Channel Four in Great Britain [or] . . . as preventing the distribution of only the footage taken of Wildmon to other producers and interviewers for use in other productions." *Id.* at 1174. The plaintiff's motion for summary judgment was accordingly denied.

- *Cleary v. News Corporation*[4]: Cleary signed a contract in 1965 with the publisher of *Robert's Rules of Order* that stated the royalty he would be paid but did not mention attributing credit to him and reserved all rights to the author. Cleary first assisted the original author's daughter-in-law to revise the book for the 1970 edition, and the title page named him as one who had assisted the author, as did the 1980 edition, on which he also provided assistance. He made no contribution to the 1990 edition, however, and no credit was attributed to him. Cleary claimed that the title page of that edition should have done so. He acknowledged, however, that attribution credit had not been overlooked or considered important at contract formation: "[I]t was not important that there be name credit, but it became in my mind more and more important as my involvement grew and grew by considerable degrees over the period of the ensuing years."[5] When he signed the contract, he did not insist upon receiving attribution credit. Later, he discovered more value in such credit and decided he did want it after all.[6] Cleary decided against attribution as a benefit and later changed his mind. This is a clear case of regret over initially rejecting a potential benefit. The hazard was the absence of a commitment by the publisher to give Cleary attribution credit; his decision not to ask for it enabled the hazard to occur.

Benefit Oversight and Rejection

A benefit is a discrete value or utility that is realized from a transaction when successfully completed. In *Wildmon,* the benefit to Yule was value, the revenue to be received from broadcasting and rebroadcasting the program; to Wildmon it was utility, control that ensured the use of the interview material promoted his cause. The control of subsequent broadcasts for Wildmon would have been additional to his control over the interview material in subsequent productions and for Yule additional to the value he received from the initial broadcast of the original program. Overlooking such additional or incremental value or utility is a lost

[4] 30 F.3d 1255 (9th Cir. 1994).

[5] *Id.* at 1264.

[6] The court denied him credit, however, holding that the absence of the attribution clause in the contract warranted the conclusion that the publisher "did not intend to contract to give Cleary name credit." *Id.* at 1263.

opportunity. Once missed, the other party is unlikely to cede it because in many transactions, as in *Wildmon*, one party's loss is another party's gain. This zero-sum game in incremental benefit allocation in a transaction underscores the importance of identifying and selecting benefits no later than contract formation. In other transactions, completion of additional tasks may be required to yield the additional benefit, and those efforts will likely increase the performing party's costs. In the best case, a party will identify all such potential incremental benefits; in the worst, it misses them all. A hazard occurs when a potential benefit is omitted, as the party that would have enjoyed the benefit may later come to regret the omission.

Transactions in which a party could have augmented the anticipated value or utility and later regretted its failure to do so include the following:

- A separate, often closely associated, value could have been realized.
- Additional value might be realized in the future had the present transaction been differently structured.
- Separate value in the information about the transaction may be realized or its realization is controlled by the other party.
- Value to one party's reputation from doing business with the other is controlled by the other.

The preceding list is not exhaustive but illustrative of incremental value and utility, the oversight of which is often regretted after contract formation.

Associated Benefits. A party may anticipate that because it will realize one benefit, especially the principal benefit, it will or should realize another benefit. This will often be the case where one benefit cannot realistically be realized without the other. Such other benefit is a discrete value that might require separate tasks to be completed for it to be realized. In that case, it should be unbundled and identified as a distinct potential benefit so that the list of anticipated benefits is clear and the costs associated with each can be identified and calculated. It may also be a benefit that is often realized when another benefit is realized, even though different tasks must be completed for its realization. Overlooking or rejecting such an associated benefit creates a hazard, the omission of the benefit.

The following illustrate associated benefits that were overlooked:

- *Allen v. Kaiser Aluminum and Chemical Corp.*[7]: A seller supplied a machine that met the expressly stated performance specifications—that the technology provided would be "sufficiently developed to permit commercial operation." The contract disclaimed all other warranties. The machine could not be operated safely without changes.[8] The buyer claimed the machine should have been capable of safe operation. The claim was, in effect, that one benefit—that a machine conformed to the specifications—included a second—that the machine must also operate safely. This is also a case in which the realization of the first benefit, use of the equipment as specified, was not realistically possible without realization of the second benefit, safe operation of the equipment. Assuming the first included the second benefit enabled the hazard to occur.
- *H.M. Holdings, Inc. v. Rankin*[9]: A seller conveyed real property, the title to which was to be "clean" and merchantable. The buyer claimed the seller thereby warranted that the soil on the property was physically clean and clear of contaminants. The claim that clean title entitled the buyer to clean soil is that the one benefit somehow necessarily included the other.[10]
- *Carlock v. Pillsbury Co.*[11]: Häagen-Dazs (HD) licensed Carlock (C) to sell HD's ice cream at a specific site and agreed to impart to C the necessary know-how to operate an HD store and to prepare and sell HD ice cream and other frozen desserts. C claimed, in a class action suit against HD, that "know-how" included the skills needed to improve the profitability of his store and that HD had failed to impart these skills. The claim was that training in the know-how of the franchisor's business, a narrow benefit, included training in how to operate a profitable business, a more expansive benefit.[12]

---

7 585 F. Supp. 154 (E.D. Mo. 1984).

8 An employee was killed using the equipment. The buyer unsuccessfully claimed that a warranty that the equipment was safe to use should be implied, even though the only express warranty given was that technology provided shall be "sufficiently developed to permit commercial operation" and all other warranties were expressly disclaimed.

9 70 F.3d 933 (7th Cir. 1995).

10 The buyer's claim was unsuccessful. The contract stated the land was otherwise sold "as is."

11 719 F. Supp. 791 (D. Minn. 1989).

12 The court dismissed his claim, holding that C had received what HD had committed to provide: the manual and training in how to prepare and sell HD's ice cream and other products. The missing task that C tried to shoehorn into "know-how" was training

Learning to operate an ice cream store was confused with the development and management of a successful business.

In all three cases, oversight of the additional benefits resulted in missing the additional tasks that would have had to have been completed for those benefits to have been realized: design and fabrication for safety in the first, remediation in the second, and management training in the third.

Future Benefits. A benefit that cannot be realized at contract formation but might be at a future time, a future benefit, may be additional to that anticipated in the then-current transaction. Like an associated benefit, a future benefit may or may not add value to one party's benefits without subtracting value from the other's benefits. Such a benefit may or may not be identifiable at contract formation because the technology for producing it does not then exist. Few such benefits enter the parties' contemplation when planning a transaction because they usually seem too speculative and remote to warrant time and effort to plan for their realization. Overlooking or rejecting such a benefit is still a hazard even though the probability may be low that a party will come to regret not devoting the time and effort to identify and protect them.

The following illustrate omissions of future benefits that proved problematic with hindsight:

- *Pantry Pride Enterprises, Inc. v. Stop & Shop Companies, Inc.*[13]: A sublessee granted its sublessor a right of first refusal on an assignment of the sublease. The sublessee operated a supermarket at the subleased site. It was one of twenty supermarkets the sublessee owned. The sublessee wanted to sell the chain of supermarkets, which would include the real property interests, and the equipment located, in the stores. The price allocated to the store on the subleased site was $571,000. The price for the sublease alone was $142,750.[14] The hazard to the sublessee was the potential for the first refusal right to apply even when the sublease was bundled

in marketing and managing the franchise business; the implicit benefit was business management skill.

[13] 806 F.2d 1227 (4th Cir. 1986).

[14] The court held the sublessor-grantee was entitled to purchase the sublease without the equipment located on the site.

with all the assets comprising the supermarket chain. The hazard was the broad first refusal right, which may have been caused by the sublesse overlooking the breadth of that right when the first refusal right was granted. In any event, the oversight resulted in the sublessee missing an opportunity to eliminate the hazard: the sale of the sublease with the business of which it was a part could have been excluded from the first refusal right. As the sublease had to be sold separately to the sublessor, the sublessee lost the incremental value that would have been realized had the sublease been included with the sale of the other supermarket chain assets.

- *Cragmere Holding Corp. v. Socony-Mobil Oil Co., Inc.*[15]: A lessor agreed in a lease that it would not allow another tenant to operate a business on its property that competed with the tenant's business within an agreed distance of the tenant's leased site. The lessor later acquired a parcel of land adjacent to the leased site that was within the agreed distance. The tenant claimed the additional parcel was also subject to the noncompete restriction.[16] The hazard to the landlord was the potential for the noncompete restriction to extend to any additional adjacent parcels within the agreed distance acquired by the landlord. The cause of the hazard was the broadly worded noncompete restriction. The landlord's oversight of the application of the restriction on any additional adjacent land within the agreed distance that it might purchase contributed to the creation of the hazard. Acquiring the additional parcel was a further cause of the harm. As the tenant was correct, the lessor lost the additional rent it could have realized from renting the additional parcel to a competing business.
- *Coca-Cola Bottling Co. of Elizabethtown, Inc. v. Coca-Cola, Inc.*[17]: The contract between Coke and a number of bottlers required each gallon of the syrup supplied by Coke to contain a fixed quantity of cane or beet sugar, based on a 1921 consent decree. The price charged to the bottlers was partly based on the published market price of beet sugar. In 1987, Coke began unilaterally substituting high-fructose corn syrup for sugar because the corn syrup had

[15] 65 N.J. Super. 322, 167 A.2d 825 (N.Y. App. 1961).

[16] After the lessor purchased additional property adjacent to and within 1,000 feet of the leased parcel, it sought a judicial declaration that it could be used to operate a service station. The court held the restriction extended to the subsequently acquired parcel.

[17] 988 F.2d 386 (3d Cir. 1993).

become available, did not alter the taste, and cost less. Coke continued to calculate the price based on sugar. The bottlers objected to the substitution. The hazard to Coke was a fixed formula for the syrup that precluded using substitutes that might yield cost savings. The decision not to consider or oversight of the potential use of substitutes in 1921 enabled the hazard to occur. Had Coke been entitled to substitute syrup for sugar without the bottlers' consent, it alone would have enjoyed, and the bottlers would not have enjoyed any, of the additional, resulting value. Otherwise, it had to come to terms with the bottlers over how the additional value would be shared.[18]

Information Benefits. Information that two parties engage in an exchange and the details of that exchange have value distinct from the benefits that drive the parties to transact with each other. Information one party receives from the other party may be the benefit the latter expects to realize. Such is the case where one party licenses another to use proprietary information.[19] The parties expect value to be created by

---

18 The bottlers sued for breach of contract, claiming Coca-Cola breached by substituting the syrup for sugar without their agreement, and alternatively, the contract should be re-formed to allow use of the syrup and pass the savings through to the bottlers. The bottlers were awarded damages by the district court. The appeal court affirmed the finding of breach, but because the bottlers had suffered no loss, reduced the judgment to $1. The court said of the alleged mutual mistake, "The fact that the parties failed in 1921 to anticipate and provide for the development of satisfactory sweeteners, other than sucrose, does not mean that they made a mutual mistake in reducing their shared intent to writing when they specified the sweetener for Coca-Cola Bottlers' Syrup would be 5.32 pounds sucrose per gallon. The fact that they based the price of the syrup on the market price of sucrose with a mark-up in absolute terms, instead of a percentage mark-up, is evidence to the contrary." *Id.* at 405.

19 *E.g.*, Sunds Defibrator AB v. Beloit Corp., 20 U.S.P.Q.2d 1633, 930 F.2d 564 (7th Cir. 1991), where the agreement pursuant to which Sunds licensed Beloit to manufacture and sell pulp washers in North America using Sunds' nonpatented technology prohibited each party from disclosing and using technical information received from the other party "in any manner, except to the extent necessary to accomplish the purposes of this Agreement." Sunds developed a competing pulp washer and offered to sell it in Taiwan at a price lower than that offered by Sunds. Sunds sued for breach of contract; and the trial court awarded damages and ordered Beloit to withdraw its other bids to sell pulp washers around the world. The appeals court upheld the award and order, holding the license agreement prohibited Beloit's use of technical information disclosed to it even if it could have shown it was in the public domain and Beloit was permitted to disclose it.

the use of that information. That information and its value differ from the information about the parties and their deal. Value in information about the parties and deal can be realized by adding a party's name to a customer, client, partner, or other list used for marketing or by compiling statistical data about that and similar deals that can be sold or otherwise used by financial and other advisors and rating agencies.[20]

The utility or value in such information flows to the party or parties that can exploit it. That may or may not be the same as the party who controls that exploitation. The possibilities are:

- one party controls the exploitation by both parties of all information about itself, the other party, and the transaction,
- both parties jointly control the exploitation by either party of all such information, and
- each party is free to exploit such information.

Control over such information is a zero-sum game: the control one party has over information comes at the expense of the other party. In all three instances, both parties can realize the potential value of such information, but its ability to do so varies with control over its exploitation of such information. In the first, the controlling party alone decides when information about itself, the other party, or the transaction may be exploited. In the second, neither can exploit such information and realize its value without the agreement of the other. In the third, both are free to realize the value of such information without having to obtain the other's consent. Neither party has control over the other party's exploitation in that situation.

The following cases illustrate how control over the flow of information about each of the parties and their transaction can be an important benefit to one or both parties, independent of the other benefits the parties expect to realize:

---

[20] *E.g.*, All West Pet Supply Company v. Hill's Pet Products Division, Colgate-Palmolive Co., 847 F. Supp. 858, amended 842 F. Supp. 1376 (1994), where the distributor of pet food products claimed the manufacturer was contractually obligated to keep information about the distributor's customers confidential after termination of their distribution contract. The court held that the contractual obligation to keep the information confidential terminated with the contract.

- *Grunseth v. Marriott Corp.*[21]: A lobbyist and candidate for governor stayed at a hotel in Washington D.C. A reporter obtained a copy of the receipt for that night's stay and published a story that the candidate had stayed the night with a woman with whom he was having an affair. The information about the candidate's stay had value to the reporter. Possibly, the candidate assumed the facts concerning his stay were private, though there was no contract with the hotel to that effect. The hazard to the candidate was his lack of control over the information. The causes of the harm were the hotel's disclosure of the information to the reporter and the reporter's use of the information. The hotel and party were each at liberty to use the receipt—information about the candidate's stay—as it saw fit. His oversight resulted in his missing whatever opportunity he might have had to insist upon the information about his stay remaining private. To that extent, his oversight enabled the hazard to occur.[22]
- *Personal Touch, Inc. v. Lenox, Inc.*[23]: Personal Touch (PT) designed a commemorative plate, contracted with Lenox (L) for its manufacture at $35 per plate, and organized a marketing campaign. L published a brochure that included a picture of the prototype of the plate and a price of $20. The design of the plate had value to L distinct from the value to be received from sales to PT. It hoped to generate additional sales to third parties. That information is likely to have had similar value to PT. Where PT assumed it alone controlled flow of the information about the design, L assumed each party was free to use it as it saw fit. The contract was silent on the issue.[24] The absence of control over the information imparted to L was a hazard for PT. The cause of the loss was PT's publication

---

[21] 872 F. Supp. 1069 (D.C. 1995).

[22] The candidate sued the hotel, claiming breach of an implied contract to keep information about his stay confidential. The court dismissed the claim. "There is no evidence in this record to prove the existence of such an implied contract. Plaintiff never made nondisclosure of his hotel receipts a condition of his stay at the . . . hotel." *Id.* at 1073.

[23] 708 F. Supp. 108 (E.D. Penn. 1989).

[24] PT canceled its order with L and demanded that L withdraw the brochure. When L refused, PT unsuccessfully sued, claiming L had a duty implied by trade usage and the covenant of good faith and fair dealing to keep information about the commemorative plate confidential. The court found no evidence of a trade usage and was unwilling to hold the duty of good faith and fair dealing implied a confidentiality obligation.

of the design and price. PT's oversight resulted in missing the opportunity to avoid the hazard.

- *Hoffman v. L & M Arts*[25]: The seller of a valuable Mark Rothko painting displayed in a museum sold it privately, rather than through an auction, to avoid publicity about her financial condition. The buyer agreed to "make maximum efforts" to keep all aspects of the sale confidential indefinitely. Nearly three years later, the buyer consigned the painting to public auction at Sotheby's, causing the seller the very embarrassment she had sought to avoid. The information about the sale had value to the buyer, as it could realize a higher price by selling at a public auction at Sotheby's. It was also useful to the seller, as its disclosure would and did embarrass her. The case was one in which one party, the seller, expected to control all dissemination of information about her and the sale, even though doing so might require controlling future sales and information about those sales because any such sale would reveal that she had sold the painting.[26] Because the buyer paid less for the painting than if he had bought it a public auction, he received value for the value given in the confidentiality agreement. He may have underestimated or later regretted the value he gave when agreeing to an indefinite term for the confidentiality agreement.

Reputation. The fact that a party engages in a transaction or that the transaction is with a particular counterparty may enhance or harm a party's reputation or good will. That effect has value to the party whose reputation is affected. That value is part and parcel of the benefit the party expects to receive when the good reputation of the party completing a task is material to the principal value the other party expects to receive. A producer of a movie, television program, concert, or performance enlists a star to perform because of the additional value his or her reputation brings to the performance.[27] When the reputation of the

[25] 774 F. Supp.2d 826 (N.D. Tex. 2011).

[26] The seller sued for breach of the confidentiality agreement, claiming that the publicity about the sale would allow an inference to be drawn that the seller had sold to the person offering to sell through the auction. The court held the claim was plausible and denied the buyer's motion to dismiss.

[27] *E.g.*, in RKO Radio Pictures, Inc. v. Jarrico, 128 Cal.App.2d 172, 274 P. 2d 928 (Cal. App. 1954), a longtime associate of a screenwriter testified before a congressional committee investigating communist activities in the motion picture industry that the screenwriter was a communist; the screenwriter, when called to testify, invoked his privilege against

party completing the task does not so enhance the value the other party receives, any positive or negative value is independent of the primary benefit. In either case, the potential for a transaction to damage a party's reputation is a hazard; overlooking it contributes to the hazard. In both cases, a morals clause[28] allocates and mitigates the loss of value to a party that may result from conduct by the other party.

Following are illustrations of how the conduct of a party may adversely affect the other party's reputation:

- *In re NWFX, Inc.*[29]: A company sold money orders through stores, which, as agents, issued the money orders, collected the money from the customers, held that money in trust for the company, and periodically paid it to the company less their commissions. Financially troubled, the company instructed the stores to stop selling its money orders. To minimize the loss of good will with their customers, two such stores used part or all of the sums held in trust for the benefit of the company to refund amounts paid by their customers whose money orders were dishonored or to pay amounts to payees to whom the money orders had been payable. The stores had no obligation to their customers or the payees to refund or pay on the money orders, nor did the contract expressly entitle the stores to make such payments.[30] The stores most likely

self-incrimination and refused to deny or confirm the allegation, and the motion picture production company that had hired the screenwriter to write the screenplay for a movie filed for declaratory relief, alleging the screenwriter had breached the morals clause in the contract that obligated him to "conduct himself with due regard to public conventions and morals and . . . not do anything which would tend to degrade him or bring him into public disgrace, obloquy, ill will or ridicule." The contract, which expressly recited that "essential consideration of the contract was the popularity and good reputation of appellant with the public," recognized that the value of the film could be affected by the writer's actions and reputation. *See* also RKO Radio Pictures, Inc. v. Scott, 240 F.2d 87 (9th Cir. 1957); Nader v. ABC Television, Inc., 330 F. Supp.2d 345 (S.D.N.Y. 2004).

28 *E.g.*, Charter Practices Int'l, LLC v. Robb, 2014 WL 273855 (D. Conn. 2013), where a "charter practice" or franchise agreement for a pet hospital provided, "You must conduct your business following the highest standards of honesty, integrity, fair dealing and ethics. You must do nothing that would tend to discredit, dishonor, reflect adversely upon or in any manner injure the reputation of MMI, CPI, their affiliates, or the Network [of Banfield Pet Hospitals]."

29 864 F.2d 593 (8th Cir. 1989).

30 After the company filed for bankruptcy, its trustee claimed the deductions and setoffs for such payments against the funds held in trust were not permitted under the bankruptcy code, as the contract between the company and the stores did not permit them. The court

overlooked how the company's default on its commitments to the stores' customers could damage good will with those customers, and the resulting hazard was the absence of an express right to refund and pay customers following a default by the company.

- *BP Products North America Inc. v. Twin Cities Stores, Inc.*[31]: The morals clause in a gas station lease obligated the gasoline retailer lessee "not conduct itself at any [TCS store] in a manner that, in Twin Cities' sole discretion, may reflect poorly on Twin Cities' name or business reputation or may offend an appreciable segment of the public." The retailer set its prices above those of its competitors, which drove away customers from the stores. The contract expressly reserved to the retailer the right to set prices of its products. The hazard to the lessor was the potential for the gasoline retailer to set gasoline prices that would drive away other business. The lessor, however, had not overlooked the potential negative effect of gasoline prices on other business in the stores, as the contract expressly allowed the gasoline retailer to set its prices. The lessor may have underestimated the potential negative effect of the lessee having gasoline prices higher than its competitors on other business; it had come to regret accepting the risk it had assumed.

Task Oversight and Rejection

Value-Creating Tasks. A task is to a benefit what a means is to an end. It is an act that when completed (or not completed in the case of forbearance) will contribute to realization of a benefit. It may not be the only task that must be completed for a benefit to be realized, and alternative actions may achieve the same result. When it is one of the means by which such a contribution can be made, it or its alternatives must be identified and completed. It may be a task that one party completes for the benefit of the other or for its own benefit. Ideally, it will be identified and responsibility for its completion allocated to one of the parties before or at contract formation.

held that because the stores had no obligation to their customers or the payees to refund or pay on the money orders and nothing in the contract with the company allowed them to do so, the deductions or set-offs were not allowed under the bankruptcy code. *Id.* at 596.

[31] 534 F. Supp.2d 959 (D. Minn. 2007).

When, at contract formation, a task that must be completed for a benefit to be realized is not included in the list of such tasks, a gap in that list is created. That gap is also a hazard, depending upon which party must complete the task and which will benefit from its completion. Two such hazards are as follows:

(1) The missed or rejected task is one that must be completed by one party for the other to realize a benefit.

(2) The missed or rejected task is one that must be completed by a party for it to realize a benefit.

Scenario (1) creates two potential hazards: (a) The party that anticipates realizing a benefit stands to lose that benefit or incur additional cost to have the other party complete a task if the latter is not obligated to do so. (b) The other party—which must complete the missed or rejected task—stands to incur additional cost to complete the task or liability for failing to do so. In scenario (2), the party anticipating to benefit stands to incur the additional time and cost of completing the missed task or choosing to abandon the transaction because such additional time and cost overshadow the value of the anticipated benefit. What separates scenarios (1)(a) and (1)(b), on one hand, and (2), on the other, is that in the former a party is expected to complete a task for the benefit of the other, whereas in the scenario in (2) it is expected to complete the task for its own benefit.

Following are cases that illustrate these hazards:

- *Holston Valley Hospital and Medical Center, Inc. v. The Ashford Group Ltd.*[32]: A contractor agreed to transfer a hospital's data from a Honeywell to an IBM computer. While the contract required the hospital to provide readable computer tapes, it did not state which of the parties was to render those tapes usable on the IBM machine. Either party could convert the data, but this would require considerable time and cost to complete. The contractor abandoned the contract when the hospital failed to provide such tapes. Both parties overlooked conversion of the data on the tapes (assuming neither identified the task and chose not to allocate it to one or the other). The contractor expected the hospital to

[32] 661 F. Supp. 72 (E.D. Tenn. 1986).

convert the data on the tapes. Had it been correct, the case would illustrate the hazard in (2), where the hospital overlooked a task it had to complete to realize its anticipated benefit (and for the contractor to perform, transferring the data to the new computer). The hospital expected the contractor to convert the data. The case thus illustrates a potential scenario (1)(a) and an actual scenario (1)(b): the hospital and the contractor each overlooked a task that the hospital successfully claimed the contractor had to perform for the benefit of the hospital.[33]

- *Cenex, Inc. v. Arrow Gas Service*[34]: Cenex purchased Arrow Gas's propane business for a base price of $1.6 million, paid at the closing, subject to adjustment depending upon the actual number of gallons of propane gas Cenex sold during the two-year period following the closing date. The purchase price was reduced by $.40 per gallon for each gallon below 6,000,000 gallons of propane sold, up to a total of $200,000, and increased by $.40 per gallon for each gallon above that figure, up to a maximum of $400,000. The total amount of propane sold in the applicable two-year period following the closing date was 4,603,100 gallons, resulting in a payment due to Cenex in the amount of $200,000. The acquisition contract did not specify what, if anything, Cenex was required to do to promote sales. The seller overlooked the tasks the buyer had to complete to boost sales so that the maximum earn-out payments became due and payable. No effort by Arrow Gas was required.[35] The case illustrates the scenario in (1)(a): Cenex lost the additional payments because Arrow Gas did not have to make any particular effort to boost sales.
- *Sonoran Scanners, Inc. v. PerkinElmer, Inc.*[36]: Sonoran Scanners, Inc. (SSI) developed a high-speed computer-to-plate (CTP) technology it hoped to market to the newspaper and graphic arts industries

[33] The hospital sued the contractor for breach of contract. The district court held as a matter of law that because the hospital "was admittedly inexperienced in using IBM equipment and since [the contractor] represented itself to be experts, the Court finds it unreasonable to believe that Holston Valley [the hospital] would hire experts to convert the computer programs but would reserve the most difficult conversion task for its own inexperienced staff." *Id.* at 74.

[34] 896 F. Supp. 1574 (D. Wyo. 1995).

[35] The court, granting summary judgment to the acquirer, held the seller had submitted no evidence that the covenant of good faith and fair dealing had been breached.

[36] 585 F.3d 535 (1st Cir. 2009).

and, by 2000, it built a prototype machine that would save its users significantly in the long-term. It failed to sell any machines because they were expensive and potential customers had concerns about SSI's ability to support a new technology. Short of cash, indebted to its suppliers and other creditors, and having exhausted its founder's $3.5 million investment, SSI sold its business to PerkinElmer, Inc. (PEI) for $3.5 million paid at closing, a significant portion of which went to SSI's creditors, and an additional $3.5 million in "earn-out" payments over five years: $750,000 if three machines were sold in the first year, $1.5 million (less the prior earn-out payment) if ten machines were sold during the first two years, and additional payments if the CTP machines yielded certain margins. PEI also hired SSI's founder under a separate employment agreement for $150,000 per year plus up to $6.6 million in bonuses, calculated in a manner similar to the earn-out payments.[37] Three and a half years later, during which time only one CTP machine had been sold, PEI shut down the CTP business and laid off the associated staff, including the founder. Neither contract, however, specified what, if anything, PEI was to do to develop and promote the CTP business. Still, as SSI and the founder successfully claimed, PEI had to reasonably help SSI and its founder to earn their earn-out payments.[38] What those tasks included had been overlooked by both parties. Because PEI was obligated to help the founder and the seller earn the earn-out payments, the outcome was the opposite of *Cenex*, and the case illustrates scenario (1)(b); both parties overlooked a task the buyer had to perform for the seller's benefit.

- *Stevedoring Services of America, Inc. v. Marvin Furniture Manufacturing, Inc.*[39]: A tenant leased a warehouse to store foam rubber used to manufacture mattresses. After the lease was signed, the fire department insisted upon the installation of a "one-hour"

---

[37] *Id.* at 537–38.

[38] SSI and the founder claimed PEI had an implied duty "to make good faith and reasonably competent and diligent efforts to develop, market, and sell [the] CTP products." *Id.* at 539. The federal district court granted summary judgment to PEI, but the appeal court reversed, ruling, "There was no language in the agreement negating an obligation by PerkinElmer to use reasonable efforts or conferring absolute discretion on PerkinElmer as to the operation of the business. Under these circumstances, we find that PerkinElmer had an implied obligation to use reasonable efforts to develop and promote SSI's technology." Id at 544.

[39] 54 Wn. App. 424, 774 P.2d 44 (Wash. App. 1989).

separation barrier and a sprinkler system to protect the building from the fire hazard created by the storage of the foam rubber. The tenant nowhere claimed the landlord was responsible for the improvements. The landlord's task was delivery of possession of the leased premises. Although the tenant did not expect to do so, one of its tasks was to make changes that would enable it to store foam rubber at the site. In this case the party would have completed the task for its own benefit. The case illustrates scenario (2).[40]

The hazard in each of the preceding cases is an omission from the list of tasks and the terms of the contract of the task that had to be completed by one of the parties. Assuming the party could have identified and eliminated the omission but for the oversight, its oversight enabled the omission to become a hazard.

Value-Preserving Tasks. In addition to those that must be completed for a benefit to be realized, certain additional tasks when completed will enhance or protect that benefit from diminution after its initial realization. The hazards are comparable to those in scenario (1): for the party expecting to realize a benefit, the hazard is the possibility the other party will not complete the additional task that will protect that benefit in scenario (1)(a). The hazard for the other party is having to complete a task it did not expect to complete in scenario (1)(b).

The following illustrate such tasks:

- *Bessemer Trust Co. v. Branin*[41]: Branin was a shareholder in a financial services firm that sold substantially all its assets, including its client accounts, to Bessemer, was employed by Bessemer for a short while thereafter, and left to join a third financial services firm. One of his former clients contacted him and met with representatives of his new firm and him to decide whether to transfer its account to

[40] When the tenant was unsuccessful at persuading the fire department the fire code did not require these changes, it vacated the building and terminated the lease, claiming the changes required by the fire code were economically unfeasible and the lease had been frustrated by the fire department's actions. The trial court granted the landlord's motion for summary judgment. The appeal court affirmed the judgment, holding that in the absence of an attempt to resolve the dispute with the fire department through the applicable administrative procedure, it could not claim frustration of contract.

[41] 16 N.Y.3d 549, 925 N.Y.S.2d 371, 949 N.E.2d 462, 211 N.Y. Slip. Op. 03307 (N.Y. 2011).

Branin's new firm. The contract was silent on what contact Branin could have with his old clients. The parties may have overlooked what marketing and business the sellers could do with their former clients after the closing. They had an implied obligation not to solicit their former clients, however.[42] To that extent, they had a task they had to complete that they had not specified in the contract. The sellers were permitted to trade with their former clients whom they had not impermissibly solicited. To that extent, Bessemer had missed a task it might have required of them.[43] How a seller was to respond to solicitations from his former clients without breaching the implied duty not to solicit was a fact to be determined in each case.[44] The hazard to the buyer was the potential for the sellers to receive business from their former clients, business which the buyer expected to have after the sale. Oversight of or a decision to ignore that potential enabled it to result in a loss.

- *Dushkin v. Desai*[45]: Desai formed a small community, appointed himself as its leader, and for twenty-five years presented himself as its authentic guru, "a 'teacher and object of veneration' who

[42] Bessemer sued in the New York state court; the case was removed to federal district court, which referred to the New York Court of Appeals the question of whether an 'improper solicitation' occurred as a result of "(1) the active development and participation by the seller, in response to inquiries from a former client whose good will the seller has voluntarily sold to a third party, in a plan whereby others at the seller's new company solicit a client, and (2) participation by the seller in solicitation meetings where the seller's role is largely passive." 16 N.Y.3d 549, 551-2, 925 N.Y.S.2d 371, 374, 949 N.E.2d 462, 465.

[43] "Moreover, the seller of a business is free to subsequently compete with the purchaser and even 'accept the trade of his former customers, provided that he does not actively solicit such trade'. . . . To militate against these risks, which extend beyond the limited scope of a seller's 'implied covenant,' a purchaser is free to negotiate an express covenant, reasonably restricting, for instance, a 'seller's right to compete in a particular geographical area or field of endeavor.'" 16 N.Y.3d 549, 557, 925 N.Y.S.2d 371, 377, 949 N.E.2d 462, 468 (citations omitted).

[44] The court held "We conclude that, while a seller may not contact his former clients directly, he may, 'in response to inquiries' made on a former client's own initiative, answer factual questions. Furthermore, under the circumstances where a client exercising due diligence requests further information, a seller may assist his new employer in the 'active development . . . [of] a plan' to respond to that client's inquiries. Should that plan result in a meeting with a client, a seller's 'largely passive' role at such meeting does not constitute improper solicitation in violation of the 'implied covenant.' As such, a seller or his new employer may then accept the trade of a former client." 16 N.Y.3d 549, 559–60, 925 N.Y.S.2d 371, 380, 949 N.E.2d 462, 470.

[45] 18 F. Supp.2d 117 (D. Mass. 1998).

attains his status in part through several forms of abstinence, including refraining from sexual activity and material pursuits." In fact, he had sexual affairs with some of his followers and received a portion of the revenues from the community's operations. During the last fifteen years of its operation, the community had 15,000 paying guests a year and a staff of 250 resident members who worked for room and board and a small stipend, largely out of dedication to Desai. The contract between Desai and his staff nowhere prohibited his hypocritical behavior,[46] though the utility of the counseling was diminished by his behavior when it became known. The hazard to the followers was the absence of any restraint on the guru's actions; their oversight of or decision to ignore the potential for such actions enabled him to behave hypocritically with impunity.

- *Cordonier v. Century Shopping Plaza Associates*[47]: A lease for a space in a shopping mall obligated the lessor to lease two large spaces to a chain supermarket and a chain drug store, respectively. The lessor leased such spaces as required, but the tenants vacated. The lessee claimed the lessor was also obligated to keep such spaces continually rented to such stores. One of the lessee's anticipated benefits was a volume of foot traffic in the shopping mall commensurate with that which had a chain supermarket and a chain drug store. The lessee identified one task the landlord could complete (the landlord had to lease spaces to a chain supermarket and chain drug store), but missed another (these spaces had to be so leased repeatedly, whenever a supermarket or drug store tenant vacated).[48] Unlike the two previous cases, where value or utility is preserved by forbearance from actions that diminish the same, value is preserved, in this case by actions by the landlord.

---

[46] When the facts came to light, fourteen of his followers sued, claiming, among other things, breach of contract, in particular that the implied covenant of good faith and fair dealing obligated him to live to the standards he professed to follow. The court dismissed the claim, holding "nothing in the allegations indicates that any contract specifically required Desai to adhere to a particular code of conduct or abjure any specific behavior to maintain his status." *Id.* at 123.

[47] 82 Cal. App.3d 991, 147 Cal. Rptr. 558 (Cal. App. 1978).

[48] The court held the lessee was entitled to introduce evidence that an obligation to keep spaces leased to a chain supermarket and drug store should be implied.

Condition and Contingency Oversights

Conditions and contingencies can be overlooked during transaction planning. A condition is a circumstance that exists at contract formation and impedes or facilitates the completion of a task or realization of a benefit. Oversight of a condition may result in ignorance of how a benefit or task is impossible or more or less difficult or expensive to complete. A contingency is an event that occurs after contract formation. The occurrence of a contingency alters the conditions that facilitate or impede benefit realization or task completion. Oversight of a contingency may or may not have an adverse effect on a transaction, depending whether it occurs.

The following cases illustrate condition and contingency oversight:

- *Griffith v. Brymer*[49] and *Krell v. Henry*[50]: In the first case, Griffith hired a room from Brymer to view King Edward VII's coronation procession. Unknown to either party, an hour earlier a decision had been reached to cancel the parade.[51] Before and at contract formation, the hazard to the renter was a condition: that there was no longer scheduled a parade to watch. After contract formation, the condition, together with the parties' actions, resulted in losses for the parties. In the second case, the parade was canceled after the renter agreed to rent the room to watch the parade. The hazard that existed at and after contract formation was a contingency: the potential for the parade to be canceled, whatever the reason. Oversight of the condition in the first case and the contingency in the second precluded opportunities to address the hazards.[52]
- *Grenall v. United of Omaha Life Ins. Co.*[53]: Grenall paid a single, substantial premium for an annuity payable in monthly installments for the rest of her life. Unknown to her, she had a fatal disease when she bought the annuity. She died after receiving only three

---

49 19 T.L.R. 434 (1903).

50 *Supra* ch.1, note 24.

51 Justice Robert Samuel Wright held the agreement was made on the "missupposition of facts" and void. 19 T.L.R. 434.

52 Lord Justice Vaughan Williams described the cancelation of the coronation procession as "an event 'of such a character that it cannot reasonably be supposed to have been in the contemplation of the contracting parties when made.'" 72 L.J. (K.B.) 794, 797, 89 L.T. 328, 331, 19 T.L.R. 711, 713.

53 165 Cal. App.4th 188, 80 Cal. Rptr.3d 609, 08 Cal. Daily Op. Serv. 9581 (Cal. App. 2008).

> payments. Because the disease had been contracted before contract formation, it was a condition that affected the value of the annuity to the annuitant. The hazard to the annuitant was her illness that would eventually prevent her from realizing anywhere near the amount she anticipated. Her ignorance of her condition precluded her acting to avoid the loss that would result from the hazard.[54]

More detailed descriptions of contingencies that may be overlooked are described in chapters 10, 11, and 12.

Commitment and Responsibility Gaps

Commitment Gaps. A contractual commitment is a promise to complete or forbear from completing certain actions or to cause an outcome or result or a warranty that an outcome or result will occur. To the extent a party commits to do any of the foregoing, it assumes responsibility for certain of the losses the other party incurs because it fails to do so, subject to contract law principles that discharge or excuse it from performance.

A task to be completed by one party for the benefit of the other may be identified but no commitment given to complete it. Either the commitment has been overlooked by the party for whose benefit it would be completed or, if the commitment has not been overlooked, such party decided to proceed without it. The latter is an instance of rejection. The opposite side of the coin is that a party gives a commitment without recognizing that it has done so or, if it has recognized that it has, it later regrets having done so. The latter is another instance of remorse.

City of Yonkers v. Otis Elevator Co.[55] illustrates a commitment gap. Yonkers induced Otis, who had been located there since 1853, to remain, using its urban renewal powers to facilitate expansion of Otis' plant by acquiring and transferring to Otis land adjacent to the Otis factory. In exchange, Otis renovated and expanded its plant. Changes in technology during the next few years rendered the plant obsolete, and six years later Otis closed it. The contract did not include an express promise by Otis

---

[54] The administrators of her estate sought to rescind the contract on the ground that her decision to purchase the annuity was based on a mistake of fact: her ignorance of her illness. Her estate's claim was dismissed, the court ruling that, as a matter of law, "A contracting party bears the risk of a mistake when the agreement so provides or when the party is aware of having only limited knowledge of the facts relating to the mistake but treats this limited knowledge as sufficient."

[55] 844 F.2d 42 (2nd Cir. 1988).

to continue its operations in Yonkers for any period of time and none was implied. Yonkers had identified the task it wanted Otis to perform, continued operation at its location, but overlooked getting a commitment from Otis to do so.[56] The resulting hazard to Yonkers was the potential for Otis to leave before Yonkers had realized all anticipated benefits. The cause of harm to Yonkers was Otis' decision to leave Yonkers. Yonkers' oversight of Otis' lack of commitment enabled the hazard to occur, assuming it would have insisted upon a firm commitment for Otis to remain had it recognized the omission. Had an implied commitment by Otis been found, Otis would have overlooked it, finding itself with a burden it did not expect it had.

The terms obligor, obligee, promisor, promisee, and obligation are inapplicable where no commitment or promise has been made. Completion of a task may be obligatory or optional. A task is optional when the party expected to complete a task for the benefit of the other party is not liable for any such losses that flow from a failure to complete the task. When optional, no obligation exists, and the party expected to complete it is not an obligor. The task may be for the benefit of the party completing it or the other party. When it is for the benefit of the party completing it, it cannot be an obligation and the party completing it is not an obligor. It may be an obligation only when the task must be completed by one party for the benefit of the other. For convenience, a party expected but not obligated to complete a task for the benefit of the other is referred to as a "putative obligor" and the party expected to so benefit a "putative obligee."

Sequential Tasks. A task may be one in a sequence of tasks to be completed by the same party and can be completed only if each of the preceding tasks is completed. All the tasks must be completed for the other party to realize its anticipated benefit. If a commitment gap exists as to any one of these tasks, it creates a commitment gap as to all the tasks that follow it. This will be the result even if the party is committed to completing the later tasks. The hazard to the party for whose benefit a task will be completed is the gap in the commitment to complete the earlier task. In

[56] The city sued the company for breach of an implied promise to continue its operations there for a reasonable period of time, the contracts not having stated that the company was obligated to remain there. The court declined to imply such promise, while recognizing the purpose of the contract was to keep the company operating there. "The letter of intent . . . contains a clear distinction between 'goals' and 'commitments.' Otis' continuing presence was only a goal, not a commitment." *Id.* at 47.

addition, the fact that a party has a commitment to complete an earlier task does not ensure it has a commitment to complete a later one.

The following cases illustrate how the existence or absence of a commitment to complete an earlier task affects the commitment to complete a later, sequential task:

- *Nalle v. Taco Bell Corp.*[57]: Premises were leased "for the purpose of conducting thereon the business of a TACO BELL retain (sic) food outlet and for incidental purposes related thereto, or for any other legally permissible business or commercial venture as shall be provided by Lessor in writing." The rent was the higher of a fixed amount or a percentage of the gross receipts of the restaurant. The lessee stopped operating a restaurant on the premises after seventeen years, began using the site to store materials for the business, which it operated elsewhere, and paid the fixed rental amount. Two tasks were sequential and had to be completed in order for the lessor to realize the maximum benefits of its lease: (1) the lessee had to operate a restaurant on the site, and if it did, (2) it had to pay a percentage of its receipts as rent (if higher than the fixed rent). If the lessee had no commitment to complete (1), it effectively had no commitment to complete (2). Apart from the statement about how the premises could be used, the lease did not expressly state if there was a commitment to operate a restaurant on the site.[58]
- *Cenex, Inc.*[59]: This case is previously summarized.[60] The purchase price of a business increased or decreased depending upon the gross sales of the business after closing. Two tasks were sequential and had to be completed in order for the seller to realize the full

[57] 914 S.W.2d 685 (Tex. App. 1996).

[58] The lessor sued, unsuccessfully claiming the lessee was obligated to continue operating a restaurant on the premises, either under the wording of the lease or the implied covenant of good faith and fair dealing. The court held the obligation to operate a restaurant at the site would not be implied where the fixed rent was substantial. "[The lessor] Jim Ray, the original lessor and Nalle's predecessor in interest, stated in an affidavit submitted by Nalle that the minimum rent covered his financing obligations. In addition, the lease obligated Taco Bell to pay taxes, insurance, repairs, and upkeep expenses. Evaluated at the time the lease was signed, this fixed rent was sufficiently adequate and substantial to prevent the implication of a covenant of continuous operation." *Id.* at 689.

[59] 896 F. Supp. 1574 (D. Wyo.1995).

[60] *See* text accompanying notes 34 and 35.

benefit of the sale: (1) sufficient effort had to be made to sell a quantity of products that ensured the price would be increased by the maximum amount, and (2) the price increase had to be paid. It is conceivable that the buyer might do nothing to maintain or increase sales and the targets still be met, but that would be a scenario where the completion of (1) was not essential to the completion of (2). In effect, the business would generate sufficient sales notwithstanding the absence of effort by the buyer. If the completion of (1) was essential to the completion of (2), the absence of a commitment to complete (1) left the buyer at liberty to avoid payment of any price increase.

- *City of Yonkers.*[61]: This case is previously summarized.[62] Three tasks had to be completed for the city to realize its benefits: (1) it had to transfer the adjacent land to Otis, (2) Otis had to renovate and expand its plant, and (3) Otis had to remain and operate there. Yonkers had a commitment to complete (1) and Otis (2) but not (3). That Otis was obligated to complete (2), a substantial investment, did not imply a commitment to complete (3), however.

Buyer's Remorse

Regret over decisions about benefits, tasks, conditions, contingencies, and responsibility occur after contract formation, while implementation is in progress, or when the deal is completed. In the latter case, the regret may be that a better deal was not struck or, if the outcome was unsuccessful, regret over decisions that led to such outcome.

Buyer's Remorse. A party may have second thoughts about the deal it has struck at any time after contract formation. Those second thoughts may be about its choice of the benefits it expects, the benefits the other party expects, the tasks it or the other party must complete, and the commitments it has given to complete the tasks it must complete for the benefit of the other party or the lack of commitments by the other party to complete the tasks it must complete. The hazards to one party are that it may come to regret its choices or the other party may come to regret its choices.

---

[61] 844 F.2d 42 (2nd Cir. 1988).

[62] *See* text accompanying note 55.

Following are examples of regret that occurred immediately after contract formation, in the first case over benefits chosen and in the second over the tasks a party committed to complete:

- *Empire Gas Corp. v. American Bakeries Co.*[63]: In response to the increase in gasoline prices in the late 1970s, a bakery agreed to have its fleet of delivery trucks converted to propane by a gas company, following which the gas company would supply all of the bakery's propane gas requirements. A few days later, the bakery changed its mind about the project and never ordered the conversion of any of its trucks. The report of the case does not explain why the bakery abandoned the project so soon after contract formation. If, as seems likely, the cost savings no longer appeared as important as they had at contract formation, perhaps because management modified its priorities, the case illustrates remorse over the chosen benefits.[64]
- *Resource Management Co. v. Weston Ranch and Livestock Co.*[65]: Four brothers were the shareholders and officers of a company that owned 8,000 acres of ranch land in Utah. After they were asked if they would lease their properties for oil and gas exploration and production and two of the brothers signed leases separately for parcels they owned, one of the brothers met the president of Resource Management Co. (RMC), a consulting firm, at a cattlemen's convention. Months later, he and the four brothers met for three days and negotiated a two-page consulting agreement, obligating RMC to prepare evaluations of the company's land and provide advice on proposals and negotiations for mineral leases. The contract generously gave RMC a two percent interest in all hydrocarbons produced on the subject property, an undivided one percent interest to all other minerals produced on the property, thirty-one percent of the royalties in excess of fourteen and one-half percent received by the owners, and thirty-one percent of all cash or other income or consideration received by the owners from the

[63] 840 F.2d 1333 (7th Cir. 1988).

[64] The gas company successfully sued for breach of contract, and the bakery appealed, arguing that because theirs was a requirements contract, it was allowed to reduce its requirements, to nothing if it chose to do so in good faith; its commitment was to buy whatever gas it chose to buy from the gas company. Judge Richard Posner explained the bakery could not reduce its commitment simply because it had second thoughts about the project; it needed to show it had legitimate business reasons for eliminating its needs. Because the bakery offered no such reasons, its reversal of its position on the project breached the contract.

[65] 706 P.2d 1028 (Utah 1985).

sale, leasing, or other development of the minerals underlying the real property. A year and a half passed, during which the brothers and the company negotiated and executed several mineral leases without asking RMC for assistance. The brothers apparently wanted advice on the best terms of mineral leases and found it elsewhere. Their remorse was over the high fees they agreed to pay RMC. This case illustrates how quickly after contract formation a party comes to regret the task it has committed to complete when it learns it ceded more than normal value.[66]

Following are examples of regret over benefits, tasks, and commitments that came after the performance had been partly or wholly completed:

- *Cleary*[67]: This case is previously summarized.[68] Cleary acknowledged that he had considered attribution credit but did not think important enough to ask for at contract formation: "[I]t was not important that there be name credit, but it became in my mind more and more important as my involvement grew and grew by considerable degrees over the period of the ensuing years."[69] The case illustrates remorse by a party over its omission of a benefit.
- *Greenfield v. Philles Records, Inc.*[70]: The Ronnettes music group signed a contract with Philles Records in 1963, giving the latter "the right to make phonograph records, tape recordings or other reproductions of the performances embodied in such recordings by any method now or hereafter known." In the late 1980s, interest in the Ronnettes' music revived, and Philles Records licensed some of their records for use in movies and television and master

[66] The company and the brothers, through their lawyer, claimed they were never bound by the contract with RMC, and if they were, RMC had breached it. They argued the contract was unconscionable because RMC had received far more than its services were worth, so it seemed in retrospect. The Utah Supreme Court held for RMC, ruling, "When viewed in light of the circumstances as they existed . . . when the instant contract was executed, we cannot say that the contract was so unfair or oppressive in its mutual obligations as to shock the conscience. The contract was essentially like other contracts dealing with that particular subject matter. The [brothers], before contracting with RMC, recognized that they needed advice and assistance in dealing with oil companies and their land men." *Id.* at 1043–44.

[67] 30 F.3d 1255 (9th Cir. 1994).

[68] *See* text accompanying note 4.

[69] 30 F.3d at 1264.

[70] 98 N.Y.2d 562, 750 N.Y.S.2d 565, 780 N.E.2d 166 (2002).

recordings through a new process referred to in the industry as "synchronization."[71] The case illustrates how the potential for a future benefit can be identified and allocated in a contract, how the value one party gains is the other party's loss, and how a party who does not know the value of a benefit, because it is speculative at contract formation, may come to regret its decision to cede it to the other party.

- *Davis v. General Foods Corp.*[72]: Davis wrote to General Foods to indicate she had an idea for making flavors to be used in the household for making ice cream. General Foods replied, "We shall be glad to examine your idea for a new food product, but only with the understanding that the use to be made of it by us, and the compensation, if any, to be paid therefor, are matters resting solely in our discretion."[73] General Foods used her recipe and paid her nothing. Davis sued.[74] While knowing that General Foods had no commitment to pay, Davis expected to receive compensation if her recipe was used. The case illustrates how a party comes to regret not obtaining from the other party a commitment to complete a task that will yield the benefit.
- *U.S. v. Bethlehem Steel Corp.*[75]: Fleet agreed to build vessels for the government for price equal to its actual cost plus one-half the difference between the estimated and actual costs. After completion, the government refused to pay the profit portion of the price when it learned the difference would be approximately 22 percent of the shipbuilder's actual costs (excluding any profit Bethlehem Steel made selling the steel to its shipbuilding subsidiary), claiming the shipbuilder had misrepresented its estimated costs, and even if it had not done so, the half-savings clause was unconscionable. The unconscionability defense illustrates how a party, in this case the

[71] Ronnie Greenfield, one of the Ronnettes, claimed the contract did not give such rights to Philles Records. The trial court ruled for Greenfield, a decision upheld by the appeal court. New York's highest court affirmed, finding the language in the contract quoted above gave Philles Records the "right to reproduce the performances by any current or future technological methods."

[72] 21 F. Supp. 445 (S.D. N.Y. 1937).

[73] *Id.* at 446.

[74] After General Foods used her recipe and paid her nothing, she sued. District Judge John Clancy held for General Foods, while noting, in passing, "the plaintiff in disclosing her recipe relied upon the good faith and sense of fairness of the defendant corporation to recompense her for the value of the recipe." *Id.* at 447.

[75] 315 U.S. 289, 62 S. Ct. 581, 86 L. Ed. 855 (1942).

government, came to regret its commitment to complete a task for the benefit of the other party—paying the profit portion of the price—having made the commitment in desperation.[76]

Busted Deals. Blame and regret are common reactions to an unsuccessful transaction outcome, especially when the transaction is important to one or both parties. Regret over a decision is an acknowledgment that the party could have done better by making a decision that could have either avoided the unsuccessful outcome or mitigated its resulting losses. Hindsight enables a party to spot where a different decision would have yielded a favorable result. It may regret not having fully appreciated the probability or significance of a potential adverse outcome of its decision at contract formation.

Following are cases that illustrate such remorse:

- *Emerson v. Adult Total Community Services, Inc.*[77]: Emerson, an 83-year-old man, elected to live in a one-bedroom apartment (and not a personal care unit where a nurse was on duty in the personal care wing twenty-four hours a day) in a retirement residence community and receive meals and certain services. He paid an $83,000 entrance fee and monthly fees. He suffered a stroke five and one-half months later, following which he lay undiscovered for two days in his apartment and died two weeks after his discovery. Clearly, the outcome for Emerson was unsuccessful. While the report of the case does not indicate whether he regained consciousness to regret his decision—to forego the protection of a nurse on duty 24-hours a day—his estate did so on his behalf.[78] This is an example of a deal gone sour because a party decided against choosing the appropriate benefit: more attention in the personal care wing.

---

[76] The Supreme Court held for the shipbuilder. Justice Black noted, "[T]his, so far as we know, is the first instance in which government has claimed to be a victim of duress in dealings with an individual." He added, "The profits made in these and other contracts entered into under the same system may justly arouse indignation. But indignation based on the notions of morality of this or any other court cannot be judicially transmuted into a principle of law of greater force than the expressed will of Congress." 315 U.S. at 308–9.

[77] 842 F. Supp. 152, reconsideration den. 848 F. Supp. 44, *aff'd.* 39 F.3d 1169 (E.D. Penn 1994).

[78] His executors unsuccessfully claimed breach of contract, namely that the community had failed to provide monitoring services that would have resulted in his immediate discovery after his stroke, and rescission, that the entrance fee was unconscionable where the resident had lived in the community for only six months.

- *Stedman v. Hoogendoorn, Talbot, Davids, Godfrey & Milli*[79]: A North Carolina client asked his Chicago attorney to ascertain quickly (within 72 hours) if a Minneapolis rare coin dealer had any negative history, such as a bankruptcy, civil or criminal investigation, litigation, or conviction of any kind. The attorney hired a Wisconsin private investigator to conduct the investigation. The investigator collected information available electronically and reported his findings, highlighting the gaps in the information and his strong reservations. The client ignored the warnings and bought coins from the dealer that proved to be counterfeit. Only a search on site of the records of criminal convictions in the county where the dealer lived would have revealed his conviction for fraud. The client knew what benefit it hoped to realize (sufficient evidence concerning the coin dealer's character) and knew the tasks that had to be performed (a search of the county records) to ensure the benefit was realized, but the client chose not to have that task completed to save time and money, hoping the task was unnecessary.[80] This is an example of a deal gone sour because a party rejected a task the other would have had to perform for its benefit.

OVERSIGHT AND REJECTION RISK MANAGEMENT

The hazards that go unnoticed due to oversights and decisions a party comes to regret may be avoided, mitigated, and allocated through the use of the following:

- diligence that identifies that which would otherwise be missed,
- a cooling-off period that allows a party to further reflect on its efforts, possibly catching what it missed or decisions it will come to regret,

[79] 843 F. Supp. 1512 (N.D. Ill. 1994).

[80] The client sued his attorney for breach of contract, claiming that he would not have bought the rare coins had he known of this conviction. The attorney moved for summary judgment, and the court granted the motion, finding the attorney had not breached the contract by selecting the investigator. The court added the client had decided to proceed with the investment notwithstanding the strong reservations voiced by the investigator and attorney. The client was the putative obligee, the attorney the putative obligor, and the on-site search of the county court records the task that the client could have had completed once it received the investigator's report and recommendations. He rejected that task, hoping it was unnecessary in that it would not reveal any criminal convictions.

- disclaimers of commitments, which allow a party to escape responsibility for oversights and decisions it might come to regret,
- low standards of performance, which minimize a party's commitment to perform,
- amendments to correct oversights and decisions it comes to regret, and
- termination of contracts that are so flawed by oversights and decisions the party has come to regret that termination is preferable to continuing.

Diligence

Diligence will mitigate, if not avoid, most of the benefit, task, and commitment oversight and remorse risks previously described. Identifying a benefit, task, or commitment eliminates the risk it will be missed. For example, had Wildmon (in *Wildmon*[81]) identified control over subsequent broadcasting of the original program as an additional benefit he expected to realize, he could have included it in the contract. Had the parties identified the conversion of the data as a task that had to be completed in *Holston Valley Hospital and Medical Center, Inc.*,[82] responsibility for completing that task would have likely been allocated to one or the other party, and possibly the fee would have been adjusted accordingly, or there would have been no deal. In *Bessemer Trust Co.*,[83] had the parties identified and recognized the importance of the potential for the sellers to recover their clients' business at another firm, they could have detailed when it would be permissible. Decisions will still have to be made whether to include or omit a benefit, task, or commitment. Investigating and analyzing the possible outcomes of such decisions one way or another will further mitigate the benefit, task, and commitment remorse risks. This text does not attempt to summarize the diligence that might or should be done to identify and assess benefit, task, and commitment oversight and omission risks in any specific transaction or type of transaction.

---

81 *See* text accompanying notes 1–3.

82 *See* text accompanying notes 32 and 33.

83 *See* text accompanying notes 41–44.

Cooling-Off Period

A period following contract formation before a contract becomes effective or, if effective at contract formation, during which a contract can be terminated with impunity allows a party to reflect upon the deal before committing to proceed with the implementation phase. It would have been useful in *Resource Management Co.*,[84] where shortly after contract formation the mineral lessors learned how much they had agreed to give their consultant. Having agreed to terms, they could have checked with other advisors, such as their attorney, as to whether the compensation they agreed to pay was excessive. The cooling-off period would not have been helpful in *U.S. v. Bethlehem Steel Corp.*,[85] where the government did not learn of the high compensation until Fleet's performance under the contract had been completed. In *Grenall*,[86] the annuitant might have discovered her fatal illness during a cooling-off period. In both *Resource Management Co.* and *Grenall*, only diligence, on the level of fees in the first and the annuitant's health in the second could have revealed the hazards, though that could have been done before contract formation in both cases.

Commitment Disclaimer

Contract interpretation principles are the primary tools for allocating responsibility for oversight of, and regret over, decisions about benefits, tasks, condition, contingencies, and responsibility. A benefit or task that has been omitted, whether it has been overlooked or deliberately excluded, can be included by an implied term. Technically, the term was present in the contract from contract formation, and the later determination that the term was implied is a recognition that it was there from the beginning. For example, in *City of Yonkers*,[87] Yonkers claimed a duty on Otis to continue operations in the city should have been implied even though none was stated in the contract. The court declined to rescue Yonkers by implying the missing term. Responsibility for the risk of the absence of a commitment to complete the task—remaining in

[84] *See* text accompanying notes 65 and 66.

[85] *See* text accompanying notes 75 and 76.

[86] *See* text accompanying notes 53 and 54.

[87] 844 F.2d 42 (2nd Cir. 1988).

Yonkers—was thus allocated to Yonkers. In *Cenex*,[88] the seller claimed the duty of good faith and fair dealing implied a duty to use reasonable efforts to generate revenues that would yield the additional purchase price. The court's refusal to imply such a term allocated to the seller responsibility for the risk that the buyer had no commitment to promote propane sales. In *Sonoran Scanners*,[89] in which the court held the buyer had such a duty, the court allocated responsibility for the risk to the buyer.

An express disclaimer of any commitment can be used to mitigate the chance that a commitment will otherwise be implied by the application of contract interpretation principles.[90] A disclaimer negates or limits a party's responsibility for losses that result when a task has not been completed or a desired result has not been achieved. A commitment disclaimer may be broad or narrow:

- A party may commit to complete a task but disclaim that its effort will yield or contribute to yielding an anticipated benefit, thereby disclaiming responsibility for losses that occur because the desired result is not achieved.
- A party may commit to complete a task but disclaim any commitment to complete the task when applicable contract principles excuse or discharge its performance.
- A party may disclaim any commitment to complete a task.

A disclaimer creates a commitment gap to the extent one party still hopes or expects the other party to complete a task and no commitment to complete it or to complete it as anticipated is given. The party that accepts the disclaimer assumes the risk that the task for which no commitment to complete is made will not be completed or the outcome of completion of a task will not be as anticipated.

---

88 *See* text accompanying notes 34, 35, 59, and 60.

89 *See* text accompanying notes 36–38.

90 Black's Law Dictionary defines disclaimer of warranty as "[a]n oral or written statement intended to limit a seller's liability for defects in the goods sold." Black's Law Dictionary 562 (10th ed. 2014). Because warranties are given in a wide variety of transactions, in all of which they may be disclaimed, a definition limiting disclaimers to sale of goods transactions is too narrow. The definition in the text is adapted from the quoted definition.

Seegers v. Pioneer Hi-Bred International, Inc.[91] illustrates how a disclaimer limits an obligor's commitment. A seed company supplied corn seeds to farmers who agreed to grow the crop and deliver it to the seed company. The farmers planted the seeds. When grass began to encroach on the crop, they treated the grass with a pesticide, also supplied by the seed company. The pesticide damaged the crop.[92] Their contract with the seed company provided that the farmers "accept full responsibility for performance of such materials [fertilizers and pesticides] both to this crop and any succeeding crops."[93] Once the seed company accepted orders for seeds, it was obligated to supply them. That did not commit the seed company to ensure the seeds achieved any result, and the express disclaimer negated responsibility for the result falling below the farmers' expectations. The case illustrates the disclaimer described in the first bullet.

By disclaiming any commitment to complete a task, a party also reserves until the time for completion is to begin a right to decide whether to complete that task. It thus enables a party that is uncertain about whether it has identified or made good decisions about all the benefits that might be realized, the tasks that must be completed, and the costs of completing them, and the conditions and contingencies that might affect their completion to wait until the last possible moment to decide to commit or to complete a task without committing to do so. Following are three cases that illustrate such use of disclaimers:

- *Flight Concepts Limited Partnership v. The Boeing Company*[94]: Flight Concepts granted a Boeing subsidiary an exclusive worldwide license to manufacture and sell a "multirole" aircraft, the design for which was owned by Flight Concepts, in return for a royalty payment of $150,000 per aircraft sold by Boeing, such license to continue for ten years from the date of first sale. Before granting the license, Flight Concepts had unsuccessfully approached the Italian government and other aircraft manufacturers. The license not only did not

[91] 997 F. Supp. 1124 (N.D. Ind. 1998).

[92] The farmers sued the seed company for breach of contract. The court, granting summary judgment in favor of the seed company, held the quoted provision controlled liability for losses that resulted from the use of the pesticides, and the farmers, not the seed company, accepted that responsibility.

[93] *Id.* at 1126.

[94] 819 F. Supp. 1535 (D. Kan. 1993).

obligate Boeing to produce any aircraft, it stated clearly that Boeing had no such obligation.[95] Boeing disclaimed any commitment to use the licensed intellectual property. Boeing produced no aircraft using the design and terminated the license after two years. Flight Concepts had identified the benefit it hoped to realize (profits from aircraft sales), the task to be completed to realize that benefit (production and sale of the aircraft), and the commitment it needed from Boeing to get that task completed, but it failed to get Boeing to commit to produce and sell them and later regretted this unsatisfactory outcome.[96] Flight Concepts also unsuccessfully claimed Boeing had an implied duty, based on its duty to act in good faith and fair dealing. The disclaimer effectively trumped the contract interpretation principle that would have implied such duty. The case illustrates the disclaimer in the third bullet.

- *MJ & Partners Restaurant Ltd. Partnership v. Zadikoff*[97]: Michael Jordan, a famous basketball player, granted a partnership that owned and operated restaurants an exclusive license to use his name, voice, and likeness at a restaurant in the Chicago area and in a separate letter agreement reserved to himself "the right to review and approve each additional restaurant opportunity on a case-by-case basis."[98] The restaurant was a success and the partnership opened a second restaurant using Jordan's name in Chicago without his prior approval. The right to review and grant or refuse consent in its sole discretion negated any commitment

---

95 The relevant term read, "It is the intent of the parties hereto, in consideration of the terms and conditions herein, that BMAC shall be under no obligation whatsoever to produce and/or sell Licensed Product(s) and/or any product utilizing Licensor's Know-How during any part of the term of this License Agreement, and the License Agreement shall not be terminable by Licensor for BMAC's failure to produce and/or sell Licensed Product(s) and/or any product utilizing Licensor's Know-How." *Id.* at 1541.

96 Flight Concepts sued, asserting various claims based on what Boeing had said or not said during the negotiations, as well as the contract; the court granted Boeing summary judgment on all claims. Flight Concepts argued that the duty of good faith and fair dealing implied in every contract obligated Boeing to produce the aircraft and that this implied duty overrode the exclusion clause. Dismissing this claim, the court said the exclusion clause "precludes the plaintiffs from contending that they had a reasonable expectation of any implied protection. The concept of good faith became irrelevant on these matters." *Id.* at 1551.

97 995 F. Supp. 929 (N.D. Ill. 1998).

98 *Id.* at 930.

by Jordan to allow the use of his name by the partnership.[99] The partnership also unsuccessfully claimed that Jordan had an implied duty to consent, given the success of the first restaurant, based on the duty of good faith and fair dealing. The express reservation trumped the principle that would have implied such duty. The case illustrates the disclaimer described in the third bullet.

- *G. Golden Associates of Oceanside, Inc. v. Arnold Foods Co., Inc.*[100]: Golden Associates (GA) sold the technical information for making a flat bread product it had developed and associated trademarks in exchange for a percentage of the net sales proceeds of the flat bread products sold by the buyer. The contract also stated that the buyer knew best how to develop, manufacture, and sell such products. It further stated that the buyer "shall have complete and total discretion in determining the manner and extent to which it will manufacture, distribute, sell or promote the [p]roducts, and grant licenses of its rights."[101] The buyer produced and sold the flat breads for a little over a year and ceased production. Arnold Foods (AF) acquired the buyer and resumed production for eighteen months and ceased production. About the same time, AF acquired another company that produced flat bread products under its own name. The quoted language disclaimed any responsibility to do anything with GA's products. Less clear, however, was whether the disclaimer allowed AF to favor competing products.[102] That

---

99 Jordan sued the partnership for violation of his rights. The partnership argued that because he had profited considerably from the first restaurant he could not withhold his approval of his use of his name at the second. Judge James Moran, holding Jordan had reserved absolute discretion to decide when his name would be used, recognized that Jordan's discretion extended to deciding whether the benefits that might flow to him from his deal with the partnership were worthwhile relative to other deals he might strike: "The 'monetary benefits' Jordan has received or could possibly receive from [the partnership] pale in comparison to the international value of Jordan's name. It is not 'unreasonable,' then, for Jordan to want to strictly control the use of his name so that he could make decisions about its licensing that would allow him to achieve the highest possible financial return." *Id.* at 934.

100 870 F. Supp. 472 (E.D.N.Y. 1994).

101 *Id.* at 474.

102 GA sued AF, claiming the acquisition of a competitor breached the contract, in particular the implied covenant of good faith and due diligence. AF unsuccessfully sought summary judgment, contending nothing in the contract barred it from acquiring a competitor and the quoted language negated implying any duty to promote GA's flat bread. The court agreed that the contract could not be read to bar AF's acquisition of a competitor but did not agree that the duty of good faith and due diligence should not be implied.

disclaimer was qualified, however, by application of the duty of good faith and fair dealing, which implied a commitment not to favor such competing products. The case illustrates a qualified version of the disclaimer described in the third bullet.

Performance Standards

A party may commit to act in a certain manner when endeavoring to complete or completing a task. The task might not be completed when the commitment is to act in a certain manner when endeavoring to complete a task. By accepting a commitment from the obligor to complete a task in a certain manner, the obligee assumes responsibility for the risk that performance will be completed—the obligor will act in the prescribed manner when completing the task—but the result of such completion may not yield the result the obligee hopes for. For example, a lawyer who represents a client in a trial commits to perform to a standard but does not thereby assure the client of a favorable result. A gap exists between the lawyer's commitment to represent the client and the client's desired outcome of the efforts made during such representation, and nothing can be done to close that gap. It may do all that is required and yet complete a task that does not contribute toward benefit realization, or it may fail to complete a task that even if completed would not necessarily so contribute. That commitment gap is increased by lowering the standard of performance: the lower the standard, the wider the gap. For example, were the lawyer to commit only to act honestly, disclaiming all other assurances about its competence, it would have set a low bar for its performance, leaving the client to hope for a successful outcome with little reason to do so. The standard to which an obligor is expected to perform determines the gap between a compliant obligor's performance and the contribution the completed task is expected to make to the realization of the benefit the obligee expects or hopes to realize.

Chemical Bank v. Security Pacific National Bank[103] illustrates the gap between a low performance standard and the level of performance expected by an obligee. An agent bank filed a form financing statement

---

The court read the clause to say GA "would have the benefit of [the buyer's] expertise and [the buyer's] commitment to act for the 'mutual benefit' of the parties. Under this interpretation, [the buyer] would not have had the right to act solely in its benefit without consideration of [GA's] interests." *Id.* at 477–78.

[103] 20 F.3d 375 (9th Cir. 1994).

to perfect a security interest in its own name but not in its capacity as agent for the syndicated banks. As a result, the syndicated banks did not have a perfected security interest in the debtor's assets, a failure that the court characterized as negligent and a breach of a fiduciary duty. The contract between the agent and the syndicate banks stated the agent would be liable only for its gross negligence and willful misconduct. Any lower standard would have been unenforceable. The agent bank failed to complete the required task, perfecting the syndicated banks' security interest, but such failure did not amount to a breach because it was not gross negligence. By accepting the lower standard of performance, the syndicate banks assumed responsibility for the risk the agent bank's compliant performance would not yield or even contribute to the anticipated benefit, a perfected security interest. The agent bank correspondingly reduced its risk of liability for its inept efforts to perfect the security interest.

Contract Modification

Contract amendments can be used to fill in gaps created by oversight and rejection and not filled by terms implied by contract interpretation principles. A modification is a "change to something; an alteration or amendment."[104] Modification and amendment are used interchangeably with regard to contracts. Any term of a contract may be modified as specified in the contract or in the absence of such a provision as permitted by law.

Because a modification, when effective, can add to or change the terms in a contract, it trumps the allocation of risk implied by the application of contract interpretation principles. It can also reverse decisions made at contract formation that a party later regrets. Missed and omitted benefits, tasks, and commitments can be added to the contract after contract formation. Benefits, tasks, and commitments that come to be regretted after contract formation can be deleted or modified, short of terminating the contract.

That procedure may be the mutual agreement of all parties, a percentage of the parties, or one party. The party that controls the amendment procedure also allocates benefit, task, and commitment oversight, and remorse risks. If, by amendment, an obligee can unilaterally

---

[104] Black's Law Dictionary, *supra* note 90, 1156.

add benefits, tasks, and commitments to be completed by the obligor, the latter will be responsible for completing such tasks and commitments. The omission of anticipated benefits, tasks to be completed by the other party, and commitments to complete those tasks that the obligee has come to regret after contract formation can be added or modified. Conversely, an amendment procedure can allow an obligor to modify or delete tasks and commitments it agreed to complete. If it missed such a task, the deletion enables the obligor to correct its oversight. If it included such a task and later regrets the inclusion, the amendment procedure allows it to assuage its regret. The party or parties that decide what contract amendments are allowed also decide when benefit, task, and commitment hazards can be eliminated and thereby have the power to allocate responsibility for the risk of their continuation after contract formation.

Between these two extremes, unilateral and mutual amendments, are compromises that give the other party a voice in any decision about an amendment and limit the decision-making authority of the party authorized to unilaterally modify the contract. The decision-making party may be required to notify the other party of the amendment or consult with or obtain the consent of such other party. That consent may be withheld in the discretion of the consenting party or only with reason. A decision to modify terms might be limited by a reasonableness requirement: the amendment must be reasonably related to a condition or contingency.

The following cases illustrate unilateral modification procedures:

- *Rodman v. Safeway Inc.*[105]: Safeway's standard terms and conditions for online purchases stated:

  > [Safeway] reserves the right to, from time to time, with or without notice to you, in [Safeway's] sole discretion, amend the Terms and Conditions for use and purchases regarding the online shopping services. Any amendment by [Safeway] will be effective only as to orders you place after [Safeway's] revisions of these Terms and Conditions as displayed on the Web site.

  The terms and conditions also stated Safeway "has no responsibility to notify you of any changes before any such changes are effective."

[105] Case No. 11-cv-03003-JST. (N.D. Cal. 2015).

In 2010, Safeway modified its policy for pricing products sold online, charging a premium for such products where it previously priced products at the prices in its physical stores. In 2011, Safeway notified its customers that it had modified its online pricing policy: "Please note before shopping online at [Safeway.com] that online and physical store prices, promotions, and offers may differ." After discovering a discrepancy between prices for products sold online and those in physical stores, Rodman sued, claiming the higher online prices breached the terms of service for online purchases. Safeway's unilateral amendment procedure proved ineffective because the changes had not been clearly brought to the customer's attention.[106] Because the customers had to assent to the changes by continuing to purchase online, Safeway used the amendment procedure to change terms applicable to future transactions. The procedure enabled it to unilaterally avoid oversight and other hazards in those future transactions. Because the amendment procedure did not change the terms of past or existing transactions, it did not enable Safeway to allocate to the customers responsibility for risks from oversight and other hazards in those transactions.[107]

- *Marriott Corp. v. Dasta Construction Co.*[108]: Marriott hired a contractor for a fixed price to complete the exterior skin work on a fast-track hotel construction project. "[T]he architectural plans and specifications are designed and modified as the building's actual construction progresses" in a fast-track project.[109] The parties thus acknowledged that the drawings and specifications had gaps without knowing what those gaps were. The contract excluded nearly all entitlements to change orders. Still, the contractor had to provide sufficient workers to comply with the schedule, even if the order of the work changed; the contractor had to suffer the

[106] "Regardless of the version of the Special Terms that Class Members viewed when they registered with Safeway.com, it is undisputed that Class Members were not provided with conspicuous notice that changes had been made to the Special Terms at the time those changes were made. Therefore, those changes represent an offer to which the class members never expressed assent, and class members were therefore not bound by those changes."

[107] *E.g.*, Rodriguez v. Instagram, LLC, 2013 WL 3732883 (N.D. Cal. 2013).

[108] 26 F.3d 1057 (11th Cir. 1994).

[109] *Id.* at 1060.

> additional costs that resulted from delays caused by Marriott, whether by negligence or otherwise, and other events, such as fires and storms, and the contractor had to bear additional costs, foreseen and unforeseen, including from unforeseen and unusual obstructions. Marriott frequently and significantly changed the plans and the order in which the work was done, resulting in the contractor being unable to use its workforce efficiently. Other problems occurred, for the most part stemming from the fast-track nature of the project. When the contractor had exhausted its funds, it submitted an "efficiency claim" for $1.5 million (its original bid was just over $3 million). Marriott refused to pay any of the claimed amount. By allowing Marriott to unilaterally amend the drawings and specifications for the portion of the project the contractor had to complete, the contractor assumed responsibility for the risks—task oversight and omission risks—that tasks appropriate to the project that were not yet identified therein would be identified and added later, as they were.

The full import of the allocation of responsibility for oversight and rejection risks effected by the unilateral amendment procedure in *Marriott Corp.* depended upon the compensation terms with which it was combined. The contractor assumed responsibility for the risk that its actual costs might exceed its estimated costs when it agreed to complete the work for a fixed price. It was not entitled to additional compensation for the changed or added tasks. The greater the discrepancy between its anticipated and actual costs for the additional tasks, the greater losses and responsibility for the risk assumed by the contractor.

Had the contractor been compensated on the basis of a price for each unit by which tasks were measured, it would have assumed responsibility for a different financial risk: the risk that its cost per unit for the additional tasks would have been higher than anticipated, perhaps because each additional unit would have more difficult to complete than estimated. Because its compensation would not have been calculated on the basis of the actual scope, the contractor would not have assumed the risk that the scope was greater than anticipated. Had the contractor been compensated on the basis of its costs plus a profit, it would have been compensated for the additional tasks on the same basis. The contractor would have passed back to Marriott responsibility for the financial risk that the cost of completion might be greater than anticipated. The contractor assumed responsibility for the greatest risk under the unilateral amendment procedure when it agreed to perform for a fixed price, whatever the changes, and would have assumed the least risk had it performed for a cost-plus price.

Contract Termination

A contract may state when and how it may be terminated or rescinded, which may be upon the agreement of the parties, the occurrence of certain events, or the decision of one party. In this last instance, a party can, in effect, terminate its commitment at any time, subject to the terms permitting termination. A party allowed to terminate for convenience can do so because it missed or regrets its choice of benefits, tasks, or commitments and prefers to terminate instead of continuing with the transaction.

In the absence of breach or other terms to the contrary, termination leaves the parties where they stand at the time of termination, each having to bear its costs of performing until that time and to forego whatever further benefits might have been realized. By terminating, a party reduces potential losses that might result or are resulting from oversight and rejection hazards. The other party suffers the loss of its investment in the transaction and its potential benefits. To that extent, it also bears responsibility for benefit, task, and commitment oversight and remorse that adversely affect the terminating party. Termination is a "nuclear" option for eliminating risks as it destroys all potential benefits that might be realized by both parties from the terminated transaction. Responsibility for losses that result to a party that result from termination by the other party can be shifted to the terminating party by having it pay a fee or compensation upon termination.

The following cases illustrate how the exercise of unilateral termination rights both eliminate hazards for the terminating party and burden the nonterminating party with a share of the resulting losses:

- *Piantes v. Pepperidge Farm, Inc.*[110]: For 24 years, Piantes distributed Pepperidge Farm, Inc.'s (PFI's) baked goods in certain suburbs of Boston under a consignment agreement. PFI asked Piantes to sell a portion of its franchise "route" because PFI wanted to introduce a new product and decided Piantes, being already overstretched,

[110] 875 F. Supp. 929 (D. Mass. 1995).

lacked the capacity to deliver the additional product. Piantes rejected the offer. The contract allowed PFI to terminate at any time and without cause but required PFI to pay Piantes 125 percent of the fair market value of the franchise, as determined by a panel of arbitrators. PFI terminated the agreement.[111] The potential hazard to PFI at contract formation was the chance that PFI's commitment to Piantes would impair realization of a new benefit at a future date. That potential hazard became a hazard that threatened losses when the new product was developed and the contract with Piantes impeded its distribution. Those potential losses were mitigated by the broad termination right PFI had reserved. The hazard to Piantes at contract formation was the unilateral termination right. To the extent PFI had to compensate Piantes, it, not Piantes, bore responsibility for Piantes's losses upon termination; and to the extent such compensation was less than Piantes's losses, Piantes bore responsibility for them.

- *United Airlines, Inc. v. Good Taste, Inc.*[112]: A contract between a caterer and an airline had a three-year term but allowed either party to terminate upon 90 days' prior written notice.[113] The caterer invested approximately $1 million in equipment to perform under the contract. Sixteen months later, the airline gave 90 days' termination notice.[114] The caterer unsuccessfully claimed the airline had to exercise the termination right reasonably, consistent

[111] Piantes sued PFI for breach of contract, claiming the termination, inter alia, breached the implied covenant of good faith and fair dealing. The court granted the motion for summary judgment, holding, "This contractual remedy [payment of 125 percent of fair market value] makes it virtually impossible for PFI to take the kind of unfair advantage of Piantes which other franchisees have suffered, since PFI is obliged to pay Piantes in excess of the economic value of what he is losing." *Id.* at 940. Having the unilateral termination right enabled PFI to dictate the routes operated by the franchisees, thus maximizing their value to it.

[112] 982 P.2d 1259 (Alas. 1999).

[113] "The term of this Agreement shall commence on May 1, 1988, and shall continue for a period of 3 years(s) [sic]; provided, however, either party may terminate this Agreement upon ninety (90) days' prior written notice." *Id.* at 1262.

[114] The caterer successfully sued for breach of contract, arguing the implied covenant of good faith and fair dealing prohibited termination of the contract without a good reason. The Alaska Supreme Court reversed the judgment, holding the airline was entitled to summary judgment on the issue, as the caterer "could not reasonably expect something other than what it expressly bargained for: a contract expressly terminable for any cause or no cause upon ninety days' notice." *Id.* at 1267.

with its, the caterer's, expectations. The report of the case does not explain why the airline terminated. It may have had remorse over the deal. Still, the case illustrates how a broad, unilateral termination right allowed the terminating party to terminate its commitment upon short notice and thus mitigate whatever risk had occurred. The termination right was also a hazard to the caterer because it would, as it did, lose its investment and potential benefits without any compensation.

- *Ace Flying Service, Inc. v. Colorado Department of Agriculture*[115]: A contract for the spraying of one million acres of insect-infested lands for 13.75 cents per acre provided, "[t]he State and its cooperators may terminate this contract at any time subject only to the service guarantee herein specified." The guarantee obligated the state to pay fixed amounts for aircraft that the agency requested to spray, had been readied for flying to the point they were on the airstrip, but did not spray because of unforeseen conditions. The contractor incurred $32,532.18 in expenses and sprayed 243,792 acres for which it received $32,518.65 for the acreage sprayed, plus the sum of $1,500, upon termination of the contract. As in the previous case, the report does not indicate why the state agency terminated the contract. The case also illustrates how a broad termination right allowed the state to mitigate any benefit, task, or commitment oversight or remorse risks. Finally, it illustrates how the losses that the nonterminating party may suffer as a result of termination can be mitigated by compensation paid by the terminating party.

[115] 348 P.2d 962 (Colo. 1960). The contractor sued the state agency, claiming it was entitled $24,653.03 as preparatory expense on the unsprayed acreage, together with $16,939.51 for lost profits. The agency moved to dismiss the claim, the trial court granted the motion, and the court upheld the ruling on appeal. The state supreme court agreed, holding, "The obligations of the parties in the event of a termination were clearly stated in the contract. With full knowledge thereof, the plaintiff calculated its costs and was low bidder on the contract. Hence, the price was not dictated by defendants, but was the offer of the plaintiff. It is not unlikely that other bidders took the termination clause into consideration in making their bids, thus making it possible for plaintiff to underbid them and obtain the contract, which was plain in its terms." *Id.* at 965.

4

Information and Assumption Risks

INFORMATION AND ASSUMPTION HAZARDS

Incorrect Information, Processing, and Assumptions

Decisions about transactions are based on information or assumptions in lieu of information or a combination of both. Information, here used in the broadest sense, includes any thought communicated about a matter, the correctness of which can be verified at contract formation or later.

Collecting and evaluating information about a transaction always has a cost. In a complex transaction, where a party will never have all the information that might be compiled about that deal, its diligence costs must be controlled, especially because the marginal value of the information collected will decrease. A party must decide when it has sufficient information to make decisions about that deal. It will usually rely on such information unless the party doubts its reliability.

In the best case,

- all information on which a party relies is correct,
- it correctly investigates, evaluates, and processes whatever information is received, and
- any assumption on which it relies is correct.

In the worst case,

- any information on which a party relies is incorrect,
- it incorrectly processes some or all of the information, and
- any assumption on which it relies is incorrect.

Between these extremes are twenty-five other combinations of these three hazards. The simplest three are the focus of this chapter.

These three combinations are (1) reliance upon incorrect information, processed correctly, and not supplemented by assumptions; (2) reliance upon correct information incorrectly processed; and (3) little or no information, correct and correctly processed as far as it goes, but supplemented by an incorrect assumption upon which a party relies. In all instances, the hazard is the *reliance* upon such information or assumption. The causes of (1) are the counterparty or third parties, and the causes of (2) and (3) will be the party.

Following are cases that illustrate hazards (1), (2), and (3), respectively:

- *OnBank & Trust Company v. FDIC*[1]: A government agency became the conservator of an insolvent savings and loan association, transferred the mortgage loans the association had made to its customers into a trust, offered to sell interests in the trust, and described the loans in a prospectus that overstated the total principal amount of the loans by approximately $1,000,000, or two percent. The buyer relied upon the stated amount when bidding for the portfolio.
- *Smith v. Zimbalist*[2]: Zimbalist, a prominent violinist and collector of rare violins, visited Smith, another violin collector, inspected two of his violins, declared they were made by Stradivarius and Guarnerius, respectively, asked Smith what price he would accept for the violins, and agreed to pay $8,000 in installments. The buyer made and relied entirely upon his own evaluation of the violins. In fact, the violins were imitations. The information available, the violins, was incorrectly examined.
- *Backus v. MacLaury*[3]: A livestock breeder decided to bid at an auction on a calf he intended to use to breed a herd, though

[1] 967 F. Supp. 81 (W.D.N.Y. 1997).

[2] 2 Cal.App.2d 324, 38 P.2d 170 (Cal. App. 1934).

[3] 278 A.D. 504, 106 NYS 2d 401 (N.Y. App. 1951).

the calf was then too young for its fertility to be determined. No information about the fertility of that specific calf was available. Each bidder had to make an assumption that the calf was or might be or was not or might not be fertile. The assumption was knowingly made. A rational bidder who assumed the calf was fertile, as did the bidder in the case, would bid an amount higher than one who assumed otherwise. The latter might not bid at all. The bidder's assumption proved incorrect.

Benefit Misconceptions

A benefit is misconceived when its expected value or utility is more or less than can or will be realized. The misconceiving party may or may not be the one who will realize the benefit. A hazard occurs when a party relying upon such misconception expects to receive more value or utility than can or will be realized. A hazard should not occur because one party expects the other to receive less than can or will be realized unless it would have realized extra value had such excess not accrued to the benefit of the other party or it could also have received more value in exchange without giving more.

A party misconceives a benefit because (1) the information the party receives and on which it relies about such benefit is incorrect, (2) the party incorrectly processes good information and relies upon its conclusion about such benefit, or (3) the party makes and relies upon an incorrect assumption about such benefit.

Following are two cases that illustrate reliance upon incorrect information, a feature of hazard (1):

- *OnBank & Trust Company v. FDIC,* which is previously described.[4] The prospectus overstated the total principal amount of the loans the buyer received.
- *Conti v. Winters*[5]: The seller stated the car had not been driven more than 3,500 miles, and the odometer read between 3,400 and 3,500 miles, when, in fact, the car had been driven more than 15,000 miles before being purchased by the seller.

---

4 *See* text accompanying note 1.

5 86 RI 456, 136 A.2d 622 (R.I. 1957).

Following are three cases that illustrate incorrect processing of information, a feature of hazard (2):

- *Smith v. Zimbalist*, which is previously described.[6] Both the seller and buyer wrongly concluded the violins were authentic and more valuable than they were.
- *Beachcomber Coins, Inc. v. Bosket*[7]: A coin dealer examined a dime purportedly minted in 1916 at Denver for 15 to 45 minutes and then paid the seller, another coin dealer, $500. The *D* on the dime had been counterfeited.[8] This case also illustrates scenario (1).
- *Tamplin v. James*[9]: Drawings made available at an auction described a parcel of real property as one of three lots occupied by a tenant. Without checking the drawings and specifications, a buyer offered to buy the parcel immediately after the auction on the mistaken belief that he was buying all the property occupied by the tenant—that is, all three lots. The buyer incorrectly concluded that because the tenant occupied three lots, all three were offered. He also failed to check his conclusion against the drawings.[10]

Following are four cases that illustrate incorrect assumptions, a feature of hazard (3):

- *Backus v. MacLaury*, which is previously described.[11]
- *Griffith v. Brymer*[12]: This case is summarized in chapter 3.[13] Griffith (G) agreed to hire a room from Brymer (B) to view King Edward VII's coronation procession. Unknown to either G or B, an hour

6 *See* text accompanying note 2.

7 166 N.J. Super. 442, 400 A.2d 78 (N.J. 1979).

8 The buyer sued for rescission when he discovered the error, claiming mutual mistake of fact. The trial court held that, had the parties been aware of any uncertainty about the authenticity of the coin, the risk would have been assumed by one of the parties; however, because they had no doubt of its authenticity, neither party assumed the risk it was not authentic and the buyer was entitled to rescission, even if its investigation had been negligent.

9 (1880) 15 Ch.D. 215; 43 L.T. 520; 29 W.R. 311, aff'd 215 Ch.D. 219 (Ch. Div. 1880).

10 In an action for specific performance by the seller, Baggallay L.J., deciding in favor of the seller, held the buyer was not justified in relying upon the fact that the lots were occupied without checking the drawings or specifications.

11 *See* text accompanying note 3.

12 19 T.L.R. 434 (1903).

13 *See* text accompanying ch. 3, notes 49–52.

earlier a decision had been reached to cancel the parade. The renter, having no information about and giving no thought to the prospect of a cancellation, assumed the parade remained scheduled.[14]

- *Hecht v. Batcheller*[15]: Two hours before a seller sold a promissory note to a buyer, the debtor on the note made an assignment for the benefit of creditors. The value of the note diminished, if not disappeared, with the debtor's assignment. Neither party knew of the debtor's insolvency at the time of the sale.[16] The buyer, having no information about the debtor's insolvency, assumed otherwise.
- *Grenall v. United of Omaha Life Ins. Co*[17]: This case is summarized in chapter 3.[18] Grenall paid a single, substantial premium for an annuity payable in monthly installments for the rest of her life. Being ignorant of her fatal illness, she assumed that she had no condition that would shorten the period over which she would receive annuity payments.

That the buyer in the first case knew of his assumption and the parties in the latter three did not does not change the hazard. None of the parties had any information about the condition adversely affecting the value or utility that was expected to be realized. He or she proceeded on the basis of an incorrect assumption.

Task Misconceptions

A task to be completed is misconceived when a party expects that such task can be completed when it cannot, when a different task will be completed, when a different method will be used to complete the task, or when the time, effort, or cost of completing a task will be different. All such possible misconceptions about a task, which might be referred to as task information and assumption hazards, can be categorized by each

[14] Justice Wright held the agreement was made on the missupposition of facts and void.

[15] 167 Mass. 335, 17 N.E. 651, 9 Am. St. Rep. 708 (Mass. 1888).

[16] The buyer sued for rescission, claiming mutual mistake of fact; the court rendered judgment in its favor; and the seller successfully appealed to the Massachusetts Supreme Court, which held that because the mistaken assumption was not about the "existence or identity of the thing sold," the buyer was not entitled to rescission.

[17] 165 Cal. App.4th 188, 2007 N.Y. Slip Op. 09545 (Cal. App. 2008).

[18] *See* text accompanying ch. 3, notes 53 and 54.

and a combination of the following three facts: whether the party who relies upon such information is the source of the incorrectness in the information or assumption, whether the party expected to complete the task is also the party relying upon erroneous information or assumption, and whether the task is to be completed for the party relying upon such information or another party.

First, such misconceptions occur because:

(1) the information a party receives about such task is incorrect,

(2) a party incorrectly processes information about such task, or

(3) a party makes an incorrect assumption about such task.

Second, the party who receives and relies upon incorrect information, incorrectly processes information, or makes an incorrect assumption will be either:

(a) the party who is expected complete the task or

(b) the other party (who is not expected to complete the task).

Both parties can receive and rely upon incorrect information, have incorrectly used information, or made an incorrect assumption, in each case about a task. That possibility is (a) and (b) combined. It is also the classic case of mutual mistake.[19] It is not here considered as a separate variation because each of the two variations of which it consists is separately considered. The three types of mistake or misconception can be combined with the two variations to yield six information and assumption hazard scenarios: for example, hazard (1)(a) occurs when the party expected to complete a task receives incorrect information about that task.

Third, the hazards also vary with the party for whose benefit the task is being completed:

(i) The task is for the benefit of the party completing it and the result is adverse to it if completion is impractical, will not yield the anticipated benefit, or will be more onerous or costly than anticipated, or

---

[19] *E.g.*, Sherwood v. Walker, 66 Mich. 568, 22 N.W. 919 (Mich. 1887), limited to its facts in Lenawee County Bd. of Health v. Messerly, 331 N.W.2d 203, 209 (Mich. 1982).

(ii) the task is for the benefit of the party not completing it, and ignoring potential liability for breach by an obligor, the result is adverse in this scenario when it expects to complete a less onerous or costly task than the one it will or is required to complete.

Based on the three variables, a matrix of the twelve scenarios is conceivable. Each such scenario is referred to as follows by the combination of numbers and letters previously used. For example, scenario (1)(a)(ii) refers to a scenario where (1) incorrect information is (a) received and relied upon by the party completing the misconceived task (ii) for the benefit of the other party. For convenience, the description of these twelve scenarios are grouped into six categories as follows.

(1) *Incorrect information about a task received by party completing it*: The first two scenarios are receipt by a party of incorrect information about the task it is expected to complete. The source of the incorrect information may be the other party or a third party. These are scenarios (1)(a)(i) and (ii). Following are two illustrations of these scenarios:

- *J.I. Hass Co., Inc. v. Jones-Teer*[20]: A contractor advised a successor subcontractor that the work by the prior subcontractor, who had been terminated, was satisfactory. The new subcontractor agreed to finish the work of that prior subcontractor for a fixed price. In fact, much of the prior subcontractor's work was unsatisfactory and had to be redone.[21]
- *In re Schenck Tours, Inc.*[22]: A party bid on a parcel of real property based on an estimate received from its expert that the costs of remediating pollution of the parcel would be approximately $250,000. It learned from another bidder that the cost was more likely $2.5 million.

In the first case, the subcontractor was an obligor whose obligation to the contractor was to complete the predecessor's unfinished work. This

[20] 755 F.2d 1264 (6th Cir. 1985).

[21] When the subcontractor found it had to correct the prior subcontractor's work to proceed with its work, it claimed it was entitled to receive $500,000 additional compensation for correcting defects in the painting work of the prior subcontractor and sued for breach of contract. The trial court found the contractor misrepresented the prior subcontractor's work, though it had not done so fraudulently, awarding the subcontractor a judgment of $17,920. The appeal court reversed the judgment, holding that the subcontractor had reason to know of the defects before it signed the subcontract.

[22] 69 B.R. 906 (E.D. N.Y. 1987).

is scenario (1)(a)(ii) (where the party completing the task for the other party's benefit receives and relies upon incorrect information). In the second, remediation was not an obligation, though it was necessary for the buyer to use the parcel after it had paid for it and thus to realize its benefit. Its obligation to its seller was to pay the price. The buyer was not an obligor but a party having to complete a task to realize a benefit. This is scenario (1)(a)(i) (where a party completing a task for its own benefit receives and relies upon incorrect information). Also, in the first case, the subcontractor received incorrect information from its counterparty, whereas in the second the buyer received it from its expert. Here we treat the buyer and its consultant as independent parties. In each case, the task was incorrectly described to the party obligated or otherwise expected to complete it.

(2) *Incorrect information about a task received by party not completing it*: The second two scenarios are receipt by a party of incorrect information about the task the other party is expected to complete. These are scenarios (1)(b)(i) and (ii). Scenario (1)(b)(i) (a party completes a task for its benefit while the other party relies upon incorrect information about that task) can occur but should not create a risk to the party receiving incorrect information. Its reliance upon the incorrect information neither diminishes its benefits nor alters its tasks or their completion costs.

CERAbio LLC v. Wright Medical Technology, Inc.[23] illustrates these scenarios. A company sold its business for two payments of $1.5 million each and royalties, the first payment to be made at closing and the second when the buyer had verified that its sole product could be made following the protocol agreed by the parties. After closing, the parties learned the sole supplier of a key ingredient used to make the product no longer supplied it. The seller believed that with an immaterial change to the protocol and the use of a new ingredient the product could be produced. The buyer was unwilling to make the change.[24] The seller was not obligated to run a test protocol. Its doing so satisfied a condition that obligated the buyer to make the second payment. Completion of the task thus contributed to the seller's ultimate benefit realization: receipt of the full price. This aspect of the case illustrates scenario (1)(b)(i): the buyer had incorrect information about a task the seller would perform for its own benefit. Running the test protocol also benefited the buyer by proving the product could be produced. This

---

23 410 F.3d 981 (7th Cir. 2005).

24 The buyer was unwilling to make the change and claimed fraud. The seller sued for the second payment and royalties, and the buyer counterclaimed for fraud. The trial court dismissed the buyer's claim and the jury awarded a verdict in favor of the seller.

aspect of the case illustrates scenario (1)(b)(ii): the buyer, based on incorrect information received from the seller about the protocol, expected the seller to complete the protocol specified in the agreement, not an alternative workaround, to prove for the buyer's benefit that the product could be produced.

(3) *Information about a task processed incorrectly by party completing it*: The fifth and sixth scenarios are the incorrect use of information by a party about a task it is expected to complete. These are scenarios (2)(a)(i) and (ii). Following are cases that illustrate these scenarios:

- *White v. Berrenda Mesa Water District of Kern County*[25]: A contractor misread the technical data about the condition of a site on which construction was to be undertaken and underestimated the scope of work. The data were good, but the reading was faulty.[26]
- *Bowser, Inc. v. Hamilton Glass Co.*[27]: A subcontractor agreed to fabricate glass reflectors in conformity with specifications provided by the contractor but misunderstood the reference to "Spec. 93-24794." Thinking it was a parts number and not the specification for the glass, the subcontractor produced reflectors that did not conform.[28]
- *Covich v. Chambers*[29]: Before buying a site on which he intended to build a residential neighborhood, the buyer walked the perimeter of the site and noticed that gravel had been excavated and that a swamp was located nearby. He chose not to dig test holes or to perform percolation tests to determine the water table. After his purchase, he found the water table unsuitable for sewage and septic systems. His investigation of the site was to determine its suitability for development, the benefit of his purchase, not to benefit the seller or to confirm any statements by the seller about the site. He thus incorrectly assessed

[25] 7 Cal. App.3d 894, 87 Cal. Rptr. 338 (Cal. App. 1970).

[26] For discussion of the outcome of the case, *see* the text accompanying notes 54–56.

[27] 207 F.2d 341 (7th Cir. 1953).

[28] When sued by the contractor for its additional costs in obtaining the reflectors from another source, the subcontractor claimed its error was an excusable mutual or unilateral mistake of fact. The trial court awarded a judgment in favor of the contractor and the appeal court confirmed, holding, "so far as the terms of the contract are concerned, there was no mistake. There is a plain agreement to manufacture the article according to certain specifications. This the defendant promised to do and this it failed to do."

[29] 8 Mass. App. Ct. 740, 397 N.E.2d 1115 (Mass. App. 1979).

conditions that materially affected completion of a task he had to complete to realize that benefit.[30]

The first two cases illustrate scenario (2)(a)(ii) (party having to complete a task for the benefit of the other party incorrectly uses information to define that task). In each case, the contractor incorrectly used the available information and, as a result, incorrectly defined the work it had to complete as an obligation performed to benefit the other party. The last case illustrates scenario (2)(a)(i) (party having to complete the task for its benefit incorrectly uses information to define that task): the buyer's inept investigation led to a conclusion that development of the site—a task the buyer had to complete—was feasible at its estimated costs and would thus yield the anticipated benefits.

(4) *Information about a task processed incorrectly by party not completing it*: The seventh and eighth scenarios are incorrect processing by a party of information about the task the other party is expected to complete. These are scenarios (2)(b)(i) and (ii). Scenario (2)(b)(i) (a party completes a task for its benefit while the other party erroneously processes good information about that task) can also occur but should not create a risk to the party incorrectly processing information. Its reliance on the incorrect information neither diminishes its benefits nor alters its tasks or their completion costs.

U.S. v. Spearin[31] illustrates scenario (2)(b)(ii). A government agency provided plans and specifications it prepared for work to be completed by a contractor. The work included diversion and relocation of a section of a sewer, which increased stress on a dam in the sewer system not mentioned in the plans or specifications. The pressure of heavy rains and a high tide broke the dam. Because the dam was not shown in the plans, the contractor did not include in the scope of the project any work that would support the dam. The agency was the party not completing the task that incorrectly prepared the drawings and specifications used by the contractor.[32]

---

30 The buyer sought rescission, based on mutual mistake. The court found the mistake was not mutual: "Covich did not rely on anyone else's knowledge, representations or belief as to the controlling facts concerning the water table; and that in failing to insert a similar condition in the purchase and sale agreement, Covich voluntarily assumed the risk as part of his bargain that the land might not have adequate drainage for the necessary septic systems." *Id.* at 750.

31 248 U.S. 132, 54 Ct. Cl. 187, 39 S.Ct. 59, 63 L.Ed. 166 (1918).

32 The government insisted that the contractor remedy the problem, and after more than a year of negotiations, during which the contractor refused to assume responsibility, the

(5) *Incorrect assumption by party completing a task*: The ninth and tenth scenarios are incorrect assumptions by parties about the tasks they must complete. These are scenarios (3)(a)(i) and (ii). Such an assumption is adverse to that party when it assumes that such task will be less onerous or costly than it will be or is required to be. The following three cases illustrate these scenarios:

- *Mineral Park Land Co. v. Howard*[33]: A contractor agreed to take from an owner's land all of the gravel and earth needed for certain construction work. After the contractor had removed approximately half the gravel it required, it took the balance from another source because, even though the owner's land contained enough material to satisfy the balance under the contract, it was below the water level and the cost of extracting it would have been ten or twelve times as much as the usual cost, and it would require drying at great expense and delay. At contract formation, the contractor had no information about the condition of the subsurface and assumed it was the same as the surface.[34]
- *General Dynamics Corp. v. U.S.*[35]: A contractor agreed to build a stealth fighter aircraft for a fixed price but later asked the government to modify the contract to a cost-plus reimbursement contract when it found its costs were likely to exceed the price and the government had not shared its "superior knowledge" about the technology. The government responded it did not have to disclose its superior knowledge because such information was a state secret.[36] The contractor had not received all relevant information

government annulled the contract. The contractor sued for sums owing to it and was awarded a judgment by the Court of Claims, which was affirmed by the Supreme Court. Justice Brandeis held "the articles [in the contract] prescribing the character, dimensions and location of the sewer imported a warranty that, if the specifications were complied with, the sewer would be adequate." *Id.* at 137. That warranty overrode the contractor's obligations to inspect and determine the conditions at the site.

33 172 Cal. 289, 156 P. 458, L.R.A. 1916 F. 1 (Cal. 1916).

34 The California Supreme Court held the contractor's failure to take the balance under the contract was excused because "where the difference in cost is so great as here, and has the effect, as found, of making performance impracticable, the situation is not different from that of a total absence of earth and gravel." 172 Cal. at 293.

35 563 U.S. 478, 179 L. Ed. 2d 957, 131 S.Ct. 1900 (2011).

36 The contractor claimed it was entitled to additional payments up to the amount of its costs, and the government claimed repayment of a portion of the amount paid. The

about the technology from the government. Either it mistakenly used what information it had or, more likely, made an assumption about the technology.

- *WRI/Raleigh, L.P. v. Shaikh*[37]: A tenant intended to convert vacant space in a shopping center into a restaurant and signed a lease, but he changed his mind when he soon learned he would have to install a grease trap considerably larger and more expensive than the one he believed the local codes required. The tenant had not inquired about what size of grease trap the codes required and assumed a smaller one would comply.[38]

The parties completing the tasks in the first two cases are obligors and their completion are performances of their respective obligations. This is scenario (3)(a)(ii) (party makes an incorrect assumption about a task it will complete for the other party's benefit). The party completing its task in the third case is not obligated to do so. Installing the grease trap was one of the tasks that had to be completed by the tenant to convert the vacant space into a restaurant, enabling the tenant to realize the anticipated benefits. This is scenario (3)(a)(i) (party makes an incorrect assumption about a task it will complete for its benefit). Its obligation to its landlord was to pay rent. Still, the three cases illustrate a party who is expected to complete a task and has no or insufficient information about it or an applicable condition and makes an incorrect assumption.

contractor claimed its default was excused by the government's failure to share its "superior knowledge" about the technology. The government claimed it did not have to disclose information about its superior knowledge because such information was a state secret. The Court of Federal Claims changed the termination for default to termination for convenience and awarded the contractor the amount it requested; the appeal court reversed; upon retrial the Court of Federal Claims upheld the default termination and denied adjudication of the superior knowledge defense; the appeal court reversed the default termination but upheld the denial of the adjudication of the superior knowledge defense; and on remand again the Court of Federal Claims allowed the default termination and the appeal court affirmed. The U.S. Supreme Court reversed, holding that neither party's claims could be adjudicated.

[37] 183 N.C. App. 249, 644 S.E.2d 245 (N.C. App. 2007).

[38] The tenant claimed his performance was thus impossible and discharged. The court disagreed, holding that because a larger grease trap could be used, he was not excused from the lease. He incorrectly assumed, apparently not based on any information, that a smaller grease trap would be sufficient.

(6) *Incorrect assumption by party not completing a task*: The eleventh and twelfth scenarios are incorrect assumptions by a party about what the other party's tasks include. These are scenarios (3)(b)(i) and (ii). Scenario (3)(b)(i) (a party completes a task for its benefit while the other party makes an incorrect assumption about that task) can also occur, but it should not create a risk to the party making the incorrect assumption. Its reliance on the incorrect information neither diminishes its benefits nor alters its tasks or their completion costs. The following two cases illustrate scenario (3)(b)(ii):

- *Smith v. Hughes*[39]: A farmer asked a manager of a horse training facility if he would like to buy oats, showing him a sample. The manager did not inspect the sample but wrote to say he would buy the whole lot at a specified price. The oats were new, not old as the manager expected. Though offered a sample, the manager proceeded with no information about the nature of the oats.[40] He must have assumed the oats the seller would deliver would be old.
- *Meda AB v. 3M Co.*[41]: A buyer of a worldwide pharmaceutical business did not ask the seller if it or its French subsidiary had any understandings with the French regulatory authorities about how the subsidiary would price a specific drug in France. Nor did the seller mention such understandings. The buyer thus had no information about the regulation of such price in France and believed none existed. While the case could be viewed as one where the available information was incorrectly processed, because the buyer did not seek any information about the understanding, treating it as one where the party made an incorrect assumption about the business the seller would deliver is also appropriate.[42]

---

39 (1871) L.R. 6 Q.B. 597, 40 L.J.Q.B. 221, 25 L.T. 329, 19 W.R. 1059 (Q.B. 1871).

40 When he received the oats, the manager complained the oats were new, not old as he expected; the farmer refused to take back the oats and sued for breach of contract. The jury was instructed that if the word "old" had not been used in the communications between the parties, they should find for the manager if the farmer believed the manager was under the impression he was agreeing to buy old oats. The court found for the manager and the farmer appealed. The Queen's Bench reversed the verdict and ordered a new trial, holding the jury instruction failed to distinguish between "agreeing to take the oats under the belief that they were old, and agreeing to take the oats under the belief that the [farmer] plaintiff contracted that they were old." The manager was not entitled to a verdict in the former instance.

41 969 F. Supp.2d 360 (S.D.N.Y. 2013).

42 The buyer sued for fraud and concealment. Finding in favor of the seller, the court "finds that [the buyer's] Meda's diligence related to drug pricing was not thorough or meticulous.

Condition and Contingency Misconceptions

Everything previously said about how incorrect information, incorrect use of information, and incorrect assumptions affect expectations about benefits and tasks can be repeated for conditions and contingencies. Because it receives and relies upon incorrect information, it incorrectly uses correct information or forms an incorrect assumption, a party may suppose that a condition that must exist or not exist or a contingency that must occur or not occur for a benefit to be realized or a task to be completed does or does not exist or will or will not occur. *Griffith v. Brymer*[43] and *Krell v. Henry*,[44] which were described in chapter 3 as examples of condition and contingency oversight,[45] respectively, also illustrate incorrect assumptions about conditions and contingencies. For the renter in the former case, the transaction was premised upon a condition that the parade was still scheduled, and in the latter upon a contingency that the parade would be held as scheduled.

Presidio Enterprises, Inc. v. Warner Bros. Distributing Corp.[46] illustrates how incorrect information about a contingency affects benefit realization. Warner touted the movie *Swarm*—a movie about the invasion of killer bees from South America into Texas, with a cast that included such famous names as Michael Caine, Richard Chamberlain, Olivia de Havilland, Patty Duke Astin, Henry Fonda, Ben Johnson, Slim Pickens, Katharine Ross, and Richard Widmark—as the "blockbuster" of the summer of 1978. The movie flopped. Warner's statements about the famous names and the story were correct. Its conclusion that the movie would be a hit, based on those facts, was wildly incorrect. The distributor formed expectations about the likely revenue from its distribution of the movie based on Warner's promotional statements and paid Warner accordingly. Like all

Indeed, though Meda was presented with thousands of documents in due diligence, it apparently never noticed the absence of European drug pricing agreements." *Id.* at 375.

43 *See* text accompanying ch. 3, note 49.

44 *Supra* ch. 1, note 24. *See* text accompanying ch. 3, notes 50 and 51.

45 *See* text accompanying ch. 3, notes 49–52.

46 784 F.2d 674 (5th Cir. 1986). Presidio paid Warner $65,000 for distribution rights for Swarm. When demand for the movie flopped and Presidio lost $56,000, it sued Warner for negligent misrepresentation, receiving a verdict for damages of $500,000, an amount that presumably included Presidio's expected profit of at least $450,000 from its box office receipts. The appellate court held, however, that whatever "blockbuster" meant, it was too vague to be actionable. More importantly, the statement about the potential success of the movie was "a prediction, not a statement of fact" and also not actionable. *Id.* at 680.

information about future events, however, its incorrectness could not be known until the time for such event to occur had passed. The hazard in the case was reliance upon information about the likely occurrence of the contingency, which in hindsight proved to be incorrect. Because financial projections often prove to be more optimistic than warranted, when tested by future events, reliance upon such forecasts is considered hazardous.

The matrix of twelve information and assumption hazards that affect expectations about tasks may be replicated for expectations and assumptions about conditions and contingencies, the existence or occurrence of which is essential to completion of a task as anticipated. The extent of the pollution in *In re Schenck Tours, Inc.*,[47] the suitability of the site in *Covich v. Chambers*,[48] and the condition of the subsurface in *Mineral Park Land Co. v. Howard*[49] are examples of incorrect information about a condition, incorrect use of correct information about a condition, and an incorrect assumption about a condition, respectively. These are versions of the hazards described as scenarios (1)(a)(i), (2)(a)(i), and (3)(a)(ii), respectively.

Fraud, Nondisclosure, and Mistake

So far, we have seen how a party's reliance upon incorrect information and assumptions and incorrect use of information can be a hazard to the party who relies on the same. Such information and assumptions are also a hazard to the other party otherwise unaffected by the hazard because the affected party may be able to rescind the contract and claim fraud. This risk will be of little concern to the con artist who hopes to get away with his deception. A legitimate enterprise, however, will be concerned about loss of the expected bargain if the contract is rescinded, liability for misrepresentation and fraud, and harm to its reputation. An understanding of these risks in a transaction requires careful consideration of how the legal principles of unilateral and mutual mistake; inadvertent, negligent, and intentional misrepresentation; fraud; and concealment may apply.

Incorrect Information Received by Party. A party that receives and relies upon incorrect information may be able to rescind the contract and claim

---

47 69 B.R. 906 (E.D. N.Y. 1987).

48 8 Mass. App. Ct. 740, 397 N.E.2d 1115 (Mass. App. 1979).

49 172 Cal. 289, 156 P. 458, L.R.A. 1916 F 1 (Cal. 1916).

damages for inadvertent, negligent, or intentional misrepresentation or fraud because of such incorrect information. The following two cases illustrate these risks:

- *Bentley v. Slavik*[50]: A violin seller told the buyer he was selling an Auguste Sebastien Philippe Bernardel violin made in 1835 with an appraised value ranging from $15,000 to $20,000, facts he honestly but wrongly believed were true as they had been certified by a reputable violin maker, authenticator, and appraiser, and he had no expertise to conclude otherwise. The buyer successfully rescinded the contract when it learned of the error.[51]
- *Hollerman v. F.H. Peavey & Co.*[52]: A franchisor prepared and circulated a brochure soliciting participation in a chicken-breeding program stating that participation "will return to the careful broiler raiser an income roughly equal to half as much as is obtained from an average size farm in the Midwest—and it will do so for about six hours of one person's attention daily." An unsuccessful participant successfully claimed the brochure was fraudulent.[53]

Information Incorrectly Used by Party. A party that incorrectly uses information may likewise be able to rescind the contract. Following are two cases that illustrate this outcome:

- *White v. Berrenda Mesa Water District of Kern County*[54]: This case is previously summarized.[55] A contractor who misread the technical data about the condition of a site on which construction was to be undertaken and underestimated the scope of work was allowed to rescind his bid.[56]

---

[50] 663 F. Supp. 736 (S.D. Ill. 1987).

[51] The court held the parties made a mutual mistake of fact that entitled the buyer to a refund of the difference between the amount paid on the price of the violin and its value. *See* also: Norton v. Popolos, 443 A.2d 1 (Del. 1982), summarized in text accompanying notes 112 and 113.

[52] 269 Minn. 221, 130 N.W.2d 534 (Minn. 1964).

[53] The court held such statements, along with others, were evidence of fraud to be considered by a jury.

[54] 7 Cal.App.3d 894, 87 Cal. Rptr. 338 (Cal. App. 1970).

[55] *See* text accompanying notes 25 and 26.

[56] The contractor discovered the error after the bids were opened and he was awarded the contract; he requested the district to allow him to withdraw his bid and return his bond, and when the district refused, he sued for declaratory relief and rescission. The trial court

- *Consolidated Rail Corp. v. Portlight, Inc.*[57]: An importer recovered $140,521 from its insurer for the loss of 68 cartons of a 368-carton shipment. The insurer in turn claimed against the carrier, which settled for $120,302.53. It later discovered that the bill of lading limited its liability to $500 per carton, for a total liability of $33,500, and successfully rescinded the settlement.[58] The carrier had overlooked or incorrectly identified and examined the documents available to it before agreeing to the settlement.

Incorrect Assumption Made by a Party. A party that makes an incorrect assumption may be able to rescind the contract for unilateral or mutual mistake of fact or claim damages for fraud or concealment.

- *Richfield Bank and Trust Co. v. Sjogren*[59]: Buyers of purification units borrowed the moneys to pay for their purchase from a bank. The bank also had the seller as a customer and knew the latter was insolvent. The seller failed to deliver units because of its insolvency. When the bank sued the buyers on the promissory note received for the loan, the buyers successfully claimed the bank had induced them by fraudulently failing to disclose the seller's insolvency that the bank knew of when the loan was made. The buyers had no information one way or the other about the seller's insolvency and assumed it to be solvent.[60]
- *Transdigm Inc. v. Alcoa Global Fasteners, Inc.*[61]: In the course of its diligence in a business acquisition, Alcoa identified the importance

denied him relief, but the appeal court reversed, holding the contractor's error was a "mistake of judgment," albeit negligent, that entitled him to rescission.

57 188 F.3d 93 (3d Cir. 1999).

58 The carrier claimed the release should be voided because of a mutual mistake of fact, a claim usually denied in cases concerning releases, since the very certainty they are supposed to bring to the dispute would be undermined; however, the court allowed the claim because the fact about the parties being mistaken concerned an existing condition, the cap on damages.

59 309 Minn. 362, 244 N.W.2d 648 (Minn. 1976).

60 The jury specifically found (1) seller's officers knew that they could not fulfill their contractual obligation to the buyers and (2) that bank's officer who approved the loan knew of the pertinent financial condition of the sellers and of the actions, concealment, and representations of the officers of the sellers in its dealings with the buyers. The bank appealed, and the Minnesota Supreme Court affirmed the verdict, holding the bank was obligated to disclose to the buyers its knowledge of the sellers' irretrievable insolvency.

61 2013 WL 2326881 (Del. Ch. 2013).

of the target's sales to one customer and asked Transdigm, the seller, about the target's relationship with its customers, in particular, if the payment terms included rebates. Transdigm knew that a principal customer would reduce its purchases by fifty percent and receive a five percent rebate but did not disclose this information to Alcoa when responding. Alcoa assumed no such rebate was given by the target to its principal customer. When Alcoa learned of these facts after the closing, it successfully claimed fraud by active concealment.[62]

INFORMATION AND ASSUMPTION RISK MANAGEMENT

In the absence of express terms in the contract, the law of intentional, negligent, and inadvertent misrepresentation; express and implied warranty; fraud; and unilateral and mutual mistake allocate the information and assumption risks in a transaction. For example, in *U.S. v. Spearin*,[63] previously summarized,[64] the contractor successfully claimed the government agency that had provided the plans and specifications it prepared for work to be completed by a contractor impliedly warranted their correctness. The contractual rules that implied the additional term, the warranty, allocated the risk that the drawings were incorrect to the government agency. In *Consolidated Rail Corp.*,[65] also previously summarized,[66] the carrier's oversight of the limitation on its liability in the bill of lading was held to be a mutual mistake of fact that entitled it to rescind the settlement. The rules applicable to mutual mistake allocated responsibility for the risk of the carrier's mistaken examination of the documents to the insurer since the settlement could be unwound. In *Presidio Enterprises, Inc.*,[67] the rule that no liability for fraud or misrepresentation lie for opinions about the occurrence of contingencies allocated to the distributor responsibility for the risk that Warner's touting of the film as a blockbuster would prove incorrect.

---

[62] *See* Prairie Capital III, L.P. v. Double E Holding Corp., 135 A.3d 35, 54 (2015), which holds that the disclaimer need not use the word "omission."

[63] 248 U.S. 132, 54 Ct. Cl. 187, 39 S.Ct. 59, 63 L.Ed. 166 (1918).

[64] *See* text accompanying notes 31 and 32.

[65] 188 F.3d 93 (3d Cir. 1999).

[66] *See* text accompanying notes 57 and 58.

[67] 784 F.2d 674 (5th Cir. 1986).

Expressly stated warranties, disclaimers, antireliance clauses, merger clauses, waivers of defenses, amendments, and termination rights, when effective, can trump or modify the risk allocations implied in the fraud, misrepresentation, and mistake rules.

Diligence

The appropriate investigation of information about benefits, tasks, conditions, and contingencies varies with the complexity and importance of the transaction to the parties. A party can investigate conditions that are knowable before or at contract formation. *Smith v. Hughes*[68] is the clearest illustration of a case where all the diligence that was needed lie in the buyer's hands; he had only to look at them. Conditions that are unknowable at contract formation can be investigated but cannot be proved or disproved at that time. Similarly, the probability that a contingency will occur can be investigated but not proved or disproved with certainty at contract formation. The diligence appropriate for any type or specific transaction is outside the scope of this text.

Diligence is the most important mitigation of misrepresentation, fraud, and concealment risks. Asking a party to assume responsibility for losses that will result from its fraud will have little value, except where that party is able and willing to compensate the defrauded party for those losses. This will be the case in a legitimate business transaction since neither party expects at contract formation to perpetrate a fraud on the other. It will not be so when fraud is central to the deal. The con perpetrating the fraud will hope to escape with the proceeds of its deceit. Absent a guaranty or similar instrument from a reliable third party, diligence is the only tool for detecting and protecting the innocent party against such a scheme.[69]

Warranties

With reference to a contract, a warranty is an "express or implied promise that something in furtherance of the contract is guaranteed by one of the contracting parties."[70] A representation is defined as "[a] presentation

---

[68] *See* text accompanying notes 39 and 40.

[69] For an example of insurance against fraud, *see* text accompanying notes 100–102.

[70] BLACK'S LAW DICTIONARY (10th ed. 2014).

of fact—either by words or conduct—made to induce someone to act, esp. to enter into a contract; esp. the manifestation to another that a fact, including a state of mind exists."[71] For convenience, the following discussion treats warranties and representations interchangeably.[72] Each confirms to the party benefiting from the representation or warranty that a party, benefit, task, condition, or contingency is or will be as represented or warranted. The party giving the warranty assumes responsibility for the risk that the matter proves to be otherwise.

Warranties can be used to allocate the information and assumption risks previously described. A warranty may be expansive, warranting that a benefit will be realized or a task can or will be completed or limited to warranting the existence of a condition that must exist or the occurrence of a contingency that must occur for a benefit to be realized or a task to be completed. A warranty that a task the warrantee will complete for its own benefit can be completed and will contribute toward benefit realization as expected allocates responsibility for the risks in scenarios (1)(a)(i), (2)(a)(i), and (3)(a)(i) to the warrantor. A warranty that a task the warrantee will complete for the warrantor's benefit can be completed as warranted allocates responsibility for the risks in scenarios (1)(a)(ii), (2)(a)(ii), and (3)(a)(ii) to the warrantor. A warranty that a task that the warrantor will complete for the benefit of the warrantee can be completed and, when completed, will contribute to the warrantee's benefit realization as expected allocates responsibility for the risks in scenarios (1)(b)(ii), (2)(b)(ii), and (3)(b)(ii) to the warrantor. Such warranties cover all the information and assumption hazard scenarios previously described, except scenarios 1(b)(i), 2(b)(i), and (3)(b)(i), which we have seen are not hazards.

A party aware of an assumption it makes can have a warranty affirm the assumed fact as true. The warranty assures the warrantee that the matter will be as assumed just as a warranty assures the warrantee that information about a matter is or will be as described. A party unaware of an assumption it makes about a matter cannot describe such an assumption and ask that the other party give an assurance that it exists

[71] *Id.* at 1493.

[72] A warranty differs from a representation: (a) a warranty is conclusively presumed to be material, whereas a representation is not; (b) a warranty must be strictly complied with, whereas substantial truth is sufficient for a representation; (c) a warranty is an essential part of a contract, whereas a representation is a collateral, usually an inducement; and (d) a warranty is usually written, whereas a representation may be oral or written. *Id.* at 1821.

as assumed. At best, a party unaware of an assumption it makes may ask for a broad assurance that other matters that would or might affect its decision to proceed with the transaction do not exist or will not occur. By giving such a warranty, the warrantor assumes responsibility for the risk that such matters exist or will occur. Warranties that allocate responsibility for the risks in scenarios (3)(a) and (b) will differ, depending whether the warrantee is aware of the assumption it makes and is warranted.

The following cases illustrate the warranties previously described:

- *Hollerman v. F.H. Peavey & Co.*[73]: This case is previously summarized.[74] The statement that participation in a chicken-breeding program "will return to the careful broiler raiser an income roughly equal to half as much as is obtained from an average size farm in the Midwest" was a warranty or representation that such benefit would be realized.[75] The case illustrates a warranty that a specific benefit will be realized. It allocated to the warrantor responsibility for the risk that the information upon which the warrantee relied about the benefit was incorrect.
- *Rhone Poulenc Rorer Pharmaceuticals, Inc. v. Newman Glass Works*[76]: An office building owner contracted with a general contractor to install glass curtainwalls, specifying that the glass had to be made by one of three named manufacturers and conform to the specifications for size, thickness, and coating, depending upon the choice of manufacturer. The coating for the manufacturer whose glass was chosen was, as it had to be, attached with a glue the product literature for which stated could normally be expected to perform in temperatures exceeding 180 degrees Fahrenheit. The contract also warranted the work would be "free from faults and defects" and obligated the contractor to remove all work the owner and its architect condemned "as unsound, defective or improper." The general contractor contracted with a subcontractor to procure and install such windows, including in its contract the specifications and warranties included in the contract with the owner. The

[73] 269 Minn. 221, 130 N.W.2d 534 (Minn. 1964).

[74] *See* text accompanying note 52.

[75] The court held such statements, along with others, were evidence of fraud to be considered by a jury.

[76] 112 F.3d 695 (3d Cir. 1997).

subcontractor purchased and installed the windows in compliance with the specifications, but before the work was completed the coating began to delaminate from the glass. By warranting that the work would be free from defects, the subcontractor assumed responsibility for the defects in the window specifications.[77] The case illustrates how a warranty can allocate responsibility for the information risk in scenario (1)(a)(ii) (warrantor warrants correctness of incorrect information it received about a task the warrantor must complete for the warrantee's benefit). Had the subcontractor not so warranted the outcome, the contractor would have impliedly warranted the specifications, and the case would have been an example of a warranty allocating responsibility for the risk in scenario (1)(b)(ii) (warrantor warrants correctness of incorrect information about a task the warrantee must complete for the warrantor's benefit).

- *Kraft Foods North America, Inc. v. Banner Engineering & Sales, Inc.*[78]: Banner, an engineering firm, supplied insulated pipe joint kits to be used by Kraft, a food manufacturer, in its installation of stainless steel tubing and other equipment to transport low-trans-fat oils to various parts of its food manufacturing plant. The engineering firm included general information about how to assemble the pipe kits, stating the maximum torque to be used. Kraft followed the directions in the general information, using the maximum torque. The result was that food produced using the new tubing was contaminated. A lighter torqueing would have been sufficient and avoided the resulting damage to the product. Banner warranted that the information provided with the kits was suitable for Kraft's purposes. The case illustrates how a warranty can allocate responsibility for the information risk in scenario (1)(a)(i) (warrantor warrants correctness of incorrect information about a task the warrantee must complete for its own benefit).

[77] The general contractor demanded that the subcontractor replace the defective windows, and when the subcontractor refused, sued for damages. The district court granted the subcontractor's summary judgment motion to dismiss the suit and its counterclaim against the contractor, but a divided appeals court reversed, holding that by expressly warranting that the windows would be free from faults and defects, the subcontract "explicitly allocated to [subcontractor] the risk that the glass would be defective." *Id.* at 697.

[78] 446 F. Supp.2d 551 (E.D. Va. 2006).

- *Merrill Lynch & Co. Inc. v. Allegheny Energy, Inc.*[79]: A seller of a commodity trading business warranted that the information provided to the buyer "in the aggregate, includes all information known to the Sellers which, in their reasonable judgment exercised in good faith, is appropriate for the Purchasers to evaluate [the target's] . . . trading positions and trading operations." The seller failed to disclose that the target's chief executive officer had embezzled $43 million from the target and had influenced the preparation of the flawed financial statements provided to the buyer. Whether the warranty was breached by the failure to disclose these facts had to be decided by trial.[80] Note that the warranty in the case was limited to what the seller knew and reasonably should disclose. It did not cover matters assumed by the buyer of which the seller was unaware or matters the seller reasonably decided it did not have to disclose. The case illustrates how a warranty can thus partially allocate responsibility for the risk in scenario (3)(b)(ii). It also illustrates how the form of warranty used to allocate responsibility for the risk that a warrantee has made an unknown, incorrect assumption differs from the form of warranty used to allocate comparable risks in the other scenarios.

Disclaimers and Related Terms

When effective, disclaimers of representations and warranties, antireliance clauses, and merger and integration clauses allocate responsibility for the risks previously described to the parties who rely upon incorrect information and assumptions or who incorrectly process information. They also limit misrepresentation, fraud, and fraudulent concealment claims. Parties who accept disclaimers and similar terms, but rely upon information or assumptions, hope that the completed task will conform to their expectations—that the information on which they formed such expectations and any assumptions they may have made are correct—but the other parties are not committed to ensuring this will be

[79] 500 F.3d 171 (2nd Cir. 2007).

[80] When sued by the seller for the purchase price, the buyer counterclaimed the seller had breached the warranty by failing to disclose the information about the chief executive officer. The trial court dismissed the counterclaim, and the appeal court reversed, holding the trial court had failed to find whether the warranty had been breached and if it had resulted in any diminution of the value of the target. *Id.* at 185.

so and are not liable for breach of warranty, misrepresentation, fraud, and fraudulent concealment.

Disclaimer. A disclaimer—words or conduct that tend to negate or limit a warranty or representation[81]—can negate any warranty that information received is correct, that the recipient of information has correctly processed it, and that an assumption is correct. Such a disclaimer allocates responsibility for the information and assumption risks, as follows:

- First, any warranty that *any benefits will be realized or that the benefits will have any value or utility* can be disclaimed. Such disclaimer allocates to the putative warrantee responsibility for the risk that any information and assumptions upon which it may have relied about such benefits may be incorrect.
- Second, any warranty that *a task a warrantee will complete for its own benefit* can be completed or will contribute toward benefit realization as expected can be disclaimed. Such a disclaimer allocates to the putative warrantee responsibility for the risks in scenarios (1)(a)(i) and (2)(a)(i) and, to the extent the warrantor may have warranted an assumption upon which the warrantee relies that it can complete a task for its own benefit, (3)(a)(i).
- Third, any warranty that *a task a warrantor will complete for a warrantee's benefit* can be completed can be disclaimed. Such a disclaimer allocates responsibility for the risks in scenarios (1)(a)(ii) and (2)(a)(ii) and, to the extent a party may have warranted an assumption by the other party that the latter can complete a task for warrantor's benefit, scenario (3)(a)(ii).
- Fourth, any warranty that *a task that will be completed by the warrantee for the benefit of the warrantor* can be completed or will contribute to the latter's benefit realization can be disclaimed. Such disclaimer allocates responsibility for the information and assumption risks in scenarios (1)(b)(ii) and (2)(b)(ii) and, to the extent the warrantor may have warranted an assumption by the warrantee that the latter can complete a task for warrantor's benefit, scenario (3)(b)(ii).

81 *Supra* ch. 3, note 90.

Such disclaimers cover all the information and assumption hazard scenarios previously described, except scenarios (1)(b)(i), (2)(b)(i), and (3)(b)(i), which we have seen are not hazards, and incorrect assumptions that have not been warranted. A disclaimer of warranties is inapplicable to assumptions that are not warranted. Assumptions, as we have seen, can be made knowingly and unknowingly at contract formation by one or both parties. Disclaimers may be insufficient to negate unilateral and mutual mistake and concealment defenses that may be available in such cases. When effective to cut off warranty claims, disclaimers may also be sufficient to eliminate certain but not necessarily all misrepresentation and fraud claims.

The following cases illustrate how effective and ineffective disclaimers may be to allocate responsibility for the risks that a party may have relied upon incorrect information or an incorrect assumption:

- *UniCredito Italiano SpA v. JP Morgan Chase Bank*[82]: Enron's officers created special purpose offshore entities that bought commodities from Enron. When the prices of such commodities dropped below agreed amounts, Enron had to repurchase them. These transactions were, in reality, disguised loans to Enron, the effect of which was to give Enron the appearance of being financially stronger than it was. JP Morgan Chase Bank (JPMC) purchased ownership interests in the offshore entities and arranged syndicated loans to Enron, aggregating to $4.5 billion. UniCredito Italiano (UCI) participated as a syndicated lender in these loans but had no information about the transactions with the offshore entities or JPMC's participation therein. The credit agreement expressly disclaimed any duty by JPMC to provide information to the participant banks: "The Paying Agent shall not have any duty or responsibility, either initially or on a continuing basis, to provide any Bank or the holder of any Note with any credit or other information with respect thereto, whether coming into its possession before the making of the Advances or at any time or times thereafter."[83] The disclaimers were effective to shield JPMC from liability for negligent misrepresentation and fraud for failing to disclose what it knew about the Enron entities and the transactions.[84] UCI received incorrect information about

[82] 288 F. Supp. 2d 485 (S.D.N.Y. 2003).

[83] *Id.* at 491–92.

[84] UCI sued JPMC for, inter alia, fraudulent concealment, breach of the duty of good faith and fair dealing, aiding and abetting fraud by Enron, negligent misrepresentation; JPMC

the Enron entities, their financial condition, and the transactions. The value it received for the fees and interest charged to Enron was less than it would have been had UCI known of the true state of affairs. UCI had no information about JPMC's investments in the offshore entities and assumed the latter's role was limited to arranging the loans. The case illustrates how a disclaimer may be effective to allocate to a party responsibility for the risk it is acting upon the basis of incorrect information and an incorrect assumption of which it is unaware.[85]

- *Stambovsky v. Ackley*[86]: After contract formation but before closing, a house buyer learned the subject property was reputedly occupied by poltergeists, a fact known to the seller, who had reported her sightings to the local press and *Reader's Digest* on three occasions during the nine years before the sale. The report of the case refers to but does not quote in full the merger, antireliance and "as-is" clauses, the latter two of which are equivalent to a warranty disclaimer. The antireliance clause or disclaimer stated, in part, that the buyer had not relied upon any representations as to the condition of the property or "any other matter or things affecting or relating to the aforesaid premises."[87] On one view, the clause did not extend to paranormal phenomena and was insufficient to negate the duty

moved to dismiss. The court dismissed the fraud and negligent misrepresentation claims, based on the provisions in the credit agreements summarized and quoted. "[E]ven if the bank Defendants had the knowledge the Complaint attributes to them, the banks had no duty to disclose it to Plaintiffs. Sophisticated parties such as Plaintiffs are held to the terms of their contracts." *Id.* at 499. The court also dismissed the argument that JPMC fell within the "peculiar knowledge exception." "Extension of the peculiar knowledge exception to defeat contractual allocations of risks away from the Defendant banks in this case because the principal (Enron) was particularly adept at concealment of its fraud would require at a minimum some factual basis for finding reasonable Plaintiffs reliance on parties on whom it agreed it would not rely in any respect in making the operative decisions." *Id.* at 501.

85 The credit agreement also included the usual boiler plate provisions stating, inter alia, the bank that issued letters of credit thereunder and its affiliates had the right to engage in transactions with Enron "with no duty to account therefor" to the participating banks, an acknowledgment of participating banks that they had not relied on the letter of credit bank in making the decision to enter into the agreement and that they would make their continuing decisions as to whether or not to take action under the agreement or letters of credit issued under the agreement "independently and without reliance upon . . . the [letter of credit bank]." *Id.* at 491–02.

86 169 A.D.2d 254, 572 N.Y.S.2d 672, 60 USLW 2070 (N.Y. App. 1991).

87 169 A.D.2d at 260.

to disclose the house's reputation to the buyer.[88] The buyer gave no thought to whether the house was reputed to be haunted and assumed it was not.[89] Responsibility for the risk that the buyer's assumption about paranormal phenomena was incorrect remained with the seller. The case also illustrates how disclaimers and antireliance clauses may be ineffective to allocate responsibility for incorrect information and assumption risks to the party relying upon such information and assumptions.[90]

Antireliance Clause. An antireliance or nonreliance clause (hereinafter referred to as an antireliance clause) is a promise by a promisor that it will not claim that it has relied upon any information it received from or was provided on behalf of the other party.[91] An antireliance clause disclaims reliance upon information received from one or more sources. A claim for breach of warranty or misrepresentation rests upon a causal connection between the breach or misrepresentation and the loss suffered by the warrantee: reliance upon the correctness of warranted or represented information. An antireliance clause severs that link since the party cannot claim it was entitled to rely upon such information. An antireliance

---

88 "As broad as this language may be, a reasonable interpretation is that its effect is limited to tangible or physical matters and does not extend to paranormal phenomena. Finally, if the language of the contract is to be construed as broadly as defendant urges to encompass the presence of poltergeists in the house, it cannot be said that she has delivered the premises 'vacant' in accordance with her obligation under the provisions of the contract rider." *Id.*

89 "Where, as here, the seller not only takes unfair advantage of the buyer's ignorance but has created and perpetuated a condition about which he is unlikely to even inquire, enforcement of the contract (in whole or in part) is offensive to the court's sense of equity. Application of the remedy of rescission, within the bounds of the narrow exception to the doctrine of caveat emptor set forth herein, is entirely appropriate to relieve the unwitting purchaser from the consequences of a most unnatural bargain." *Id.*

90 *See* text accompanying notes 112–14.

91 "The parties further declare that they have not relied upon any representation of any party hereby released . . . [Party A] or of their attorneys, agents, or other representatives concerning the nature or extent of their respective injuries or damages." "[Party A represents and warrants] . . . (a) no promise or inducement for this Agreement has been made to him except as set forth herein; (b) this Agreement is executed by . . . [Party A] freely and voluntarily, and without reliance upon any statement or representation by Purchaser, the Company, any of the Affiliates or . . . [Party B] or any of their attorneys or agents except as set forth herein; (c) he has read and fully understands this Agreement and the meaning of its provisions; (d) he is legally competent to enter into this Agreement and to accept full responsibility therefor; and (e) he has been advised to consult with counsel before entering into this Agreement and has had the opportunity to do so." Rissman v. Rissman, 213 F.3d 381, 383 (5th Cir. 2000).

clause is limited to allocating responsibility for the information risks in scenarios (1)(a) or 1(b), where incorrect information has been received, or combinations of hazards where the scenarios occur. A party that accepts an antireliance clause but still relies upon representations or warranties not expressly stated in the contract assumes responsibility for the risk they may be incorrect. An antireliance clause should also bar certain claims of fraud and misrepresentation. Because the other hazards do not result from the use of incorrect information, the antireliance clause is inapplicable. An antireliance clause does not override express warranties and, in some instances, a duty to disclose to a party that it is relying upon incorrect information or assumptions.

The following illustrate how an antireliance clause allocates responsibility for information risks:

- *Schlumberger Technology Corp. v. Swanson*[92]: Sellers sold their interests in a diamond mine joint venture and stated they were not relying upon any statement or representation by the buyer. When they later learned the diamond mine's prospects were much better than they anticipated at the time of the sale, they claimed misrepresentation. The report of the case does not describe what the buyers allegedly misrepresented, but the antireliance clause barred any such claim.[93] The antireliance clause allocated responsibility for the risk of the buyers' misrepresentation to the sellers.
- *Green Construction Co. v. Kansas Power & Light Co.*[94]: A utility provided bidders on a dam construction project with a report on the site from which soil was to be excavated but stated, in the conditions for submitting bids, that each bidder was responsible for investigating the site. The moisture content of the soil was critical to the stability of the dam. The clause read,

> [i]t must be understood and agreed that all such factors have been properly investigated and considered in the

[92] 959 S.W.2d 171 (Tex. 1997).

[93] When the sellers discovered the prospects of the venture were brighter than they supposed, they sued for misrepresentation. The jury award of compensatory and exemplary damages was reversed on appeal, the Texas Supreme Court holding, "Because the parties were attempting to put an end to their deal, and had become embroiled in a dispute over the feasibility and value of the project, we conclude that the disclaimer of reliance the [the sellers] Swansons gave conclusively negates the element of reliance." *Id.* at 180.

[94] 1 F.3d 1005 (10th Cir. 1993).

> preparation of every proposal submitted, as there will be no subsequent financial adjustment, to any contract awarded thereunder, which is based on the lack of such prior information or its effect on the cost of the work."[95]

The soil had more moisture content than indicated in the report and was allowed under the specifications; as a result, the dam, when constructed, developed cracks that could not be repaired. The utility had to replace the dam. The antireliance clause barred the contractor's claim that the soils report impliedly warranted that the soil had the moisture content stated in the report and that the error in the report necessitated a material change in the scope of work, entitling it to the contract price and extra costs.[96] The case illustrates a combination of scenarios (1)(a)(ii) and (2)(a)(ii): the contractor received incorrect information (the moisture content of the soil) about a condition material to the task it was to perform for the utility's benefit (using the soil to build a dam) but also incorrectly used the information available to it by not investigating its correctness when advised that it must do so. The antireliance clause allocated responsibility for the combined risks to the contractor.

Merger Clause. An integration or a merger clause is a "contractual provision stating that the contract represents the parties' complete and final agreement and supersedes all informal understandings and oral agreements relating to the subject matter of the contract."[97] We are not here concerned with the effectiveness of an oral agreement reached after contract formation but with information exchanged prior to that time. That information may be incorrect or incorrectly used. A merger clause excludes as evidence of the terms of the contract all prior express agreements, representations, and warranties not included in a written agreement. A party that relies upon such agreements, representations, and warranties assumes responsibility for the risk they are incorrect. Like an antireliance clause, a merger clause applies only to information given

---

95 *Id.* at 1008, footnote 1.

96 The court dismissed the claim on summary judgment, finding the utility had effectively excluded itself from all responsibility for site conditions. By accepting the bid documents, the contractor assumed the risk that moisture content of the soil was higher than described in the bid documents.

97 Black's Law Dictionary, *supra* note 70, 929.

prior to or at contract formation, which are scenarios (1)(a) and (1)(b) when such information is incorrect. Whereas a merger clause negates express warranties and representations not stated in the contract, an expansive disclaimer negates all warranties and representations not stated as express warranties therein.[98]

Waiver of Defenses. A party may agree that its obligation in a contract is absolute and unconditional, the effect of which is to bar such party from asserting any defense it may have that would otherwise permit it to refuse to perform. A party that agrees to such a waiver assumes responsibility for the risk that information about its anticipated benefits or the tasks to be completed may be incorrect; it may have incorrectly used information, or made incorrect assumptions about anticipated benefits and tasks. It also assumes responsibility for the risk that the other party may know of its reliance upon such information or assumption and not have notified it thereof. The waiver can extend to fraud, misrepresentation, and mistake claims, including claims that a party was fraudulently induced to enter into the contract.[99]

MBIA Insurance Corp. v. Royal Indemnity Co.[100] illustrates how such a waiver of defenses allocates responsibility for information and assumption risks. A bank bought student loans from a company that specialized in making such loans but had falsified the student borrowers' creditworthiness and employment history; it conspired with schools to generate as many loans as possible by altering or forging loan documents. The bank obtained policies insuring repayment of such loans. The insurer issued the policies based, in part, on representations from the company that the student loans had been made in compliance with applicable law and regulation. The policies waived in broadest possible terms all defenses the insurer might have against payment of claims under the policies.[101] The insurer sued for rescission of the policies, claiming fraudulent inducement. In turn, the bank sued the insurer, claiming breach. The trial court awarded the bank summary judgment, based on the waivers. The appeal court affirmed in part, holding the waivers

[98] *E.g.*, Wilkinson v. Carpenter, 276 Or. 311, 554 P.2d 512 (Or. 1976), holding that a merger clause barred a claim for rescission of a contract for the sale of a business based on an alleged innocent misrepresentation by the seller.

[99] Citibank, N.A. v. Plapinger, 66 N.Y.2d 90 (N.Y. 1985); Wells Fargo Bank Nw. v. TACA Int'l Airlines, 247 F. Supp. 2d 352, 360 (S.D.N.Y.2003).

[100] 426 F.3d 204 (3d Cir. 2005).

[101] *Id.* at 210–11.

precluded the insurer from asserting fraud as a defense to payment under the policies.[102] The insurer, by agreeing to the broad waiver of defenses, assumed responsibility for the risk that the originator might have provided incorrect information about the insured loans.

Limitations on Disclaimers and Similar Terms. None of the terms that enable a party to limit its liability for breach of warranty and inadvertent, negligent, and intentional misrepresentation and fraud, such as disclaimers, are fully effective in all circumstances. Such limitations, which vary among the jurisdictions, must be understood by anyone attempting to use such terms to allocate responsibility for information and assumption risks.

Following are cases that illustrate such limitations:

- *OnBank & Trust Co. v. FDIC*[103]: This case is previously summarized.[104] The prospectus also included clear disclaimers and antireliance language: the trust interests were being sold "as-is" and "without any representation or warranty except as expressly provided" in the agreement and "without recourse" against the seller;[105] the buyer was not relying upon any information received from the seller.[106] When the buyer discovered the error, it sued the seller, claiming that the seller, as servicer of the mortgage loans, knew of the discrepancy and should have disclosed it. The seller moved for summary judgment, arguing that any reliance by the buyer was unreasonable in view of the disclaimer and antireliance language. The court dismissed the motion, holding that a number of factual issues had

102 *Id.* at 212–13.

103 967 F. Supp. 81 (W.D.N.Y. 1997).

104 *See* text accompanying note 1.

105 "5.5 *Due Diligence.* Purchaser understands and agrees that it is solely responsible for conducting a due diligence investigation of the Mortgage Loans, Servicing Rights (including, without limitation, the Loan Documents) and the Certificates, and that Purchaser is buying the Certificates and the Servicing Rights 'as is' without any representation or warranty except as expressly provided in this Agreement and, except as provided in Section 2.3, without recourse against the Seller or the RTC." *Id.* at 85.

106 "5.7 *Access to Information.* Purchaser has been finished with, and has had an opportunity to review and has reviewed, all financial data, and other information relating to the Servicing Agreement, the Loan Documents, the Certificates, and the Servicing Rights requested by Purchaser. Purchaser has had any questions arising from or relating to such review answered to the satisfaction of Purchaser. Purchaser has not relied upon the Thrift, the Seller or the RTC or any of their respective employees, counsel, or agents with respect to any information regarding the Certificates or the Servicing Rights." *Id.* at 85–86.

to be tried: what each party knew during the transaction.[107] The case illustrates how an express warranty—the total value of the loans in this case—was not automatically trumped by a disclaimer.

- *McRae v. Commonwealth Disposals Commission*[108]: Upon learning that a vessel of some nature had been abandoned off the coast of New Guinea, a government commission advertised the sale of the vessel as "an oil tanker lying on Jourmaund Reef, which is approximately 100 miles North of Samarai. The vessel is said to contain oil." In fact, the vessel was a barge, as the buyer discovered after he incurred some cost mistakenly searching for a tanker. The commission was willing to refund the price paid by the buyer, but the buyer also wanted compensation for his costs of searching for the vessel and sued when denied such compensation. The terms of the sale included a clear disclaimer: "While every effort shall be made to describe the property correctly, the Commonwealth shall not be liable for compensation or otherwise by reason of any misdescription or alleged variation of property delivered, from sample or property inspected."[109] Other clauses stated that the goods "are sold as and where they lie with all faults" and no warranty is given as to "condition description quality or otherwise."[110] These disclaimers, the Australian High Court held, however, did not override by the "promise by the Commission that there was a tanker in the position specified."[111]
- *Norton v. Popolos*[112]: A seller agreed to sell, and a buyer agreed to buy, a lot in an industrial park. The buyer explained he intended to store petroleum products in barrels and tanks. The seller indicated that the property was subject to restrictions, a copy of which he

[107] "There are a number of issues of fact in this case that simply cannot be resolved on a motion to dismiss. In general, these issues relate to: what information was known to RTC, but not to OnBank, prior to the formation of the contract; whether that information was 'peculiarly within' RTC's knowledge, and whether it was available to OnBank; whether RTC made any material misrepresentations to OnBank; and OnBank's ability to have discovered the discrepancy between the Certificate Principal Amount and the actual loan balance prior to the date on which the servicing rights and obligations were transferred to OnBank." *Id.* at 87. The case was eventually settled before these factual issues were tried. United States District Court, W.D. New York, Docket 6:95cv06640.

[108] [1951] Argus L.R. 771, 84 C.L.R. 377 (High Court of Australia 1951).

[109] *Id.* at 382.

[110] *Id.* at 398.

[111] *Id.* at 410.

[112] 443 A.2d 1 (Del. 1982).

said he would supply but never did before the contract was signed. When the buyer learned that special approval of the local building committee would be required for the intended use, he applied for but was denied that approval. He demanded the return of his deposit and attorney's fees. Because the contract included a merger clause and a contingency that the property may have a specific zoning designation, which it had, but did not include any representation or warranty as to the restrictions on its use, the trial court held for the seller. The Delaware Supreme Court reversed, holding the seller had innocently misrepresented the zoning designation by not disclosing that the restrictions that required the special approval of the local building committee. Referring to the antireliance clause as a merger clause, the court said the "better rule" is that "even if a sales contract contains a merger clause, a buyer may rescind the contract if it resulted from an innocent but material misrepresentation by a seller."[113] The antireliance clause was ineffective to allocate to the buyer responsibility for the risk the seller had provided incorrect information.

- *Stambovsky*[114]: This case, which is previously summarized,[115] illustrates how a disclaimer or antireliance clause may be ineffective to allocate to a party responsibility for the risk it is acting upon the basis of an incorrect assumption about anticipated benefits of which the other party is aware.[116]

---

[113] *Id.* at 7. *See also,* Slomin's, Inc. v. Wilson, C.A. No. 07-07-0217 (Del. Com. Pl. 2009), where a homeowner who was contemplating moving to Pennsylvania asked and was told by a home alarm company that it serviced all of Pennsylvania, and on that basis signed a 5-year service contract. When he moved to Pennsylvania, he learned service was not available in that state and cancelled the contract. The alarm company sued, and the home owner introduced evidence of the statements made by the company before the contract was signed; the company objected, citing the merger clause in the contract. The court held the evidence was admissible to show a mutual mistake of fact. The court said of the merger clause, "[B]ecause of the nature of the standardized contract and the oral statements of the sales representative, it is unlikely that this contract represents the real intentions of the parties." The case should have been decided on the ground the homeowner was induced by a misrepresentation, albeit innocent or negligent.

[114] 169 A.D.2d 254, 572 N.Y.S.2d 672, 60 USLW 2070 (N.Y. App. 1991).

[115] *See* text accompanying notes 86–90.

[116] "Where, as here, the seller not only takes unfair advantage of the buyer's ignorance but has created and perpetuated a condition about which he is unlikely to even inquire, enforcement of the contract (in whole or in part) is offensive to the court's sense of equity. Application of the remedy of rescission, within the bounds of the narrow exception

Amendments

An amendment can correct an incorrect description of or an incorrect assumption about a benefit or task. An amendment procedure favors a party by allowing it to revise the details of the tasks that must be completed. This will be the obligor in scenarios (1)(a)(ii), (2)(a)(ii), and (3)(a)(ii): the party charged with completing the task for the benefit of the other party has incorrect information, has incorrectly used information, or made an incorrect assumption about a task, respectively. After contract formation, it discovers it cannot complete the task as expected. An amendment or change order procedure allows the obligor to correct the description of the task. An amendment procedure will favor the obligee in scenarios (1)(b)(ii), (2)(b)(ii), and (3)(b)(ii): the obligee has incorrect information, has incorrectly used information, or made an incorrect assumption about such task, respectively. After contract formation, it discovers the task cannot be completed or will not yield the desired benefit, in each case, as expected. An amendment or change order procedure allows the obligee to correct the description of the task. An amendment procedure is unnecessary for scenarios (1)(a)(i), (2)(b)(i), and (3)(b)(i): in these scenarios, after contract formation a party discovers that a task it will complete for its own benefit, usually after the other party has performed its obligations, cannot be completed as expected or will not yield the desired benefits. But since it can choose whether and how to complete such task, a contractual amendment procedure is unnecessary.

The amendment procedure allocates responsibility for information and assumption risks to a party to the extent it has no control over the amendment and must bear responsibility for the increased risks that the amended task cannot be performed and increased costs in performing. If an obligor can revise the details of a task it must complete in scenarios (1)(a)(ii), (2)(a)(ii), and (3)(a)(ii), such changes are adverse to the obligee, and no compensation is given to the obligee for suffering such diminution, the obligee bears responsibility for the information and assumption risks. If an obligee can revise the details of a task the other party must complete in scenarios (1)(b)(ii), (2)(b)(ii), and (3)(b)(ii), such changes are adverse to the obligor, and no compensation is given

to the doctrine of caveat emptor set forth herein, is entirely appropriate to relieve the unwitting purchaser from the consequences of a most unnatural bargain." *Id.*

to the obligor for incurring such incremental risk and cost, the obligor bears responsibility for the information and assumption risks.

The following illustrate how an amendment procedure allocates information and assumption risks:

- *Marriott Corp. v. Dasta Construction Co.*[117]: This case is described in chapter 3.[118] The case combines scenarios (1)(b)(ii) and (2)(b)(ii), and possibly (3)(b)(ii): Marriott was the obligee, the contractor the obligor, and Marriott's ability to correct errors in and embellish the plans and specifications as the work progressed the amendment procedure. Such errors could have been incorrect information Marriott had received, errors by it while developing the design and specifications, and incorrect assumptions about the conditions at the site. Since it controlled the process for changing the plans and specifications and the contractor was not entitled to extra time or cost, the procedure allocated nearly the entirety of responsibility for these information and assumption risks to the contractor.
- *Net2Globe Int'l, Inc. v. Time Warner Telecom of New York*[119]: Time Warner Telecom of New York (TWTNY) was a domestic carrier that owned no international cables or routes of its own and subcontracted with international carriers for international service to its customers. Net2Globe Int'l (NG2) was a reseller whose customers' communications were carried by TWTNY. The contracts between TWTNY and N2G incorporated the domestic carrier's applicable tariffs. The tariffs stated fixed rates for the reseller's customers' calls. One tariff, however, reserved to the domestic carrier

  > the right to discontinue service, limit service, or to impose requirements as required to meet changing regulatory or statutory rules and standards, or when such rules and standards have an adverse material affect [sic] on the business or economic feasibility of providing service, as determined by the Company in its reasoned judgment.

  After contract formation, TWTNY discovered that the rate subcontractors charged it for international calls to cellular phones

---

117 26 F.3d 1057 (11th Cir. 1994).

118 *See* text accompanying ch. 3, notes 108 and 109.

119 273 F. Supp. 2d 436; 2003 U.S. Dist. LEXIS 11950 (S.D.N.Y. 2003).

was almost five times the rates for routing international calls to land lines. TWTNY passed such higher charges through to N2G, based on the quoted tariff.[120] The case illustrates scenario (3)(b)(ii): TWTNY seemingly had no information about the subcontractors' right to charge the higher rate and assumed the subcontractors' charges for calls to landline and cellular phones were the same. TWTNY was the obligee, N2G the obligor, and TWTNY's right to change the rate a limited right to modify N2G's obligation. Responsibility for the incorrectness of TWTNY's assumption about its subcontractors' rates was thereby allocated to N2G.

Termination

Termination of a contract can mitigate the potential losses likely to result from the hazards described in this chapter just as it can stem the losses that might result from other hazards. A termination right favors an obligor in scenarios (1)(a)(ii), (2)(a)(ii), and (3)(a)(ii): a party has agreed to perform an obligation based upon incorrect information, incorrectly used information, or an incorrect assumption about a task. After contract formation it discovers it cannot complete the task as expected. Termination allows it to avoid completion of the task. A termination right favors the obligee in scenarios (1)(b)(ii), (2)(b)(ii), and (3)(b)(ii): the obligee has agreed to the obligor's performing an obligation based upon incorrect information, incorrectly used information or an incorrect assumption. After contract formation the obligee discovers the task cannot be completed or will not yield the desired benefit, in each case, as expected. Termination allows the obligee to mitigate its losses by stopping further performance by it and the obligor. The comments in chapter 3 about termination rights generally apply to such termination rights.

[120] "The section's use of the disjunctive conjunction, 'or,' which, along with the preceding comma, setting off a second conditional clause, indicates that two propositions are being delineated—one for circumstances involving changing rules and standards and another involving materially adverse effects of regulatory rules and [**20] standards irrespective of any change." *Id.* at 447.

5

Uncertainty Risks

UNCERTAINTY HAZARDS

Uncertain Expectations

Uncertainty is defined as "[t]he quality, state, or condition of being in some degree of serious doubt" and "anything that is indefinite, indeterminate, or dubious."[1] First, one or more conditions and contingencies that affect task completion and benefit realization may be in serious doubt or indeterminate at contract formation. The lack of information about such conditions and contingencies creates uncertainty about what actually exists in the case of a condition and what will occur in the case of a contingency. Second, independent of whether conditions and contingencies are known, a task or benefit may be indefinitely or vaguely conceived at contract formation; no one can definitely say which actions will complete such a task or the value that must be realized. It will be difficult or impossible to say if the task has been completed or the benefit realized.

The intentions or expectations stated in a contract can be clear or vague, they can be concordant or discordant, and they can be inadvertently or intentionally so: clear or vague and concordant or discordant. Certainty is at its best when, at contract formation:

---

[1] BLACK'S LAW DICTIONARY 1756 (10th ed. 2014).

- A party's expectations about the benefits it should realize, the tasks to be completed by all parties, the commitments to complete those tasks, and responsibility for unknown conditions and contingencies are sufficiently specific that there is no reason for doubting what is required.
- The other party understands and accepts those expectations.

The expectations are clear and concordant and known to be so. Uncertainty is at its worst when

- Whatever expectations a party has about such benefits, tasks, commitments, and responsibility are vague.
- The other party does not understand or accept those expectations.

The uncertainty described in the first bullet is the party's expectation at contract formation: the party does not know what it will expect when after contract formation its ideas about the transaction have evolved into more specific expectations. The hazard is proceeding with only vague expectations, whether or not the party knows how vague its expectations are. The uncertainty in the second bullet is whether the party's expectations will prevail in the event they are disputed by the other party. The hazard is proceeding with discordant expectations, whether or not the party is aware of them.

The following cases illustrate such uncertainties.

- *Cummings v. Dusenberry*[2]: House buyers told their sellers they wanted to buy a "year-round house." This was not a term of art in the real estate trade. The sellers sold the buyers a house in which the windows leaked and let in flies, the roof leaked badly during rains, and the walls dripped with condensation in the winter. At contract formation, the buyers had a vague notion of the house they expected to buy, but after living in it for some time came to expect a house without such shortcomings. The sellers viewed the buyers' expectation of a year-round house to be meaningless, like a "good house," "nice location," or house the buyer will be "happy with."[3] The sellers did not accept the buyers' revised expectations

[2] 129 Ill. App.3d 338, 472 N.E.2d 575 (Ill. App. 1984).

[3] The house buyers sued for rescission, claiming breach of warranty (because a year-round house implied a warranty of habitability) and unilateral mistake. The court, while rejecting the implied warranty, allowed rescission on the grounds of unilateral mistake, holding, "Although the question of what constitutes a 'year-round' home is somewhat a question

of a habitable house. The case illustrates uncertainty as described in both bullets.

- *Harlequin Enterprises, Ltd. v. Warner Books, Inc.*[4]: A writer who created a fictional character who decimated mafia gangsters agreed that his publisher could publish books in the series written by other authors. At contract formation, his publisher recognized it would be best protected by, and asked the writer for, a commitment not to write any work that competed directly or indirectly with sales of the series.[5] The author accepted the proposal but reserved "the right to create and/or write works for others, other than works which would compete with the sale of the action-adventure series contemplated in [the contract]." The writer later agreed to write a new series for another publisher centered on a "psychic detective" and based on "mystical and supernatural themes, mixing parapsychology and the occult with detective suspense and sex."[6] The first publisher had hoped the writer would not write a new fiction series that would erode sales of its action series and, if he did, its view of the limitation would be accepted by a court.[7] In effect, the parties decided not to decide, at contract formation, what the contract should require of the author. The author had more than a vague but less than a certain notion of the works he might write, while the publisher had a clear idea of what it hoped he would not write.

of personal taste, there was evidence in the record that this home was built as a vacation house, and was not suitable for winter use by a young family." *Id.* at 344.

4 639 F. Supp. 1081 (S.D.N.Y. 1986).

5 Don Pendleton, who authored a highly successful "Executioner" series of 38 action novels based on a character who hunted down and killed mafia gangsters, agreed that Harlequin could continue publishing new novels in the series, which, because the mafia had been decimated in the earlier novels, was expanded to include terrorists and other crazies and was labeled as the "Gold Eagle" series, the ideas for which would come from Pendleton but the writing would be by authors hired by Harlequin; in return, Pendleton would be paid a royalty on each book sold. Unusually, the contract prohibited Pendleton from competing directly or indirectly with the Executioner series, but, at Pendleton's request, reserved to him "the right to create and/or write works for others, other than works which would compete with the sale of the action-adventure series contemplated in this Agreement, which Pendleton may publish or cause to be published in any language throughout the world." *Id.* at 1084.

6 *Id.* at 1084.

7 "Harlequin's people claim that they knew that paragraph 8 would allow Pendleton to write in the future, but understood that his interest was limited to publishing inspirational, non-fiction works." *Id.* at 1087.

The case also illustrates uncertainty as described in both bullets, though to a lesser extent than that described in the first than in the second bullet.

Vague expectations may be attributable to the following:

- Lack of sufficient experience and expertise to shape a party's ideas into a clear expectation. *Cummings* illustrates such inexperience.
- Insufficient time or effort devoted to planning the details of the transaction. Contract formation may come too early to the transaction, with the result that the parties have still to crystallize their expectations. The parties may be unwilling to invest the time and effort to reach a detailed agreement on all issues. *Harlequin Enterprises, Ltd.* illustrates such an unwillingness: they chose to leave open what the author would be allowed to write rather than resolve the issue at contract formation. Transaction planning, negotiation, and documentation, like diligence, takes time and money, both of which are limited resources that must be rationed, no matter how important the transaction is to the party. In addition, negotiating terms ancillary to the principal benefits of the transaction risks upsetting agreement on the principal matters. Vagueness of expectation may be a price a party is willing to pay for time and cost savings during transaction planning, negotiation, and documentation.
- Uncertainties about the conditions and contingencies that significantly affect any effort to describe the benefits that might be realized or the tasks that have to be completed. How such uncertainties affect that effort is explained in the following section.

Whatever the cause of uncertainty, the hazards remain the same: a party proceeds with a transaction with a vague idea of the benefits, tasks, commitments, or responsibility for conditions and contingencies, or an idea of the foregoing that differs from that of the other party.

The following cases are additional illustrations of the uncertainties described in the first two bullets.

- *Coto-Matic, Inc. v. Home Indemnity Co.*[8]: Coto-Matic's founder and general manager (H) saw a machine in Los Angeles that created a semiautomatic process that painted small pieces of sheet metal.

[8] 354 F.2d 720 (10th Cir. 1965).

He decided to develop a machine in Kansas that would uniquely operate an automated process: coiled metal would be unwound, treated in a series of tanks, dried in a tower, painted by a paint applicator, baked in an oven, and rewound or coiled, all operating through a connecting and timed system. He asked a contractor to quote a price for fabricating such a machine based on a loose description of how it would perform. The contractor quoted a price and later agreed to fabricate the machine, incorporating that description into the contract and a list of components. When tested, by feeding the metal coils into the machine, it had to be stopped, adjusted, and restarted. The contractor made adjustments but H was still dissatisfied with the result.[9] The case illustrates a vague idea that stemmed from lack of expertise: H had done no more than describe the dimensions and his concept of the operation of the machine, which had not previously been fabricated. Either he or the contractor had to assume responsibility for the risk the machine, the technical details of which were so vaguely described, would not meet his expectations.[10]

- *GLS Development, Inc. v. Wal-Mart Stores, Inc.*[11]: Wal-Mart, a retail chain store, after agreeing with a developer that the latter would develop a site for one of its stores, asked the developer to transfer its development rights to another developer, offering as consideration $500,000 and "a few" additional projects to work on. The developer transferred its rights but never received the payment or a new project.[12] The case illustrates uncertainty about what Wal-Mart and

9 Coto-Matic sued for damages, claiming the contractor had failed to produce the continuous finishing system called for in the contract. The appeals court upheld the trial court's verdict in favor of the contractor. "We conclude, therefore, that the obligation of [the contractor] Industrial was not to accomplish an unqualified end result for a continuous finishing system in that phrase's broad sense but was limited to a contractual obligation to fabricate a mechanically suitable machine capable of meeting the parties' concept of a five-stage operation properly coordinated in time and function and in accord with the contractually agreed upon plans and specifications." *Id.* at 725.

10 "It is difficult to comprehend that either the contractors or the owners contemplated building such a unique piece of machinery with only its size and dimensions in mind—disregarding for contract purposes whether it would actually and ultimately process and paint metal as originally conceived." *Id.* at 724–25.

11 944 F. Supp. 1384 (N.D. Ill. 1996).

12 The choice of "a few" reflected the store's preliminary thinking about what it might do for the developer, which was so highly conceptual it was too vague to be enforceable.

the developer expected by the term "few projects." At best, each had only a vague idea about what it hoped for. The vagueness of the words "few projects" created another risk, discussed in chapter 6, that the legal formalities for creating a binding commitment had not been satisfied. As a result, Wal-Mart had no commitment to give any projects to the developer. In this case, the uncertainty could have been eliminated by devoting time to specify the few projects before contract formation. Complex projects are often vague ideas in their inception and evolve with careful planning. Contract formation arrived too early for the developer, who accepted uncertainty about what tasks Wal-Mart would perform.

Condition and Contingency Uncertainty

Condition Uncertainty. A condition, the existence or nonexistence of which affects task completion or benefit realization, is uncertain when a party lacks sufficient information at contract formation to determine whether such condition exists. Such information may or may not be available; or the condition may or may not be knowable at contract formation. Either way, the existence of the condition is unknown to the party having to decide whether and how to proceed with a transaction. This predicament was described as scenario (3)(a) or (b) in the last chapter: in scenario (3)(a), a party has insufficient information about a condition affecting the completion of a task it must complete; in scenario 3(b), a party has insufficient information about a condition affecting the completion of a task the other party must complete. In each case, it makes an assumption about the condition. That assumption may be favorable, that the condition exists, or unfavorable, that it does not. Because that assumption may prove to be incorrect, proceeding on the basis of such an assumption may be also a hazard. In short, the solution—making an assumption about a condition to resolve uncertainty about that condition—swaps one risk, uncertainty, for another, an incorrect assumption.

Following are cases that illustrate condition uncertainty risk.

- *Laidlaw v. Organ*[13]: A tobacco buyer received news that a treaty had been signed ending the 1812 war between Britain and the United States. He bought tobacco from a merchant ignorant of this news

[13] 15 U.S. (2 Wheat.) 178, 4 L.Ed. 214 (1817).

in New Orleans, where tobacco prices were depressed because the port had been blockaded. The seller asked the buyer "if there was any news which was calculated to enhance the price or value of the article about to be purchased." The buyer did not respond; the seller nonetheless agreed to sell. The price of tobacco increased 30 percent to 50 percent the following day. The uncertainty, whether the war and resulting blockade continued, did not affect the task the seller was to perform, sale of the tobacco. It affected the value the seller would realize and the corresponding task the buyer had to complete, payment of the price. The transaction was scenario (3) (a) (ii) if the seller assumed the war continued and the port remained blocked. Whether or not he did, he accepted the risk the tobacco was worth more than the price he received.[14]

- *Kennedy v. Reece*[15]: A contractor agreed to drill a hole for a water well to a depth of 400 feet for a fixed price. It encountered hard rock at a depth of 130 feet. It started over at another location, where it drilled to a depth of 270 feet and encountered further hard rock. It abandoned the work. Two other contractors were willing to drill at a third location to the depth of 400 feet. The uncertainty, the hardness of the subsurface, affected the contractor's task and cost, as more time and effort was required to drill a third hole.[16] The case was also scenario (3) (a) (ii) if the contractor assumed it would not have to drill more than one hole. The contractor had assumed responsibility for the risk its costs would exceed its fixed price unless its performance was excused.[17]

The uncertainties about whether hostilities continued and the extent of rock in the subsurface became hazards at contract formation. In the first case, the seller had to agree upon a price while unable to determine if a condition depressing the price of his tobacco continued. Had he been

[14] The seller sued for rescission. Chief Justice Marshall held for the buyer, saying, "The court is of opinion that he was not bound to communicate it. It would be difficult to circumscribe the contrary doctrine within proper limits, where the means of intelligence are equally accessible to both parties." 15. U.S. at 194.

[15] 225 Cal.App.2d 717, 37 Cal. Rptr. 708 (Cal. App. 1964).

[16] The contractor sued for breach of contract, and the owners counterclaimed for breach by the contractor. The trial court found the contractor had breached the contract. The appeal court held the finding was supported by the evidence.

[17] The court held the defenses of impossibility and impracticability were unavailable because two other contractors were willing to drill the hole at another location. 225 Cal.App.2d 717, 724-7.

able to index the price to a market that reflected relevant conditions, he would have been able to avoid uncertainty risk. In the absence of such an index, he would have to assume the risk the tobacco was worth more than the agreed price, whatever that price might be, but the higher that price the less the chance of selling too low. Put another way, any increase in compensation paid to the seller would have diminished the seller's potential losses from uncertainty risk. In the second example, the contractor assumed uncertainty risk by fixing his price without knowing how many holes he would have to drill. The uncertainty risks in these cases could have been traded for incorrect assumption risks, that is, assumptions about the existence or nonexistence of the condition. If not, the uncertainty risks remained and responsibility for them was assumed by the seller in *Laidlaw* and the contractor in *Kennedy*.

Contingency Uncertainty. As observed, a contingency is always uncertain because the occurrence of a future event is to some degree unpredictable. The best information about a contingency forecasts the probability of its occurrence but cannot predict its occurrence with certainty. As such, whether a contingency will occur will be unknown to the party having to decide whether and how to proceed with a transaction. This is also the predicament described as scenarios (3) (a) and (b) in chapter 4: because it cannot confirm that a contingency will occur, a party might make an assumption about the contingency. However, because that assumption may prove to be incorrect, proceeding with a transaction on the basis of such an assumption is also a hazard.

The more possible outcomes of a contingency, the occurrence of which will affect benefit realization and task completion, the more difficult the description at contract formation of the specific benefits that may be realized and tasks that must be completed. Planning for a contingency that has two results entails just that: determining what task, if any, should be completed for each outcome. For example, two outcomes of a lottery ticket purchase are possible: the winning numbers drawn correspond to those on the ticket or they do not. The ticket buyer might plan for both outcomes or make an assumption about the outcome and plan accordingly. As the variations of an outcome multiply, planning for each becomes impractical at some point and the resulting uncertainty is a tolerable necessity. A transaction that contemplates more than one action over a period of time further complicates planning because a number of contingencies, each with multiple outcomes, may be relevant. Identifying all the potential outcomes of each contingency or combination of contingencies may be difficult, let alone specifying how a party must act in response to each outcome. Assumptions might be made, but they may be unrealistic in view of the uncertainties. Uncertainty about the outcome of the contingencies results in uncertainty about what tasks must be completed and the benefits that will be realized. Expectation uncertainty, itself a hazard, may be the result of condition and contingency uncertainty. The hazard is uncertainty about contingencies that result in uncertainties about the potential benefits and tasks.

Following are cases that illustrate such contingency uncertainty.

- *Western Geophysical Co. of America, Inc. v. Bolt Associates, Inc.*[18]: A licensee of a patent for an air gun device designed to provide a source of sound for use in underwater seismic exploration agreed to use its best efforts to promote the licensing and sublicensing of the product. After the first one and one-half years, during which time the licensee redesigned the device to eliminate technical shortcomings affecting its performance for shallow reconnaissance surveys or oceanographic mapping, one of its two uses, the licensee concluded superior devices were available in the market for such purpose and did not attempt to market it for that use. The licensee also attempted to develop a "system" for the other use for the device, deep penetration seismic exploration, as it judged that the users of such devices for such exploration were not interested in the device without a system. The licensee never completed this effort. When no one had been licensed after three and one-quarter years, the licensor terminated the license. The licensor claimed the licensee had not done enough to promote the product.[19] The case illustrates how the nature and extent of the tasks to be performed were uncertain due to contingencies: one contingency was the full development of the technical capabilities the air gun and another was the availability of similar devices in the market. Both contingencies had several potential outcomes.

---

[18] 584 F.2d 1164 (2nd Cir. 1978).

[19] The licensor sued for breach of contract, claiming the licensee had not used best efforts. In particular, waiting until a system had been developed to seek licensees fell short of what best efforts required. The federal district court, recognizing different promotional plans might be adopted, awarded a judgment in favor of the licensee; and the appeals court upheld the judgment, holding, "The phrase 'best efforts to promote licensing' indicates a degree of discretion in the selection of the promotional plan." *Id.* at 1171.

- *DaimlerChrysler Motors Co., LLC v. Manuel*[20]: An automobile dealer agreed with the manufacturer to build a new dealership facility at an agreed-upon location. The manufacturer agreed it would use its best efforts to litigate or settle any protest against such new location that was lodged before a state commission by another dealer. In fact, another dealer did protest the new location before a state commission, even though it had previously waived its right to protest the location of new dealerships. The manufacturer sued the protesting dealer in federal court, which remitted the dispute to the state commission. Eventually, the manufacturer settled with the protesting dealer. The dealer claimed the manufacturer waited too long to reach such settlement.[21] The case illustrates how a contingency creates uncertainty about when and how a task should be completed. At contract formation, the manufacturer could not have stated how aggressively it would litigate before settling the protest, as that could have tipped its hand to the protesting dealer.[22] It also had to wait until a dealer protested, as only then could it assess the potential reaction to litigation by the protesting dealer, the courts, and state commission.[23]
- *Middleton v. California Co.*[24]: Land in the amount of 4,600 acres was leased for oil and gas exploration and production for a one-eighth royalty. Only 30 wells on 400 acres were drilled during the first 18 years of the lease, but they produced more than 17,000,000

[20] 362 S.W.3d 160, 172 (Tex. App. 2012).

[21] The relocating dealer successfully claimed it was entitled to compensation for profits lost during the resulting delay because the manufacturer could have settled sooner. "[T]he goal or objective of the best efforts provision in the AESSA [the contract], in light of the agreement as a whole, was for Chrysler to use its best efforts to litigate or settle the Meador protest in such a period of time that Manuel could establish the South Arlington dealership by January 1." *Id.* at 172.

[22] "The question is not whether Chrysler should have litigated, as we agree that was its right. Rather, the question is when did Chrysler's choice to litigate to the exclusion of making any efforts toward settlement become unreasonable." *Id.* at 177.

[23] "Chrysler argues that the AESSA [the contract] did not obligate it to pay any money to [the protesting dealer] Meador, that it had no contractual obligation to use the $50 million it had allocated to its budget to settle protests by dealers, and that it could simply have 'ignored' settling with Meador until it had fully litigated its pending federal court and administrative proceedings. Chrysler reasons that [the relocating dealer] Manuel's position (and the trial court's finding of failure to use best efforts) imposed 'an additional burden' on Chrysler of settlement." *Id.* at 176.

[24] 237 La. 1039; 112 So.2d 704 (La. 1959).

barrels of oil and yielded payments of more than $4,000,000 in royalties to the lessors. Very little was done on the remainder of the leased land. When the lessors were offered a one-sixth royalty by another oil company for a lease of a portion of the leased area not developed by the first oil company, they invoked a clause in the lease allowing termination if the operations were not conducted in accordance with the lease. The alleged breach was the failure to use reasonable diligence to drill on every part of the leased premises.[25] It seems likely that because the mineral lessors did not contemplate exploration and production proceeding according to a specific drilling plan, none having been agreed at any time, they had vague expectations about the rate at which the mineral lessee would explore and develop producing wells. That changed when a better deal was offered for the undeveloped portion of the premises.[26] The case illustrates a combination of condition and contingency uncertainty: at contract formation, the extent of the crude oil reserves was unknown (a condition) and the cost of exploration and production and the price at which such oil could be sold (contingencies) were unknown.

In none of the three cases was it practical at contract formation to state in reasonable detail all the tasks that were to be completed by the licensee, manufacturer, and mineral lessee. The various outcomes of all the contingencies made that effort unrealistic. In all three cases, the contingencies—the development of the technology and the market for such air guns in *Western Geophysical Co. of America, Inc.*, the reactions of the other dealer to litigation in *DaimlerChrysler Motors Co., LLC*[27] and the extent of the resource, the cost of production, and the price of crude oil in *Middleton*—were potential hazards before contract formation. They became hazards at contract formation when the parties decided

[25] It was well-settled law in Louisiana, where the land was located, that "a mineral lessee must develop with reasonable diligence every part of the leased premises, having due regard for the interests of all contracting parties, or surrender the lease." *Id.* at 710.

[26] A divided court held for the mineral lessee. Justice E. Howard McCaleb observed, "In this connection it is apt to point out that, considering the large acreage of land covered by the lease, it is apparent that neither the lesser (sic) nor the lessee contemplated that an immediate development of the land was feasible or practicable. And we think it evident that the parties assumed that the securing of production from all parts of the tract would require considerable time after the initial production was obtained." *Id.* at 708.

[27] *See* text accompanying notes 20–23.

to proceed with the transactions notwithstanding the uncertainties. They became hazards at contract formation to both of the parties in all three transactions because the tasks to be completed either had not been specified, as in *Middleton*, or vaguely specified as in the other two cases. In *Western Geophysical Co. of America, Inc.*, the best efforts obligation allocated to the licensee responsibility for the risk that it would have to do more to develop and market the air gun than it anticipated and to the licensor responsibility for the risk that the licensee would have to do less than anticipated. In *DaimlerChrysler Motors Co., LLC*,[28] the best efforts obligation allocated to the manufacturer responsibility for the risk it would have to settle earlier and for more money than anticipated and to the dealer responsibility for the risk it would have to wait longer while the litigation dragged on longer than anticipated. None of the parties could be certain what would be required of the licensee, manufacturer, or mineral lessee.

UNCERTAINTY RISK MANAGEMENT

Diligence

Examination of the potential benefits and tasks during the planning phase should drive a party to clarify its expectations about the benefits it hopes to realize and the tasks the parties must complete to realize them. In a case where a party has insufficient experience or expertise, as did the general manager in *Coto-Matic, Inc.*, it might recognize the uncertainties in its plans. It might abandon the effort or enlist help to guide the detailed planning of the tasks and benefit. Identifying and forecasting contingencies that determine what tasks will have to be completed will also help crystallize expectations about benefits and tasks, although because contingencies do not occur until after contract formation, no definitive statement of such expectations is realistic when a task is largely undertaken in reaction to a contingency.

In a transaction in which there are critical conditions and contingencies that are unknown and unknowable at contract formation, diligence will help to identify these unknowable uncertainties and their impact on a party's expectations about the potential benefits and corresponding tasks. *Middleton*[29] is an example: in view of the large area

[28] *See* text accompanying notes 20–23.

[29] *See* text accompanying notes 24–26.

covered by the mineral lease and the absence of accurate information about the crude oil reserves, the cost of exploring, developing, producing, and marketing crude oil, the extent and pace at which the mineral lessee would proceed was bound to be uncertain at contract formation. Diligence can mitigate, if not eliminate, expectation uncertainty where the conditions and contingencies that shape expectations about benefits and tasks are knowable or, if unknowable, are few or insignificant. It mitigates uncertainty to a lesser extent when unknowable conditions and contingencies make crystallization of benefits and tasks unrealistic at contract formation. As noted in previous chapters, this text, while repeatedly emphasizing the importance of diligence to transaction planning, does not explain the diligence appropriate for any transaction.

Define Benefits and Tasks or Process

Contract interpretation principles, especially those applicable to clear terms that can be given their plain meaning, vague and ambiguous terms that require additional evidence and speculation to give them meaning in specific cases, and the implied duty of good faith and fair dealing allocate the uncertainty risks previously described. For example, in *Coto-Matic, Inc.*,[30] a case of expectation uncertainty previously summarized,[31] contract interpretation principles called for the contract to be classified as one that limited the contractor's contractual obligation to fabricate a mechanically suitable machine capable of meeting the parties' concept of a five-stage operation properly coordinated in time and function and in accord with the contractually agreed upon plans and specifications or as one to accomplish an unqualified end result for a continuous finishing system mentioned in the contract. Those principles implied that responsibility for the uncertainty risk—what was required to achieve that end and whether doing so was feasible—was assumed by the company in the former and by the contractor in the latter.

In *Middleton*, also previously summarized,[32] where the extent of the resource and the costs and returns of developing them were uncertain, contract interpretation principles would, in the absence of exceptional circumstances, have implied a term that the lessee had to develop with reasonable diligence every part of the leased premises, having

[30] 354 F.2d 720 (10th Cir. 1965).

[31] *See* text accompanying notes 8–10.

[32] *See* text accompanying notes to 24–26.

due regard for the interests of all contracting parties, or surrender the lease. In exceptional circumstances, the term implied was that the lessee had to develop the lease with reasonable diligence. The former principle implied the uncertainty risks had been assumed by the lessee, and the latter implied the risk had been assumed by the lessor so long as the lessee reasonably developed the acreage. Such principles create the framework for managing the uncertainty risks previously described.

A party that recognizes benefit and task uncertainty in a transaction has two alternatives or strategies for managing that risk:

- State some or all of the tasks either vaguely or clearly in the contract.
- State clearly a process for defining some or all of the tasks in the contract as and when it becomes necessary to decide on benefits and tasks.

Although it is seemingly inconsistent for a party having only vague expectations to clearly define the tasks to be performed, whether by it or the other party, both strategies are available for both uncertainty hazards previously described.

Define Benefits and Tasks. A statement of the tasks to be completed may be clear or vague.

- A clear statement defines each of the tasks with sufficient specificity that each party can understand what is required of it and the other party. The risk to a party that has vague expectations at contract formation is that when its expectations crystallize as the transaction evolves, they will vary from what the contract requires. It will be, and such party assumes the risk it will be, required to give more or accept less than eventually expected.
- A statement of tasks will be sufficiently vague as to encompass nearly all the possible actions that might have to be completed by one or both parties during the course of implementing a transaction. The risk to a party that has vague expectations at contract formation is the same as the previous bullet: as expectations crystallize, they may vary from what the other party expects, which may be what the contract requires. *Middleton*[33] is one example: the mineral lessors

[33] *See* text accompanying notes to 24–26.

came to expect a faster pace of development of the leased acreage. *DaimlerChrysler Motors Co., Ltd.* is another example: the dealer came to expect a quicker settlement by the manufacturer than the manufacturer did. The risk to a party that has clear expectations at contract formation is that they may vary from what the other party expects, which may be what the contract requires. In either event, in the worst case, it will be required to give more or accept less than eventually expected. An additional risk, as illustrated by *GLS Development, Inc.*,[34] is that the vague wording may fail to satisfy the legal formalities of contract formation, and thus not create a binding commitment.

A difference between the two strategies is that there is certainty about what the contract requires in the first but not the second.

Define with Certainty. A party that is uncertain about the benefit it expects to realize or the task it expects to be completed can, notwithstanding such uncertainty, state in the contract that a specific task will be completed in the hope that it will prove to be the correct one. If there is uncertainty about a condition or contingency that affects the description of a benefit or task, a specific task can still be described, again, on the hope that the condition or contingency will be as supposed. If the party stating or accepting such statement is the obligor, it runs the risk of having to give more than it ultimately expects. If the party stating or accepting such statement is the obligee, it runs the risk of receiving less than it ultimately expects to receive. *Laidlaw* is an example: the price of the tobacco could be fixed, notwithstanding the uncertainty about the hostilities, but stating a fixed price allocated responsibility for the uncertainties about the conditions to the seller.

The contracts in the following cases also used clear statements of tasks when one or both parties had uncertain expectations about what such tasks included.

- *State ex rel. Santa Fe Sand & Gravel Co. v. Pecos Construction Co., Inc.*[35]: A subcontractor agreed to "furnish all plant, labor and equipment required to perform" a mass excavation and backfilling for a project for a fixed price. The subcontractor underestimated the volume of mass excavation. The subcontractor claimed the contract was vague

[34] *See* text accompanying notes 11 and 12.

[35] 86 N.M. 58, 519 P.2d 294 (N.M. 1974).

on the scope of the mass excavation, and it should be compensated for the additional work. The case illustrates how a clear statement of a task to be completed managed uncertainty about a condition that determined the scope of work. By agreeing to do all excavation for a fixed price, the subcontractor assumed responsibility for the risk the work would exceed its estimate.[36] It may also illustrate scenario (2)(a)(ii) described in chapter 4 (party incorrectly processes correct information about a task it must complete for the other party's benefit).

- *Austin v. Cotten*[37]: Austin hired Cotten, an engineer, to consult on a street improvement project for which it would pay him 8.1 percent of the total project cost, not to exceed $28,800, calculated as a percentage of an estimated project cost of $358,000. The limitation on his fees was increased twice, as the total costs exceeded the estimates. The consultant asked, but the city refused, to delete the limitation.[38] When the total project cost exceeded $980,000, the consultant claimed additional compensation, contending that the limitation was based on a mistake of fact, that the estimated total project cost was reliable.[39] The case illustrates how a contingency, in this case development of the scope of the project, generated uncertainty over the extent of tasks to be completed, the effort required of the consultant. It further illustrates how that risk was managed by a clear statement of the task the consultant was to complete—all the consulting work on the project: the consultant assumed responsibility for the risk that the effort required would exceed the initial estimate.[40] Finally, the case may illustrate scenario (1)(b)(ii) described in chapter 4 (Cotten relied upon incorrect

[36] "Since the uncertainty of the volume of the excavation and backfill was the responsibility of appellant, this uncertainty was a risk which appellant assumed as part of the bargain." *Id.* at 297.

[37] 509 S.W.2d 554 (Tex. 1974).

[38] *Id.* at 556.

[39] The jury awarded the consultant additional compensation, but the Texas Supreme Court set aside the verdict, holding the mistake of fact doctrine does not apply when the parties, at contract formation, recognized the uncertainty concerning the scope of the services and limited the compensation, as they had in this case. The contract described the consultant's scope in sufficiently broad terms that it included all design services required for the street improvement project. *Id.* at 559.

[40] "No reason is perceived why the City would have insisted that plaintiff's proposal be qualified by a stated maximum fee except that the City foresaw that construction costs

information received from the city about the scope of the work he had complete for the city's benefit).

- *TPS Technologies, Inc. v. Rodin Enterprises, Inc.*[41]: A property owner estimated 1,000 tons of contaminated soil would have to be removed to remediate a site and hired a contractor to remove all contaminated soil for a fixed amount per ton of soil removed. The contractor removed 902.12 tons during the first phase and 916.19 tons during the second phase. The owner objected to the invoice for the second phase, claiming that the environmental permit limited the scope of work to 1,000 tons. The case illustrates how uncertainty over a condition creates uncertainty over the scope of the tasks to be completed. It is also an example of how a unit price contract can be used to manage that uncertainty risk: Had the scope been limited to phase one as the owner contended, the owner would have been responsible for the risk that a second phase had to be undertaken, but it would not have been committed to paying the contractor for that work. Because the scope had not been limited, the owner assumed responsibility for the risk that a second phase had to be executed.[42] The case may illustrate scenario (3)(b)(ii) described in chapter 4 (the property owner relied upon an incorrect assumption about a task the contractor had to complete for the property owner's benefit).

The previous cases further illustrate how the method of compensation, when combined with a specific description of the task to be completed, allocates responsibility for the uncertainty concerning the scope of the task. If the value it receives for completing a task is fixed, the scope of which task is uncertain, the obligor risks having to give more time and effort than anticipated for the fixed amount; it bears responsibility for uncertainty risk. The discrepancy between what it anticipated giving and

---

might exceed the estimate and was unwilling to assume the risk of higher engineer's fees." *Id.* at 558.

41 816 F. Supp. 345 (E.D. Pa. 1993).

42 The court found the contract clearly obligated the contractor to remediate all of the contaminated soil on the property. "Under Florida law, which provides that 'a unit price contract provides for payment of the actual amount work done . . . where the precise amounts needed are not known at the inception of the project,' . . . there is no question that [the contractor] TPS is entitled to be compensated for performing its contractual obligation to remediate all of the soil that [the owner's representative] Dunn determined was contaminated." *Id.* at 350.

what it must give to complete the task is its loss. If the value varies with the actual scope but is fixed for each hour, item, or other unit of measure, the obligor assumes responsibility for the risk that its unit cost will be higher than anticipated, perhaps because each unit is more difficult to complete than anticipated. Because such value is also calculated based on the actual scope, it does not assume responsibility for the risk that the scope will be greater than anticipated. If the value is based on the obligor's costs of completing the task, the obligor has passed back to the obligee responsibility for the risk that the scope and the effort of completion may be greater than anticipated.

Define with Uncertainty. A party that is uncertain about the benefit it expects to realize or the task it expects to be completed can state such tasks in the contract with such ambiguity that whatever it later decides should be the benefits and tasks will be included in the contract. The contract "reflects" the party's own vague expectations. *Cummings,*[43] *Coto-Matic, Inc.*[44] and *GLS Development, Inc.*[45] are examples. A party that is certain about the benefit it expects to realize or the task it expects to be completed could also adopt such strategy, though it would make sense as a hedge against the risk that it may later find it was wrong and the description of the tasks should have been different. Vague contractual language does not specifically allocate responsibility for the uncertainty risk to either party. *Middleton*[46] is an example: the mineral lessors assumed responsibility for the risk that exploration and production could proceed at a pace slower than they wished, and the mineral lessee assumed responsibility for the risk that exploration and production might have to proceed at a pace faster than it wished. Words such as "material," "materially adverse," and "reasonable" do not indicate what must specifically occur or be done for an event or act to be material, materially adverse, or reasonable. Their meaning is decided on a case-by-case basis. *DaimlerChrysler Motors Co., LLC*[47] is also an example. Their exact meaning—what they will mean in the circumstances in which a dispute over their meaning arises—cannot be predicted at contract formation. Their initial effect is to defer to a later date (when the event

[43] *See* text accompanying notes 2 and 3.

[44] *See* text accompanying notes 8–10.

[45] *See* text accompanying notes 11 and 12.

[46] *See* text accompanying notes to 24–26.

[47] *See* text accompanying notes 20–23.

must occur or the party must complete the task described by the vague language) the determination of what specifically it means. Each party bears responsibility for the risk that the meaning ultimately given to the language varies from its ultimate expectations.

Bloor v. Falstaff Brewing Corp.[48] further illustrates the risk to an obligor whose obligation to use best efforts is defined as and when the obligor must act. A purchaser of a brewery production and distribution business agreed to pay, as part of the purchase price, a royalty per barrel of the brands sold. It also agreed to use its best efforts to promote and maintain a high level of sales of the brands. Four years later, during which the operations of the brands lost $22 million, even though advertising and sales were increased, a new buyer assumed control of the brands' operations and, following a strategy used for marketing its own brands, cut costs by reducing advertising and the number of distribution centers. Where in the year prior to the new buyer's assuming control sales increased 2.4 percent, sales declined during the new buyer's first two years by 29.72 percent and 45.81 percent, respectively, but had a net income of $8.6 million. The seller successfully claimed the new buyer's emphasis on profit over sales of the brands breached the best efforts obligation. The parties could not have detailed at contract formation how much the buyer should spend each year on marketing the products, as the potential effectiveness of such efforts would depend upon a range of factors, all contingencies, which yielded uncertainty about the extent to which marketing efforts would promote sales. The best efforts commitment left for later resolution what specifically the buyer was required to do. Both parties assumed responsibility for uncertainty risk, although the seller ultimately prevailed.

Define Process. Instead of defining the benefits and tasks and stating how responsibility for unknown conditions and contingencies should be allocated, a contract can prescribe a process by which one or more parties define benefits and tasks as expectations are clarified. Such process is similar and economically equivalent to the amendment procedure described in chapter 3. A technical difference is that an amendment changes an existing contractual term, where a process for defining tasks clarifies, eliminates ambiguity in, and supplements existing terms. A process can specify when decisions about benefits, tasks, condition, and

---

48 601 F.2d 609, 26 UCC Rep. Serv. 281 (2nd Cir. 1979).

contingencies may or must be made, who may make and participate in making them, and limitations on decision-making authority.

Single Party, Sole Discretion. The best and worst cases are the same procedure: one party has sole discretion to decide the benefits that will be realized, the tasks to be completed and when and how they will be completed, and responsibility for conditions and contingencies. The procedure is best for the decision maker and worst for the other party. The obligee, as decision maker, decides what task the obligor must complete and when and how they will be completed. The obligor, as decision maker, decides what tasks it will complete and when and how it will complete them. Uncertainty risk is mitigated, if not eliminated, for the decision maker because it can decide how such uncertainty is to be resolved. For the other party, however, the uncertainty risk is traded for another: the risk that the decision maker may properly decide in a way that was unexpected by the other party. This risk is explained and illustrated with cases in chapter 7.[49]

Single Party, Limited Discretion. The risk to a party of an adverse decision by the other party when the latter is the sole decision maker can be mitigated by requiring that the decision conform to a minimum standard. One of the most common is that the decision be reasonable. This standard allows a party to question the reasons for a decision. Because the decision maker has discretion to resolve uncertainties falling with that discretion, the discretion still mitigates uncertainty risk; however, because the exercise of that discretion must conform to a standard the meaning of which is itself uncertain at contract formation, uncertainty has not been entirely eliminated. Such limitations on discretion are discussed in chapter 7 and are mentioned here to indicate their effect on uncertainty risk.[50]

Multiple Parties. A procedure can give both parties a voice in decisions that resolve uncertainties. One common requirement is that the decision maker consult the other party before making its decision. Such consultation may be simple or elaborate. A second procedure, typified by joint venture decision-making, requires collaboration by the parties and extends participation in decision-making: the venture parties periodically exchange information, meet, and decide certain matters. In joint ventures, such decision-making may be formal and regulated: some decisions may

[49] *See* text accompanying ch. 7, notes 18–30.

[50] *See* text accompanying ch. 7, notes 46–57.

be required to be by majority, others by a supermajority, and still others by unanimity of the parties or interests. In other contexts, depending upon the nature of the transaction and the relationships of the parties, collaboration may be more or less formal than in joint ventures. An agreement to agree on a future matter is the simplest and most extreme form of joint decision-making, giving each party total discretion to accept or reject the other party's proposals. A refusal to agree is a decision that is adverse to the party seeking agreement.

Collaborative decision-making trades one uncertainty risk for another. Uncertainty about the tasks to be completed is a risk because, at contract formation, a party may commit to complete or to accept completion of a task while being uncertain about whether that is the task that it will ultimately expect to be completed and whether the task is what is needed when its expectations crystallize. Decision-making eliminates that risk for a party when the procedure itself is certain because the parties know how uncertainties will be resolved. This is true for both the decision maker and the other party. The latter, however, assumes the risk of decisions adverse to its interest. Decision-making does not eliminate the risk if the outcome is unpredictable because a decision maker must collaborate or decision makers must agree on their decisions but have no commitment to do so. The irony of agreements to agree that are found to be too vague to be enforceable is that the outcome of such unenforceability is that the party's refusal to agree is effective. Uncertainty about benefits, tasks, commitments, conditions, or contingencies is traded for uncertainty about the decisions that should resolve such uncertainty.

Termination

Uncertainty risks can be mitigated by termination, cancellation, or rescission of a contract just as such devices manage benefit and task oversight and rejection and commitment gap risks. A termination or equivalent right enables a party to make a choice after contract formation it would not otherwise have made. An obligor whose expectations at contract formation were uncertain and who later finds its task is more onerous than it expects, having deepened and clarified its expectations, can choose to terminate, abandoning the transaction. The obligee who has expectations at contract formation that were uncertain and who, having deepened and clarified its expectations, finds the benefits less than expected or its task greater than expected may choose to terminate, abandoning the transaction. Such termination right can be broadly formulated to allow a party to terminate for any reason or be narrowly focused on a condition or contingency, permitting termination only if the condition that must exist does not exist or the contingency that must not occur occurs. Unless the contract imposes a termination fee or similar charge on the terminating party, each party bears uncertainty risk to the extent it loses all costs incurred in preparing for and proceeding with the transaction through the date of termination as well as the anticipated benefits. If the contract also imposes a termination or similar fee, the terminating party incurs that as an additional loss. The termination or equivalent right enables the terminating party to allocate such sharing of responsibility for task uncertainty risk between the parties.

6

Commitment Risks

ENFORCEABILITY RISKS

A contractual commitment must be enforceable and allow recovery for certain of the losses that result from breach. A defect in the effectiveness of a commitment is a hazard for an obligee and an unpredictable windfall for an obligor.

A fully effective commitment will satisfy three standards:

- First, all the formalities necessary to create it have been completed such that an arbitrator or court will enforce it in accordance with its terms in a proceeding brought by the obligee against the obligor.
- Second, it states the actions that must be completed with such certainty that there can be no reasonable doubt about what is required, and any dispute about what is required can be resolved in favor of an obligee in a summary proceeding.
- Third, the administration of justice—the administration of the substantive and procedural rules applicable to a commitment—by the courts or arbitrators is sufficiently stable and predictable that the parties can expect enforcement of the commitment according to its terms.

Enforceability Hazards

A commitment is "enforceable" when all the requirements have been satisfied for it to be enforceable by the party seeking to enforce it against the party against whom enforcement is or will be sought in the jurisdiction in which enforcement is expected. A party may have to comply with formalities to be an obligor in a transaction, the other party may have to comply with different formalities to be an obligee, both parties may have to comply with additional formalities for the contract to be enforceable, and the terms of the contract may have to comply with substantive standards to be enforceable.

Obligor. A starting point of a list of the formalities to be satisfied for a party to be bound as an obligor is the textbook defenses personal to it. If it is an entity, it must exist; it must have legal capacity to form a contract; it must have authority to form a contract; it must be authorized to form the contract; it must have competence to understand the contract; it must not be laboring under a mistake, fraud, duress, or corruption that vitiates consent; and unless it is capable of waiving and has waived its rights, it must not be a sovereign or similar entity that is immune from legal process. The hazard for the obligee is the existence of any such circumstance at contract formation that entitles an obligor later to disavow its commitment.

Chemical Bank v. Washington Public Power Supply System[1] illustrates how critically important these formalities are to binding the obligor to a commitment. Washington Public Power Supply (WPPS) issued bonds in the face amount of $2.25 billion to finance the construction of two nuclear power plants, the electricity that was expected to be generated from which had been sold to participating utilities. Each such utility had to pay its share of various payments made by WPPS, whether or not the plants generated electricity. Nineteen of these participants were Washington public utility districts and another nine municipal corporations. Their statutory powers authorized them to "enter into contracts or compacts with any operating agency or a publicly or privately owned public utility for the purchase and sale of electric energy or falling waters."[2] If, as the trustee for the bondholders claimed, the cities and districts had authority under the quoted language to agree to pay for a participating interest in the electricity generated by the plants even when no electricity was

[1] 99 Wn.2d 772, 666 P.2d 329 (Wash. 1983).

[2] RCW 43.52.410; quoted in 99 Wn.2d 772, 783.

generated, they were authorized and bound by the agreements. However, that was not the case, as the cities and utility districts successfully claimed; they lacked authority under the quoted language to agree to pay for their participating interests and were not authorized and not bound by the agreements.[3] Similar claims and conclusions were made and drawn concerning other statutory powers granted the cities and districts. At contract formation, the hazard to the bond holders was the districts' and cities' lack of clear authority to pay for their participating interests. The bond holders assumed responsibility for the risk that the contracts might not have been authorized. That hazard would have passed had the courts determined that the districts and municipalities were authorized or, as happened, the hazard would have resulted in harm to the bond holders once the courts determined the districts and cities lacked such authority.

Obligee. An obligor may be bound by its commitment but the obligee may be unable to enforce it because it has failed to satisfy a formality that entitles it to do so. A starting point of a list of such formalities are the licenses and approvals it requires to engage in a business or transaction in which it is engaged and taxes and other fees it may have to pay in connection with such business or transaction. A real estate agent must obtain a license from a real estate licensing board, a lawyer a license from the state bar, a contractor a license from the contractors' licensing board, and a vendor of alcoholic beverages a license from the alcohol beverage control agency. In addition, a government may require all who engage in business in its jurisdiction to register, qualify to do business there, and pay taxes. A person who engages in such activities without the applicable license or registration may be subject to fines, penalties, and other sanctions.

In certain instances, the failure to have the required license or registration when it contracts to engage in such activities may preclude it from enforcing the contract: an unlicensed real estate agent may not collect his or her commission, an unlicensed attorney may not collect his or her fees, an unlicensed taxi company may be unable enforce a contract to buy taxi medallions, an unlicensed lender may be unable to recover the principal loaned and accrued interest, and an unregistered business may be unable to enforce any contracts in the courts of the jurisdiction where it is required to register and pay taxes. The hazard for the obligee

[3] "The unconditional obligation to pay for no electricity is hardly the purchase of electricity. We hold that an agreement to purchase project capability does not qualify as a purchase of electricity." 99 Wn.2d 772, 784.

in these transactions is the existence of any such circumstance at contract formation that entitles an obligor later to bar the obligee from enforcing the obligor's commitment, except where the obligee is allowed to correct its shortcoming and enforce the contract.

Brack v. Omni Loan Company, Ltd.[4] illustrates the serious consequences of an obligee's failing to comply with such local licensing requirements. Located in Nevada, but through an office in California, Omni loaned between $900 and $1800 each to members of the military who were nonresidents stationed in California. Omni asked the California Commissioner of Corporations to rule that it was not required under California law to obtain a license to make such loans. The commissioner refused the request. Nonetheless, Omni made loans pursuant to agreements that chose Nevada law to govern their terms. A class action was filed against Omni in California by a nonresident military member borrower stationed there, claiming, inter alia, that Omni had failed to comply with the California license requirement. This was a case where the obligee knew of the potential application of, and rejected complying with, a licensing requirement, deciding intentionally to take the risk it might apply. If, as Omni claimed, Nevada, and not California, law applied because California had no fundamental interest in transactions with nonresident military members stationed in that state, Omni would have assumed responsibility for the risk a license was required, but the hazard would have passed. But, as the class plaintiff successfully claimed, California law trumped the Nevada choice of law clause in the loan agreement and Omni was required to have obtained the license; Omni had assumed responsibility for the risk it would have to obtain the license. The contracts made in violation of this requirement were void.[5]

Contract Formation. Every legal system prescribes certain formalities that must be satisfied for an obligor to be bound and for the obligee to have corresponding rights. The basic formalities of contract law are taught in a contract law course: a contract must be embodied in an offer and the offer must be accepted; consideration or an equivalent must be received for it to bind a party, unless the contract is signed under seal or set forth in a deed; and a contract for certain transactions must be in writing and signed by the party against whom enforcement is sought. Other formalities, specific to types of transactions, require more

[4] 164 Cal. App.4th 1312, 80 Cal. Rptr.3d 275, 08 Cal. Daily Op. Serv. 9178, 2008 Daily Journal 10 (Cal. App. 2008).

[5] *Id.* at 1327.

specialized knowledge of the law applicable to those transactions. For example, a disclaimer of warranties in a sale of goods contract may have to be stated in a format that visibly sets it apart from other terms; a guaranty may have to include a statement as to the maximum amount of the guarantor's liability; the description of collateral in the granting clause of a security agreement may have to use specific words to be effective; a sale of securities in an initial public offering requires detailed disclosures about the issuer, its management, its industry and related matters; a franchise contract may have to disclose certain information to the franchisee; a contract between an attorney and the attorney's client may have to disclose how fees will be calculated; and certain clauses may have to be signed or initialed separately from the signature to the contract. Still further formalities may be mandatory for the effectiveness of an agreement or instrument: it may have to be notarized; it may have to be filed, registered, or recorded in designated public registries; and stamp and other taxes may be payable, often based on the value of the transaction. Approval of a government agency might be required. Failure to comply with these formalities may result in liability for fines and penalties and may be a hazard to the enforceability of the contract by the obligee.

Wallace Hardware Company, Inc. v. Abrams[6] illustrates the potential cost of overlooking or ignoring all the potential formalities that may apply to contract formation. Located in Tennessee, Wallace agreed to provide wholesale hardware goods and services to retail hardware stores and a line of credit to buy such goods and services to Tri-County located in Kentucky. The Abrams brothers who owned Tri-County also signed personal guaranties, guaranteeing Tri-County's obligations to Wallace. The contracts chose Tennessee law to govern their terms. The guaranties would not have been valid under Kentucky law because they did not specify the maximum amount guaranteed or the date on which the guaranties terminated, both of which were required under Kentucky law.[7] Had Kentucky law been applicable to the guaranties, notwithstanding their choice of Tennessee law, as the guarantors claimed and the district court judge ruled,[8] Wallace would have borne the consequences of the guaranties not complying with the Kentucky law requirements. It was a risk Wallace most likely overlooked, assuming that Tennessee, not

6 223 F.3d 382 (6th Cir. 2000).

7 Ky. Rev. Stat. Ann. § 371.065(1); quoted in 223 F.3d 382, 398-9. *See* Osborn v. Griffin, 865 F.3d 417, 443-4 (6th Cir. 2017), holding that Kentucky law should be applied.

8 223 F.3d 382, 389.

Kentucky, law was applicable. In this case the hazard passed because that assumption proved correct, though not without litigation and an appeal. Wallace could have had the guaranties comply with both Tennessee and Kentucky law so that risk of unenforceability—due to noncompliance with the Kentucky law formalities—was avoided altogether.

Contract Terms. Every legal system circumscribes freedom of contract by voiding or allowing parties to void agreements that violate the system's important policies. Textbook examples with which lawyers are familiar include contracts that facilitate the commission of a crime or tort or violation of a law, contracts that charge interest at a rate in excess of the legal maximum rate, contracts to acquire indebtedness for the purpose of initiating proceedings, and contracts that unfairly restrict competition. Additional examples include liquidated damages that penalize breaches rather than compensating losses; indemnity provisions that violate policies against indemnifying parties for wrongdoing; waivers of rights to minimum wages, class actions, and mechanics liens; and exculpatory clauses and releases from and limitations on liability. In each of these examples, a commitment is fatally defective because it cannot be enforced against the party purportedly bound by it: the lender may have no right to insist upon payment of interest, the obligee may have no right to collect on the debt, the promisee may have no right to insist upon compliance with the restrictions on competition, the nondefaulting party has no right to insist upon payment of the liquidated damages, the indemnified party has no right to indemnification, and the employer has no right to refuse to pay the minimum wage. In addition, the taint of the clause may infect the contract, allowing termination by one or both parties. The hazard to the obligee is creating a commitment that the obligor can void.

National Glass, Inc. v. J.C. Penney Properties, Inc.[9] illustrates what is often the minimal cost to the putative obligee of overlooking or ignoring the potential unenforceability of a contractual term in a jurisdiction whose laws might apply. National Glass, Inc. (NGI), as a subcontractor and supplier of labor and materials for a project located in Maryland for $90,000, petitioned to file a mechanics lien for the $56,579.00 balance. It waived all its mechanic lien rights under a subcontract that chose Pennsylvania law to govern its terms.[10] The waiver was valid under

[9] 336 Md. 606, 650 A.2d 246 (Md. App. 1994).

[10] "Subcontractor hereby waives and releases all liens or right of liens now existing or that may hereafter arise for any and all work or labor performed or material furnished under

Pennsylvania, but not Maryland, law. Had the choice of Pennsylvania law been enforceable under Maryland choice of law principles, the mechanics lien waiver would have been enforceable. The contractor would have taken the chance that the choice of Pennsylvania law and the waiver were effective and succeeded; the hazard would have passed. But Maryland law applied, and the mechanics lien waiver was unenforceable, as was held; the contractor's gamble failed.[11] However, because it could not otherwise have eliminated the subcontractor's mechanic lien rights, it lost nothing by including the clause. This was not a case where by modifying the contract the waiver would have been effective under Maryland law. The contractor was not subject to a penalty for including the Pennsylvania choice of law and mechanics lien waiver in the contract. The contractor could hope that, given the uncertainty concerning the enforceability of the choice of law and waiver, the subcontractor would comply with the waiver, just as a putative obligor might complete a task that it has not committed to complete. Whether a party should rely upon the complacency or ignorance of its counterparty is another question, but the strategy of doing so may come at little or no cost to the obligee.

Enforceability Risk Management

Enforceability risks are initially managed by the legal rules that facilitate or impair the enforceability of a commitment, determine when an obligor has satisfied the requirements that bind it to a commitment, and specify the requirements an obligee must satisfy to enforce a commitment. When effective, waivers; choice of law, savings, and severability clauses; and termination rights enable modification of these rules and the risk allocations they effect.

---

this Subcontract, upon said facility, or monies due or to become due to Contractor, and agrees to furnish a good and sufficient waiver of lien in proper form for filing from every person or entity furnishing labor or materials for this Project under Subcontractor." 336 Md. 606, 609, 650 A.2d 246, 247.

11 The circuit court dismissed NGI's petition for failure to state a claim upon which relief could be granted because the provision in the subcontract waiving the right to claim a mechanic's lien precluded NGI from obtaining a mechanic's lien. NGI filed a motion for reconsideration of the dismissal. That motion was denied. NGI appealed to the Court of Special Appeals. Prior to that court's consideration of this case, the Maryland Court of Appeals issued a writ of certiorari and dismissed the appeal. Following that dismissal, the circuit court dismissed NGI's petition with prejudice. NGI appealed that final order. The Maryland Court of Appeal reversed that order.

Diligence. Diligence is the most effective method of managing the enforceability risks previously described. Except where there are shortcomings in a legal system, all the requirements that must be satisfied to form a contract that an obligee will be entitled to enforce against the obligor are knowable prior to contract formation. Any enforceability hazards should be identifiable and avoidable before that time. The hazard in *Chemical Bank*[12]—the absence of statutory authority to purchase the participating interests in the plants—would have been difficult to avoid while continuing to participate; however, unless it was eliminated, the plants and bond holders did not have commitments they could enforce. As in previous chapters, this text repeats the importance of thorough diligence while not attempting to detail what it includes in any specific transaction.

Waivers. Subject to certain limitations, at contract formation an obligor may waive certain of the defenses that it may have as a result of the hazards previously described. A shortcoming in an obligor's existence, capacity, authority, and competence at contract formation cannot be waived in the contract since it cannot be bound by such contract. At contract formation, an obligor may be able to waive whatever immunity from legal process it may have. A shortcoming in an obligee's compliance with a requirement that entitles it to enforce a contract might be validly waived, depending upon such matters as whether compliance therewith is intended to protect the obligee. An obligor might agree to pay the obligee fees or other compensation for its performance notwithstanding that the obligee may not have all the required licenses. The obligor might waive any right to refuse to make such payment. Because the purpose of the licensing requirement is to protect the public from individuals plying a trade for which they are not qualified, the waiver may be effective in cross-border transactions in which the individual has a qualification in one jurisdiction but not necessarily in all jurisdictions affected by the transaction.[13]

---

[12] *See* text accompanying notes 1–3.

[13] "Should property(ies) that are listed on Addendum "A" be located in a state other than the state of Washington then owner expressly acknowledges that they are not knowingly entering into an agreement which is illegal by contracting with real estate broker which is not licensed in state (sic.) where facilities are located. In addition, Client agrees to waive any such provision that would allow for a contest of fees based on the fact the Consultant is not licensed as a real estate broker in the state where facilities are located." Erwin v. Cotter Health Centers, Inc., 135 P. 3d 547, 550 (Wash. App. 2006); rev'd, aff'd 167 P.3d 1112 (Wash. 2007).

A waiver cannot breathe life into a contract that is void ab initio for illegality, but it may preserve a contract that is voidable in limited conditions: a guarantor can agree its obligation under a guaranty is absolute and unconditional,[14] and an obligor on a note[15] and a lessee under a lease may likewise do so, by agreeing it will pay as stated in the note or lease come "hell or high water."[16] The absolute and unconditional obligation effectively waives the guarantor's right to terminate an otherwise voidable guaranty.[17] This is also the case for the note or lease obligation, where the hell or high water clause waives the obligor's right to terminate a voidable obligation. A waiver, when effective, puts the parties in the position they would have had had the hazard not occurred in the first instance and allocates to the obligor responsibility for the risk that its commitment may have defects that would otherwise have enabled it to escape liability for failing to fulfill it.

Representations and Warranties. A representation or warranty cannot shift responsibility for the commitment risks previously described. Representations and warranties by an obligor that it exists, it has capacity and authority to execute the contract and to perform its obligations, it has been duly authorized to do so, and it has duly executed the contract are commonplace and purport to affirm the facts so represented and warranted and to allocate to the warrantor responsibility for the risk that the facts so warranted are incorrect. If, however, an obligor does not exist or have the capacity or authority such that it cannot properly execute the contract, it cannot overcome the defect by warranting there is none. No

---

14 "By its plain terms, in broad, sweeping and unequivocal language, the guaranty forecloses any challenge to the enforceability and validity of the documents which establish defendant's liability for payments arising under the purchase agreement, as well as to any other possible defense to his liability for the obligations of the Agra businesses." Cooperatieve Centrale Raiffeisen-Boerenleenbank, B.A., & C. v. Navarro, 25 N.Y.3d 485, 494, 36 N.E.3d 80, 15 N.Y.S.3d 277, 2015 N.Y. Slip Op. 04753 (N.Y. 2015).

15 Bankers Trust Co. v. Litton Systems, Inc., 599 F.2d 488 (2nd Cir. 1979), where the lessor's assignment of photocopier leases provided the assignee's rights under the leases would be independent of any claims or offsets against the lessor.

16 "The Lessee's obligation to pay all rent and all other amounts due hereunder and to perform all the terms hereof shall be absolute and unconditional and shall not be affected or reduced by any circumstances, including . . . any set-off, counterclaim, recoupment, defense or other right which the lessee may have against the lessor." Wells Fargo Bank Nw. v. TACA Int'l Airlines, 247 F. Supp. 2d 352, 355 (S.D.N.Y.2003).

17 Cooperatieve Centrale Raiffeisen-Boerenleenbank, B.A., & C. v. Navarro, 25 NY 3d 485, 36 NE 3d 80, 15 NYS 3d 277 (N.Y. 2015); Citibank, N.A. v. Plapinger, 66 N.Y.2d 90 (N.Y. 1985).

contractual term can be included at contract formation that will allocate to the obligor responsibility for the risk that it lacks existence, capacity, or authority. Similarly, a representation and warranty that the terms are valid and enforceable cannot validate a contract that is void ab initio for illegality, though, like a waiver, it may preserve a contract that is voidable in limited conditions.

Choice of Law Clause. When effective, a choice of law clause can mitigate and eliminate certain of the commitment risks previously described. First, the law of a jurisdiction applicable to an entity might limit or prohibit an entity's waiving its immunity from legal process, while the law of another jurisdiction may permit a more expansive waiver. Second, the law of a jurisdiction may require that certain formalities be complied with for a contract to be valid thereunder, while the law of another jurisdiction may not require such compliance. *Wallace Hardware Company, Inc.*[18] illustrated such a difference in laws: Kentucky law required that a guaranty state the maximum amount and termination date, but Tennessee law did not. Third, the law of a jurisdiction may require that an obligee comply with certain local laws before it can enforce a contract against an obligor, while the law of another jurisdiction may not require such compliance. *Brack*[19] illustrated such difference in laws: California law required that the lenders obtain a license from a California authority, but Nevada law did not. Fourth, the law of a jurisdiction may void or allow the parties to void a term of a contract, while the law of another might not. *National Glass, Inc.*[20] illustrated such difference in laws: Pennsylvania law allowed the waiver of mechanics lien rights, but Maryland law did not. In each of these instances, the agreement to the choice of laws that would enforce a commitment over the law of another jurisdiction that would not effectively waived the fatal defects in the commitment under the laws of the other jurisdiction, to the extent the choice of law was itself enforceable.[21] In *Brack,* the choice of Nevada law was not enforceable in a California court applying California choice of law principles.

---

[18] *See* text accompanying notes 6–8.

[19] *See* text accompanying notes 4 and 5.

[20] *See* text accompanying notes 9–11.

[21] *E.g.*, Hodes v. S.N.C. Achille Lauro, 858 F.2d 905 (3d Cir. 1988), where the plaintiff, a passenger on a vessel, unsuccessfully contended her claims arising out of the death of her husband while aboard the vessel should not be subject to Italian law or heard in an Italian court, as provided in the contract, because, inter alia, the Italian court would enforce the $10,000 limitation on the vessel owner's liability to passengers.

Savings Clause. A savings clause rescues a term otherwise illegal or invalid by automatically reforming it to be valid. An example is a usury savings clause in a loan agreement, which states that if the interest rate exceeds the maximum rate permitted by law, the rate will be automatically reduced to the maximum.[22] Another example is a clause that pares back the duration or geographical scope of a covenant not to compete that would otherwise be invalid. By reforming a defective commitment, the savings clause effectively preserves that which is valid from the taint of the offending portion.

A saving clause mitigates and allocates the risk of illegality by limiting the scope of the clause to that which is legal. Where a term or contract may be void or voidable because it violates a policy, the savings clause limits the unenforceability of such term or contract to the portion that is illegal. The party that would have benefited from the illegal or unenforceable term mitigates its loss: only the portion of the bargain that is illegal or unenforceable is lost (and this loss is due to the illegality or unenforceability of the bargain); the portion that is legal or enforceable is preserved. To that extent the balance of the term or contract remains enforceable, the victim of the illegal term or contract assumes or is allocated the risk of illegality when agreeing to a savings clause. Because the savings clause, when effective, insulates the party benefiting from the illegal or unenforceable clause from losses beyond what is illegal or unenforceable, in the absence of other sanctions it has little incentive not to overreach and include such terms.[23] A savings clause might be unenforceable for that reason.[24]

---

[22] *E.g.*, "If the loan secured by this Security Instrument is subject to a law which sets maximum loan charges, and that law is finally interpreted so that the interest or other loan charges collected or to be collected in connection with the loan exceed the permitted limits, then: (a) any such loan charge shall be reduced by the amount necessary to reduce the charge to the permitted limit; and (b) any sums already collected from Borrower which exceeded permitted limits will be refunded to Borrower. Lender may choose to make this refund by reducing the principal owed under the Note or by making a direct payment to Borrower. If a refund reduces principal, the reduction will be treated as a partial prepayment without any prepayment charge under the Note." Robert Joseph Phillips Living Trust v. Scurry, 988 S.W.2d 418, 420 (Tex. App. 1999).

[23] *E.g.*, Robert Joseph Phillips Living Trust v. Scurry, 988 S.W.2d 418 (Tex. App. 1999), where the court held the savings clause applied to reduce the rate of interest and preserved the validity of the promissory note.

[24] *E.g.*, Richard P. Rita Personnel Services Int'l, Inc. v. Kot, 229 Ga. 314, 191 S.E.2d 79 (Ga. 1972), refusing to reform the covenant not to compete to make it valid.

Severability Clause. A severability clause excises an invalid term from the contract while preserving the validity of remainder of the other terms and conditions.[25] Where a savings clause revises the invalid term to be valid, the severability clause removes the term entirely from the contract.[26] Unlike the saving clause, which might not be enforced, the severability clause is generally effective, though its application may be denied in certain instances where the term being excised is fundamental to the contract. The severability clause thus mitigates the potential loss to the obligee from fatal flaws in the obligor's commitment.

Termination. An obligee may prefer to terminate a contract when it finds that the obligor's commitment has one or more of the commitment defects previously described. An obligee who has not materially performed its obligations is unlikely to have a reason to do so under a contract to which its obligor is not bound because at contract formation it did not exist or have the capacity or authority to enter the contract, and these shortcomings cannot be corrected. An obligee who has not materially performed its obligations and is barred from enforcing a contract because it failed to comply with a licensing or other requirement will also have little reason to perform unless it can cure the deficiency. The party who is disadvantaged by the illegality or unenforceability of a term may likewise want the option of canceling the bargain because it will not get all that it anticipated. For example, a loan agreement might state that the agreement will terminate if the interest rate is usurious, and the loans will have to be repaid. The savings clause enables the lender to

[25] *E.g.*, "Any provision of this Lease which is prohibited or unenforceable in any jurisdiction shall, as to such jurisdiction, be ineffective to the extent of such prohibition or unenforceability, without invalidating the remaining provisions hereof. To the extent permitted by applicable law, Lessee hereby waives any provision of law which prohibits or renders unenforceable any provision hereof in any respect." Frankenmuth Mutual Insurance Company v. Escambia County, Florida, 289 F.3d 723, n.8 (11th Cir. 2002).

[26] *E.g.*, Frankenmuth Mutual Insurance Company v. Escambia County, Florida, 289 F.3d 723 (11th Cir. 2002), where a computer lease provided the lease would terminate if the county lessee failed to appropriate funds to pay the rent and the county would not lease or purchase substitute equipment for the remainder of that and the following appropriation period. After the county comptroller, who approved and signed the lease, was fired and charged with malfeasance in connection with the lease, the county clerk who replaced him repudiated the lease, claiming the nonsubstitution clause was invalid under the state constitution and rendered the lease invalid. The court held the inclusion of the severability clause demonstrated the parties' intent that clauses were severable, and the nonsubstitution clause did not go to the essence of the lease. *Id.* at 729.

recover interest to the extent allowed; termination permits it to exit the transaction because it cannot realize the full expected value. Termination enables the obligee to mitigate the losses it might suffer as a result of the obligor's commitment having the defects previously described.

COMMITMENT UNCERTAINTY RISKS

Commitment Uncertainty

Separately, a commitment is certain when its description of the actions required to fulfill it are reasonably clear. A commitment lacks certainty when the terms chosen are susceptible to more than one meaning. This may be due to the words chosen, which are vague or ambiguous, or the legal system, the substantive rules, or the administration of which lack predictability. Chapter 5 describes vague and ambiguous terms used to document uncertain expectations about tasks to be completed. Vague and ambiguous terms may be used even when expectations are certain because of poor drafting or to avoid revealing intentions. An uncertain commitment may result in the obligor having no commitment to do what the obligee expects. A certain commitment will entitle the obligee to a summary judgment or an equivalent order after the briefest of proceedings. An ambiguous commitment will require longer proceedings to decide what actions are required in the circumstances. More evidence may be needed to decide what the parties intended by their choice of words.

Ambiguous terms may be inadvertently chosen to specify a task even though a party has clear expectations of what actions that task includes; their use does not reflect uncertainty about the tasks the party expects to complete or to be completed. They are drafting oversights or shortcuts. The choice is inadvertent when such party is unaware of the potentially different meanings that might be given the term. As a result, it is also unaware of the risk that the term might include actions different from those expected to be performed. The textbook case *Frigaliment Importing Co.*,[27] summarized in chapter 1,[28] is an illustration: the terms used to describe the chickens to be bought and sold included birds suitable for broiling and frying. The seller and buyer each had a specific expectation about the birds that would be

[27] 190 F. Supp. 116 (S.D.N.Y. 1960).

[28] *See* text accompanying ch. 1, notes 3–14.

delivered, but the words chosen to describe them failed to eliminate other birds that might be delivered instead. The textbook case *Raffles v. Wichelhaus*[29] is another example. The correspondence between the buyer and the seller referred to cotton to be delivered "ex Peerless" from Bombay at Liverpool. Each party clearly had in mind a vessel named *Peerless* departing from Bombay but on different dates. While each party had a quite specific expectation about the vessel from which the cargo was to be delivered, the term "ex Peerless" was thus fatally unclear, covering both vessels. It seems unlikely that in either case either party recognized the potential for "ex Peerless" or "chickens" to have more than one meaning.

Commitment Uncertainty Risk Management

The contract interpretation rules that determine when a term is ambiguous and the admissibility of evidence to understand its meaning allocate responsibility for the risk created by ambiguity. An ambiguity inadvertently included in a contract is equivalent to an oversight hazard. Although the party has a clear expectation of the benefit, task, or commitment it expects to realize or be fulfilled, it misses the ambiguity in its choice of words and the hazard it creates. This is not a case where the ambiguity in the contract attempts to allocate responsibility for the risk of uncertainty in the party's expectations. Inadvertently drafted ambiguity risk is best managed by diligence and the terms described for managing oversight risks in chapter 3: amendments and termination.

COMMITMENT MISTAKE RISKS

Drafting Mistakes

The statement of a commitment in a contract may fail to reflect one or both parties' expectations. A party has clear expectations about the terms it expects the contract or other document to include, but such terms are not stated as expected.

Benefits and tasks described in a contract may reflect a party's expectations based on incorrect information, incorrectly processed

---

[29] 2 Hurl. & C. 906, 159 Eng. Rep. 375 (Ex. 1864).

information, or incorrect assumptions. Those expectations are superseded by expectations formed when the error is discovered. A term may also incorrectly state an expectation formed based on correct information correctly processed, but somehow misstated in the contract. Such errors are:

- preparation mistakes, where a party drafting or preparing a contract omits to include a term, includes the wrong term, or misstates a term in a contract, and
- reading mistakes, where a party does not read or misreads or misunderstands what another party has written in a contract.

Such an error is also a hazard to the commitment because it does not state what the party expected it to state. The hazard to the obligor is that the drafting or reading error will commit it to do more than it anticipated and the hazard to the obligee is that the obligor will be committed to do less than it anticipated. Responsibility for the losses that result from a condition or contingency may have been allocated differently in the contract than one or both parties expected.

Preparation Errors. Preparation errors include clerical, tabulation, calculation, and other drafting errors and omissions in the terms of the offer, acceptance, contract, or related document: for example, writing down as the price per pound what was intended to be the price per ton.[30] *Donovan v. RRL Corp.*[31] further illustrates a clerical error in stating a term. A car dealer advertised in a local newspaper "a 1995 Jaguar XJ6 Vanden Plas," specifying the color and vehicle identification number, but inserting the word "SAVE" for the price. Four days later, the car dealer's advertising manager asked the newspaper to delete the listing for the car and to list a 1994 Jaguar XJ6 with a price of $25,995. Employees of the local newspaper did not replace the listing of the 1995 Jaguar with the description of the 1994

[30] *E.g.*, Hume v. U.S., 132 U.S. 406, 10 S. Ct. 134, 33 L. Ed. 393 (1889), where a printed form stated the price per pound, the reference to per pound was to be struck and replaced with per shuck, but the change was not made. The contractor claimed it was entitled to 60 cents per pound as stated in the contract, notwithstanding that the price was 40 times the market value of the corn.

[31] 109 26 Cal.4th 261, 27 P.3d 702, Cal. Rptr.2d 807 (2001).

Jaguar, but did replace the word "Save" with the price of $25,995. This amount was $8000 to $10,000 less than the amount for which such car was selling elsewhere. A buyer visited the dealer's lot, inspected the 1995 Jaguar, and offered $26,000, but the dealer countered with $37,000. Expecting to resell the car for $37,995, the buyer refused and sued the dealer for breach of contract. If the dealer was bound by the terms of the advertisement, it assumed responsibility for the risk of the error; if not, responsibility for the risk was borne by the potential buyer.[32] Inadvertently omitting a line item when calculating a price or incorrectly totaling the amount is an example of a tabulation and calculation error. For example, in *M. F. Kemper Construction Co. v. City of Los Angeles*,[33] a contractor, when preparing its bid on a public works project, inadvertently omitted $301,769 from its worksheet, resulting in the bid totaling $780,305, in contrast to three other bids for $1,049,592, $1,183,000, and $1,278,895.[34] Responsibility for the risk of such clerical and tabulation errors is borne by the party preparing the document if it

[32] The municipal court held the newspaper advertisement for an automobile was a valid contractual offer that the customer could accept by tendering payment of the advertised price, but in the present case there was no valid offer because defendant's unilateral mistake of fact negated the dealer's intent. The appellate department reversed the judgment for the defendant. The appeal court agreed with the appellate department's holding. The California Supreme Court reversed, holding that while the advertisement would ordinarily be an offer the buyer could accept, the mistake in the advertisement negated the dealer's intent to offer the car at the advertised price. While it was true the dealer had failed to proofread the advertisement and such "an omission might constitute negligence, it does not involve a breach of defendant's duty of good faith and fair dealing that should preclude equitable relief for mistake." *Id.* at 831.

[33] 37 Cal.2d 696 (Cal. 1951).

[34] Two days after the bids were opened, the contractor discovered its omission and withdrew its bid. The bid terms included a provision that stated, "After bids have been opened and declared, except with the consent of the officer, board or City Council having jurisdiction over the bidding, no bid shall be withdrawn. . . ." Nonetheless, the contractor was allowed to cancel its bid. The board refused to allow, and the contractor sued for, cancellation of the bid. The trial court held in favor of the contractor and the California Supreme Court affirmed, holding, "There is no reason for denying relief on the ground that the city cannot be restored to status quo. It had ample time in which to award the contract without readvertising, the contract was actually awarded to the next lowest bidder, and the city will not be heard to complain that it cannot be placed in status quo because it will not have the benefit of an inequitable bargain." *Id.* at 703.

is bound by the mistaken or omitted term[35] and by the other party if the party preparing the document may terminate the contract.[36]

Boston Edison Co. v. Federal Energy Regulatory Commission[37] illustrates how a term can be inadvertently omitted from a complex contract where considerable skill and effort goes into its preparation. A utility constructed a nuclear power plant, the output from which was sold to its thirteen municipal customers pursuant to long-term power purchase contracts. The price at which the electricity was sold consisted of two charges: a capacity charge, the intent of which was to recover the capital and finance costs of construction of the plant, and a monthly energy charge, the intent of which was to recover the operating costs of the plant. A clause in the contract stated the general intention that the customers "would pay 'the sum of all of the costs incurred' by the utility" in the construction and operation of a power plant. The contract also included a detailed list of the items that the utility was allowed to include in its calculation of each of the factors. For example, the interest charges on the financing were limited to the 'weighted average of interest rates of all bond issues existing at the time of commercial operation of the Unit, revised as required to reflect refinancings of debt issues existing at the time of the commercial operation date.'"[38] No mention was made of

---

[35] In City of Newport News v. Doyle and Russell, Inc., 211 Va. 603 (Va. 1971), the contractor discovered a $100,000 error in his concrete bid and sought to withdraw his bid after the agency had opened the bids. Referring to the quoted clause, the Virginia Supreme Court held the contractor was bound by its bid. "The quoted language is not limited to a mistake of judgment. It plainly means any mistake in the bid, and includes a mechanical mistake. Thus, it was within the contemplation of the parties that the risk of mistake in the bid was to be borne by the bidder. Manifestly, the purpose of the quoted language was to avoid the precise claim now advanced by the defendants [bidder]." *Id.* at 607. But not all courts reach this result. For example, the regulations applicable to the bids in M. J. McGough Co. v. Jane Lamb Memorial Hospital, 302 F. Supp. 482 (S.D. Iowa 1969), stated, "Negligence on the part of the bidder in preparing the bid confers no right for the withdrawal of the bid after it has been opened." *Id.* at 487. The court, citing a number of cases, held, "It is sufficient to say that provisions such as these have been considered many times in similar cases and have never been held effective when equitable considerations dictate otherwise." *Id.*

[36] The court characterized the mistake as one of fact and allowed the contractor to withdraw the bid. "As we have seen, such a bid is in the nature of an irrevocable offer or option, but the offer is subject to rescission upon proper equitable grounds, and the cases recognize no distinction between public and private contracts with regard to the right of equitable relief." 37 Cal.2d 696, 704.

[37] 856 F.2d 361 (1st Cir. 1988).

[38] *Id.* at 364.

interest on the financing of additional plant equipment that had been acquired. The utility nonetheless included such interest in its calculation of the monthly charges.[39] The contract was not ambiguous but clear on what could be included in the calculation. Had the utility the right, based on the general statement that it was to recover its costs, to include in the calculation items not specifically listed in the formula, responsibility for the risk of an item having been omitted from the contract would have be borne by the municipal customers. The municipal customers' successful claim that additional amounts not specifically listed in the formula could not be included in the charges, however, implied that responsibility for the risk of such omission was borne by the utility; it was not permitted to include the additional interest in the calculation of the monthly charges.[40]

Review Errors. Review errors are the mirror image of preparation errors: a party may miss a term in a contract or misunderstand what a term says or means. For example, a mortgagor may fail to see that a mortgage specifies one property when it was expected to specify another.[41] A party may understand a term to mean one thing when it means another. For example, a term in a contract that states that its duration is indefinite sometimes means that the contract is terminable at the will of either

[39] When the utility billed the municipal customers, the latter filed a complaint with the Federal Energy Regulatory Commission for an order declaring such charges impermissible and ordering a refund of those of such charges paid. The commission ruled in favor of the municipal customers, the utility petitioned for a rehearing, the commission denied the motion, and the appeal court affirmed the commission's ruling.

[40] Reconciling this provision and the omission of the interest on additional equipment, the court said, "It is true that the parties clearly meant that BECO re-cover all costs as defined in the Contract. There is nothing in the language of the introductory paragraph, however, which exhibits any collective desire to contravene the plain wording of the payment equation and the financing formula, or to treat PAI differently than other items of investment expense." *Id.* at 366.

[41] *E.g.*, Balistreri v. Nevada Livestock Production Credit Association, 262 Cal. Rptr. 862, 214 Cal.App.3d 635 (Cal. App. 1989), where mortgagors failed to read the deed of trust in which they encumbered one property believing they were encumbering a different property. The trial judge held in favor of the mortgagees in an action to cancel the deed of trust, but the appeal court reversed, holding the mortgagees mistakenly induced the mortgagors to believe they were encumbering the property they expected to encumber, notwithstanding that they had not read the deed of trust. The mortgagors' expectations of the property to be encumbered did not match the deed of trust, which was clearly described the property and did match the mortgagee's expectations. The mortgagee's expectation was thus mistaken.

party. A party that expects a contract to continue forever, past his or her death, misunderstands the meaning of the term.[42] A term that was included but not expected to have been included might be overlooked. A term that was not included but was expected to have been included may have been omitted, and such omission overlooked. The hazard in these instances is the failure to read—parties frequently do not bother to read their contracts before executing them—or to read and understand correctly the terms of the contract or other document that creates the commitment.

Five of the cases in the litigation generated over three and a half decades by a form contract used by National Utility Service (NUS) for its electricity-saving consulting services illustrate such review risks.[43] NUS was hired, in each case, to review its client's electricity bills for some or all of the client's manufacturing facilities and "to submit recommendations for all possible savings and refunds on [the client's] costs of electricity [and] make a detailed analysis of all factors in [the client's] costs and advise where refunds and reductions can be obtained."[44] The client had to approve any recommendation. Any recommendation that was "acted upon" by the client entitled NUS to fifty percent of the client's savings on its electricity bills over five years. In two cases, the clients (Whirlpool and Chesapeake) were already considering specific actions that would increase the power factor at certain plants before they signed NUS's form; they so advised NUS and included clauses in the contract that excluded savings at those plants from the fee. Nonetheless, NUS recommended that these actions be taken and

42 Puretest Ice Cream, Inc. v. Kraft, Inc., 806 F.2d 323 (1st Cir. 1986), where the franchisor's representative told a potential franchisee that "[w]e want you to retire in the business and we want your children to retire in the business." The franchisee claimed the term barred the franchisor from terminating the franchise. The term was held, construed most favorably to the franchisee, to mean the franchise continued indefinitely; it could be terminated at will under Indiana law, which applied. No cause was required for the exercise of such termination right.

43 National Utility Service v. Whirlpool Corp., 325 F.2d 779 (2nd Cir. 1963); National Utility Service v. Northwestern Steel and Wire Co., 426 F.2d 222 (7th Cir. 1970); National Utility Service v. J.R. Sexton, Inc., 1989 W.L.R. 343048 (D. Conn. 1989); National Utility Service v. Callahan Mining Corp., 799 F. Supp. 1004 (N.D. Cal. 1990); National Utility Service v. Blue Circle, Inc., 739 F.2d 52 (2nd Cir. 1992); National Utility Service v. Sunshine Biscuits Inc., (N.J. App. 1997); and National Utility Service v. Chesapeake Corp., 45 F. Supp.2d 438 (D.N.J. 1999).

44 National Utility Service v. Callahan Mining Corp., 799 F. Supp. 1004, 1005.

claimed the clients waived the exclusions.[45] Whirlpool prevailed on a directed verdict motion in the first,[46] and Chesapeake defeated NUS's summary judgment motion in the second.[47] In both cases, the clients, having reviewed the form, saw the potential that they would have to pay for electricity savings that did not flow solely from NUS's analysis and recommendations and narrowed NUS's scope of services for which they would have to pay the contingent fee. In each of three other cases, NUS recommended the clients (Callaghan, Sexton, and Blue Circle) apply for a rate different from the one at which electricity was then being delivered, a rate that would result in considerable savings. Callaghan had already requested the lower rate but did not mention this to NUS.[48] Callaghan also used the form letter prepared by NUS to augment its request to the utility for the lower rate. Callaghan spotted the overlap between the services under the NUS form and its prior efforts but did nothing to narrow the scope of services. In another case, the utility had previously advised Sexton of the availability of the lower rate and Sexton omitted to mention this to NUS;[49] and in the third, where Blue Circle would have had to modify its plant to change to the rate recommended by NUS, the utility created a variation of the rate recommended by NUS that Blue Circle could use without changes to its plant.[50] In these latter three cases, the client missed or chose to ignore that NUS was duplicating services the clients were already receiving. NUS claimed it was entitled to its contingent fee and succeeded on a motion for summary judgment in all three cases. Each of Callaghan, Sexton, and Blue Circle could have excluded from the fee the savings that had been or were, during the term of the agreement with NUS, recommended by the clients' utilities, thus linking the effort for which NUS was compensated to its specialized knowledge of energy savings and analysis of the client's operations. Instead, however, Callaghan, Sexton, and Blue Circle accepted the form with no effort to reduce the NUS scope of services. In failing to do so, they created the risk that they would receive and have to pay for tasks performed by NUS that made no contribution to their energy savings.

---

[45] National Utility Service v. Whirlpool Corp., 325 F.2d 779, 780; National Utility Service v. Chesapeake Corp., 45 F. Supp.2d 438, 442.

[46] National Utility Service v. Whirlpool Corp., 325 F.2d 779, 781.

[47] National Utility Service v. Chesapeake Corp., 45 F. Supp.2d 438, 453.

[48] National Utility Service v. Callahan Mining Corp., 799 F. Supp. 1004, 1005.

[49] National Utility Service v. J.R. Sexton, Inc., 1989 W.L.R. 343048, 2.

[50] National Utility Service v. Blue Circle, Inc., 739 F.2d 52, 55.

In all five cases, the clients had clear expectations that they would not have to pay NUS for electricity savings that resulted from their own or others' efforts before NUS was hired; in the first two cases, Whirlpool and Chesapeake narrowed the contract to reflect their expectations; and in the last three, Callaghan, Sexton, and Blue Circle failed to do so. Responsibility for the risk of the discrepancy between those expectations and the terms of the contract was borne by them.

Commitment Mistake Risk Management

Contract interpretation rules and the unilateral and mutual mistake of fact doctrines allocate the preparation and review error risks previously described. A commitment that binds an obligor to perform as promised allocates to it responsibility for the risk it may have been mistaken about what was promised in the absence of defenses. The obligee, who cannot expect more or less than was promised, also assumes responsibility for the risk it may have been mistaken about what was promised. The *NUS* and the *Boston Edison Co.*[51] cases illustrate this risk allocation. That risk allocation is trumped by the risk allocations implied by the application of the legal doctrines of unilateral and mutual mistake of fact and good faith and fair dealing: responsibility for the risk is shifted from the party who would otherwise have been bound by the mistaken terms to the other party or both parties. The *Donovan*[52] and *M. F. Kemper Construction Co.*[53] cases illustrate this allocation of responsibility for risk. That risk allocation might be trumped still further by a clause that states the parties are responsible for the completeness and accuracy of the terms and are bound by the terms as stated even if they are mistaken.[54] When effective, the clause allocates responsibility for the risk of mistake to the party who errs in the preparation or reading of the term or contract. But

[51] *See* text accompanying notes 37–40.

[52] *See* text accompanying notes 31 and 32.

[53] *See* text accompanying notes 33 and 34.

[54] *E.g.*, "No plea of mistake in the bid shall be available to the Bidder for the recovery of his deposit or as a defense to any action based upon the neglect or refusal to execute a contract." City of Newport News v. Doyle and Russell, Inc., 211 Va. 603, 604 (Va. 1971). The charter of the City of Los Angeles stated, in part, "After bids have been opened and declared, except with the consent of the officer, board or City Council having jurisdiction over the bidding, no bid shall be withdrawn, but the same shall be subject to acceptance by the city for a period of three months. . . ." 37 Cal.2d 696, 699, 235 P.2d 7 (Cal. 1951).

as the *Donovan* and *M. F. Kemper Construction Co.* cases illustrate, this risk allocation might not be enforced in all cases.

Because a preparation or review mistake is inadvertent, it is equivalent to an oversight hazard. Although the party has a clear expectation of the benefit, task, or commitment it expects to realize or be fulfilled, it misstates the term in the case of a preparation error or misses or misreads the word in the case of a review error. Inadvertent mistakes in drafting and review are best managed by diligence and the terms described for managing oversight risks in chapter 3: amendments and termination.

LEGAL SYSTEM RISKS

Legal System Hazards

The institutional framework for creating a commitment—the substantive and procedural rules that govern the transaction and any disputes concerning the parties' rights and obligations, together with the institutions that administer them—reinforces, enhances, or diminishes the certainty of the contractual terms. In the latter case, the rules and institutions are hazards to a transaction.

Substantive Law Uncertainty. The substantive legal rules of jurisdictions applicable to commercial transactions may be sufficiently specific and internally consistent that the commitments that are governed by such rules are clear and the outcome of any dispute under a well-drafted contract reasonably predictable. The more specific and consistent the substantive law that governs commercial transactions, the greater is the predictability of the application of that law in specific cases. English and New York laws applicable to commercial deals are often touted as examples of the former. A legal system's rules can be so broadly and vaguely conceived that the parties cannot understand what is expected under their contract or predict the outcome of any such dispute. Sharia'ah principles of the legal regime in The Kingdom of Saudi Arabia are considered examples of the latter.[55] Because of their high level of abstraction, such rules allow

[55] "The legal regime in The Kingdom of Saudi Arabia includes Sharia'ah principles that are often expressed in general terms, providing a Saudi Arabian adjudicatory body with considerable discretion as to how to apply such principles." Affidavit of Mohammed Al-Sheikh quoted in In re Aramco Services Co., No. 01-09-00624-CV., Tex. App. LEXIS 2069, 2010 WL 1241525 (Tex. App. 2010).

claimants to argue for different outcomes in cases where the outcomes are reasonably predictable in other legal systems. Vague and inconsistent legal rules, like vague terms in a contract, are hazards to a transaction, as the meaning given the terms of a contract may vary from what was expected. Any commitment that is governed by such rules is less certain than one governed by more certain and predictable legal rules.

Even the most advanced legal systems have unsettled or novel questions, the resolution of which is uncertain and possibly finely balanced beforehand.[56] In such cases, more than one outcome is possible, and the legal system has still to decide which it will be. An educated guess or opinion might be given about how such a question will be resolved, but so long as the issue remains undecided, uncertainty exists about the applicable substantive rules of the jurisdiction. In so far as such uncertainty affects a commitment, it is also a hazard to and weakness in that commitment.

U.S. ex rel. Shakopee Mdewankaton Sioux Community v. Pan American Management Co.[57] illustrates such uncertainty. A Native American tribe hired a contractor to manage a gambling operation on the tribe's reservation. The tribe and contractor asked the Bureau of Indian Affairs (BIA) to review and approve the contract. The bureau declined both, deciding that its approval was not required for such a contract, which was compared to a contract for managing a bingo hall on a reservation. Contracts to manage casino operations on reservations were a recent development, and the need for approval had not been decided by the courts. When the validity of the contract was later challenged because such approval was lacking, a court decided the BIA's approval of such management contract had been required, the contract was illegal, and neither the court nor the BIA was estopped from holding it unenforceable. Because the BIA's approval was a legal formality that had to be complied with for the tribe's commitment to be enforceable, the uncertainty at contract formation about the need for that approval was serious shortcoming in the law applicable and a hazard to the transaction.

---

[56] *E.g.*, Bhatnagar v. Surrendra Overseas Ltd., 52 F.3d 1220 (3d Cir. 1995), where the court acknowledged that the question of whether "extreme delay in an alternative forum renders that forum inadequate for purposes of assessing a forum non conveniens motion" was one of first impression. *Id.* at 1222.

[57] 616 F. Supp. 1200 (D. Minn. 1985), appeal den. 789 F.2d 632 (8th Cir. 1986).

Administrative Uncertainty, Bias, and Advantages. The administration of the substantive law by the courts, arbitrators, or other authorized institutions can enhance or diminish the certainty of a commitment in a transaction. A consistent, fair, and impartial application of confusing or vague rules can establish predictability and certainty absent in the rules themselves. By examining and comparing decisions resolving transaction disputes, parties can predict the likely outcome of any dispute in their transaction.

Conversely, an opaque, biased, or inefficient administration of the substantive law can undermine the certainty and predictability of clear rules and aggravate the uncertainty of vague rules. The application of Sharia'ah principles in The Kingdom of Saudi Arabia is an example of an administration of justice lacking transparency and predictability, as decisions of the adjudicators are neither cited in later decisions nor publicly reported.[58] An example of bias is a special law enacted in Nicaragua for harms caused by exposure to the chemical compound dibromochloropropane used by U.S. firms in their operations there. The law stipulated that the chemical was conclusively presumed to have caused the sterility in afflicted claimants who had been exposed to the chemical; claimants were entitled to minimum damages; defendants had to post a $100,000 bond to participate in the litigation and $15 million, within 90 days, to guarantee payment of compensation and the plaintiffs' costs; defendants were allowed only three days to answer the complaint, the parties eight days to present evidence, and the court another three days to issue its verdict.[59] Less extreme are the disadvantages a party or class of parties have in court proceedings: employees and consumers may be able to participate in class actions and to have their claims heard by sympathetic juries. The aggregation of claims into a class action gives the employee and consumer plaintiffs leverage they would not otherwise have in any settlement negotiation and litigation because the amount of the claim is multiples of what any single individual might have. The defendant employer and credit card issuer has more to lose if it ignores the claim. The class action plaintiff's attorney whose remuneration is calculated as a percentage of any settlement or verdict is motivated to press the class

[58] "Previous decisions of Saudi Arabian adjudicatory bodies are not considered to establish a binding precedent for the decision of later cases; the principle of stare decisis is not accepted in The Kingdom of Saudi Arabia. In addition, decisions of various Saudi Arabian adjudicatory bodies are not generally or consistently indexed and collected in a central place or made publicly available." Affidavit of Mohammed Al-Sheikh quoted in In re Aramco Services Co., No. 01-09-00624-CV., Tex. App. LEXIS 2069, 2010 WL 1241525 (Tex. App. 2010).

[59] Osorio v. Dole Food Co., 665 F. Supp.2d 1307, 1314–15 (S.D. Fla. 2009).

action case in a way it would not with that of a single individual. The elimination of a jury as the arbiter of facts removes an audience that may be more sympathetic to one party than a judge or arbitrator. Long delays in adjudicating or reaching final resolution of disputes undermines the predictability of the applicable rules because of the potential changes in parties, evidence, and adjudicators during the course of adjudication.[60] Such shortcomings in the dispute resolution process impair certainty of the commitments. As such, they are hazards to both parties, except to the extent unpredictability, bias, and inefficiency tend to favor a one of them.

Multiple Proceedings. The location of parties to a transaction in different jurisdictions nourishes uncertainty about where the proceedings to resolve any dispute will take place. The jurisdictions in which the parties are located are potential choices. Any third jurisdiction that allows one or both parties to initiate proceedings is also a potential choice. The formation of more than one contract between the parties for their deal can result in separate proceedings for each contract unless the disputes concerning the different contracts can be consolidated into a single case.[61] Parties may also have claims that, while related to their contract,

[60] Sablic v. Armada Shipping Aps, 973 F. Supp. 745 (S.D. Tex. 1997), where the court dismissed a motion to dismiss an action filed by a Croatian seaman for an injury that occurred, and for which he was treated, in Colombia while unloading a Panamanian-flagged vessel owned by a Panamanian corporation, operated by a Danish corporation, and chartered by a Connecticut corporation. The seaman's employment contract chose Croatian law and provided for disputes to be subject to the Croatian courts. "Croatia is a war-torn country that, while making great strides towards recovery, is simply too unstable for this Court to find it to be an adequate forum for Plaintiff's suit." *Id.* at 748.

[61] *E.g.*, Karaha Bodas Company v. Perusahaan Pertambangan Minyak Dan Gas Bumi Negara, 364 F.3d 274, 294 (5th Cir. 2004); enforced Karaha Bodas Company v. Perusahaan Pertambangan Minyak Dan Gas Bumi Negara, 465 F.Supp.2d 283 (S.D.N.Y. 2006); aff'd 500 F.3d 111 (2nd Cir. 2007). Karaha Bodas Company (KBC), a project company, agreed in one contract with the state-owned oil and gas company, Perusahaan Pertambangan Minyak Dan Gas Bumi Negara (Pertamina), to develop, build, and operate a geothermal electricity generating plant, and with Pertamina in a second contract agreed to sell to the state-owned electricity generating, transmitting, and distributing company, Perusahaan Listrik Negara (PLN), the electricity generated by the plant. After the Indonesian government suspended the project, KBC initiated arbitration against Pertamina and PLN. Disputes under both contracts were to be resolved under the UNCITRAL rules in Geneva, Switzerland, although the contracts did not provide for consolidation of the claims thereunder. The arbitrators consolidated the claims, however; and Pertamina objected to the awards against it on this, among other grounds. The U.S. federal district court held the consolidation was valid in this instance: "Due to the integration of the two contracts and the fact that the Presidential

do not arise under their contract, such as claims of misrepresentation and fraud. Such claims might be adjudicated in separate proceedings. The jurisdiction in which the assets against which any court judgment may have to be enforced are located is also a potential choice and separate proceeding. Any uncertainties about the body that will resolve and the process it will follow in resolving all the disputes in a transaction are hazards to the commitments in that transaction.

Legal System Risk Management

Choice of Law. A choice of law clause states both parties agree that their contract will be governed by the rules of the legal system they designate in the contract.[62] The validity and meaning of the terms of the contract are determined according to the rules of the designated legal system. Legal rules of a jurisdiction that would void or allow a party to void terms of the contract or add requirements that must be satisfied for the contract to be enforceable can be avoided by choosing the laws of another jurisdiction to govern the contract. This use of a choice of law clause to avoid risks has limitations and itself creates risks. First, the freedom to choose the laws of a jurisdiction to govern a contract is limited; the choice will not always be enforceable.[63] When the enforceability of a choice of law

Decrees, the consequences of which are at the origin of the dispute, affected both of them, the initiation of two separate arbitrations would be artificial and would generate the risk of contradictory decisions. Moreover, it would increase the costs of all the parties involved, an element of special weight in the light of difficulties faced by the Indonesian economy, to which counsel for [Pertamina] legitimately drew the Arbitral Tribunal's attention." 364 F.3d 274, 294 (2004).

[62] *E.g.*, "This Agreement . . . shall be governed by, and construed in accordance with, the laws of the State of New York, without regard to conflict of laws principles." IRB-Brasil Resseguros, S.A. v. Inepar Investments, S.A., 20 N.Y.3d 310, 982 N.E.2d 609, 958 N.Y.S.2d 689, 2012 NY Slip Op 8669 (N.Y. 2012).

[63] *E.g.*, Putnam Leasing Co., Inc. v. Pappas, 2014 NY Slip Op 24283, 46 Misc.3d 195, 995 N.Y.S.2d 457 (N.Y. App. 2014), where a Connecticut leasing company leased a car to a Connecticut resident but provided for the lease agreement to be governed by New York law and for disputes to be heard in the New York courts. The court held that, applying The Restatement (Second) of Conflict of Laws § 187(2), Connecticut, not New York, law should govern the lease. 46 Misc.3d at 202. The court noted an exception existed under General Obligations Law § 5-1401, which has "allow[ed] parties without New York contacts to choose New York law to govern their contracts" if the transaction "in the aggregate" involves "not less than two hundred fifty thousand dollars." The exception was inapplicable to the lease, however.

clause is questionable, the clause becomes a hazard to the transaction. Second, the laws of a jurisdiction may apply whatever the contract says about the choice of law because of the location or the parties or assets concerned. Whatever law had been selected to govern the contract, the consent requirement would have remained in *U.S. ex rel. Shakopee Mdewankaton Sioux Community* because the tribe is located in the United States and remains subject to federal law whatever the contract might stipulate to the contrary. There was no system to choose for that contract (with a tribe) that would have enabled the parties to avoid the consent requirement.

A choice of law clause, when effective, also enables parties to avoid the unpredictability of the rules of a legal system risk whose rules are highly vague or undeveloped. The choice of the laws of an alternative jurisdiction with reasonably certain rules eliminates the uncertainty risk associated with the rules that would otherwise apply. If the legal uncertainty favored one party—it was better off with the commitment highly uncertain—the choice of a legal system with certainty favors the other party. The party that uncertainty would have favored foregoes whatever advantage the uncertainty gave it.

Choice of Forum. A choice of forum clause states that disputes arising under a contract will be heard before the courts or arbitral tribunal designated in the contract. An arbitration agreement is an agreement to arbitrate disputes arising under the contract, whereas a choice of forum clause is an agreement to resolve such disputes in a specified forum. Arbitration proceeds under rules and at a location specified by the parties and is a private arrangement between the parties; court proceedings are subject to the procedural rules of the jurisdiction where the court is located and are often public. The choice of arbitration precludes initiating other proceedings, other than to enforce the arbitration agreement and the award, interim measures to preserve the status quo, and other claims expressly excluded by the arbitration agreement.[64] A choice of forum may be exclusive[65] or nonexclusive: the former allows

[64] *E.g.*, "You and we retain any rights to self-help remedies, such as repossession. You and we retain the right to seek remedies in small claims court for disputes or claims within that court's jurisdiction, unless such action is transferred, removed, or appealed to a different court. Neither you nor we waive the right to arbitrate by using self-help remedies or filing suit." Sanchez v. Valencia Holding Co., 61 Cal.4th 899, 908, 190 Cal. Rptr.3d 812, 353 P.3d 741 (Cal. 2015).

[65] *E.g.*, "It is agreed by and between the passenger and the Carrier that all disputes and matters whatsoever arising under, in connection with or incident to this Contract shall

proceedings to be initiated and conducted only in the chosen forum; the latter designates the chosen forum as one in which proceedings may be initiated and conducted but allows proceedings elsewhere.

Choice of forum and arbitration clauses can mitigate the administrative uncertainty and bias risks previously described. Such clauses also implicitly waive any advantage a party would otherwise have in a court proceeding, such as a class action and jury trial.[66] The risk that an arbitration or court proceeding will be incompetently administered or biased in favor of a party is mitigated by choosing an arbitral system or courts that are reputed for their independence, neutrality, and efficient and fair application of the rules. The federal and state courts in New York and the English courts are reputedly examples of such fora for commercial disputes. The International Chamber of Commerce, the London Court of International Arbitration, and the American Arbitration Association reputedly operate well-established and accepted arbitration regimes in international commercial and financial centers. Insofar as one party might be advantaged by uncertainty and bias in the administration of justice, it loses that advantage by the choice of an independent forum for dispute resolution. The arbitration agreement or an exclusive choice of forum clause also mitigate the risks that one or more of the parties will race to initiate litigation in a court most favorable to it, because the sole proceeding must be arbitration or in the chosen forum. The potential for delay that might result from the case being heard in a jurisdiction where delays are protracted will be minimized, if not avoided, by the choice of a forum, the procedural rules and administration of which mandate expeditious dispute resolution. The choice of arbitration under the auspices of a reputable arbitration regime, taken together with provisions for consolidation of related arbitration proceedings and the choice of

be litigated, if at all, in and before a Court located in the State of Florida, U.S.A., to the exclusion of the Courts of any other state or country." Carnival Cruise Lines, Inc. v. Shute, 499 U.S. 585, 587–88 (1991). "This note shall be construed in accordance with and governed by the laws of the state of New York. Maker irrevocably submits to the exclusive jurisdiction of the state and federal courts located in the state of New York to . . . settle any disputes, which may arise out of or in connection herewith and with the debt documents. . . ." VFS Financing, Inc. v. Elias-Savion-Fox, LLC, 2014 WL 676582, 73 F.Supp.3d 329, 337, 59 Employee Benefits Cas. 2473 (S.D.N.Y. 2014).

66 *E.g.*, "If a dispute is arbitrated, you will give up your right to participate as a class representative or class member on any class claim you may have against us including any right to class arbitration or any consolidation of individual arbitrations." Sanchez v. Valencia Holding Co., 61 Cal.4th 899, 908, 190 Cal. Rptr.3d 812, 353 P.3d 741 (Cal. 2015).

the New York or English courts as the exclusive forum, mitigate the legal risks previously described.

The choice of forum and arbitration clauses can be a hazard for a party, for example, when a forum or tribunal slants the proceedings toward a party whom the selected judges and arbitrators favor. Similarly, the choice of an arbitral system or courts that are reputed to consistently decide in favor of a class is a hazard for the party not belonging to that class. It indicates a pattern of decision-making unfavorable to that party, even if the selected judges and arbitrators are not proven to have been biased in favor of, to have conflicts of interest favoring, or have been corrupted by the class that prevails.

The risk of multiple proceedings may be mitigated by choice of law and forum clauses and arbitration agreements expanded to include other aspects of the transaction not falling directly under the contract and by clauses that allow multiple proceedings to be consolidated.[67] An expanded choice of law clause, when enforceable, has the effect of directing the court or arbitrator to apply the law of the chosen jurisdiction and precluding the application of the rules of any other jurisdiction to their contract and other aspects of the transaction as to which claims are asserted. Just as a choice of law clause may be expanded to include claims associated with the transaction, such as misrepresentation, fraud, and concealment, an arbitration agreement and a choice of forum clause may be extended to noncontract claims associated with the transaction and potentially even unrelated claims.[68] If the arbitration agreement also allows one or more parties to consolidate additional arbitration

---

[67] *E.g.*, "This Agreement was made and entered into in the State [of] Georgia and all rights and obligations of the parties hereto shall be governed by and construed in accordance with the laws of the State of Georgia." Banek, Inc. v. Yogurt Ventures U.S.A., Inc., 6 F.3d 357, 359 (6th Cir. 1993). The court held the choice of law clause was broad enough to cover the related franchisee's fraud and misrepresentation claims. "Had these claims only been tangentially related to the franchise relationship, we would be much more inclined to find the choice of law provision not applicable. The claims of fraud and misrepresentation that plaintiff has asserted here are directly related to the franchise agreement." *Id.* at 363.

[68] The following clause was included in a bank account agreement: "Any dispute regarding whether a particular controversy is subject to arbitration, including any claim of unconscionability and any dispute over the scope or validity of this agreement to arbitrate disputes or of this entire [customer] Agreement, shall be decided by the arbitrator(s)." The court held the clause was broad enough to warrant allowing the arbitrator to decide if a tort claim for an injury to the plaintiff was subject to arbitration even though she had closed her account three years before her injury. Hawkins v. Region's, 944 F. Supp.2d 528, 530 (N.D. Miss 2013).

proceedings, with other parties and under related contracts, the potential for multiple, conflicting court proceedings is mitigated.

Locating assets against which an arbitral award or court judgment can be enforced in the jurisdiction in which such award or judgment is likely to be issued mitigates the risk of having to initiate separate proceedings in the jurisdiction in which the assets would otherwise be located. The reverse is also possible: a party could agree to resolve disputes under a contract in the courts of the jurisdiction where the counterparty's assets are located. In doing so, however, the party may be foregoing the advantage of having the case heard in its home jurisdiction; it may also be assuming the risks that the procedural rules will favor the counterparty and that there may be bias and corruption in the local courts.

While tangible assets, such as plant and equipment, cannot be relocated to a party's preferred jurisdiction for resolving disputes, certain intangible assets can be. Cash, for example, can be deposited in bank accounts located in the jurisdiction where the creditor is located and prefers to have disputes resolved; and, in principle, a judgment against the obligor should be enforceable against such account. (Obtaining security over the account helps prevent third parties from imposing liens on and trumping the creditor's potential levying on such accounts. It may also provide recourse without having to obtain an arbitral award or judgment.) Ownership of tangible assets located in another jurisdiction may be vested in an entity incorporated in the jurisdiction in which dispute resolution proceedings are favored and the shares or other equity interests of such entity pledged to the creditor in that jurisdiction, enabling the creditor to indirectly enforce its arbitral award or judgment against those assets by levying against such shares or equity interests. If the law of the jurisdiction where the tangible assets are located requires that such assets be owned by an entity formed under that jurisdiction's law and those laws are unclear or tilted against the creditor, it might be possible for that entity to be owned by an intermediate entity formed under the law of still another jurisdiction so that the creditor's objective is achieved: it might have a pledge of shares of an entity formed under the laws of a jurisdiction whose substantive and procedural laws enable it to readily enforce an arbitral award or judgment against those shares. While such complexity creates its own risks—compliance with the laws of several jurisdictions, potential tax liability in more than one country, etc.—it indicates how the risk of multiple proceedings can be mitigated in transactions straddling more than one border.

Part III

Counterparty Risks

7

Discretion Risks

ADVERSE-PARTY DISCRETION HAZARDS

Adverse-Party Discretion

Discretionary acts "involv[e] an exercise of judgment and choice, not an implementation of a hard-and-fast rule exercisable at one's own will or judgment."[1] A decision guided by a rule for which there is but a single outcome is not discretionary; however, if more than one outcome is possible and must be accepted by others, then the authority to make the decision is committed to judgment or discretion. We are here concerned with the hazard such discretion creates, whatever the reason for its grant.

As described in chapter 5, discretion allows a party, alone or together with other parties, either

(1) to decide a matter, such as a benefit, task, commitment, or responsibility for a condition or a contingency for itself or the other party or

(2) to veto the decision of such party, often by requiring a party's consent to such a decision.

[1] Black's Law Dictionary 565 (10th ed. 2014).

Following are cases that illustrate the types of discretion previously described:

- *Computronics, Inc. v. Apple Computer, Inc.*:[2] In its contract with its dealers, Apple, a computer manufacturer, reserved "the right to appoint other authorized dealers and resellers, and to make direct sales to anyone at any time without notice or liability to Dealer." Apple sold computers to a university at a discount and allowed the university to sell them to staff and students. The dealer objected to Apple's decision. The case illustrates the first type of discretion: Apple could choose to seek the benefits of direct sales to universities, even at a discount and even though such sales competed with the dealer, eroding the dealer's benefits.[3]
- *Pacesetter Motors, Inc. v. Nissan Motors Corp. U.S.A.*:[4] An auto dealer agreed to sell its auto dealership for approximately $500,000 to a buyer who wanted to move the location. To complete the sale, the seller had to obtain the manufacturer's consent, such consent not to be unreasonably withheld. The manufacturer refused its consent because the site at which the transferee intended to operate was too close to another dealer. The dealer sold the dealership to another buyer for $250,000. The case illustrates the second type of discretion: the manufacturer could veto the dealer's decision to sell, subject to having reasons for doing so.[5]

One party's discretion is the other party's hazard: the former's decision has the potential to diminish the latter's interests in the transaction, contrary to the latter's expectations about how such discretion was to be exercised. As we have seen, the allocation of potential benefits in a

---

[2] 600 F. Supp. 809 (W.D. Wis. 1985).

[3] When the dealer sued for breach of contract, the court held the quoted language "reserved to [the manufacturer] itself the broadest possible latitude to sell to whomever it pleased under whatever terms it chose." *Id.* at 813.

[4] 913 F. Supp. 174 (W.D. N.Y. 1996).

[5] The dealer sued the manufacturer for wrongfully withholding its approval, claiming proximity to an incumbent was not a valid reason for denying consent. The manufacturer moved for summary judgment, which the court granted. "[The manufacturer] Nissan clearly possessed the right to evaluate any proposed sale in accordance with what Nissan deemed to be its best interests. 'Location' was expressly stated as being a criterion relevant to Nissan's determination that a prospective buyer could meet its obligations under a franchise agreement." *Id.* at 179.

transaction can be a zero-sum game: one party's benefit comes at the other party's loss of economic opportunity or value, apart from any tasks such other party must complete. In such transactions, one party's anticipated benefits are at the mercy of the other party's decisions to the extent of such discretion.

Such hazards are divisible by the party having discretion and the matters its discretion it can affect.

(a) The party, alone or together with other parties, may decide
  (i) the benefits it will realize,
  (ii) the tasks it will perform,
  (iii) the commitments it will have to complete such tasks, and
  (iv) how it will respond to contingencies; or

(b) the party may, alone or together with other parties, decide
  (i) the benefits the other party will realize,
  (ii) the tasks the other party will perform,
  (iii) the commitments the other party will have to complete such tasks, and
  (iv) how the other party will respond to contingencies.

Computronics, Inc. illustrates the combination of the facts in scenario (1)(a)(i) (party decides what benefits it will realize), and *Pacesetter Motors, Inc.* illustrates (2)(b)(i) (party decides whether to veto other party's decision about benefits that the other party hopes to realize). When combined with (1) (party decides) and (2) (party vetoes by refusing consent), the decisions in (a) and (b) yield sixteen scenarios or hazards created by adverse parties having discretion.

Following are cases that illustrate five of these sixteen scenarios:

- *Lenape Resources Corp. v. Tennessee Gas Pipeline Corp.*[6]: A pipeline company agreed to take, or pay for if not taken, a portion of gas produced by producers from gas reserves committed under a gas sale agreement. The contract permitted the producers

[6] 870 S.W.2d 286; rev'd 925 S.W.2d 565; 1996 Tex. LEXIS 40; 39 Tex. Sup. J. 496; 29 U.C.C. Rep. Serv. 2d (Callaghan) 759; 137 Oil & Gas Rep. 630 (Tex. 1990).

> "[t]o operate its property free from any control by [the pipeline company] Buyer in such a manner as [the producers] Seller, in its sole discretion, may deem advisable, including without limitation, the right, but never the obligation, to drill new wells, to repair and rework old wells, and to plug any well or surrender any lease or portion thereof when no longer deemed by Seller to be capable of producing gas in paying quantities under normal methods of operation."[7]

Some 10 years later, the producers increased production from two wells, one of which was low producing, to five wells, significantly boosting production. Whereas before the production increase the pipeline company never paid more than $300,000 for gas produced in any single year, after the increase, it paid $89,000,000 for gas produced in one year.[8] The case illustrates scenarios (1)(a)(ii) (producers decide how much gas they will sell) and (1)(b)(ii) (producers decide how much gas the pipeline company will buy or for which it will pay a take-or-pay payment).

- *Anderson v. Automatic Sprinkler Corp.*[9]: An employment contract included the following clause relative to the award of bonuses:[10]

> The award of any direct incentive is entirely within the discretion of the corporation and nothing contained herein will be construed to the contrary. . . . With respect to those representatives whose employment with the corporation is terminated [for reasons other than their disability or

---

7 925 S.W.2d at 576.

8 The pipeline sued for declaratory relief that, inter alia, it was not obligated to take gas or pay for gas not taken in the quantities produced by the sellers. The trial court granted a partial summary judgment for the sellers. The court of appeals reversed the trial court's summary judgment on the Uniform Commercial Code issue, holding that the contract was an output contract subject to the good faith and proportionality restrictions in the UCC. The Texas Supreme Court reversed, holding the contract was not an output contract because the take or pay payment was "for the exclusive dedication of reserves for a fixed period of time." *Id.* at 578. The court held that the contract "anticipates that the Sellers may drill new wells in new depths and horizons and increase production and delivery capacity in discovering new reserves." *Id.* at 571.

9 147 Ga. App. 236, 248 S.E.2d 507 (Ga. App. 1978), sub. nom. Automatic Sprinkler Corp. v. Anderson, 243 Ga. 867, 257 S.E.2d 283 (Ga. 1979).

10 *Id.* at 867.

retirement], the payment or nonpayment of all or any direct incentive installments previously set aside but unpaid to them at the time of their termination, will rest completely in the absolute and final discretion of the Compensation Committee of the Board of Directors."

A sales representative terminated his employment. The compensation committee decided not to award any incentive compensation, giving no reasons. The case illustrates scenario (1)(a)(ii): the employer had discretion to decide how much, if any, bonus compensation it would be obligated to pay a former employee.[11]

- *Ehredt Underground, Inc. v. Commonwealth Edison Co.*[12]: A contract under which a utility agreed to pay a contractor a fixed price for work required the contractor to use employees who belonged to a union acceptable to the utility. To mollify the union that represented its employees, the utility advised the contractor that the union must belong to the AFL-CIO. As a result, the contractor had to choose a union whose members received wage rates 90 percent more than the rates for the union the contractor proposed but was not affiliated with the AFL-CIO.[13] The case illustrates scenario (2)(b)(ii) (the utility had to approve the contractor's choice of the union the members of which would perform the contract).
- *Flight Concepts Limited Partnership*[14]: This case is summarized in chapter 3.[15] The case illustrates scenario (1)(a)(iii): the licensee had discretion to decide, when if at all, it would be committed to use the licensed intellectual property.

---

[11] The employee sued for breach of contract, claiming the employer failed to make an honest judgment and thus abused its discretion. The employer moved for summary judgment, and the trial court granted the motion; the appeal court reversed, and the Georgia Supreme Court reversed, holding "There can be no breach of an implied covenant of good faith where a party to a contract has done what the provisions of the contract expressly give him the right to do." *Id.* at 868.

[12] 848 F. Supp. 797 (N.D. Ill. 1994).

[13] The contractor claimed the utility's refusal to accept its proposed union violated the covenant of good faith and fair dealing. The court granted the utility's motion for summary judgment, finding the utility's desire to avoid difficulty with its own union consistent with acting in good faith.

[14] 819 F. Supp. 1535 (D. Kan. 1993).

[15] *See* text accompanying ch. 3, notes 94–96.

- *Cabriolet Porsche Audi, Inc. v. American Honda Motor Co., Inc.*[16]: The agreement between a car dealer and the exclusive importer and distributor of Honda cars in the United States allowed the importer to allocate cars to dealers according to a mathematical formula. The contract stated that when cars were in short supply, "Dealer gives Distributor the right to allocate such supply in any reasonable manner Distributor deems fit in any geographical market area." Demand for Honda cars increased during an Arab oil embargo. The distributor continued to use the same formula for allocating cars to dealers. The case illustrates scenario (1)(a)(iv): the importer had discretion to decide how to complete a task it had to complete—allocation of available cars to the dealers—in the event of a contingency, the shortage of cars.[17]

Two further subdivisions of two groups of the scenarios previously described are useful. The first group constitutes the scenarios wherein a party decides its or the other party's tasks: scenarios (1)(a)(ii), (1)(b)(ii), (2)(a)(ii), and (2)(b)(ii)). This group can be divided into decisions about

(A) the tasks that must be completed and

(B) whether the tasks have been completed (or a breach or a default has occurred).

Lenape Resources Corp. and *Ehredt Underground, Inc.* illustrate the discretion described in (A) or scenarios (1)(a)(ii)(A), (1)(b)(ii)(A), (2)(a)(ii)(A), and (2)(b)(ii)(A).

---

16 773 F.2d 1193 (11th Cir. 1985).

17 The dealer sued the distributor for breach of contract when its orders went unfilled. The district court found the allocation system unreasonable and awarded judgment in favor of the dealer; the distributor appealed. The appeal court reversed, finding the allocation system and its application to the shortage reasonable. "American Honda's allocation system is a competitive one. Dealers in each zone are competing with each other for the limited number of cars sent from Japan. That an automobile distributor, naturally interested in selling as many cars as possible and encouraging its dealers to do so, should adopt such a competitive system is not unreasonable. Nor is it unreasonable that, under this competitive system, dealers that undertake to sell a maximum number of cars during a soft period are rewarded with more cars during the hot period than are dealers, like Cabriolet, that for their own reasons do not undertake to sell many cars." *Id.* at 1204.

Following are cases that illustrate three scenarios:

- *Random House, Inc. v. Curry*[18]: A contract between three authors and a publisher obligated the authors to deliver a manuscript about Jesse Jackson of approximately 100,000 words in length, "satisfactory to the [p]ublisher," not later than an agreed date. The authors delivered a manuscript. The publisher decided the manuscript was unsatisfactory, terminated the contract, and demanded repayment of the royalty advance.[19] Because, at contract formation, neither party could detail the content and style it expected in the manuscript, the authors' task was highly uncertain. That uncertainty was mitigated, if not eliminated, for the publisher by the wide latitude given it, the obligee, to decide if the manuscript prepared by the authors, the obligors, was satisfactory. The authors traded uncertainty risk for the risk the publisher would unfavorably exercise that discretion. The case illustrates scenario (1)(b)(ii)(B): the publisher had discretion to decide if the other party, the authors, had fulfilled their commitments. That discretion was also a hazard to the authors, as their investment in and anticipated royalties from the book would be lost.
- *General Electric Capital Corp. v. Direct TV, Inc.*[20]: General Electric Capital Corp. (GECC) purchased and serviced Direct TV's accounts receivable payable by its customers. The agreement provided accounts would be "characterized as written off when deemed uncollectible in GECC's sole discretion, or, if not sooner, when the account is 180 days delinquent." In response to complaints about dealer fraud and breaches, GECC wrote off $16 million of Direct TV's accounts and terminated the agreement. The case illustrates scenario (1)(a)(ii)(B): GECC had discretion to decide when its obligation to service an account had been completed, by "deeming uncollectible" and writing off accounts.[21] That discretion mitigated GECC's information

---

[18] 747 F. Supp. 191 (S.D.N.Y. 1990).

[19] The publisher sued to recover the advance and moved for summary judgment. Denying the motion, the court held that while the satisfaction clause was enforceable, the publisher's decision had to be made in good faith, and the question of whether that was the case was one of fact to be determined by the trial court.

[20] 94 F. Supp.2d 190 (D. Conn. 1999).

[21] When GECC sued Direct TV, the latter claimed the write off breached GECC's duty of good faith and fair dealing which should be implied in the agreement. The court granted GECC

and uncertainty risks—that the accounts might be subject to claims not disclosed and difficult or impractical to collect. That discretion was a hazard for Direct TV as it stood to lose the value in its receivables it expected to realize from their sale to GECC.

- *Capital Options Investments, Inc. v. Goldberg Brothers Commodities, Inc.*[22]: Linnco acted as a clearing broker for certain commodity trades and guaranteed payment for losses on trades by the commodity exchange. It cleared commodity option trades initiated by customers of introducing brokers, such as Capital Options, whose customers traded on the margin. The contracts between the clearing and introducing brokers and between the introducing brokers and their customers required the latter to "maintain such margins or collateral for [c]ustomer's accounts as requested from time to time by [the clearing broker] . . . in its sole discretion (which requests may be greater than exchange and clearing house requirements)." When, in 1987, the stock market crashed, Linnco demanded that Capital's customers double their margin requirements within five days, from $1300 to $2600 per option, even though their positions were not due until later that year and early the following year. The following month, Linnco demanded that the broker's customers further increase their margin requirements on certain options to $15,000 per option and gave them one hour to satisfy the demand.[23] Because at contract formation, Linnco could not predict changes in the commodity prices, it could not then decide the margin requirements at any time in the future. They were uncertain. That uncertainty was mitigated, if not eliminated, for Linnco, the obligee, by the discretion given it to decide the customers' or obligors' margin requirements at any time. The introducing brokers and customers traded uncertainty risk for the risk Linnco would exercise its discretion adversely to their interests. The case illustrates scenario (1)(b)(ii)(A): Linnco

summary judgment on the claim, holding such duty could not be implied where it would override the express contractual terms. *Id.* at 197. Thus while GECC had an obligation to service the accounts it purchased, it also had sole discretion to decide when those accounts were written off and no longer to be serviced.

22 958 F.2d 186 (7th Cir. 1992).

23 The demand was not met, Linnco liquidated the customers' positions, and Capital sued the clearing brokers for breach of contract. The district court granted the clearing brokers' motion for summary judgment and the appeal court affirmed.

had discretion to decide the margin or collateral the trader was required to provide at any time.

- *CIBC Bank and Trust Co. (Cayman) Ltd. v. Banco Central do Brasil*[24]: A facility agreement permitted the agent to accelerate outstanding Brazilian sovereign debt following a default if creditors holding more than 50 percent of the outstanding debt voted to instruct the agent to do so. More than 50 percent of such debt was held by a Brazilian bank that was owned more than 50 percent by the Brazilian government, also an obligor under the facility. One bank, acting on behalf of the remaining debt holders, demanded that the agent accelerate the outstanding debt.[25] This scenario is a variation on scenario (2)(a)(ii)(B): the Brazilian government through its ownership of the bank that controlled the voting rights under the facility agreement had discretion to decide when a default warranted acceleration of its debt. The discretion did not permit the Brazilian bank to declare that the Brazilian government had satisfied its obligations or was not in default, but did allow it to block acceleration, a key remedy. The hazard for the other banks was the debtor's ability to gain control over the decision to declare a default.

The second group, which includes scenarios wherein a party decides its or the other party's commitments in scenarios (1)(a)(iii), (1)(b)(iii), (2)(a)(iii), and (2)(b)(iii)), can be divided by whether the decision is about:

(X) when a commitment exists and

(Y) when that commitment is terminated.

Flight Concepts Limited Partnership[26] illustrates scenario (1)(a)(iii)(X): Boeing had discretion to decide when it would be committed to use the licensed intellectual property.

---

[24] 886 F. Supp. 1105 (S.D.N.Y. 1995).

[25] When the debt was not accelerated, the bank demanding acceleration filed suit against the agent and the Brazilian bank for breach of contract. The agent and the Brazilian bank moved for summary judgment, which was granted. The bank argued that the implied duty of good faith and fair dealing prohibited the Brazilian bank from using the outstanding debt it held to block acceleration. The court held the implied duty could not override the express provisions of the agreement, which clearly defined the Brazilian bank as a bank and required banks holding more than 50 percent of the outstanding debt to vote in favor of acceleration. The Brazilian bank had discretion as to how to vote the debt it held.

[26] *See* text accompanying notes 14 and 15.

The following cases illustrate scenario (1)(a)(iii)(Y):

- *Mirax Chemical Prod. Corp. v. First Interstate Commercial Corp.*[27]: A borrower promised to pay its lender "on demand, all or any part of the debit balance at any time." The loan agreement could be "terminated at any time by the [the lender] by written notice to the [borrower]." When the borrower incurred financial losses, the lender demanded repayment of the loan. The case illustrates scenarios (1)(a)(iii)(Y) and (1)(b)(ii)(A): the lender had discretion to terminate its commitment and to determine when the borrower had to perform by accelerating its obligation to repay outstanding loans.[28] That discretion mitigated, if not eliminated, a hazard to the lender: the uncertainty about when the borrower might be unable or unwilling to pay. The hazard for the borrower was the lender's discretion to accelerate the loans' maturity without reason at any time.
- *Boat & Motor Mart v. Sea Ray Boats, Inc.*[29]: A boat dealer sold a manufacturer's boats for more than 20 years under a dealership agreement that allowed either party to terminate upon 30 days' notice to the other party and provided that neither party was to be liable for any loss arising out of the agreement. Dissatisfied with the dealer's performance, the manufacturer notified the dealer the dealership agreement would not be renewed following expiration of its annual period. During the last year of the dealership, the dealer spent $90,000 on promotion and incurred costs of $85 per hour for warranty repairs while being reimbursed $20 per hour from the manufacturer. The case illustrates scenario 1(a)(iii)(Y): the manufacturer had discretion to terminate its commitment upon 30 days' notice notwithstanding any investments by the dealer.[30] That discretion mitigated, if not eliminated, the benefit, task, condition, and contingency oversight, remorse, and other risks to both parties, as discussed in chapters 3 to 5. That discretion

[27] 950 F.2d 566 (8th Cir. 1991).

[28] The borrower claimed breach of contract, bad faith, economic duress, and intentional infliction of mental distress. The district court granted summary judgment in favor of the lender and the appeal court affirmed, finding the contract was terminable at will by the lender.

[29] 825 F.2d 1285 (9th Cir. 1987).

[30] The dealer unsuccessfully claimed such terms were unconscionable.

was a hazard for the dealer, whose losses could be and were its investment in and anticipated profits from the dealership.

Changes in Decision Maker

A decision maker may undergo changes that have the potential to materially alter its use of its discretion when

- the party to the contract is changed,
- another party controlling the decisions made by a party is changed, or
- the personnel of the party responsible for making such decisions or performing or receiving performance are changed or their managers are changed.

The decision maker changes when it assigns or transfers the contract, often as an asset with its own value or as one of the assets or liabilities that are part of a business being transferred. The contract might also pass by operation of law to the decision maker's heirs or legatees or, if it is an entity, to its successor or owner in a liquidating distribution[31] or merger. The result is a decision maker different from that with which the other party contracted. A change of control of a decision maker occurs when its ownership interests are transferred, effecting a transfer or change of control of it without having to transfer the assets it owns; technically, the parties to the contract remain unchanged, while the owner of the decision maker has changed. A change of control can also occur without all the ownership interests in the decision maker being transferred; those responsible for its governance or management may change. When a transfer of ownership interests effects a change of control is outside the scope of this text. When there is more than one tier of entity ownership, a change of control may be effected by the transfer of the ownership interests at a higher tier level: the ultimate parent entity may transfer the ownership interests in a lower tier entity that owns the ownership interests in a still lower tier entity that owns the decision maker, or the ownership interests in the ultimate parent might

[31] *E.g.*, Trubowitch v. Riverbank Canning Co., 30 Cal.2d 335 (Cal. 1947), where an antiassignment clause in a contract for the sale of tomato paste was held inapplicable to a transfer of the contract by operation of law that occurred following dissolution of the corporation that was party to such contract.

be transferred.[32] A merger may or may not result in a change of party or control: if the decision maker is the surviving entity, no change in party occurs, though a change of control may or may not occur; and if it is not the surviving party, a change in party occurs, as the contract becomes a binding obligation of the surviving entity. A change in management occurs when a decision maker changes the individuals responsible for deciding whether to continue with a transaction and the resources to be allocated to its implementation. A change in personnel occurs when individuals not initially responsible for implementing the transaction are given such responsibility.[33]

While a change in decision maker or its owners, management, or personnel does not itself result in the decision maker's exercising discretion more adversely to the other party than it otherwise would, the possibility of such a change creates uncertainty about how that discretion will be so exercised. A changed decision maker may desire to extract more value from a transaction than its predecessor and will thus exercise whatever discretion it has to realize such value.

Following are cases that illustrate the adverse effect of changes in decision makers:

- *Lenape Resources Corp.*: This case is previously summarized.[34] During the first ten years of the term of the gas sale agreement, the producers drilled only two wells on the committed acreage, one of which was a low-producing stripper well. The mineral lessors who leased mineral rights to the producers, impatient with the low production, sued the producers for, inter alia, failing to develop the leases underlying the committed acreage. The mineral lessors and producers settled the lawsuit, agreeing that part of the committed acreage would be

[32] *E.g.*, Torrey Delivery, Inc. v. Chautauqua Truck Sales and Service, Inc., 47 A.D.2d 279 (N.Y. App. 1975), where a lease granted the lessee a right of first refusal to purchase the leased property. When the sole shareholder of the landlord died, the shares in the landlord were sold to the defendant; the landlord was merged into the defendant, which registered the title to the property in its name. The lessee claimed it was entitled to exercise its right of first refusal and purchase the property, as the purchase of the stock effected a change in the ownership of the property. The defendant's motion for dismissal was granted on appeal; the court held, "Ownership of capital stock being distinct from ownership of corporate property, it follows that the sale of such stock is not a sale of corporate property." *Id.* at 282–83.

[33] *E.g.*, Mindel v. Image Point Productions, Inc., 725 F. Supp. 189 (S.D.N.Y. 1989).

[34] *See* text accompanying notes 6 and 7.

unitized with an adjacent property. After unitization, the producers entered into a farmout agreement with two other gas producers. As a result of the farmout, these two other producers became the "sellers" under the gas sale agreement. The new producers drilled three wells, one bottomed on the committed acreage and two inside the units on acreage outside the acreage originally committed to the gas purchase agreement. The two new wells on the units were highly successful.[35] Through the farmout agreement, the producers transferred a portion of their interests in and control of development of the mineral leases to the new producers, who more aggressively developed the committed and adjacent acreage. As previously discussed, the first hazard for the pipeline company was the producers' discretion to increase production. The second was the producers' ability to transfer their interests to more aggressive producers. The buyer assumed responsibility for the risk it might have to deal with producers who would increase production.

- *Liebowitz v. Elsevier Science, Ltd.*:[36] Liebowitz "conceived of a scientific journal and persuaded the late media tycoon, Robert Maxwell, who then owned Pergamon Press, to back the idea. Publication began. Over the years, Liebowitz's ideas spawned a number of highly successful journals, all published by Pergamon under Liebowitz's direct or indirect editorship."[37] The contract was between Pergamon and Advanced Engineering Research and Development Corp. (AERDCO), an entity formed and controlled by Liebowitz, reflected "mutual confidence shared by Liebowitz and Maxwell, [and] did not contemplate the possibility that the parties would part ways."[38] "In time, however, Pergamon was sold [after Maxwell died]. Relations between Liebowitz and Pergamon's new owners soured."[39] AERDCO had "responsibility and authority for appointing and removing" editors and appointees of any of the journals but had to consult with Pergamon regarding any such appointments. An editor of one of the journals resigned. AERDCO appointed Liebowitz and his son as successors. Pergamon appointed a competing candidate, opposing Liebowitz's self-interested appointments, even though

[35] This summary is extracted from the report of the case at 925 S.W.2d 565, 568.

[36] 927 F. Supp. 688 (S.D.N.Y. 1996).

[37] *Id.* at 692.

[38] *Id.*

[39] *Id.*

Liebowitz previously served as an editor. Where Maxwell would have deferred to Liebowitz concerning the appointment of editors, the new management of Pergamon more aggressively asserted its right to participate in the appointments by seeking to block Liebowitz's.[40] The relatively insignificant hazard for AERDCO was Pergamon's limited participation in decisions to appoint new editors. Pergamon could not block but could influence those appointments. That hazard was acerbated by the potential for a change in Pergamon's ownership and management, which could, as it did, result in an unwillingness to accept AERDCO's choices.

ADVERSE-PARTY DISCRETION RISK MANAGEMENT

Adverse-Party Discretion

We observed how discretionary decision-making by one party mitigates the uncertainty risk to that party. That discretion, in turn, creates a different risk for the other party: that the decisions of the decision maker will be self-interested, in some instances, at the expense of the other party. That risk is mitigated by reintroducing uncertainty back into the transaction, by curbing the decision maker's discretion. The devices that mitigate such risk (described briefly in chapter 5) are

- processes for determining how discretion should be exercised,
- guidelines that set boundaries for the exercise of discretion, and
- requirements that the decision makers pay compensation for their exercise of discretion.

Decision-Making Process. The strongest mitigation of the risk that the adverse party will exercise its discretion in a manner unacceptable to the other party is to require that the decision maker obtain the other party's

[40] Liebowitz sued Pergamon, claiming, inter alia, his entity had the right to appoint him and his son as editors; the publisher responded that the appointments by the entity were bad faith. Both parties moved for summary judgment on the issue of who had authority to appoint the editors. The court granted Liebowitz's motion, noting, "Conceivably, if plaintiffs' (sic.) appointed a manifestly unqualified editor, such an action might be regarded as bad faith and, consequently, as a breach of contract." *Id.* at 701, n.22. Because Liebowitz served as editor-in-chief and his son had previously been on the editorial board, their appointments could not be said to be a bad faith exercise of discretion. Liebowitz was allowed to exercise his discretion, even where it clearly favored his interests. 927 F. Supp. 688, 692 (S.D.N.Y. 1996).

consent. The counterparty continues to have discretion to propose actions it or the other party may take without its decisions binding the other party unless that other party agrees to such proposal. The result is that both parties have discretion: the counterparty to propose actions and the other party to approve or veto them. As we have seen, an agreement to agree results in uncertainty about whether the parties will agree on matters as to which agreement is necessary.

As previously discussed, that uncertainty risk can be mitigated by prescribing a detailed procedure that states when and how each party may exercise its discretion or achieve specific milestones. Each party has a commitment to complete its milestone in the process of endeavoring to reach agreement while continuing to have its discretion to refuse its consent.

Following are cases that illustrate how a detailed process mitigates the uncertainty risk created by wide discretion:

- *In the Matter of the Arbitration between De Laurentiis*[41]: A producer, an author, and a distributor agreed to produce and distribute a motion picture about the South American patriot Simon Bolivar. The producer was to engage a writer or writers of the first rank to prepare a story outline, a "screen treatment," and thereafter a final scenario. The author and distributor were to consult during the preparation of the story outline and scenario. The producer was to complete a scenario in final form within three months from the date of the agreement. If the distributor did not approve the script, then the producer was to revise it. The producer undertook to make all necessary arrangements for financing, for the hiring of actors and a director, and for world distribution of the completed picture, all this to be subject to the prior approval of the distributor that promised not to withhold such approval unreasonably. The final scenario had to be accepted to all three parties.[42] The producer never hired a writer. The case illustrates scenario (2)(a)(ii)(B): the distributor and writer had to approve the final scenario prepared by the producer, thus agreeing with the producer when it had completed its tasks. It also illustrates how the consultation

41 9 N.Y.2d 503, 215 N.Y.S.2d 60, 174 N.E.2d 736 (N.Y. 1961).

42 This summary is extracted from the report of the case 9 N.Y.2d at 507.

requirement mitigated the wide latitude given the producer to perform and all three parties to approve the final scenario.[43]

- *Local 3-7 International Woodworkers v. DAW Forest Products*[44]: A buyer of a forest products business and the union representing the logging operations employees agreed upon a procedure the union and buyer were to follow when negotiating a new collective bargaining contract. The agreement allowed the union to submit within two weeks of signing the agreement a plan to keep the logging operations competitive; the buyer had to respond within an agreed period of time, indicating if the proposal had "merit;" and further procedures were to be followed, depending whether the proposal had merit. The buyer also agreed to continue logging operations unless "in the opinion of the [buyer] Company, the logging equipment is determined to be inoperative, unsafe or uneconomical to operate, [in which case] it shall be retired." Before submitting a plan, the union asked the buyer for information it said it must have to prepare a plan, but that information was not provided. The buyer purchased the business and discontinued logging operations, terminating 62 of 68 logging employees. The union demanded that the buyer continue to negotiate the collective bargaining contract. Uncertainty at contract formation about what, if any, terms on which the logging employees would continue to be employed was mitigated by a combination of procedures: one, which required the buyer and the union to follow a procedure for negotiating a collective bargaining agreement, and another, which allowed the buyer to discontinue logging operations if the logging equipment was determined by it to be inoperative, unsafe, or uneconomical to operate. Those procedures created new risks to the employees: that no agreement on the new contract would be reached, in effect a decision adverse to them, or the buyer would

[43] The distributor initiated arbitration proceedings pursuant to the contract. The producer applied to the court to stay the arbitration and to have the contract declared unenforceable as illusory. The court held the contract was enforceable because the parties "expressly promised each other to consult at reasonable times and places during the preparation of the outline and of the scenario 'to the end that both [the producer] De Laurentiis and [author] Campos may make every effort in good faith to cause to be created, within the period specified herein, a story outline, screen treatment and final scenario acceptable to both.'" *Id.* at 509.

[44] 833 F.2d 789 (9th Cir. 1987).

decide the logging operations were uneconomic, another decision adverse to them. Both of those risks were, in turn, mitigated by the enforceability of the agreement to negotiate, which enforceability limited the buyer's discretion to refuse to agree.[45] The case illustrates scenario (1)(a)(iii)(X): the buyer had discretion to determine when it would be committed to agree to a collective bargaining contract. The case also illustrates how the detailed consultation and other procedures helped to mitigate the buyer's discretion to stop negotiating with the union.

We are not here concerned with the enforceability of the agreement to agree in the first case or the agreement to negotiate in the second, though enforceability was the issue in both cases. A putative agreement that is void for vagueness is one that fails to comply with the legal formalities that create a binding commitment. Whether an agreement to negotiate or agree creates such a commitment is a question about compliance with such formalities. The question here is how that discretion to refuse to agree or to negotiate can be mitigated using consultation and other procedures. The enforceability of such an agreement is a useful indicator that the mitigation of discretion is meaningful.

Decision-Making Guidelines. Substantive standards for the exercise of discretion set boundaries by which the validity thereof is determined. The most common of such standards are good faith and reasonableness. Good faith is defined as "[a] state of mind consisting in (1) honesty in belief or purpose, (2) faithfulness to one's duty or obligation, (3) observance of reasonable commercial standards of fair dealing in a given trade or business, or (4) absence of intent to defraud or seek unconscionable advantage."[46] Reasonable is defined, in part, as "[f]air, proper, or

---

[45] The union sued for specific performance of the memorandum of agreement; the buyer claimed the agreement was too indefinite to be enforceable; the district court agreed, dismissing the suit; and the appeal court reversed. Although the court summarized the negotiation procedure outlined in the memorandum of agreement, the appeal court focused on the implied duty of good faith, holding, the "district court could determine breach of the duty of good faith consideration by examining whether the Company had exercised its 'honest judgment' or whether it had met the reasonable person standard in rejecting the Union's proposal." *Id.* at 793–94.

[46] BLACK'S LAW DICTIONARY, *supra* note 1, 808.

moderate under the circumstances; sensible."[47] Reasonableness includes good faith: a party acting reasonably is also acting in good faith.

Following are cases that illustrate how these standards limit discretion:

- *Local 3-7 International Woodworkers*[48]: This case is previously discussed.[49] The discretion to stop logging operations was also subject to the implied duty to act in good faith. The company had to consider the union's proposals in good faith and determine whether they had merit. That might also have included a duty to provide the data requested by the union.[50] Similarly, the company's discretion to cease logging was limited to instances when its logging equipment was inoperative, unsafe, or uneconomical to operate.[51] The case illustrates how a good faith limitation set boundaries on the company's discretion by obligating it to entertain and evaluate the union's proposals and continue to negotiate as long as the negotiations were fruitful. Note the contract did not expressly state that either party had to act in good faith; the limitation was implied. A party that does not want its discretion thus limited may have to exclude the implied duty.
- *Banc of America Securities LLC v. Solow Bldg. Co., LLC*[52]: A lease required the prior consent of a landlord to tenant improvements. The landlord was "not to unreasonably withhold its consent" to proposed, nonstructural changes required to render the space amenable to the lessee's business purposes. The lease also required that the landlord approve or disapprove proposed alteration plans within ten business days and that, upon substantial completion of the work, the landlord could recover its actual out-of-pocket expenses reasonably incurred in connection with such alterations. The landlord demanded a $6 million fee for its consent to alterations, an amount equal to 3 percent of the overall cost of the improvements, and sent demands to the tenant to pay the fee and notice it would not further review plans until paid. The reasonableness limitation

47 Black's Law Dictionary, *supra* note 1, 1456.

48 833 F.2d 789 (9th Cir. 1987).

49 *See* text accompanying notes 44–46.

50 833 F.2d at 794–95.

51 *Id.* at 796.

52 47 A.D.3d 239, 847 N.Y.S.2d 49, 2007 N.Y. Slip Op. 09545 (N.Y. App. 2007).

obligated the landlord to review the proposed improvements and denied him the right to demand a fee for approving them.[53] The case illustrates scenario (2)(b)(ii) while its consent was required, the landlord could not unreasonably refuse to approve the tasks the tenant proposed to complete in order to realize some of benefits of the lease. It also illustrates how the reasonableness requirement confined the landlord's exercise of discretion: it could not extract a fee when none was stated in the contract.

Decision-Making Compensation. The exercise of discretion may be conditioned upon a payment by the decision maker to the other party as compensation for some or all of its losses that result from its decision. The fee in *Banc of America Securities LLC* was not an example because the landlord was not seeking compensation for any service or reimbursement for any loss on its part. Also, because the payment was not contingent upon a breach or default by the decision maker, it was not liquidated damages or a penalty. Compensation may be nominal or substantial, and the greater the compensation that must be paid to exercise discretion one way rather than another, the more significant the deterrent on its exercise unfavorable to the party receiving such compensation.

The following are illustrations of such conditions:

- *Piantes v. Pepperidge Farm, Inc.*[54]: This case is summarized in chapter 3.[55] The franchisor was allowed to terminate a franchise upon payment of 125 percent of the fair market value of the franchise as determined by a panel of arbitrators. The case illustrates scenarios (1)(a)(i)(Y) and (1)(b)(i)(Y): the franchisor had discretion to decide when its and the franchisee's commitments could be terminated. The price of exercising the discretion was the value of the franchisee's business plus a premium.

[53] The tenant sued for an injunction to prevent termination of the lease and for damages. The trial court found that the fee was unjustified since the landlord's cost did not approach 3% of the tenant's costs; the withholding of the consent until the fee was paid was an unjustified refusal of the consent. The appeal court agreed, stating, "It is evident that the [New York] Court of Appeals did not intend economic self-interest to be applied as an expansive principle to excuse all manner of misconduct." 47 A.D.3d at 247.

[54] 875 F. Supp. 929 (D. Mass. 1995).

[55] *See* text accompanying ch. 3, notes 110–111.

- *Metered Appliances, Inc. v. Lafayette Court Apartment Corp. and Service Directions, Inc.*[56]: Lafayette leased a laundry room to Metered under a lease that gave Metered a right, upon termination of the lease, to match the terms of any new lease Lafayette proposed to enter into with a third party. Lafayette negotiated a one-year lease with a third party that gave either party the right to terminate at any time, with the lessor responsible to pay the costs of removal of the equipment and improvements. It offered this lease to Metered, who rejected it.[57] The case also illustrates scenarios (1)(a)(iii)(Y) and (1)(b)(iii)(Y): the landlord had discretion to decide when its and the tenant's commitments were terminated. The price in this instance was modest, the tenant's cost of removing its equipment.

Changes in Counterparty

Changes in a counterparty can acerbate two hazards: the adverse party's exercise of its discretion, as described in this chapter, and an obligor's or putative obligor's completion of the tasks it is expected to complete, as described in the next chapter. Changes in a party may result in its being less able or willing to perform such tasks. Measures that mitigate the risks created by changes in an obligor include all those that mitigate the risks created by changes in an adverse discretionary decision maker. For that reason, such measures are explained in the next chapter.

---

56 35 Misc.3d 1238(A), 954 N.Y.S.2d 760 (Table), 2012 WL 2122368, 2012 NY Slip Op 51038(U) (N.Y. Sup. Ct. 2012).

57 Metered claimed it was not a bona fide offer and was designed to defeat its first refusal right. The third party testified that it accepted the lease because it was confident Lafayette would be satisfied with its service and not exercise the termination right. The court granted the motion for summary judgment on the breach of contract claims, holding Metered had not proven the one-year lease was not bona fide. The short term and termination right enabled the landlord to decide at any time if the benefits of the lease with the selected lessee were worthwhile, relative to the benefits it might realize from other laundry service providers.

8

Performance Risks

PERFORMANCE HAZARDS

Black's Law Dictionary defines performance as "[t]he successful completion of a contractual duty, usu. resulting in the performer's release from any past or future liability"[1] and default as "the omission or failure to perform a legal or contractual duty."[2] The chances that an obligor will not so perform or will so default are performance risks. A performance hazard is a condition (or circumstance that exists at contract formation) or contingency (or event that occurs after contract formation) that indicates the obligor might not perform as expected.

Willingness, Ability, and Execution

An obligor's default will be attributable to one or more of the following causes:

- its lack of intent or desire or its unwillingness to perform when performance is due,

[1] Black's Law Dictionary 1319 (10th ed. 2014).

[2] *Id.* at 507.

- its lack of financial, technical, and other resources to perform or its inability to perform when performance is due, and
- its lack of diligence or care when performing, or its incompetent or inept performance.

Performance hazards are conditions and contingencies that indicate the obligor lacks or will lack at the time performance is due a willingness or ability to perform or will lack sufficient diligence when performing. Such conditions and contingencies may occur earlier than breach, anticipatory breach, and repudiation.

Unwillingness and Inability to Perform. An unwillingness or inability may be the result of a condition that exists at contract formation or it may be the result of a contingency that occurs later. Such condition or contingency may cause an obligor to immediately lose its willingness or ability to perform or may portend a future loss of such willingness or ability. In the latter case, additional contingencies, acts, and events may have to occur before the obligor becomes unwilling or unable to perform. Until that time, one or more such conditions and contingencies evidence uncertainty about such willingness and ability.

The following cases illustrate such conditions and contingencies:

- *Channel Master Corp. v. Aluminum Ltd. Sales, Inc.*[3]: A seller agreed to sell a quantity of aluminum ingots each month for five years, knowing that it did not have sufficient supplies and intending to sell only supplies not sold to other buyers. The intent not to sell was a condition that existed at contract formation. The harm would come to the buyer on the first date delivery was due; before that time, the seller's lack of intent was a hazard to the buyer.[4] Unwillingness to perform was a condition at contract formation.

[3] 4 N.Y.2d 403, 176 N.Y.S.2d 259, 151 N.E.2d 833 (N.Y. 1958).

[4] Unable to sue on the contract, which had not been reduced to writing as required by the statute of frauds, the buyer sued for fraud. The New York Court of Appeals held the action should be allowed. "If the proof of a promise or contract, void under the statute of frauds, is essential to maintain the action, there may be no recovery, but, on the other hand, one who fraudulently misrepresents himself as intending to perform an agreement is subject to liability in tort whether the agreement is enforcible (sic) or not." *Id.* at 408.

- *In re Newport Offshore, Ltd.*[5]: Newport, a ship repair firm, agreed to complete alterations and repairs to Long's vessel. It had competent welders on staff but assigned incompetent welders to the work because of commitments to other vessel owners, with the result that the repairs to Long's vessel were incompetently performed. A hazard occurred at contract formation when Newport committed to repair more vessels than it had competent staff to do the repairs. If, at that time, Newport expected to assign its incompetent welders to the vessel's repairs, it did not intend to perform as it had committed to do. If, at that time, Newport had not decided the repairs to which it would assign the incompetent welders, it was neither willing nor unwilling to perform. That would come later when it had to appoint the staff to repair Long's vessel.[6] The hazard existed at contract formation because the overcommitment created the chance Newport would not assign competent welders when it finally had to assign welders to the job, even if it hoped they would satisfactorily complete their tasks.
- *Resource Management Co.*[7]: This case is summarized in chapter 3.[8] A company that owned 8,000 acres of ranch land in Utah and its shareholders negotiated a two-page consulting agreement that generously compensated the consultant. The company and the brothers later decided not to use the consultant's services, claiming the contract was unconscionable because the consultant would receive far more than its services were worth.[9] The hazard, the decision not to use the consultant, occurred whenever they changed their minds; that resulted in harm on the first occasion they entered into a mineral lease without consulting the consultant. Their unwillingness to perform most likely occurred sometime after contract formation but before performance was due.
- *Trans World Airlines, Inc. v. Skyline Air Parts, Inc.*[10]: TWA solicited bids for certain boost pumps it once had as spare parts but had

---

[5] 155 B.R. 616 (Bankr. R.I. 1993).

[6] Long submitted a claim for breach of contract in the bankruptcy proceeding for Newport. The trustee opposed the claim and the bankruptcy court found Newport was negligent in repairing Long's vessel and breach the contract with Long.

[7] 706 P.2d 1028 (Utah 1985).

[8] See text accompanying ch.3, notes 65 and 66

[9] Supra ch. 3, note 66.

[10] 193 A.2d 72 (D.C. App. 1963).

sold and shipped them two months earlier; it accepted the winning bid.[11] Its inability to perform was a condition at contract formation.

- *Christy v. Pilkington*[12]: Buyers of an apartment building paid a down payment at contract formation and expected to borrow the balance of the purchase price; however, after contract formation, they became unable to do so.[13] Like many real property purchasers, residential and investment, the buyers were not expected to have all the cash needed to purchase the property when the contract was signed but to be able to raise the necessary funds when they needed to do so. Because the borrowers were presumably qualified at contract formation to obtain the loan, the change in their financial condition was the cause of their failure to perform. The buyers lost their ability (or qualifications) to acquire the capability (funds necessary to pay the purchase price) after contract formation.
- *Tri-State Transmission and Generation Association, Inc. v. Shoshone River Power, Inc.*[14]: A cooperative utility obligated to buy all its electric power requirements from a power-generating cooperative seller decided to go out of business and sell its assets. The generating cooperative seller obtained an injunction to restrain the sale without the court deciding if the buyer was obligated to continue its business. The utility lost its willingness to perform when it decided to sell its assets and would have lost its ability to perform had it sold them, in both cases after contract formation.

Inability and Infeasibility. Inability to perform differs from infeasibility of performance. The legal distinction between objective and subjective impossibility is useful here: impossibility is objective when a task cannot be completed by anyone and subjective when it can be completed but not

[11] TWA canceled the contract and, when sued, unsuccessfully claimed mistake of fact and impossibility as defenses. The court, unsympathetic to TWA, held, regarding the mistake defense, "If there were a mistake in the case before us, it was not mutual. Trans World knew, or should have known, of the superior right of the third party to which it had previously sold the subject matter." Likewise, the court dismissed the impossibility defense: "The inability to perform was the sole responsibility of appellant, brought about by its negligent and careless omission to check over a period of time that the subject matter offered and sold to appellee was still in its possession."

[12] 224 Ark. 407, 273 S.W.2d 533 (Ark. 1954).

[13] Their income from their car business had so declined they could not qualify for the loan.

[14] 805 F.2d 351 (10th Cir. 1986).

by a specific obligor.[15] Like objective impossibility and impracticability, completion of a task is infeasible when no one (person or entity) can complete a task as contemplated by the parties (in the quantity and quality required, at the time and cost projected) and feasible when someone can. Unlike impossibility, infeasibility is a matter of degree: a task impossible to complete under certain conditions may be capable of completion under other, more relaxed conditions. Infeasibility may exist at contract formation or occur later.

The following cases illustrate the distinction between inability and infeasibility:

- *B's Co., Inc. v. B.P. Barber & Assoc., Inc.*[16]: A subcontractor hired to install two pipes under a river according to the plans and specifications provided by a county's engineers tried twice and failed, but another subcontractor who was brought in successfully laid the pipes using a different method. If the pipes could not have been and were not installed according to the plans and specifications provided the first subcontractor (and were modified for the second subcontractor), as the subcontractor claimed, the work asked of the first subcontractor would have been infeasible. If the pipes could have been so installed, as the contractor successfully claimed, the first subcontractor lacked the skills (or ability) to lay the pipes because it tried twice.[17]

---

15 "Impossibility of performance of a contract may be classified as objective impossibility (the thing cannot be done) or as subjective impossibility (I cannot do it). It is generally well settled that subjective impossibility, that is, impossibility which is personal to the promisor and does not inhere in the nature of the act to be performed, does not excuse nonperformance of a contractual obligation." The B's Co., Inc. v. B.P. Barber & Assoc., Inc., 391 F.2d 130, 137 (4th Cir. 1968). "The impossibility which will, or may, excuse the performance of a contract must exist in the nature of the thing to be done. It must not exist merely because of the inability or incapacity of the promisor or obligor to do it." White Lakes Shopping Center, Inc. v. Jefferson Standard Life Ins. Co., 208 Kan. 121, 124, 490 P.2d 609 (Kan. 1971).

16 391 F.2d 130 (4th Cir. 1968).

17 The first subcontractor claimed the pipes could not be installed according to the plans and specifications, and these were modified for the second subcontractor; as the plans and specifications were implicitly warranted to be correct, the contractor was responsible. The court found the plans and specifications allowed the subcontractor to decide upon the method and did not mandate installation that was impossible to complete. After reviewing the difficulties experienced by the first subcontractor, the court concluded, "[T]he trial judge found that [the work] ... was not impossible to perform. It appeared most difficult

- *U.S. v. Wegematic Corp.*[18]: A contractor agreed, but failed within the agreed time, to design, build, and deliver to a federal government agency a "truly revolutionary" computer system. The government sued for damages. In response, the contractor argued the project was impractical from the outset and another year and between one million and one and one-half million dollars would have been needed to complete the work, and even then the outcome would have been uncertain. The court held for the government. The case illustrates a task that as conceived was infeasible and perhaps impossible at contract formation.

Infeasibility, like impossibility and inability, is a risk to an obligee, that the performance it expected from the obligor will not be forthcoming. Like impossibility and inability risks, responsibility for infeasibility risk must be allocated to one or both parties. As illustrated in *U.S. v. Wegematic Corp.*, an obligor may assume responsibility for the risk its performance is infeasible.

Inept Performance. An obligor may have both the will and ability to perform but nonetheless fail to do so. Such failure cannot be attributed to inability or unwillingness, interference by third parties, or other external causes. For example, in *TCBY Systems, Inc. v. RSP Co., Inc.*,[19] a frozen yogurt franchisor disapproved a location proposed for a franchise store in a suburb of the Twin Cities suggested by the franchisee and proposed two locations in Minnesota outside the Twin Cities, even though its only location outside the Twin Cities in that state was failing. Based on an investigation by an inexperienced division manager, it approved an alternative location in central Minnesota proposed by the franchisee, even though the location did not meet the minimum demographic criteria the franchisor required in its internal guidelines. The franchise business failed. A reasonable interpretation of the events is that the franchisor had the resources to help choose a good franchise location but failed to use them on this occasion.[20] Performance is inept

or perhaps impossible for [the first subcontractor] but apparently a routine operation for an experienced operator in the field, ... [the second subcontractor]." *Id.* at 137.

18 360 F.2d 674 (2d Cir. 1966).

19 33 F.3d 925 (8th Cir. 1994).

20 When the franchise business failed, the franchisee sued the franchisor for breach of the obligation in the franchise contract to provide reasonable assistance in the site selection. The jury awarded a verdict in the franchisee's favor; and the appeal court upheld the verdict.

when the only logical conclusion is that an obligor could have performed but simply did not do so. The explanation for the failure lies in the skills, experience, and knowledge of the individuals charged with performance

Information, Assumption, and Uncertainty Risks

Information and Assumption Risks. A party may believe a performance hazard does not exist when it does because it has incorrect information about an obligor's identity or intent or ability to perform, it may have correct information about such matters but process such data incorrectly, or it may have no or insufficient information about such matters and make an incorrect assumption about them. Such a mistaken party may be the obligor, in which case it has incorrect information, incorrectly processes correct information, or makes an incorrect assumption about its own ability to perform. Such a mistaken party may be the obligee, in which case it has incorrect information, incorrectly processes correct information, or makes an incorrect assumption about the other party's ability to perform. Such hazards are comparable to the information and assumption hazards described in chapter 4, concerning benefits and tasks.

The following are cases that illustrate a combination of such information and assumption and performance hazards:

- *Sassower v. Blumenfeld*[21] illustrates an obligor who had incorrect information about its own ability to perform. A property buyer believed he had sufficient funds in his investment account with Bernie Madoff's firm to pay the $1,800,000 purchase price of a home, based on statements provided by Madoff's firm. Because Madoff's scheme was fraudulent, the buyer had no funds in the account he could use to pay such price.[22] The case is summarized further in chapter 10.[23]

[21] 24 Misc.3d 843, 878 N.Y.S.2d 602, 2009 N.Y. Slip Op. 29198 (N.Y. S. Ct. 2009).

[22] The buyer deposited $180,000, which he agreed to forfeit if he failed to pay the balance. Madoff's fraudulent scheme was discovered between the times the buyer signed and closed, leaving the buyer with no cash and, because he had lost his investments, with no ability to borrow moneys with which to pay the balance. He asked for a refund of the deposit, claiming impossibility excused his performance. The court, holding for the seller, muddled through the impossibility defense, finding the buyer "has utterly failed to provide any details as to the amounts lost, the nature of his lost investments, or the actual state of his current finances and assets." *Id.* at 848.

[23] See text accompanying ch. 10, notes 7 and 8.

- *Trans World Airlines, Inc. v. Skyline Air Parts, Inc.*[24] also illustrates an obligor who had believed it had the ability to perform when it did not. The airline wrongly believed it had the spare parts to sell, an error attributable to its failure to check its own records.
- *Bliven v. The New England Screw Co.*[25] illustrates an obligee who wrongly assumed its obligor had the intent and ability to perform. A manufacturer received six orders from a buyer for screws that stated the dates by which the buyer expected delivery. As was its custom and practice, the seller accepted the orders, even though it knew it could and would not fill, and had no intention of filling, them until it had filled all prior orders, also overdue. The buyer sued for breach of contract. The court held that because the seller's custom and practice was widely known, the buyer was charged with knowing such practice. The obligee did not know of such practice and incorrectly assumed the obligor was willing and able to perform the order as stated.

Uncertainty Risks. Incidents that occur prior to default by the obligor that adversely affect willingness and ability to perform may be evidence that the obligor will not or is unlikely to perform when performance is due. The existence of a condition at contract formation or the occurrence of an incident later may correlate to an obligor or obligors in general losing or suffering an impairment of their willingness or ability to perform. The fact that an obligor has previously performed ineptly when completing similar tasks for an obligee or third parties may be evidence that it will repeat such performance, even though it has on other occasions performed satisfactorily. That correlation may also be weak or strong, depending upon the extent to which willingness and ability are impaired and the proximity to the time when performance is due. The stronger the correlation between previous and future inept performances, the stronger is the evidence that performance will likely be inept. Incidents that precede and correlate with unwillingness, inability, and inept performance are hazards to performance. The more irreversible the impairment of willingness or ability, the stronger is the evidence that performance is unlikely. In all but the clearest of cases, whether a hazard has occurred and whether there is strong evidence that

[24] 193 A.2d 72 (D.C. App. 1963).

[25] 23 How. 420, 64 U.S. 420, 16 L. Ed. 510 (1859).

a commitment will not be fulfilled will be uncertain. Such uncertainty hazard is comparable to the uncertainty hazards described in chapter 5, concerning conditions and contingencies.

Following are cases that illustrate a combination of uncertainty and performance hazards:

- *McCloskey & Co. v. Minweld Steel Co., Inc.*[26]: A subcontractor who had agreed to furnish and erect all of the structural steel required on two buildings to be built on the grounds of a state hospital and to furnish all of the long span steel joists required in the construction of one of the two buildings became concerned about the tightening of the steel market after trying unsuccessfully to purchase steel from Bethlehem Steel, U.S. Steel, and Carnegie-Illinois and asked the general contractor for help to procure the steel, hoping for assistance from a state authority. The subcontractor's difficulty acquiring the required quantity of steel in the market may have been due to a condition that existed at contract formation or a contingency that occurred later, when the market tightened. In either case, the subcontractor's difficulty may have been evidence that the subcontractor would fail to procure the steel, though this was not a foregone result. The hazard was not irreversible. The risk to the general contractor was that the longer it waited for the subcontractor to fail, the more difficult and less likely it would be able to avoid all or to reduce its losses.[27] Conversely, the risk to the subcontractor was that the earlier the general contractor terminated, the earlier the general contractor foreclosed whatever chance the subcontractor had to succeed, even if against the

[26] 220 F.2d 101 (3d Cir. 1955).

[27] The subcontract did not state a date by which the steel was to have been delivered. A clause, however, allowed the general contractor to set the dates for delivery to avoid late completion. The contract also allowed the general contractor to terminate if the subcontractor should "at any time refuse or neglect to supply a sufficiency . . . of materials of the proper quality, . . . or fail, in the performance of any of the agreements herein contained." The general contractor treated the request for help as an anticipatory breach, terminated the contract, procured the steel from Bethlehem, and brought in new subcontractors to do the work contemplated by the agreement with the subcontractor. The general contractor sued the subcontractor for breach. At completion of the trial, the judge granted the subcontractor's motions for judgment on the grounds the general contractor had failed to state a cause of action, holding the subcontractor had not anticipatorily breached by requesting help. The appeal court affirmed.

odds.[28] Until the situation was clear one way or the other, that the subcontractor could or could not perform, uncertainty about its ability to perform continued.

- *KMC Co., Inc. v. Irving Trust Co.*[29]: Irving made loans to KMC, a wholesale grocery business, based on a percentage of the value of KMC's inventory and receivables; the maximum outstanding amount was not to exceed $3.5 million. The loans were secured by KMC's inventory and accounts. KMC asked Irving to increase the maximum to $4 million to enable it to pay its suppliers but was refused. It then requested a loan of $800,000 to cover outstanding checks and was refused, even though the aggregate outstanding loans would be below the $3.5 million limit. No prior notice had been given that loans below the maximum would be refused. The bank officer was concerned that not all checks would be cleared, KMC's financial condition was precarious, and the bank would not be repaid. Unable to pay its obligations, KMC became bankrupt and was liquidated.[30] If the bank officer had been correct that KMC could not pay all its bills with its available cash and the maximum amount of borrowings under the line of credit, a hazard had occurred—KMC was insolvent or potentially so—and refusing the loans would have mitigated its potential losses that would have resulted when KMC filed for bankruptcy. But, as KMC successfully claimed, the bank officer was incorrect and KMC could have paid all its bills, no such hazard existed, only a potential hazard at worst; the bank had overreacted.[31] Uncertainty about

[28] "Despite the circumstances there is no indication in the letter that [the subcontractor] Minweld had definitely abandoned all hope of otherwise receiving the steel and so finishing its undertaking. One of the mentioned producers might have relented. Some other supplier might have turned up." *Id.* at 104.

[29] 757 F.2d 752 (6th Cir. 1985).

[30] KMC had not repudiated or breached. The uncertainty was whether its financial condition had so deteriorated as to indicate it was or would become unable to repay the bank. An inadequate response might increase its risk of default by KMC, though because the bank was fully secured that risk was not considered significant. An overreaction by the bank to the uncertainty would put it in breach, as it did.

[31] KMC sued Irving for breach of contract, claiming Irving had a duty to perform in good faith, and that duty was breached by failing to give advance notice it would not make advances when it was fully secured and had a blocked account into which KMC's funds were paid. The magistrate who tried the case awarded a verdict in favor of KMC, and Irving unsuccessfully appealed.

KMC's ability to repay the loans existed for a short while, during which time the bank's officer acted precipitously.

Changes in Party. Chapter 7 describes how changes of or in a party that has discretion can be a hazard to the other party. A change *of* party occurs when a contract is transferred to a third party, by assignment, distribution, merger, or otherwise. A change *in* a party occurs when the ownership or control of that party is transferred, the management of that party or the personnel in that party responsible for implementation of a contract is changed. Any such change of or in a party does not automatically alter its willingness or ability to perform or result in inept performance. The changed party may find the benefits of the contract as attractive as and the burdens no more burdensome than its predecessor. Until the details of a change are known, the obligee cannot assess the potential effect of a change on the obligor's potential performance. A contract that allows a change of or in a party creates uncertainty for the other party about whether such a change will occur. It also becomes a more significant hazard to the other party when a change occurs and adversely affects the obligor's willingness or ability to perform or the standard of its performance. Responsibility for the losses that result from such a change, however, may or may not remain with the changed party.

The following illustrate how such changes become hazards and how responsibility for such hazards are allocated:

- *Travellers International AG v. Trans World Airways, Inc.*[32]: Travellers, which began in 1972, developed certain package tours, agreed with TWA that it would continue to develop such tours, sell them to TWA, and produce brochures for marketing them. TWA agreed to provide the air transportation for and to market such tours. TWA also agreed to decide the number of tour passengers each year, not less than 100,000. In practice, the parties met annually and planned the number and content of the tours and brochure content. In 1985, Carl Icahn acquired control and in 1986 became chairman of the board of TWA. The owner of Travellers decided to sell the company and offered it to TWA. Icahn declined the offer, uncertain about expanding TWA's business in that direction. A year later, Icahn offered to buy Travellers from its new owner at

[32] 722 F. Supp. 1087 (S.D.N.Y. 1989).

the price he paid for it, but the new owner declined to sell. Icahn investigated how profitable Travellers' business was and how TWA could develop the land tour package business inside the airline. He decided to develop that business but recognized that the arrangements with Travellers would first have to be "cleared up." TWA terminated the contract, citing two grounds: the departure of a number of management employees at Travellers and the operation of a cruise program with SAS.[33] The case illustrates how a change of control of a party can prompt regret over the benefits ceded to the other party,[34] in this instance the profit realized by Travellers from flights arranged with TWA. The potential for an investor, such as Icahn, to acquire control of TWA was a hazard to Travellers from contract formation and became more significant when Icahn acquired control, threatening TWA's willingness to continue to perform the contract with Travellers. Because it was not at liberty to repudiate its commitments to Travellers following a change of control, TWA remained responsible for any losses that resulted from TWA's repudiation or breach (the outcome of any change in intent about performing).

- *Comdisco Disaster Recovery Services, Inc. v. Money Management Systems, Inc.*[35]: Comdisco agreed to provide disaster recovery services for Money Management. Comdisco was obligated to maintain fully operational computer centers as a backup for customers, such as Money Management, whose businesses were dependent on computers. Money Management paid a monthly subscription fee for the service. Money Management was acquired by and became a subsidiary of SunGuard Data Systems, Inc., which had another subsidiary that was a chief competitor of Comdisco. Money Management stopped paying monthly fees to Comdisco and signed a new agreement for such services with the

[33] Travellers sought a permanent injunction to prevent termination. The court held neither of the events cited by TWA breached the contract and granted the requested injunctive relief.

[34] The court, at the outset of its discussion of the issues, noted, "In an exercise of candor and reality, TWA has urged, appropriately, that the driving force for the termination was the economic effect of the Contract as perceived by Icahn. Regrettably for TWA, however, even assuming the effect was as believed by Icahn, Travellers' profit does not provide a ground for contract termination." *Id.* at 1096.

[35] 789 F. Supp. 48 (D. Mass. 1992).

SunGuard affiliate.[36] Money Management claimed that Comdisco would have unfair access to SunGuard's proprietary information if it continued to provide disaster services to Money Management. The hazard to Comdisco was the potential change in control of its client, Money Management, who, as a result of such change, would be unwilling to continue performing. The case is similar to *Travellers International AG.* Assuming Comdisco might have had access to SunGuard's proprietary information as a result of the acquisition of Money Management, the potential hazard to SunGuard was acquiring a contract or business with a contract with a competitor that might result in that competitor receiving an advantage. Both hazards occurred. Money Management assumed responsibility for both risks, not having a right to terminate upon the occurrence of a change in its control.

- *Alternative Thinking Systems, Inc. v. Simon & Schuster*[37]: A publisher contracted with a company, the president of which authored a work the publisher was to publish. The author died shortly after the manuscript was accepted. The publisher decided against publishing the book because the author would not help in marketing. The case illustrates how the loss of a key person in one party can potentially so change the benefits for the other party that it wishes to reassess the value the transaction has for it. The hazard to the publisher was the loss of the author's participation in the marketing of the book. It assumed responsibility for that risk in the absence of a right to terminate upon the death of the author.[38]

---

36 Comdisco sued for breach of contract; Money Management claimed that because Comdisco would have access to SunGuard's proprietary software and confidential information, the purpose of the contract had been frustrated and performance had become impossible. The court granted Comdisco summary judgment on the issue, holding frustration was not applicable when the party claiming the defense controlled the occurrence of the frustrating event, the event was foreseeable, Money Management's information was protected by the obligation in the contract to keep such information confidential, and Comdisco's performance had not lost its value to Money Management because it still received disaster recovery services.

37 853 F. Supp. 791 (S.D.N.Y 1994).

38 The company sued the publisher for breach. Because a clause in the draft contract that specifically gave the publisher a right to terminate—"[t]he Publisher shall not be obligated to publish the Literary work if, whether before or after acceptance thereof, supervening events or circumstances since the date of this agreement have, in the sole judgment of the Publisher, materially adversely changed the economic expectations of the Publisher

- *Mindel v. Image Point Productions, Inc.*[39]: A production company recruited and hired a director to direct television commercials for one year. Shortly after his hiring, the production company fired the executive who had recruited and supervised the director. When the director learned of the firing and replacement of the representative, he indicated he would try working with the new representative; however, after asking for that individual to be replaced with someone he preferred and being refused, he complained he could not work with the designated replacement and quit the production company. His refusal to work with the replacement representative was held to repudiate the contract. The potential for a change in his supervisor was a hazard to the director because the new supervisor might be more difficult to work for than the executive who hired him. That harm occurred when a new supervisor was appointed with whom the director had difficulty working. The director assumed responsibility for the risk that such hazard could occur unless he could approve the replacement supervisor or otherwise terminate the contract upon the appointment of a new supervisor. He had neither of such rights.

PERFORMANCE RISK MANAGEMENT

The primary purposes of managing performance risks are

- to allocate responsibility for the uncertainty that occurs when conditions and contingencies indicate that an obligor may be sliding toward an unwillingness or inability to perform or will incompetently perform,
- to reduce the chance of an obligor's failing to perform, and
- once such failure occurs, to reduce the losses the obligee ultimately suffers therefrom.

in respect to the Literary Work at the time of the making of this agreement"—had been deleted during negotiation, the company argued the publisher could not terminate. The company moved for summary judgment, based in part on the deletion of the quoted clause, but the motion was denied because the court had not received any evidence explaining the deletion.

[39] 725 F. Supp. 189 (S.D.N.Y. 1989).

Performance Risk Allocation

Information and Assumption Risk Allocation. The chance that a party may be mistaken about its or the other party's willingness or ability to perform is managed like other information and assumption risks. By committing to perform, an obligor assumes responsibility for the risk that it is not then willing or may later become unwilling to perform. It also assumes responsibility for the risk it may be laboring under incorrect information, have incorrectly processed good information, or made an incorrect assumption about its ability to perform or its capability of later acquiring such ability. *Sassower*[40] and *Trans World Airlines*[41] illustrate the allocation of responsibility for such risks to the obligor. Responsibility for that risk allocation is modified when the unilateral or mutual mistake doctrine applies, and the obligor is permitted to terminate the contract. The textbook case *Couturier v. Hastie*[42] illustrates such an allocation of responsibility: A factor sold a cargo of corn shipped for delivery in London and described as "of average quality," when at the time the cargo no longer existed because it had been removed while the vessel was in Tunis, having deteriorated while en route; the seller was held not liable for breach because at the time of sale it could not and did not know that the cargo no longer existed. *Bliven*[43] illustrates an allocation of responsibility for an incorrect assumption about the obligor's willingness and ability to the obligee.

The risk allocations previously described can be modified still further by a warranty that the obligor will perform or has certain or all of the resources it needs to perform or a disclaimer that it does not. The warrantor assumes responsibility for the risk it does or will not have the ability, and the obligee, by accepting the disclaimer, assumes responsibility for the risk the obligor does not have whatever is disclaimed.

Gulf Oil Corporation v. Federal Power Commission[44] illustrates how a warranty that an obligor can or will perform trumps its claim it labored under a mistake of fact concerning its ability to perform. A gas supplier

---

[40] See text accompanying notes 21–23.

[41] See text accompanying notes 10 and 11.

[42] 8 Exch. 40; 155 ER 1250, 22 L.J. (Ex.) 97 (1852); reversed sub nom. Hastie v. Couturier, 9 Exch. 102, 156 ER 43 (1853); *aff'd* 5 H.L. Cas. 673; 10 ER 1065, 25 L.J. (ex.) 253; 28 L.T. (O.S.) 240; 2 Jur. (N.S.) 1241 H.L.; 12 Digest (Repl.) 414 (1856).

[43] See text accompanying note 25.

[44] 563 F.2d 588 (3d Cir. 1977).

dedicated a gas field to a contract to sell gas and warranted to its buyer "to have available for delivery . . . on any day or days" a minimum quantity of gas. Both it and the buyer wrongly assumed the reserves in the field from which it expected to supply gas would be sufficient. The seller lacked the ability to produce sufficient gas from the field as it had assumed. Upon discovering the error, the supplier claimed it was entitled to relief on the basis of mutual mistake of fact. The court dismissed the supplier's argument: "We believe that the existence of a warranty as to the availability of gas completely forecloses equitable relief based on a mistake as to the availability of gas."[45] The court did not discuss if the mutual mistake doctrine would have otherwise excused the supplier's supply shortage. The supplier also claimed the impracticability of performance doctrine applied. Again, the court held the warranty precluded the excuse.[46] If either doctrine had applied, the warranty overrode the excuse and preserved the allocation of responsibility to the gas supplier.

Uncertainty Risk Mitigation. Terms and principles comparable to those that manage the uncertainty risks described in chapter 5 manage the risks that a condition or contingency has on or may adversely affect an obligor's willingness or ability to perform. Such principles include those that enable an obligee to decide when an obligor has partially and materially breached, anticipatorily breached, and repudiated a contract and allow it to respond to such incidents and other incidents that fall short of breach, anticipatory breach, and repudiation. Contractual terms that state when incidents are breaches and how an obligee may respond to them supplement such principles.

An obligee has two broad strategies for managing uncertainty performance risks: first, the contract can reserve to the obligee as much discretion as the obligor will allow for the obligee to decide from time to time that an action must be taken and what actions shall be taken to prevent or respond to incidents that portend a breach. As discussed in chapter 5, this is the preferred method of managing uncertainty risks, though it allocates responsibility for risk to the party not making the decisions the risk that the obligee will decide adversely in ways unexpected. Second, the contract can state what actions and incidents

---

[45] *Id.* at 600.

[46] *Id.*

will constitute breaches and the remedies to which the obligee may resort to prevent and respond to the same. The strategies may be combined.

The following are two cases that illustrate such strategies, stating when incidents are breaches and granting the obligee discretion to determine when a breach has occurred.

- *R.W. Power Partners, L.P. v. Virginia Electric and Power Co.*[47]: A contract obligated a power generator, which sold electricity to a utility to maintain a standby letter of credit in the agreed amount at all times as security for its obligations to the utility. The first letter of credit was issued by a bank for the first year and renewed by that bank for the second. That bank decided not to renew the credit for the third year, and it expired without a replacement. Five days later, the utility terminated the contract, citing a clause that allowed it to do so if the generator failed to "perform any of its obligations." The following day the new issuer delivered the letter of credit to the utility.[48] That letter of credit did not allow the beneficiary to draw on a bank in Virginia, as required; the credit was amended the next day. The generator's efforts to replace the letter of credit, its performance, had been incompetently executed, but delays notwithstanding, no harm had come to the utility or was imminent when it terminated the contract. Had the contract been read literally to allow the utility to terminate for such a breach, as the utility claimed, the utility would have achieved a high level of certainty about when it had a right to terminate. The generator would have assumed responsibility for the risk any minor breach, even one that did not indicate a loss was likely, could result in its loss of its investment in the transaction. In fact, the contract was no longer financially desirable to the utility, which wanted to terminate it. By reading the contract to allow the utility to terminate only when it suffered actual harm from a breach, as the generator successfully claimed, uncertainty about when a partial breach might indicate a potential material breach and stipulated as a ground for terminating the contract crept back into the contract. The utility would have to wait until a breach could or was likely to result in the loss of the anticipated benefits,

47 899 F. Supp. 1490 (E.D. Va. 1995).

48 The generator successfully sued for declaratory relief that the contract had been wrongfully terminated. The court held the utility could not terminate as it purported to do.

and this it could not do because a new letter of credit was about to be issued.[49]

- *Indiana v. International Business Machine Corp.*[50]: A state agency contracted with IBM to

> establish centralized service and call centers for the processing of welfare applications, enable remote electronic access to the system, provide the [s]tate a paperless document system, create systems to combat fraud and improve Indiana's poor welfare-to-work record and lower administrative costs.[51]

Twenty-seven months after signing the contract, the state requested IBM to adopt a "corrective action plan" to resolve 36 "issues" with its performance:

> excessive wait times at local offices and for appointments, incorrectly categorized imaged documents, high staff turnover, inaccurate and incomplete data gathering, scheduling problems, clients not receiving mailed correspondence, poor communication to all staff, unresolved help-ticket requests and untimely application and redetermination processing times.[52]

Four months later, the agency and IBM agreed on such a plan. Two months later, the agency concluded that while IBM had improved its technology and added more staff, it had not improved the timeliness of processing applications for food stamps, Medicaid, and other benefits. A month later, the agency terminated the contract for cause. The contract, referring to the state's anticipated

---

49 "It is undisputed that [the utility] . . . suffered no damage as a consequence of the fact that there was no letter of credit in place from June 30, 1995 to July 6, 1995 and that injury, actual or potential, to [the utility] . . . in consequence of the breach was not considered in deciding to terminate the Agreement." *Id.* at 1494.

50 4 N.E.3d 696 (Ind. App. 2014), Med & Med GD (CCH) P 304, 801, *aff'd* in part, vacated in part, 51 N.E.3d 150 (Ind. 2016).

51 *Id.* at 153.

52 *Id.* at 156.

benefits as "policy objectives," elaborated upon their meaning and stated eight "standards" by which performance would be measured. One such standard was the "[d]etermination by the State of [IBM]'s satisfactory performance of the Services and the Delegated Activities." The agency could terminate the contract for convenience or cause, in the latter case for material breach. In particular, a material breach included:

> a series of breaches of [IBM]'s obligations, none of which individually, constitutes a breach of this Agreement which is material considering this Agreement as a whole, but which, in view of [IBM]'s history of breaches, whether or not cured, collectively constitute a breach of this Agreement which is material when considering this Agreement as a whole.[53]

Whereas the parties may have been uncertain about the extent to which partial breaches could justify termination by the state, the clause empowered the state to decide when termination was justified. The clause also allowed the state to focus on partial breaches to the exclusion of the benefits the agency received from IBM's otherwise satisfactory performance. IBM was clearly doing something right, though not everything. As the state claimed, it could ignore those benefits and focus on IBM's shortcomings, the cumulative effect of which could be interpreted as an indication that ineptness on IBM's part might well continue. By accepting the provision, IBM assumed responsibility for the risk that its minor breaches could, when accumulated and determined by the state in the exercise of its discretion, entitle the state to terminate even though the state was realizing the material benefits of its contract.[54]

---

[53] *Id.* at 155.

[54] The agency sued for breach of contract. The trial court found the agency failed to prove that IBM materially breached the contract and that IBM had substantially performed the contract. The state appeal court reversed the trial court on the material breach issue, finding that IBM materially breached the contract. The Indiana Supreme Court held the trial court erred in finding that IBM had not materially breached the contract, as it ignored evidence that the agency was dissatisfied with IBM's performance.

Mitigation of Risk of Breach

The risk that an obligor will fail to perform a task can be reduced or eliminated by the following:

- completion of that task before contract formation,
- substituting a third party for the obligor to complete that task,
- having a third party commit to perform that task when the obligor fails, and
- regulating the obligor's actions to preserve its willingness and ability to perform that task.

Advance Performance. Performance risks can be mitigated or eliminated by having an obligor complete some or all of its performance before or when the contract is executed. Full performance before or concurrently with contract formation assures the obligee at the time that nothing further remains to be done by its counterparty.

The following are examples of such advance performance:

- payment in full of the premium on an insurance policy for the term of coverage before the policy is issued,[55]
- payment in full of the price of goods to be delivered or land to be conveyed before the goods or land are delivered,[56] and
- payment of the freight for shipping goods before the goods are accepted by the carrier.[57]

---

55 "The reports are replete with instances where company agents, as here, obtained payment of the full annual premium in advance on the broad representation that there would be interim coverage pending the company's investigation of the application and its action thereon." Allen v. Metropolitan Life Ins. Co., 44 N.J. 294, 208 A.2d 638 (N.J. 1965).

56 *E.g.*, Catalano, Inc. v. Target Sales, Inc., 446 U.S. 643,100 S. Ct. 1925, 64 L. Ed. 2d 580 (1980), where beer wholesalers were liable under antitrust laws for price-fixing for allegedly agreeing to require their buyers to pay in advance for wholesale beer deliveries.

57 "As a general rule, the carrier has the option to demand payment of freight in advance or on delivery. And, as there is a lien on the goods to secure the payment of charges, it is often a matter of indifference whether the freight is collected at the beginning or at the end of the transportation." Wadley Southern Railway Co. v. Georgia, 235 U.S. 651, 59 L. Ed. 405, 35 S. Ct. 214 (1915).

When an obligor cannot rescind the contract and recover such a payment, breach and repudiation are impossible. Obligor performance risks—intent not to pay and inability to pay—have been eliminated.

Partial completion before or at contract formation can also mitigate counterparty performance risk: the risks are eliminated to the extent of such performance at such time and continue to the extent such performance remains uncompleted. Down payments on the price of goods or land or rent for space are common examples. The higher the down payment proportion of the total price, the greater is the reduction of the counterparty performance risks.

Before or at contract formation, payment in full into a trust or escrow from which funds are to be released upon satisfaction of agreed conditions also mitigates performance risks. A three-party agreement identifies the obligor who has deposited funds into the escrow; it identifies a stakeholder, a trustee or escrow agent, which holds the escrowed fund, and obligates it to disburse such funds according to the terms of that agreement to the obligor, obligee, or both; and it entitles the obligee to receive such funds when the escrow agent must disburse them. Because the obligor must deposit funds into the escrow before or at contract formation, the risk that it will fail to make such payment is eliminated. Risks still exist, however: an obligor who breaches might dispute the obligee's right to keep any deposit or down payment as unenforceable liquidated damages, and an obligor or a third party might dispute an obligee's right to receive payment from the escrow fund, blocking such payment until the dispute is resolved. The escrow agent may fail to perform the escrow agreement.

Substitute for Obligor Performance. Performance risks can be mitigated by removing the obligor as the party expected to perform one more tasks and having either the obligee or a third party—one who would perform the task anyway or who is considered at least as reliable as the obligor—assume responsibility for completion of such tasks. Common arrangements for redirecting performance are as follows:

- A payment or performance a third party would make to an obligor is redirected to an obligee.
- A payment that an obligee would make to an obligor that, in turn, would perform by paying a third party is redirected to that third party.

The third party's performance in the first instance and the obligee's in the second substitute for the obligor's. The risk that an obligor does or will not have the will or ability to perform is entirely eliminated. The simplicity of the arrangement is that the third party and obligee assume very little additional responsibility: they are already obligated to make the payment, and that obligation is slightly modified by redirecting payments to an obligee or third party.

The following illustrate such arrangements and some of the risks they create.

- *Bituminous Construction, Inc. v. Rucker Enterprises, Inc.*[58]: An owner agreed with a subcontractor to make checks payable to both the contractor and subcontractor. When the owner settled litigation with the contractor by paying the latter the agreed amount, it breached its agreement with the subcontractor, which had not been paid in full under the subcontract. The arrangement protected the subcontractor against diversion by the contractor of payments received from the owner. The owner assumed responsibility for an incremental risk: that it would forget to make the checks payable to both the contractor and subcontractor.
- *In re Halmar Distributors*[59]: A lender required that a borrower's customers make their payments directly to a lockbox under the control of the lender. Such payments included proceeds from the sale of products supplied by a supplier that retained a security interest therein. When the supplier learned of the lockbox, it successfully claimed the lender, by controlling the lockbox, had converted the proceeds of collateral in which it had a security interest.[60] The customers assumed responsibility for the incremental risk they might mistakenly pay the borrower. The lockbox thus protected the lender against diversion by the borrower of payments from its customers but not against the supplier's claim. That was a separate risk, discussed in chapter 11.[61]

---

58 816 F.2d 965 (4th Cir. 1987).

59 968 F.2d 121 (1st Cir. 1992).

60 The bankruptcy court ruled in favor of the lender; the supplier successfully appealed. The court held that the supplier had revived the seniority of its security interest in the products it supplied and the proceeds thereof in the lockbox when it objected to the deposit of proceeds from the sale of its products into the lockbox.

61 See text accompanying ch. 11, notes 134–36.

- *McDraw, Inc. v. CIT Group Equipment Financing, Inc.*[62]: A lender and borrower agreed the former would directly pay the borrower's supplier the purchase price for equipment the lender would buy from and lease back to the borrower but would not assume any of the borrower's obligations to the supplier. Before the supplier received the final payment, the borrower defaulted under its agreement with the lender, which refused further advances and eventually foreclosed on the equipment.[63] The arrangement mitigated the risk that the lender would make loans to a borrower that was in default and eliminated any risk the borrower would divert payments intended for the equipment supplier.

A third party can also be brought into the transaction to perform a duty, the obligor's duty, it would not otherwise have to perform. Such a third party contracts with the obligee and thereby assumes an obligation to the obligee it would not have otherwise but for its participation in the arrangement that substitutes for the obligor's performance. Payment through a documentary letter of credit is an example: the issuer of the credit had no obligation to pay the beneficiary before issuing the credit. Payment by the issuer to the beneficiary upon a draw under the credit substitutes for payment by the obligor. The issuer is brought into the transaction to eliminate the risk the obligor account party may be unwilling or unable to pay when payment is due.

However, because a letter of credit or similar instrument is a contract between the issuer and the beneficiary thereof, the demand for payment thereunder must comply with the conditions stated therein. The obligee, as beneficiary under the credit, thus assumes responsibility for a new risk: that its demand thereunder for payment might not comply with such conditions, that the issuer might wrongfully refuse to pay, or a combination of both. In principle, such refusal could be due to an unwillingness or inability to pay, though most often it is due to ineptness in performing under the credit. Responsibility for one set of risks is swapped for another: obligor unwillingness and inability to pay risks are traded for the risks of obligee ineptness in presenting its demand under

[62] 157 F.3d 956 (2d Cir. 1998).

[63] The supplier sued the lender for the final payment, claiming the lender had been unjustly enriched by its supply of the equipment; the lender moved to dismiss, which motion was granted; and the appeal court affirmed.

the credit and the issuer's unwillingness, inability, and ineptness. Such trade is rarely considered a bad one for an obligee.

Philadelphia Gear Corp. v. Central Bank[64] illustrates such a risk swap. A bank issued a documentary letter of credit for the account of a buyer in favor of a seller of goods. The seller demanded payment under the credit for goods it claimed were delivered. Payment was refused because the demand did not conform to the terms of the letter of credit. The defects in such demand, however, were curable, but the bank kept the documents. The bank had been substituted for the buyer as payor for the goods, eliminating the risk the buyer would fail to pay, but creating risks that the seller would fail to demand payment in accordance with the credit and that the bank would incompetently process that demand.[65]

Guaranties. A third party can assume secondary responsibility for performance by an obligor by agreeing to perform when the obligor repudiates or fails to perform. Responsibility is secondary because the obligor remains responsible for the initial performance of the obligations and the third party is obligated to perform only after the primary obligor repudiates or breaches the contract. The most common examples of such third-party responsibility are guaranties and surety bonds: A guaranty is "[a] promise to answer for the payment of some debt, or the performance of some duty, in case of the failure of another who is liable in the first instance; a collateral undertaking by one person to be answerable for the payment of some debt or performance of some duty or contract for another who stands first bound to pay or perform."[66]

A guarantor or the like is brought into the transaction by a fresh agreement, such as a guaranty, and the obligee must comply with whatever conditions it includes to make a demand for performance thereunder by the guarantor or surety. Unlike a third party's performance described in the preceding paragraphs that eliminates or reduces the occurrence

64 717 F.2d 230 (5th Cir. 1983).

65 The seller sued the bank. The district court found that, notwithstanding that the demand did not conform as the bank concluded, the bank was liable because the defects in such demand were curable and the bank kept the documents. The appeal court reversed, holding that since a condition of the bank's obligation to pay was tender of documents that strictly conformed, the district court erred in finding the bank liable.

66 Black's Law Dictionary, *supra* note 1, 821.

of a breach, a guarantor, surety, or issuer does not become obligated to perform until after the breach occurs. Such an instrument does not eliminate the risk of repudiation or breach; it reduces the losses the obligee may suffer as a result of the breach. A reliable third party is added to the parties to which the obligee has recourse to mitigate such losses. The addition of a reputable third party as a guarantor, such as a bank, financial institution, or government or international agency, may deter or help to deter an obligor from repudiating or breaching a contract, as the obligor will desire to preserve its reputation among such institutions and agencies.

Private Regulation. A contract can burden an obligor with commitments to do what is necessary or helpful to acquire and maintain its willingness and ability to perform. The obligor thereby promises to take actions that are expected to avoid the occurrence of performance hazards, acts that could dissipate the obligor's willingness and ability. Unlike tasks that when completed contribute to realization of desired benefits by the obligee, the completion of regulatory tasks does not directly contribute to the realization of benefits; such completion preserves or facilitates the acquisition of the ability and willingness to complete such tasks. A breach of a regulatory covenant is an indicator the obligor may or will be unwilling or unable to perform when performance is due. Examples of activities that are occasionally regulated by outright prohibition or other restrictions include

- going out of business and liquidation, which eliminate ability to perform;
- transferring all or substantially all the obligor's assets;
- transferring the material resources that are expected to be used to perform;
- granting security to creditors in its assets, which will give some creditors priority over others and reduce the assets from which the obligee may be able to recover; and
- paying dividends to shareholders, which diverts cash that can be used to pay an obligee or other creditors or otherwise to fund the costs of performance.

A description of the appropriate regulatory covenants for any specific or type of transaction are beyond the scope of this text.

Prohibitions on Assignments and Changes of Control. Regulatory covenants and conditions subsequent are the principal terms by which changes of or in parties are regulated. The most common covenants and conditions include

- a prohibition of the assignment by an obligor of the contract or any interest therein;
- a condition subsequent that states a change of control of the obligor entitles the obligee to terminate the contract or to declare the obligor to have breached or defaulted and to exercise remedies; and
- a prohibition of any change in the obligor's personnel responsible for its performance.

As discussed in chapter 7, such regulation is important to a party when the other party has discretionary decision-making powers under a contract, as such regulation may enable such party to control who has or determines the use of those powers. Regulation is also important to an obligee, as it can also help ensure that when an obligor or control or the key personnel of an obligor has been changed, the obligor will be no less willing and able to perform than before such changes were made.

The following cases illustrate how such prohibitions may be structured and applied:

- *James v. Whirlpool Corp.*[67]: A distribution agreement that was annually renewed required the manufacturer Whirlpool's approval of any changes in the distributor's direct or indirect ownership, management, or control. Another clause allowed Whirlpool, upon a change of control or management of the distributor, to treat the contract as terminated. Whirlpool tightly regulated with whom it did business by reserving the right to terminate annually and by reserving the right to approve transfers of interests in its distributors. A distributor notified Whirlpool that its owners proposed selling its shares and requested Whirlpool's consent, which was refused. At the end of the year, Whirlpool

[67] 806 F. Supp. 835, 839 (E.D. Mo. 1992).

refused to renew the contract.[68] The contract was an asset of the distributor, the value of which could be realized only by a transfer of the contract or sale of the company, allowed only with Whirlpool's consent. Whirlpool could thus deprive the distributor of all value in its contract by refusing its consent. It could also do so by refusing to renew the contract. Responsibility for both risks was assumed by the distributor.

- *Carte Blanche (Singapore) Pte Ltd. v. Carte Blanche International, Ltd.*[69]: A franchise agreement prohibited assignment by either party and required the franchisor's consent for "any transfer of shares within the family of companies belonging to the [named] . . . group." Some of the franchisee's shareholders transferred their shares to a family holding company, and that holding company's shares were transferred to a publicly listed company in Malaysia. The franchisor notified the franchisee that the transfers breached the anti-assignment and share restriction clauses and filed for arbitration. Like the contract in the previous case, the franchise agreement was an asset of the franchisee, the value of which could only be realized by the transfer of that agreement or shares in the franchisee, allowed only with the franchisor's approval. If, as the franchisor claimed, any share transfer breached the covenant, the franchisor enjoyed tight control over who the franchisee included as its owners. But, as the franchisee successfully claimed, transfers within the family did not materially breach the covenant, the franchisor controlled only material changes in the franchisee. The implication was that the franchisor assumed responsibility for the risk of immaterial ownership changes in the franchisee notwithstanding language to the contrary in the franchise agreement.[70]

68 The distributor sued, claiming the refusal of the consent to the sale of its shares breached the contract. Both partiers sought summary judgment. The court granted Whirlpool's motion and denied the distributor's. The court said, "The Agreement does not require Whirlpool to provide justification for its decision to reject transfer." *Id.*

69 888 F.2d 260 (2d Cir. 1989).

70 The arbitrators held that the ownership transfers did not constitute breaches or were immaterial or had been waived. The court affirmed these findings, holding that a share transfer did not violate the antiassignment clause. The court also held a transfer of shares within the family of companies without the required consent was not a material breach and did not justify termination of the contract.

Mitigation of Losses

Mitigation of damages is a legal doctrine that "induc[es] a plaintiff, after an injury or breach of contract to make reasonable efforts to alleviate the effects of an injury or breach."[71] Independent of such duty, an obligee might plan its efforts to minimize the losses it could suffer from a failed transaction and, to the extent permitted, to maximize its recovery of compensation from the breaching party.

Self-Help Remedies. A self-help remedy is defined as "[an] attempt to redress a perceived wrong by one's own action rather than through the normal legal process."[72] The advantage to an obligee of such remedies is that because their exercise is outside the legal process, the obligee, not the courts or other official or institution, controls the execution of the process and has the potential to save time and cost since the legal process is usually more cumbersome and expensive.

Such actions include:

- suspension of performance, defined, in part, as "[an] act of temporarily delaying, interrupting, or terminating something,"[73]
- set-off, defined, in part, as "[a] debtor's right to reduce the amount of a debt by any sum the creditor owes the debtor; the counterbalancing sum owed by the creditor,"[74]
- step-in rights, defined as performance by the obligee or its representative for the benefit of the obligor an obligation it failed to perform or ineptly performed,
- enforcement of security or foreclosure, defined as "[to] terminate a mortgagor's interest in property,"[75] and
- termination of the contract, defined as the "act of ending something."[76]

[71] Black's Law Dictionary, *supra* note 1, 1154.
[72] *Id.* at 1566.
[73] *Id.* at 1676.
[74] *Id.* at 1581.
[75] *Id.* at 762.
[76] *Id.* at 1700.

The following illustrate such self-help remedies:

- *Clem Marine Towing, Inc. v. Panama Canal Co.*[77] illustrates a right to suspend performance, which right was implied: The lessee of a vessel learned the lessor had missed a payment on the leased vessel mortgage and had encumbered the vessel with two additional mortgages. The lessee, concerned that it would not be able to buy the vessel when it exercised its purchase option, notified the lessor it was suspending payments until it received assurances the lessor was able to pay its mortgage payments.[78]
- *In re SemCrude, L.P.*[79] illustrates the exercise of broad setoff rights. The contracts between a refiner and service provider and three subsidiaries of the parent debtor provided

> in the event either party fails to make a timely payment of monies due and owing to the other party, or in the event either party fails to make timely delivery of product or crude oil due and owing to the other party, the other party may offset any deliveries or payments due under this or any other Agreement between the parties and their affiliates.

When the service provider and its subsidiaries filed for bankruptcy, the refiner owed $1,405,878.40 to one subsidiary and was owed $3,302,806.03 and $10,228,439.34 by two other subsidiaries, respectively. The refiner applied to the bankruptcy court to set off

---

77 730 F.2d 186 (5th Cir. 1984).

78 The lessor filed suit for the missed payment. The lessee, as provided in the lease, tendered the purchase price for the vessel at the end of the lease, subject to the lessor providing merchantable title; the lessor failed to respond. The mortgagees holding the vessel mortgages notified the lessee they intended to foreclose on the vessel; the lessee purchased the mortgages. The district court awarded judgment against the lessee, who appealed; and the appeal court reversed, holding that under Uniform Commercial Code section 2-609, "[the lessee] PCC need only prove it had reasonable doubt that [the lessor] CPMT would provide merchantable title, and need not prove, for example, that CPMT was insolvent, so long as the doubt is otherwise reasonable." *Id.* at 189. The court held the clause providing "Payment of Charter Hire shall not be foregone or suspended by reason of the happening of any event whatsoever except a total loss of the Vessel" was subject to the lessee's right to suspend performance.

79 399 B.R. 388, 171 Oil & Gas Rep. 646, 51 Bankr. Ct. Dec. 20, Bank. L. Rep. P.81 (Bankr. Del. 2009).

what it was owed by the debtor against what it owed the debtor's affiliates. The court denied the petition on the grounds that the debts were not "mutual debts" within the meaning of section 553 of the Bankruptcy Code, as only debts owing to and from the same persons are mutual. Nevertheless, such triangular setoff rights might be permissible when the party against whom such rights are exercised is not insolvent.

- *Charter Practices International, LLC v. Robb,*[80] which is summarized in chapter 3,[81] illustrates step-in rights to operate a business: A "charter practice" or franchise agreement for a pet hospital provided:

  > In order to prevent any interruption of the operation of the Hospital that would cause harm to the Hospital or to the reputation of the Network, You [the franchisee] authorize [the franchisor] CPI or its designee to step in to operate the Hospital if, in CPI's reasonable judgment: . . . CPI decides that significant operational problems exist which require CPI to operate the Hospital for a time.

  The franchisor moved for a temporary restraining order to prevent a franchisee interfering with its taking over the franchisee's operations in response to the practice of administering half-doses of vaccines and using the remaining dose on other animals. The order was granted. The case also illustrates how an obligee may have to resort to legal process to exercise a step-in right when the obligor resists the same.

- *Jackson Trak Group, Inc. v. Mid States Port Authority*[82] illustrates step-in rights exercised to remedy defective construction work. In reliance upon the following provision in a contract for construction work, the owner seized equipment belonging to the contractor:

  > OWNER MAY CORRECT DEFECTIVE WORK. If contractor fails within a reasonable time after written notice of ENGINEER to proceed to correct and to correct defective

[80] 2014 WL 273855 (D. Conn. 2013).

[81] See text accompanying ch. 3, note 28.

[82] 242 Kan. 683, 751 P.2d 122 (Kan. 1988).

> Work or to remove and replace rejected Work as required by ENGINEER in accordance with paragraph 00713.11, or if CONTRACTOR fails to perform the work in accordance with the Contract Documents (including any requirements of the Progress schedule), OWNER may, after seven days' written notice to CONTRACTOR, correct and remedy any such deficiency. . . . To the extent necessary to complete corrective and remedial action, OWNER may exclude CONTRACTOR from all or part of the site, take possession of all or part of the Work, and suspend CONTRACTOR'S SERVICES RELATED THERETO, TAKE POSSESSION OF CONTRACTOR'S tools, appliances, construction equipment stored at the site or for which owner has paid CONTRACTOR but which are stored elsewhere. CONTRACTOR shall allow OWNER, OWNER'S representatives, agents, and employees such access to the site as may be necessary to enable OWNER to exercise his rights under this paragraph.

While the authority had given notice to the contractor to correct defective work, the contractor disputed that the work was defective and ultimately prevailed in arbitration.

Security. Security can serve as an obligee's sword, ensuring that assets will be available for recovery by the obligee should it have to recover compensation from the obligor. Enforcement of security is also a self-help remedy when the obligee can seize and sell the collateral without legal process. Security also serves as a shield, earmarking and protecting from the claims of the obligor's other creditors assets to pay the obligee's claims; security protects the priority of its claim relative to other creditors. Security thus mitigates the risks that the obligee will not recover compensation due it and that other creditors will reduce that recovery.

The greater the ease with which collateral may be liquidated, the more attractive as security it will be to the obligee. Cash and cash equivalents held by an obligee will be the most attractive security because the obligee has little more to do than apply such cash to the amounts owed to it by the obligor. Cash and cash equivalents held by a third party as a stakeholder will be a slightly less effective self-help remedy because, while the collateral is still liquid, the terms on which the stakeholder is permitted to use or release the cash will likely restrict the obligee's ability to receive payment.[83] Marketable securities will be slightly less liquid, only because they must be sold before cash is available to apply to the obligations. The risk is that such securities will be difficult to liquidate or realize less value than expected. An account or other debt owed by a third party to an obligor in which the obligee has security is less liquid than marketable securities because the account debtor's obligation, willingness, and ability to pay will be uncertain until a demand for payment is made. Still, such collateral is relatively liquid because self-help is limited to notifying the account debtor that payment should be made to the obligee and collecting payment if the account debtor fails to pay. The number of obligors and difficulty collecting payment will increase the effort required by the obligee and make the remedy less attractive.

Other intangible assets, such as patents, trademarks, copyrights, trade secrets, licenses to use the foregoing, licenses to operate a business, and securities not traded on a market, will be less liquid because an effort to locate a buyer will have to be made, and their disposition may be subject to rules that ensure their value is realized. Moveable tangible assets with a ready market, such as nonperishable inventory, equipment, and consumer goods, such as motor vehicles, may be attractive collateral because a ready market of buyers exists; however, potential difficulties locating, collecting, and selling such collateral may be subject to restrictions that make such items less attractive. Other moveable tangible assets, such as artworks, may be less liquid and require more effort to sell. Immoveable assets, such as real property and land, may also have a market in which disposition may be easily carried out but the rules for disposition may restrict how a sale is conducted and may limit the obligee's recourse for any deficiency following the sale. Disposition of a large infrastructure project may be possible in a limited market, making the task of enforcing security daunting. Collateral that requires a special license to own, use, or operate, such as a business selling alcoholic beverages or operating

---

[83] *E.g.*, In re Milano Textiles, Inc., 38 B.R. 964 (Bankr. D. Mass. 1984), where a debtor's funds were ordered by a court to be held in escrow in a bank account in the name of one of the secured parties, who paid its attorney fees from the account without authorization from the court. The debtor claimed the payment was an improper use of the funds in the account, and the bankruptcy court agreed, finding, "It is clear from the terms of the intercreditor agreement and the court order that all five secured lenders had an interest in the collateral and that the court did not want the money disbursed until their respective rights could be determined." *Id.* at 967.

a television or radio station or a pharmaceutical business will have a limited market of potential buyers and additional regulatory hurdles to be overcome for enforcement of security. The risk mitigation effected by security depends on the value relative to the debt to be collected and the liquidity of the collateral.

However, because security is always enforced to pay a debt, that debt must be liquidated. A debt is liquidated when its amount has been determined by agreement or by operation of law.[84] An obligation to repay a loan is nearly always liquidated because the amount of the debt is easily calculated; if the maturity of the debt can be accelerated, the debt will include the unpaid principal balance of the loan, accrued and unpaid interest thereon, and any unpaid fees and costs that the obligor is obligated to pay. When a secured obligation is the payment of damages that flow from a breach of contract, the amount of such damages may not always be liquidated at the time of breach because the amount of such damages may be uncertain; the amount of the debt to be paid from the security will be unknown. In the absence of obtaining a judgment or arbitral award for the damages resulting from the default, the obligee will have to estimate the amount it is owed. It runs the risk of demanding too much or too little when seeking to enforce its security. One solution is to agree on the amount of the liquidated damages at contract formation, thus eliminating the uncertainty about the amount that will be owed upon breach or repudiation and that can be realized through enforcement of the security. Because liquidated damage clauses are not always effective, the use of such a clause to liquidate the damages may trade uncertainty over what is owed for uncertainty over whether the liquidated damages clause is effective; the liquidated damages clause may swap one uncertainty risk for another. The risks associated with liquidated damages provisions are discussed in the chapter 9.[85]

Suspension and Termination. By suspending its commitment in response to a performance hazard, an obligee can avoid or minimize further investment in a transaction until it has determined the obligor is willing and able to perform. By terminating its commitment in response to a performance hazard, an obligee stops all further investment in the transaction. As previously discussed, the contract must either vest discretion in the obligee to decide when a hazard has occurred that

[84] BLACK'S LAW DICTIONARY, *supra* note 1, 489.

[85] See text accompanying ch. 9, notes 2–16.

permits it to suspend or terminate or describe clearly the incidents that will permit it to do so. The longer an obligee must wait to decide if a performance hazard will result in inability or unwillingness to perform, the more difficult it may be to avoid the breach and the resulting losses. A contractual term that allows an obligee to declare breach sooner rather than later enables it to reduce the chance of not realizing its desired benefits and the extent of its losses. For example, if the general contractor in *McCloskey & Co.*[86] had the right to declare the subcontractor in breach and terminate at the first sign that the subcontractor was having difficulty, it would have been able to bring in replacement suppliers and subcontractors and complete the project on time, thus realizing the benefits it expected to realize from the subcontract. At the same time, a term that allows the obligee to declare a breach and terminate after waiting for events to more clearly demonstrate a loss of willingness or ability allocates to it responsibility for the risk of waiting for so long and no longer: the loss of potential benefits may become irreversible with the passage of the period the obligee must wait. It also allocates to the obligor responsibility for the risk that it may be able to retrieve itself and complete performance when due. The obligor assumes responsibility for this risk when the contract allows the obligee to declare a breach and terminate before the loss of willingness or ability is irreversible.

[86] See text accompanying notes 26 and 27.

9

Liability Risks

LIABILITY HAZARDS

An obligee who expects to realize a specified amount of value from a transaction will expect compensation at least in that amount from its obligor when the latter's breach causes an unsuccessful outcome and loss of such value. If, at contract formation, the extent of those damages cannot be determined because conditions and contingencies are unknown at that time, then the compensation that the obligee may expect remains to be determined until the conditions are known and the contingencies have occurred; the damages are uncertain. When such damages are known, whether at contract formation or later, the applicable law may not allow the obligee to recover all its losses. Such damages are irrecoverable. At contract formation, the hazard to the obligee is the uncertainty of the damages it may recover for breach and the losses it may be unable to recover under applicable legal rules. Uncertainty is also a hazard to an obligor, because at contract formation it may be unable to determine the amount of its potential liability. The law also may allow the obligee to recover damages that the obligor did not anticipate could be awarded for breach of contract. The hazards to the obligor are damages that are uncertain or unexpectedly recoverable.

Inadequate and Excessive Compensation

The relief to which a party is entitled under the applicable law may fall short of or exceed that party's expectations. The relief falls short of expectation when the value of the relief available to a party injured by a breach of contract is less than the value it expected to realize and would have realized had the transaction been successfully completed. For example, in the textbook case *Hadley v. Baxendale,*[1] the owners of a flour mill in Gloucester lost five days' revenue because the carrier delayed delivery of their broken crank shaft to engineers in Greenwich but were not entitled to compensation for their lost profits, having not made the carrier aware that their mill was shut down until a new crank shaft was delivered. The owners were not entitled to compensation for value they expected to but did not realize because the operations resumed five days later than expected. The hazard to the mill owners was the limitation on the damages they could recover from the carrier for breach; the risk was the chance that they might suffer those losses.

The relief exceeds a defaulting party's expectation when the value of the relief available to a party injured by a breach of contract exceeds the losses the defaulting party expected the injured party to incur as a result of its default. For example, if, in *Hadley v. Baxendale,* the carrier had been held liable for the mill's lost profits, the mill owners would have received compensation for losses the carrier did not expect the mill owners to incur had the transaction been unsuccessful. The hazards are the discrepancies between the rules that determine the damages to which the injured party is entitled and either its expectations as to damages it should recover or the defaulting party's expectations as to the damages for which it should be liable. The hazards occur when the parties crystallize their expectations about such damages.

Uncertainty

At contract formation, the parties may or may not have sufficient information to forecast the losses that will likely result from an obligor's breach of contract. If a party has sufficient information, it should have reasonable certainty about the defaulting obligor's liability. Such obligor should be able to understand the extent of its potential liability and

[1] 9 Exch. 341, 23 L.J. (Ex.) 179, 23 L.T. (O.S.) 69, 18 Jur. 358, 2 W.R. 302, 2 C.L.R. 517, 17 Digest (Repl.) 91 (1854).

the obligee the extent of its potential losses and compensation. A party may have insufficient information to forecast such damages because the conditions and contingencies that will significantly affect the extent of the losses that result from a breach are unknown at contract formation and vary so widely that calculation of damages is not reducible to a formula. That information may or may not be available, depending upon whether the applicable conditions and contingencies are knowable at contract formation. An obligor, understanding uncertainty about forecasting the losses that result from breach, may have only vague expectations about its potential liability. An obligee, understanding this uncertainty, may have only vague expectations about its possible losses. Each party's expectations about liability and compensation might not crystallize before breach, at which time the parties are likely to disagree about the extent of losses and liability. Such uncertainty about liability and compensation is another instance of condition and contingency uncertainty and is a hazard to each party at contract formation.

An additional uncertainty that concerns litigants is the unpredictability of the cost of litigation or an arbitral proceeding and the amount of compensation that might be awarded as damages in a trial, by judge or jury, or an arbitral proceeding. The cost and effort required for a trial, arbitration, or other dispute resolution proceeding, which will depend upon the complexity of the dispute and the actions of the disputing parties, will be unknowable contingencies at contract formation. The potential for a dispute, taken together with the potential costs of resolving it, is a potential hazard at contract formation. The unpredictability of court, arbitration, and other decisions about compensation may be attributable to those institutions and not entirely to the peculiar facts or legal issues in the disputes. This is an instance of the uncertainty described in chapter 6: inept, biased, or corrupt administration of justice that undermines the certainty of legal rules and the parties' commitments in a contract. The solutions to that uncertainty risk, discussed in chapter 6, apply to the unpredictability of decisions about liability and compensation attributable to incompetent, biased, and corrupt administration of justice.

LIABILITY RISK MANAGEMENT

Contract law rules that govern the damages to which a party is entitled following a material breach by the other party allocate responsibility for the risk that its losses may exceed the amount of compensation to which it is entitled. To the extent effective, express terms in a contract can modify such risk allocation. An obligor assumes responsibility for the risk that damages that fall within the conditions and limits exceed the amount for which it anticipated it could and would be liable. The most common strategies for limiting liability, summarized in this chapter, include

- liquidated damages, which, when enforceable, stipulate the amount of compensation that the injured party may claim,
- damage exclusions, which limit or exclude types of damages for which recovery is permissible,
- remedy limitations and exclusions, which require that an obligee resort to specific remedies and not others,
- limits on money damages, within agreed bands or maximum amounts,
- limits on the persons and assets to which recourse for damages is permissible,
- private statutes of limitations that limit the periods within which claims must be asserted, and
- periodic releases, which extinguish claims that existed prior to the release.

Liquidated Damages

Liquidated damages, defined as "[a]n amount contractually stipulated as a reasonable estimation of actual damages to be recovered by one party if the other party breaches,"[2] can mitigate uncertainty about the damages that can be recovered for a breach of contract. At contract formation, the choice for each party is between continuing with that uncertainty and making assumptions about the conditions that will exist when a breach occurs and estimating the damages that will likely occur. The obligee trades responsibility for such uncertainty risk for another: responsibility for the risk that actual damages may be more than the agreed amount. The obligee self-insures its losses above the agreed amount when its recovery is limited to that amount. No such trade is made, however, when the obligee can recover the excess. The obligor trades uncertainty risk for another: the risk that actual damages will be less than the liquidated

---

[2] Black's Law Dictionary 473 (10th ed. 2014).

damages when it is liable for the stipulated amount notwithstanding such discrepancy. No such trade occurs when the obligor is not liable for the excess over actual damages.

The following cases illustrate such risk allocations:

- *Noble v. Ogborn*[3]: A contract for the sale of real property provided "In the event of default by Buyer, Seller shall have the election to retain the earnest money as liquidated damages, or to institute suit to enforce any right Seller has. . . ." After the buyer breached, the seller sued for $30,383.97 in damages instead of retaining the $1000 deposit. The seller, but not the buyer, mitigated its uncertainty risk, because the seller could elect to keep the deposit or sue for actual damages; the buyer had no such choice.[4]
- *Truck Rent-a-Center, Inc. v. Puritan Farms 2nd, Inc.*:[5] A truck lease provided:

> Upon termination of this agreement, . . . Lessor . . . shall be entitled to damages, herein liquidated for all purposes . . . as follows: (a) The sum of all rents designated as "Fixed Rental Charges" which would have become due under the normal operation of this agreement from the date of the said termination . . . including any effective renewal period; less (b) the re-rental value of said motor vehicles which is hereby agreed upon as fifty per cent (50 percent) of the sum of such "Fixed Rental Charges" as are set forth in subdivision "(a)" of this article.[6]

The lessee had an option to purchase the leased trucks, which at the time it wrongfully terminated the lease would have cost $48,134.17. Its liability for liquidated damages, however, was $92,341.79. Because the lessor's residual interest in the equipment was limited to the purchase price, the additional damages covered

---

[3] 43 Wash. App. 387, 717 P.2d 285 (Wash. App. 1986).

[4] The trial court awarded the seller $1000 plus attorney fees, and the seller appealed. The appeal court reversed, holding, "A liquidated damages clause does not preclude a party from suing for actual damages if that right is preserved in the contract between the parties." *Id.* at 390.

[5] 41 N.Y.2d 420, 393 NYS 2d 365, 361 NE 2d 1015 (N.Y. 1977).

[6] 41 N.Y.2d at 421, footnote 1.

by the liquidated damages clause were a windfall to the lessor. The clause mitigated uncertainty risk for both parties, but the lessee assumed responsibility for the risk its liability for liquidated damages could be more than the value of the lessor's residual interest at the time of breach.[7]

- *Vines v. Orchard Hills, Inc.*[8]: In 1973, a real property buyer paid $7,880 as a down payment on a purchase price of $78,700 but repudiated its obligation to pay the balance and take title to the land. The contract provided that the down payment could be retained by the seller as liquidated damages.[9] The buyer sued for his down payment to be refunded. In 1979, when the case came to trial, the property was valued at $160,000.[10] The value of the land in 1973, when the buyer repudiated, was relevant and if shown to be more than the price, would relieve the buyer of liability for damages. The liquidated damages clause operated as a limit on the buyer's liability: it could be liable for damages up to the deposit amount.[11]

Partial Breaches. A liquidated damages clause may estimate the damages an obligee suffers upon a breach that deprives it of the benefits of its bargain. This was achieved in *Noble*[12] and *Truck Rent-a-Center, Inc.*:[13] the seller in the first case hoped to realize the value of the land to be sold to the buyer, and the lessor in the second expected to realize the lease

---

7 The court held the purchase option was irrelevant to the validity of the liquidated damages provision, which was "related reasonably to potential harm that was difficult to estimate and did not constitute a disguised penalty." *Id.* at 427.

8 181 Conn. 501, 435 A. 2d 1022 (Conn. 1980).

9 "DEFAULT: In the event Purchaser fails to perform any of the obligations herein imposed on the Purchaser, the Seller performing all obligations herein imposed on the Seller, the Seller shall retain all sums of money paid under this Contract, as liquidated damages, and all rights and liabilities of the parties hereto shall be at an end." 181 Conn. at 503.

10 "The trial court relied on . . . [a $160,000 valuation in 1979] to conclude that, because the seller had gained what it characterized as a windfall of approximately $80,000, the purchasers were entitled to recover their down payment of $7880." *Id.*

11 The Connecticut Supreme Court reversed the trial court's decision, holding the buyer could submit evidence of the value of the property at the time of breach to show the seller had not suffered any loss.

12 See text accompanying notes 3 and 4.

13 See text accompanying notes 5–7.

rentals for the remainder of the lease term. Liquidated damages may also estimate the damages that result from a minor or partial breach—a partial failure to complete a task that is expected to contribute to benefit realization notwithstanding such failure or a failure to comply with a regulatory or other minor covenant. Late payment is an example of the former: the payee's damages are minor in comparison to no payment at all. Failure to deliver a notice is an example of the latter. Delay damages in a construction contract are another: late completion of a project does not necessarily substantially deprive the project owner of its anticipated benefits. Their true purpose may be to coerce performance or deter breach.

Following are two cases that illustrate the coercive character of liquidated damages for partial breaches.

- *Venitron Corp. v. CF 48 Associates*[14]: A lease provided for liquidated damages in the amount of one year's rent for any breach thereof. Since the clause covered partial and material breaches alike, the amount payable was not proportionate to all breaches.
- *Ridgeley v. Topa Thrift and Loan Assn.*[15]: A loan agreement required payment of six months' interest upon prepayment of the loan unless the borrower had paid each installment no later than 15 days after its due date; in that event, the prepayment premium was excused. When the lender demanded and collected prepayment premia from borrowers who prepaid when selling their mortgaged properties, the borrowers sued. While a prepayment premium is usually compensation for the privilege of being allowed to pay before the due date, in this case the fact that it was payable only if the borrower had been delinquent in repaying the loan tainted the provision.[16]

---

[14] 104 A.D.2d 409, 478 NYS 2d 933 (N.Y. App. 1984).

[15] 17 Cal.4th 970, 73 Cal. Rptr.2d 378, 953 P.2d 484 (Cal. 1998).

[16] The trial court held the prepayment premium was a penalty, not liquidated damages; the appeals court reversed; and a divided California Supreme Court reversed, upholding the trial court's finding. "To [the lender] Topa, moreover, the value of the disputed provision was clearly to be found in its operation as a penalty for late payment rather than as compensation for prepayment. After [the borrowers] plaintiffs made six months of interest payments (after June 21, 1991, that is), Topa would impose the prepayment charge only if during the period of the loan plaintiffs had made a late payment or were otherwise in contractual default. That contractual stipulation shows that, from Topa's viewpoint, the purpose of the threatened charge, after June 21, 1991, was to coerce timely payment

Damage Exclusions

Damages may be compensatory or punitive according to whether they are awarded as the measure of actual loss suffered or as punishment for outrageous conduct and to deter future transgressions. Damages for losses that result from a breach or repudiation of contract may be

- direct or general, defined as "damages that the law presumes to follow from the type of wrong complained of"[17];
- consequential, defined as "losses that do not flow directly and immediately from an injurious act but that result indirectly from the act"[18];
- special, defined as "[d]amages that are alleged to have been sustained in the circumstances of a particular wrong"[19];
- expectation or expectancy, defined as "compensation awarded for the loss of what a person reasonably anticipated from a transaction that was not completed"[20];
- incidental, defined by way of an example: "any commercially reasonable charges, expenses or commissions incurred in stopping delivery, in the transportation, care and custody of goods after the buyer's breach, in connection with the return or resale of the goods or otherwise resulting from the breach"; and
- exemplary or punitive, defined as "damages awarded in additional to actual damages when the defendant acted with recklessness, malice, or deceit."[21]

A contract can exclude liability for one or more of such types of damages, thus limiting liability to those not excluded. A frequent exclusion includes punitive, consequential, special, and incidental damages and precludes an obligee from seeking recovery for its lost

of interest, not to compensate Topa for interest payments lost through prepayment of principal." 17 Cal. 4th at 980.

[17] Black's Law Dictionary, *supra* note 2, 472.

[18] *Id.*

[19] *Id.* at 474.

[20] *Id.* at 472.

[21] *Id.* at 474.

profits as a result of a breach by an obligor. Such an exclusion allocates to the obligee responsibility for the risk that it might suffer losses falling into one or more of the categories of excluded damages, effectively making it the self-insurer of them.

American Nursery Products, Inc. v. Indian Wells Orchards[22] illustrates a typical exclusion of consequential damages. A seller agreed to grow and deliver 700,000 apple trees the buyer intended to use to develop a 500-acre orchard. The contract provided,

> [t]he party declaring default shall have all rights provided under the Washington Uniform Commercial Code and other applicable laws of the State of Washington and the terms and provisions of this Agreement; provided that in no event shall Grower be subject to or liable for incidental or consequential damages.[23]

The seller delivered less than the agreed quantity, and a number of those delivered were rejected and others that were accepted died. The buyer sued, and the trial court, after holding the quoted provision was unenforceable as unconscionable, awarded judgment in the buyer's favor for $2.3 million, $1.7 million of which was for lost production. The Washington Supreme Court reversed the award of consequential and incidental damages, holding the exclusion clause enforceable. The buyer had assumed the risk it would incur consequential damages from breach by the seller.

Remedy Limitations

A contract can state certain remedies that may be exercised in response to a breach and it may further state that certain remedies may not be exercised. The permitted remedies may allow or require the obligor to correct defects in its performance. The objective of such provisions is to limit, if not eliminate, liability for money damages. Such remedy exclusions are not always enforceable, however.

---

22 115 Wn.2d 217, 797 P.2d 477 (Wash. 1990).

23 *Id.* at 221.

The following illustrate such remedy limitations:

- *Frey Dairy v. A.O. Smith Harverstore Products, Inc.*[24] illustrates a repair and replace remedy limitation. A contract for the supply of a silo included as the sole and exclusive remedy for breach of the express warranty (all other warranties were disclaimed) repair or replacement of the silo, at the manufacturer's option. The buyer claimed damages for the harm to its cows caused by the condition of the silo, which breached the warranty. Had the remedy limitation been unenforceable, as the buyer claimed, it could have sued for money damages. However, because the limitation was enforceable, the buyer had assumed responsibility for the risk it could incur losses before the defects were corrected.[25]
- *Banc of America Securities LLC v. Solow Building Co. I, L.L.C.*[26] illustrates a specific performance-remedy-only limitation. A lease provided

  > Tenant hereby waives any claim against Landlord which Tenant may have based upon any assertion that Landlord has unreasonably withheld or unreasonably delayed any consent requested by Tenant, and Tenant agrees that its sole remedy shall be an action or proceeding to enforce any related provision or for specific performance, injunction or declaratory judgment or an arbitration proceeding.[27]

  The lease also provided that any dispute over tenant alterations could, at the tenant's option, be submitted to expedited arbitration. When the tenant requested the landlord's consent for tenant improvements and the landlord demanded a $6 million consent fee, the tenant sued for damages. Had the limitation previously quoted been effective even when the landlord failed to act in good faith, as the landlord claimed, the tenant would have assumed

---

[24] 886 F.2d 128 (6th Cir. 1989).

[25] The district court granted summary judgment, relying upon the repair or replace remedy, and the appeal court affirmed.

[26] 47 A.D.3d 239, 847 N.Y.S.2d 49, 2007 N.Y. Slip Op. 09545 (N.Y. App. 2007). For a summary of this case, see text accompanying ch. 7, note 52.

[27] 47 A.D.3d 239, 241.

responsibility for the risk that it could incur losses before a court could award specific performance. But, as the tenant successfully claimed, that limitation should not apply in the exceptional case when the landlord does not act in good faith. The risk allocation implied by the clause did not apply in such a case, and responsibility for the risk that its breach of contract would cause losses by the tenant remained with the landlord.[28]

- *McIntire v. Green-Tree Communities, Inc.*[29] illustrates a "no damages for delay" limitation in a construction contract. A contract to build a house provided, "[T]he Seller cannot and will not be responsible for any damages or inconveniences caused to Buyer for failure to complete residence mentioned herein by such date, regardless of the reason for such delay." The buyer had a commitment for a mortgage at a fixed interest rate of 8 percent per annum, but because completion was four months late, it had to accept a mortgage at 8-3/4 percent. Had the clause been enforceable in all circumstances, including fraudulent and willful misconduct by the contractor, as the contractor claimed, the buyer would have assumed responsibility for the risk of losses resulting from delays that breached the contract. The buyer successfully claimed, however, that the limitation should not be effective when the contractor never intended or expected to complete the work by the scheduled completion date. The buyer assumed responsibility for the risk it might suffer losses due to completion later than agreed but not when the contractor never intended or expected to complete on time.[30]

---

[28] The landlord moved to dismiss the complaint and for summary judgment on the basis of the quoted clause. The court denied the landlord's motions because the clause did not apply to a bad faith denial of the requested consent, and it was a question of fact if the landlord had acted in bad faith. The clause effectively limited the tenant to demanding that the landlord correct any breaches and allocated to the tenant the risk of losses that would result from such breaches, excluding bad faith breaches.

[29] 318 So.2d 197 (Fla. App. 1975).

[30] The buyer sued for damages, alleging the seller never intended to complete by the scheduled date. The trial court dismissed the complaint, but the appeal court reversed, holding that while the "no damages for delay" clause was enforceable, an exception existed if the seller had engaged in fraud or willful misconduct, the former of which had been alleged by the buyer.

Damage Amount Limitations

Instead of excluding liability for money damages altogether, a contract can limit liability for breach or repudiation to certain amounts. Damages must be proved, but their recovery is subject to limitations. One such limit allows recovery for amounts an obligor receives or receives during specific periods of time. Another limits an obligor's liability to amounts above a minimum and below a maximum, below and above which, respectively, damages are not recoverable. The obligee self-insures losses below the deductible and above the cap. An agreement to refund the compensation or price paid by the obligee is analogous, as it limits the damages payable by an obligor to the amount received.

The following illustrate such remedy limitations:

- *Foont-Freedenfeld Corp. v. Electro Protective Corp.*[31]: Electro Protective Corp. (EPC) installed and maintained a burglar alarm system in Foont-Freedenfeld Corp.'s (FFC) apparel store. Their contract provided:

  > [EPC] the Contractor's liability hereunder shall be limited to and fixed at a sum equal to ten percent of the annual service charge hereinabove provided for, but in no event amounting to less than the sum of fifty dollars, as liquidated damages, and not as a penalty, and this liability shall be exclusive.[32]

  The store was burgled, resulting in losses of $55,423.13. Had the limitation not been effective because it was not a valid liquidated damages clause, as FFC claimed, EPC would have been liable for an amount considerably higher than $50. As a valid limitation, however, as EPC successfully claimed, FFC assumed responsibility for its losses that resulted from a breach by EPC could exceed that limitation.[33]

---

[31] 126 N.J. Super. 254, 314 A.2d 69 (N.J. Super. 1973).

[32] 126 N.J. Super. at 257–8.

[33] FFC sued FPC for fraud and was awarded a $27,500 judgment. The appellate division reduced the judgment to $50, holding the clause was enforceable. FPC assumed the risk its losses caused by EPC's breach would exceed the $50 limitation.

- *Computrol, Inc. v. Newtrend, L.P.*[34]: Computrol, which developed custom computer software for the financial services industry, agreed to reengineer certain of Newtrend's software applications. Computrol successfully sued Newtrend for breach of contract. The contract limited "each party's liability to the other for any cause whatsoever and regardless of the form of action and whether in contract or tort, or at law or equity . . . [to] the amounts actually paid to the other under this Alliance Agreement."[35] The sum of the modified contract price for Computrol's work on one project and the cost of the work performed on another project amounted to $469,206.88. Had the words "amounts actually paid" not precluded lost profits, as Computrol claimed, Computrol might have been able to recover more than $469,206.88, though it was uncertain what those additional damages might include.[36] Regardless, implicit in Newtrend's successful claim was that Computrol had assumed responsibility for the risk its losses could exceed the fees it would receive under the contract.[37]

Recourse Limitations

The scope of persons and assets to which a party may have recourse for breach of contract can be expanded or limited by contract. First, third parties may be brought into a transaction as guarantors and indemnitors of an obligor's liabilities thereunder. Conversely, third parties—persons not party to a contract—can obtain assurances from the parties that they will not be liable for breach of that contract. Such assurances are intended to avoid claims that a third party's separateness

---

34 203 F.3d 1064 (8th Cir. 2000).

35 *Id.* at 1069.

36 On post-trial motion, the district court described proof of damages in excess of $469,206.88 as wholly speculative.

37 Computrol sued for fraud and breach of contract. A jury awarded $2,663,000 to Computrol on the breach of contract claim. On post-trial motion, the district court ruled as a matter of law that a contractual limitation of liability provision limited Computrol's breach of contract recovery to $469,206.88. The district court entered judgment in Computrol's favor in the amount of $469,206.88 plus $150,000 in attorneys' fees. The appeal court affirmed the post-trial judgment of the district court. The court held the limitation clause was "intended to foreclose all future damages, i.e., prospective lost profits." As a result, the software developer's damages were limited to amounts it had been paid prior to breach by the customer.

from a party to the contract should be disregarded and the two treated as one entity.

Hoosier Energy Rural Electric Coop., Inc. v. Amoco Tax Leasing IV Corp.[38] illustrates such a recourse limitation. Hoosier sold equipment to, and leased that equipment back from, Amoco Tax Leasing IV Corporation (Amoco Tax). The lease stated Hoosier's compensation for the equipment would be adjusted favorably if by June 30, 1983 the Internal Revenue Service issued regulations allowing the owner of the leased equipment to depreciate it over five, instead of fifteen, years. When the regulations were published on February 16, 1984, Hoosier claimed the adjustment, estimated to be between $25 million and $28 million, because the regulations were given retroactive effect and sued Amoco Corporation and Amoco Tax in an Indiana state court for unjust enrichment. When Amoco Tax filed notice to remove the case to federal court, asserting the diversity of the parties, Hoosier objected, asserting that as both Amoco Corporation and it were Indiana persons, no diversity existed. The lease, however, stated, in part, "No recourse shall be had for the payment of . . . any . . . amount payable hereunder . . . against, Amoco Leasing Corp. ([the defendant] Amoco's sole stockholder) or any other Affiliate of Amoco. . . ."[39] Notwithstanding this clause, Hoosier argued the parent corporation could be added as a party to its suit because it was unjustly enriched by the tax benefits it received from the transaction and which were referenced in the agreement. By accepting the limitation on its recourse to Amoco Tax, Hoosier assumed responsibility for the risk it would have to pursue its claim solely against that entity and in a federal court.[40]

Second, recourse for damages resulting from a breach of a contract may be further restricted to specific assets of an obligor, in which case the obligee cannot recover for its damages from the obligor's other assets. In effect, the parties identify a fund or pool of assets to which recourse is permissible to the exclusion of whatever other assets the obligor has. An example, one imposed by statute, is a limit on recourse to the

---

[38] 34 F.3d 1310 (7th Cir. 1994).

[39] *Id.* at 1315.

[40] The district court granted the motion to dismiss the parent corporation from the suit, and the appeal court affirmed. Referring to the quoted language, the appeals court said, "This language broadly applies to any claim that is in any way 'based on' the sale-leaseback agreement or otherwise 'in respect to' the agreement." *Id.* at 1316.

property that secures a loan, the proceeds from which were used to buy it. Comparable limits may be crafted by contractual terms.

The following illustrate such limited recourse:

- *In the Matter of Vintero Corp.*[41]: A debtor granted a security interest in two vessels but limited the secured party's recourse for payment of the secured debt to the collateral. The vessels were moved to another state. The secured party failed to file a new financing statement, which filing was necessary to continue perfection of such security interest. As a result, the security interest no longer had priority in the vessels, leaving the secured party without a perfected security interest or priority when the debtor became bankrupt. The secured party was still entitled to recover from the proceeds from the sale of the vessels, though after other creditors had been satisfied. It was not permitted to have recourse against other assets of the debtor. The creditor assumed responsibility for two risks any secured creditor assumes: that it would fail to maintain the priority of its security interest and that the debtor's equity in the collateral might be less than the amount owed by the debtor to it. By agreeing to limit its recourse, the creditor also assumed responsibility for a further risk—that it would need but not have recourse to any of the other debtor's assets to be repaid.
- *Chevron U.S.A. Inc. v. Belco Petroleum Corp.*[42]: Chevron held an offshore oil lease from the federal government on the outer continental shelf off the Louisiana coast. It assigned its rights under the lease to Belco in return for a one-eighth overriding royalty payment from gas produced from the field. The agreement provided Chevron would receive its royalty in-kind. It also allowed either party to take less than its share and recover the difference in "balancing" payments at a later date. Chevron was owed such a balance when the field stopped producing. Belco claimed it had no obligation to pay such balancing payments in cash. If Chevron was correct, it had recourse to all of Belco's assets for payment in cash for the balancing payments. But Belco was correct, as the appeal court ruled; Chevron had agreed to limit its recourse to the

[41] 735 F.2d 740 (2d Cir. 1984).

[42] 755 F.2d 1151 (5th Cir. 1985).

in-kind payments from the field.[43] It thereby assumed responsibility for the risk the field would not produce sufficient gas to cover the balancing payments.

A party can also limit recourse to specific assets by selecting or forming an entity to participate in a transaction as the obligor, capitalizing it with the assets to which recourse is ultimately to be had and which are or will be sufficient to cover its liabilities. The obligee may exercise all remedies against that obligor for breach of contract, receiving payment for its damages from any and all assets of that entity. Whereas, in principle, a nonrecourse obligation limits the obligee's remedies to recovery from specific assets and a full recourse obligation allows an obligee recourse against all the assets of the obligor, this difference has little financial substance when the obligor is a special purpose entity formed to implement a single project, development, or transaction, capitalized with cash, cash equivalents, and other assets, the latter of which are useful or necessary for the transaction.[44] Recourse to the entire balance sheet of the special purpose entity obligor is effectively limited to those assets.

---

43 The district court held the agreement between the parties did not provide for the situation where the field ceased production while balances were outstanding. It ruled it implied a term to achieve an equitable result. The appeal court quoted the clause in the contract that provided for balancing payments: "To allow the recovery of gas in storage and to balance the gas account of the parties in accordance with their respective interests, . . . a party with gas in storage shall be entitled to take or deliver to a purchaser its current share of the gas produced . . . plus up to 25% of the other party's share of gas production . . . until such time as that quantity of gas in storage shall be reduced to zero." The court read the clause to be clear that cash payments were not required. *Id.* at 1154.

44 "A 'single purpose entity' 'is an entity, formed concurrently with or immediately prior to the subject transaction, that is unlikely to become insolvent as a result of its own activities and that is adequately insulated from the consequences of any related party's insolvency.'" U.S. CMBS Legal and Structured Finance Criteria, Standard & Poors, May 1, 2003, at 89. Quoted in Wells Fargo Bank, N.A. v. Cherryland Mall Ltd. Partnership, 295 Mich. App. 99, 812 N.W.2d 799, 810 (Mich. App. 2011); *remanded* 433 Mich. 859, 820 N.W.2d 901 (2012). In that case the borrower, formed to own a shopping mall and obtain an $8.7 million loan from a lender, covenanted to maintain its status as a single purpose entity, which required, inter alia, that it not become insolvent. In the event the borrower failed to maintain that status the lender was entitled to full recourse against the borrower and the guarantor. The borrower became insolvent because of downturn in the market and claimed its resulting insolvency was not covered by the clause. The court held the covenant "does not require insolvency to occur in any specific manner. Rather, any failure to remain solvent, no matter what the cause, is a violation." 295 Mich. App. 99, 125, 812 N.W.2d 799, 815.

Private Statute of Limitations

The time for claiming damages for breach or repudiation may be limited to a period shorter than that otherwise permitted by law. A condition requires that notice of breach be given to the obligor within an agreed period of time. The time limitation operates as a private statute of limitations, setting a maximum time by which notice of claims must be given. Like a statute of limitations, it allocates to the obligee responsibility for the chance that it will not discover a breach until after the time for a claim has lapsed; to that extent that party self-insures the losses it sustains because it did not discover the breach.

Besicorp Group, Inc. v. Thermo Electron Corp.[45] illustrates the operation of a private statute of limitations. A subcontract between a contractor and subcontractor for the installation of an electricity-generating unit in a hospital included a warranty that read, in part, "[T]he Equipment is warranted for a period of six (6) months after delivery or 500 hours of operation, whichever first occurs, to be free from defects in material and workmanship."[46] After installation was completed, the contractor excluded the subcontractor from the site and operated the unit for 17 months and 4,000 hours before learning that the installation of the unit violated four electrical code provisions. The court held claims for these breaches of the warranty were barred by the limitations in the warranty, even if they were latent and even if the unit could not be repaired.[47] The contractor assumed responsibility for the risk the defects in the equipment might not be discoverable or discovered until after the six-month warranty period had expired.

Releases

An obligee may be required to deliver periodic releases, acknowledging that it has no claim, and releasing any claim it may have, against an obligor. Such releases are common in construction projects, where the contractor, upon receipt of periodic payment, acknowledges it has

---

[45] 981 F. Supp. 86 (S.D.N.Y. 1997).

[46] *Id.* at 91.

[47] "In the present case, the allocation of risk was especially appropriate because the System was essentially a prototype model, designed, manufactured and installed by [subcontractor] Tecogen, the value of which was substantially greater than the actual contract price." *Id.* at 101.

received payment in full for all work to date, save for retained amounts, and releases the owner of claims for such amounts. When commercial lenders agree to amendments, consents, and waivers, they sometimes ask their borrowers to acknowledge they have no claims and to release the lenders for any they might have. Any claims for damages are extinguished if the releases are properly drafted.

Sorrels Steel Co. v. Great Southwest Corp.[48] illustrates the scope of a form of releases periodically given pursuant to a construction contract. The subcontractor responsible for fabricating steel on a construction project incurred additional costs because of defects in the drawings and specifications and claimed such costs from the contractor. The contractor agreed to submit the claim to the city, which had provided the drawings and specifications. The subcontractor continued to receive defective drawings and to incur additional costs. It also received periodic payments, and executed nine releases, one of which read, in part:

> [Subcontractor] hereby releases . . . all their lien rights, claims and demands of every kind whatsoever, including any claims for extended or additional job costs and overhead and lost profits, due to any cause, including claims and demands arising from any claimed delays, disruptions or changes to the work. . . .[49]

Another form of release read, in part:

> [Subcontractor] hereby acknowledges that all materials heretofore furnished have been paid for in full, and [Subcontractor] . . . hereby remises, releases, acquits, satisfies and forever discharges [Contractor] . . . of and from any and all claims that it might have against [Contractor] . . . for furnishing materials for the aforementioned project.[50]

The subcontractor sued the contractor for its additional costs when its requested change order was not issued. If the releases covered the claims for extra costs, as the contractor claimed, then the subcontractor assumed responsibility for the risk each time it executed and delivered

---

[48] 906 F.2d 158 (5th Cir. 1990).

[49] *Id.* at 166.

[50] *Id.* at 166.

a release that it had relinquished whatever right it had to additional compensation. But, as the subcontractor successfully claimed, the releases covered only the work and claims for which it received payments; such was the nature of releases for progress payments. The releases did not alter the contractor's commitment to pay for the additional work.[51]

---

[51] The contractor claimed the releases unambiguously covered the claims for extra costs. The district court held the wording was ambiguous and did not release the contractor from claims for additional compensation due to delays in approving the subcontractor's shop drawings, because it acknowledged partial payments, five such releases were executed, and a complete release was inconsistent with the parties' intention as to payment of compensation for the delay. The court instructed the jury to decide if the releases covered the claims for additional compensation. The jury found the releases did not bar the subcontractor's recovery.

Part IV

Third-Party and Uncontrollable Event Risks

10

Supply, Offtake, and Consent Risks

SUPPLY, OFFTAKE, AND CONSENT HAZARDS

Supply Hazards

Supply is defined as "the amount of goods produced or available at a given price."[1] A supplier is "[a] person engaged, directly or indirectly, in making product available to consumers."[2] Where supply refers to a stock of goods, supplier refers to a person who furnishes such goods to consumers. Goods, services, and other items of value are furnished by firms to other firms long before they reach consumers' hands. A person obtaining such an item from another engages in a transaction. A person who obtains an item from another to fulfill a commitment to a third person engages in two transactions, one with its supplier and a second with the third party. In a supply or supply chain transaction, for purposes of this text, an obligor in one transaction is expected by its performance in that transaction to complete or to enable or help its obligee to complete a task in a second transaction. That task may be performance by an obligor of its obligation in the second transaction. It may be satisfaction of conditions that will effectuate a commitment

---

1 Black's Law Dictionary 1439 (10th ed. 2014).

2 *Id.*

to perform in the second transaction, enabling the obligee in the first transaction to realize the benefits of both transactions.

The following are examples of such supply relationships:

- *Alamance Board of Education v. Bobby Murray Chevrolet, Inc.*[3]: A car dealer successfully bid to supply school bus chassis to a number of school boards. It expected to obtain the chassis from General Motors (GM) under its contract, which stated that orders did not bind GM until they were accepted; and they were accepted when GM "released" the order for production. The supply of the chassis in the transaction between GM and the dealer, the first transaction, would have enabled the dealer to perform its obligation to the school boards in the second transaction. The case is further discussed in this chapter.[4]
- *State Fuel Co. v. Gulf Oil Corp.*[5]: During the war, kerosene shipped to the northeast United States had to be contained in barrels and carried in box cars because tankers and tank cars were in short supply. Unloading barrels increased the distributors' delivery costs. The federal government established a program to reimburse kerosene distributors for such costs, subject to a maximum amount. The supplier would credit the distributor for its excess unloading costs and apply for the reimbursement. A government-owned corporation would review the application and, if satisfied, reimburse the seller for such excess unloading costs. It could have such costs audited. Although the supply chain for the sale of kerosene was that seller and distributor were supplier and supplied, respectively, the supply chain was reversed for purposes of collecting the subsidy: the distributor supplied documentation to the supplier, and the supplier provided that documentation to the government corporation. The supplier did not have a commitment to the government corporation to supply proper documentation. The supplier had to satisfy conditions to obligate the government corporation to pay the subsidy. That reimbursement would yield the benefit of the regulatory relationship with the government corporation and one of the benefits of the contract with the

[3] 121 N.C. App. 222, 465 S.E.2d 306 (N.C. App. 1996).

[4] See text accompanying notes 12–14.

[5] 179 F.2d 390 (1st Cir. 1950).

distributor. This case, further discussed in this chapter,[6] illustrates how the supply of an item of value in a first transaction enables a party receiving that item to effectuate a third party's commitment in a second transaction, enabling that party to realize benefits in one or both transactions.

This chapter narrowly focuses on the supply transaction in which the supply of an item of value in one transaction enables or facilitates the party receiving such item to perform an obligation to a third party in the second transaction. A supply failure occurs when an obligor (P1) in a first transaction fails to supply an item of value that an obligee (P2) in that transaction expected to receive and to use to perform its obligation to an obligee (P3) in a second transaction. P2 may be unable to perform because of the supply failure. P1 may or may not be excused. In all instances P1's failure to supply the item P2 expects increases the chances that P2 will be unable to complete the task P3 expects P2 to complete in the second transaction.

Supplier Mismatch and Breach. P2's dependence upon P1 to fulfill a commitment to P3 will create the first and may create the second of the following two risks:

- a risk that P2 will be liable to P3 if P1 fails to perform its commitment to P2 and, as a result, P2 cannot fulfill its commitment to P3, and
- a risk that P1 will not be liable to P2 because P1 has not committed to perform or its failure to perform is excused, but P2's performance is not correspondingly excused or otherwise discharged.

In all cases, the chance that P1 might not perform is a threat to P2 because P2 may be unable to perform its commitment to P3. This is true even when responsibility for P1's breach has been allocated to P3. The second risk is a mismatch between P2's commitment to P3 and P1's commitment to P2. P1 might not always be liable to P2 when P2 fails to perform its commitment to P3 because P1 failed to perform its commitment to P2.

---

6 See text accompanying notes 45–47.

The following cases illustrate such mismatch and liability assumption risks:

- *Sassower v. Blumenfeld*[7]: This case is summarized in chapter 8.[8] A buyer of real property deposited $180,000 of a purchase price of $1,800,000, agreeing to forfeit the down payment if he failed to pay the balance, which he intended to pay with the cash he would receive upon liquidation of investments he had in Bernard Madoff's funds. Madoff's fraudulent scheme was discovered between the times the buyer signed and closed, leaving the buyer with no cash, and because he had lost his investments, with no ability to borrow moneys with which to pay the balance. Madoff was P1, who was obligated to supply the funds the buyer P2 required to pay the seller P3, and the contract between P1 and P2, the contract pursuant to which the buyer invested in Madoff's funds, and the contract between P2 and P3, the contract for the sale of the property. P2's commitment to P3, a firm obligation to pay the purchase price, was matched by an equally strong commitment by P1 to pay P2 the liquidated value of P2's investments. P2 had a claim against P1, the amount of which would have covered the losses recovered by P3 from P2.[9]
- *World of Boxing, LLC v. King*[10]: King (K), a boxing promoter, agreed with World of Boxing (WB), another boxing promoter, to cause boxer Guillermo Jones (J) to participate in a rematch with boxer L on a specific date. On that date, boxer J tested positive for an illicit, performance-enhancing diuretic and was disqualified from participating in the fight; the fight was canceled. J, K, and WB were P1, P2, and P3, respectively. K's commitment to WB to cause P1's participation in the fight was matched by an equally strong

[7] 24 Misc.3d 843, 878 N.Y.S.2d 602, 2009 N.Y. Slip Op. 29198 (N.Y. S. Ct. 2009).

[8] See text accompanying ch. 8, notes 21–23.

[9] The buyer asked for a refund of the deposit, claiming impossibility excused his performance. The court, holding for the seller, muddled through the impossibility defense, finding the buyer "has utterly failed to provide any details as to the amounts lost, the nature of his lost investments, or the actual state of his current finances and assets." *Id.* at 848.

[10] 56 F. Supp.3d 507 (S.D.N.Y. 2014), sum. jdgmt. on damages, 107 F. Supp.3d 265 (S.D.N.Y. 2015), *rev'd* on other grounds, Nos. 5-554-cv(L), 15-725-cv (XAP) (2d Cir. 2015).

commitment from P1 to participate. P1's breach of his contract with P2 caused P2's breach of its contract with P3.[11]

- *Alamance Board of Education*[12]: The facts in the case, previously summarized,[13] illustrate a commitment mismatch: from the outset, GM's commitment to the dealer, on which the dealer depended to perform, was conditional, unlike the dealer's commitment to the school boards, which was not conditional, creating the risk that the dealer would be unable to deliver if GM did not accept the orders and deliver the chassis to the dealer on time. As GM had not previously failed to deliver to the dealer, the dealer did not consider itself at risk when it submitted the bid. GM initially extended the dates for accepting the dealer's orders and, in turn, the school boards extended the dealer's delivery dates, but eventually GM notified the dealer that the orders would not be accepted, putting the dealer in breach.[14]
- *Evra Corp. v. Swiss Bank Corp.*[15]: A vessel charterer in Chicago agreed that if a rent payment was late, then the vessel owner in Switzerland, where payments were to be made, could terminate the charter. The day before payment was due the charterer instructed its bank (bank A) to wire transfer funds in the amount of the rent payment to the owner's bank (bank C). Bank A transferred the funds to bank B with instructions to transfer the funds to bank C, but bank B failed

---

[11] WB sued K for breach, for failing to cause J's participation as agreed. K claimed as defenses he had no control over J and supervening impossibility. The court held that because J had a history of illicit doping before fights, his testing positive was not unanticipated; impossibility was unavailable. "As the party who promised to secure [J's] Jones's participation, King [K] 'assumed the risk' of foreseeable events that might frustrate his ability to make good on that promise." *Id.* at 515.

[12] 121 N.C. App. 222, 465 S.E.2d 306 (N.C. App. 1996).

[13] See text accompanying notes 3 and 4.

[14] The dealer claimed that the parties contemplated GM as the sole source of the chassis and, that being the case, "an implied condition of its contract with plaintiffs was the ability of GM to manufacture and supply the ordered bus chassis;" that condition had failed. The court disagreed, holding the dealer "assumed the risk of its failure to supply the vehicles, as it was foreseeable that GM might not supply the bus chassis. Failure to make express provision for a foreseeable contingency in a sales contract implicitly places the burden of loss on the seller when the contingency comes to fruition." 465 S.E.2d at 311.

[15] 673 F.2d 951 (7th Cir. 1982).

to transfer the funds for reasons never explained.[16] The next day, the owner canceled the charter. The charterer initiated arbitration proceedings and the arbitrators concluded the owner was entitled to terminate the charter. The charterer then sued bank B for its damages (arbitration proceeding costs and profits lost because of cancelation of the charter). Bank B, the charterer, and the owner were P1, P2, and P3, respectively; the P1-P2 obligation was the transfer of funds to P3 and the P2-P3 contract was the charterparty. If P2's obligation to P3's was matched by a corresponding obligation by P1 to P2, then P1 would have had to deliver the funds to P3 when they were due from P2 and P1's liability for breach would have covered P2's losses under the P2-P3 contract. Such a match did not exist in this case.[17]

No Willing Supplier. Supply risk exists in transactions where the supplier has not been identified and no contract for the first transaction has been formed. P2 may need the supply of an item of value from a third party to perform its obligation to P3 and expect or hope to find a supplier after contract formation and before its performance to P3 is due. One reason for its failure may be that no supplier is willing to supply it with the value it needs, though such suppliers are willing to supply others. An example is a property buyer who must borrow moneys to pay all or a portion of the purchase price but cannot find a lender willing to extend credit to

---

[16] "No one knows exactly what went wrong. One possibility is that the receiving telex machine had simply run out of paper, in which event it would not print the message although it had received it. Another is that whoever took the message out of the machine after it was printed failed to deliver it to the banking department. Unlike the machine in the cable department that the [Bank A] Continental telex operator had originally tried to reach, the machines in the foreign exchange department were operated by junior foreign exchange dealers rather than by professional telex operators, although Swiss Bank [Bank B] knew that messages intended for other departments were sometimes diverted to the telex machines in the foreign exchange department." *Id.* at 953.

[17] The federal district court found bank C was liable to the charterer. The appeal court reversed, holding that if Illinois law applied to the claim the damages—the profits lost from the cancelation of the contract—were not reasonably foreseeable. Judge Richard Posner came close to saying the charterer had assumed the risk: "But Hyman-Michaels [the charterer] is a sophisticated business enterprise. It knew or should have known that even the Swiss are not infallible; that messages sometimes get lost or delayed in transit among three banks, two of them located 5000 miles apart, even when all the banks are using reasonable care; and that therefore it should take its own precautions against the consequences—best known to itself—of a mishap that might not be due to anyone's negligence." *Id.* at 957.

it; the failure to raise the loan is due to the buyer's lack of qualifications to borrow such amount. Whether the buyer had the ability at contract formation and lost it later does not matter. Another reason may be that no potential supplier is willing to supply the item P2 requires for its performance of its obligation to P3. As a result, performance of P2's obligation is infeasible. Such infeasibility is attributable to the absence of willing suppliers in the market. The absence of suppliers may have existed at contract formation or occur later. In either case, the absence of supply lies in the market. That risk is described in chapter 12.[18]

Mouhelis v. Thomas[19] illustrates inability of an obligor in the second transaction to find a supplier in the first. A condition in a contract for the sale of property allowed the buyer to terminate within 21 days from its execution if the buyer "submitted a true loan application and otherwise made every reasonable effort to secure a loan commitment from any source made available to him and has been unable to do so." The buyer had to notify the seller of termination within that period. The buyer applied for a loan, but because his employment had been terminated while the application was pending, the loan was denied. This, however, was after the 21-day period expired. The lender, buyer, and seller were P1, P2, and P3, respectively. The buyer either chose the wrong lender to ask for a loan, because another lender would have made the loan notwithstanding his unemployment, or he was unable to borrow from any lender because he was unemployed. In the former the buyer's problem lay with his chosen supplier, but since the lender did not commit to loan any funds, it did not breach any commitment. In the latter his problem was his inability to borrow the amount he needed. In either case, he had no supplier of the funds needed to pay the purchase price. When the 21-day period lapsed without termination, he assumed responsibility for the risk of liability to his seller for his failure to obtain those funds.[20] He had no commitment from a lender to match his commitment to his seller.

---

[18] See text accompanying ch. 12, notes 20–30.

[19] 95 Ill. App.3d 181, 419 N.E.2d 956 (Ill. App. 1981).

[20] The seller sued for the earnest money deposit and moved for summary judgment, the buyer claimed termination of his employment frustrated the contract, and the court granted the motion. The appeal court affirmed, finding that the doctrine of frustration was inapplicable where the contract addressed the contingency. "Under the contract's terms defendant buyers were to have 21 days to secure financing, and the buyers agreed unqualifiedly that if they did not serve notice of failure to procure a loan commitment upon sellers within 21 days, the contract would continue in full force and effect without any loan contingencies." *Id.* at 184.

Offtake Hazards

Offtake is the acquisition or purchase of items of value that have been acquired or produced by their seller for sale. The focus on offtake shifts from the furnishing to the acquiring of a want. Offtake enables a seller to realize some or all of the value it expects or hopes from a transaction. Just as P2 can depend upon P1 to supply items it needs to perform its commitment to P3, P2 can depend upon P3 to purchase those items to enable P2 to realize the anticipated benefit of the transaction with P1. An offtake transaction is a mirror image of a supply transaction: P1's performance as supplier in the first transaction has no value to P2 without P3's performance as offtaker in the second transaction.

An offtake failure occurs when an offtaker (P3) in a second transaction indicates it will not acquire or pay for or fails to acquire or pay for goods or services supplied by P2 that were in part or whole supplied or produced using items supplied by P1 in a first transaction, the purpose of which was to supply P3. P3's failure may or may not be excused. In all instances P3's failure to perform in the P2-P3 transaction may impair the value P2 expects to realize, unless P2 can find another offtaker at the same or better price.

Supply and offtake risk differ: a supply failure may impair or deprive the obligee in the first transaction of its ability as obligor in the second transaction to complete its commitments to its obligee in that transaction. P2 may be able to locate alternative supplies in time to perform, or it might not. The market may be such that it cannot locate any alternative supplies. An offtake failure does not affect P2's ability to perform its obligation to P1 (or P1 its obligation to P2). P3's breach or repudiation may impair or destroy the benefit P2 expects from P1's performance in the first transaction. P2 may be able to locate an alternative offtaker at the same or better price. The market may be such that it cannot locate any alternative offtakers. Whether it can or cannot locate alternative offtakers, it can pay P1 for its performance. In principle, its ability to perform is unaffected by P3's breach or repudiation.

Offtake Mismatch and Breach. The relationships P2 has to P1 and P3 also face two different sets of hazards, but they are the reverse of those described for supply transactions. The first set is acts and incidents that indicate P3 will fail to perform, excused or otherwise. This set also includes acts and incidents that indicate a loss of or potential to lose willingness and ability to perform, as described in chapter 8. The other set are chances that P2 will be liable to P1 for breach when by choice it fails to perform its obligation to P1 in the first transaction because P3 failed to perform or repudiated the second transaction. This set includes the assumption in the P1–P2 transaction of the risk that P2 will not perform in that transaction because P3 repudiated the second transaction (and P2's anticipated benefit of the P1–P2 transaction was lost). These hazards are mismatches between P3's commitment to P2 and P2's commitment to P1 and assumption of the risk of liability to P1 in the first transaction notwithstanding that P3 repudiates in the second transaction.

Following are two cases that illustrate mismatch of offtake and other commitments:

- *Peoplesoft U.S.A., Inc. v. Softeck, Inc.*[21]: A Puerto Rican software developer contracted to provide software and related services to Policia de Puerto Rico (Policia). It licensed software from a US software developer to provide those services. Policia decided not to use the Puerto Rican developer's software. The Puerto Rican developer, in turn, decided not to use the US developer's license. The US developer, the Puerto Rican developer, and Policia were P1, P2, and P3, respectively. P3, the offtaker in the P2-P3 transaction, either permissibly terminated or impermissibly defaulted on its commitment to P2. If the former, P3's commitment to P2 was weaker than P2's commitment to P1. If the latter, P3's commitment to P2 matched P2's commitment to P1, but P2 assumed responsibility for the risk P3 would breach or repudiate (though P3 was responsible for P2's losses caused by its breach). Even though P2 had a claim against P3 for breach, it was still liable to P1 for breach of the license. Note: P3's breach did not impair P2's performance under the license with P1, only its incentive to perform.[22]
- *Moore Brothers Co. v. Brown & Root, Inc.*[23]: A subcontract between a contractor and the subcontractor for a toll road project included a

21 227 F. Supp.2d 1116 (N.D. Cal. 2002).

22 The US developer sued for breach of contract, and the Puerto Rican developer asserted defenses of frustration of purpose, mistake, impossibility and impracticability of performance, mitigation of damages, failure of consideration, unconscionability, and an implied condition that Policia accept the software. The US developer moved for summary judgment, and the court granted the motion, finding that the Puerto Rican developer had assumed responsibility for the risk that Policia might fail to perform.

23 207 F.3d 717 (4th Cir. 2000).

"pay when paid" clause.[24] A payment bond was issued by a surety in favor of the subcontractor that did not include this limitation. The subcontractor requested payment for work ordered by change orders. The project owner, which depended upon receiving loans from its lenders to pay the contractor, was unable to pay the contractor for such additional work because it and the contractor had assured the lenders no such additional work was required; the contractor lacked the funds to pay the subcontractor. The subcontractor and lender were P1s (P1A and P1B, respectively), the contractor and surety were P2s (P2A and P2B, respectively), and the project owner P3. There were four contracts: (1) the P1A-P2A contract (subcontract between contractor and subcontractor), (2) the P1A-P2B contract (surety bond in favor of P1A and P2A), (3) the P2A-P3 contract (construction contract), and (4) the P1B-P3contract (loan agreement). First, the lender's contract (4) commitment did not match the owner's contract (3) commitment: the project owner had payment obligations to the contractor that the lender did not have to finance. This is an example of a supplier having a lesser commitment to perform than the supplied party has to its offtaker. Second, the contractor's contract (1) commitment to the subcontractor would not have matched the owner's contract (3) commitment to the contractor if the "pay when paid" clause was effective: the contractor had to pay only when paid by the project owner, whereas the owner had to pay the contractor all amounts due under contract (3).[25] The contractor's contract (1) commitment to the subcontractor matched the owner's contract (3) commitment to the contractor if the "pay when paid" clause was ineffective: the contractor had to pay the subcontractor, whether or not it was paid by the owner. Third, responsibility for both risks was allocated to the surety under contract (2): the surety had a commitment to pay the subcontractor whenever payment was due without regard to the "pay when paid clause."[26]

---

[24] "Notwithstanding any other provision hereof, payment by Owner to General Contractor is a condition precedent to any obligation of General Contractor to make payment hereunder; General Contractor shall have no obligation to make payment to Subcontractor for any portion of the Sublet Work for which General Contractor has not received payment from the Owner." *Id.* at 720.

[25] The district court also held that the "pay when paid" clause, while normally effective, was not effective in this case when the contractor, by its collaboration with the owner, prevented its receiving the funds with which to pay the subcontractor. This decision was upheld on appeal.

[26] The district court held that the surety was liable for the payments because the "pay when paid" clause had not been incorporated into the bond. This finding was also upheld on

No Willing Offtaker. Comparable to supply failure, offtake failure occurs when no offtaker has been identified and the contract for the second transaction has not been formed by the time an offtaker is expected to have been identified and agreed to buy. P2 may need offtake from a third party to realize the value anticipated in the first transaction and expect or hope to find an offtaker after contract formation and before its anticipated time for disposing of its items. One reason for its failure may be that no offtaker is willing to buy from P2, though such offtakers are willing to buy from others. Another reason may be that no potential offtaker is willing to buy the item P2 desires to sell. *Columbian National Title Insurance Co. v. Township Title Services, Inc.*[27] may be an example: because a few title insurers in an area had recently failed, lenders in that area were reluctant to have an insurer new to the area, seeking to develop a market, issue title policies for their loans. There was no demand for the insurer's product. Selling title insurance was feasible, though selling this particular insurer's policies was not. The absence of offtakers may have existed at contract formation or occurred later. Had lenders stopped making loans or were willing to make loans without title insurance and thus did not need title policies, the lack of demand would have been attributable to the market. Market risk—the absence of buyers for certain goods, services, and other items of value—is described in chapter 12.[28]

Additional Costs and Delays. The previous description of supply and offtake risks focuses on complete failures by a supplier to supply and an offtaker to offtake. A supplier may fall short of expectations by supplying later or at a cost higher than expected. This is a risk to the supplied party who may be unable to pass along the extra costs or time to its offtaker. An offtaker may fall short of expectations by buying later or at a lower price. This is a risk to the offtaker's counterparty who may be unable to lower the price it pays its supplier. With appropriate modifications, the previous description of supply and offtake hazards can be repeated for suppliers' late completion and completion at costs more than expected and offtakers' late completion and completion at prices less than expected.

---

appeal. *See* BMD Contractors, Inc. v. Fidelity and Deposit Co. of Maryland, 679 F.3d 643, 656 (7th Cir.), declining to follow Moore Brothers Co. v. Brown & Root, Inc., 207 F.3d 717 (4th Cir. 2000).

27 659 F. Supp. 796 (D. Kan. 1987).

28 See text accompanying ch. 12, notes 6–9.

McNamara Construction of Manitoba, Ltd. v. U.S.[29] illustrates a common mismatch between the prices a party commits to pay its suppliers and its offtaker commits to pay it. A Canadian contractor agreed to complete works on canal locks and related structures at Sault St. Marie, Michigan, for a fixed price, having estimated labor costs of $6,162,066 (out of a total estimate of $21,471,690). Laborers in the area proved far more difficult to work with than anticipated. Strikes, delays, and harassment plagued the contractor throughout the performance of the contract. The total labor costs were $14,222,624 (out of a total cost of $29,660,455). The contractor claimed compensation for the additional labor costs, contending its estimate was based on a mutually mistaken assumption about labor in the area. The laborers were P1, the contractor P2, and the government agency for which the work was performed P3. The contractor's claim was effectively that P3's commitment to P2 should be reformed to match P2's ultimate commitments to P1; P3 would thus be responsible for P2's extra costs. Had P1's commitment to P2 matched P2's commitment to P3, the laborers would not have been entitled to payments above the amount P2 estimated. No one made this claim. P2, by giving and accepting different commitments to P1 and from P3, as the government claimed, assumed responsibility for its additional costs.[30]

THIRD-PARTY CONSENT HAZARDS

Consent is synonymous with authorization, approval, and permission.[31] An essential feature of all of them for purposes of the present analysis is that consent or a like act can be given or refused; the outcome of a

---

[29] 509 F.2d 1166 (Ct. Cl. 1975).

[30] The contractor claimed additional costs due to what it characterized were "severe labor difficulties," asserting the parties labored under a mutual mistake of fact that problems would be "normal." The court dismissed the claim, stating, "What we have in the instant case, therefore, is a risk which is known to both parties and results from human inability to predict the future. The authorities are unanimous in distinguishing such risks from bona fide mutual mistakes of fact." *Id.* at 1168. In this case labor was the input that increased costs. The laborers (P1) were not as cooperative as the contractor (P2) believed they would be and unsuccessfully asked the obligee (P3) to bear that risk.

[31] Consent broadly includes "[a] voluntarily yielding to what another proposes or desires; agreement, approval, or permission regarding some act or purpose, esp. given voluntarily by a competent person." BLACK'S LAW DICTIONARY, *supra* note 1, 368. Approve is defined as "[t]o five formal sanction to; to confirm authoritatively." Id. at 123. Permission is defined as "[t]he act of permitting; the official act of allowing someone to do something." Id. at 1321.

decision whether to consent is not a foregone conclusion. A consenting person may be a private individual or entity or a government or international agency and may choose to give or deny its consent. A consent will be necessary when one or both parties are required by the contract between them or a contract with a third party or other legal obligation to obtain a consent from a third party before completing a task or realizing a benefit.

- *Specialty Tires of America, Inc. v. CIT Group/Equipment Financing, Inc.*[32] illustrates a consent required for an obligor to perform: to dispose of equipment leased to an equipment lessee who defaulted under the lease, the equipment lessor required access to the lessee's premises to deliver the equipment still located there. The equipment lessor could not deliver the equipment to a buyer without that consent.
- *Witchita Properties v. Lanterman*[33] illustrates a consent required to realize the benefits of transaction: a tenant who leased premises for the sole purpose of operating a liquor store needed and failed to obtain a liquor license and repudiated the lease. The tenant could pay rent and other obligations under the lease but could not reap the benefits without the liquor license.
- *Gerard v. Almouli*[34] illustrates a consent required because the parties agreed that it must be obtained for a party to complete a task or realize a benefit, even though such consent was not required by a contract with a third party or by any other legal obligation. A distributor agreed to be the exclusive distributor of small-sized halogenated aerosol fire extinguishers for North America, South America, Central America, Germany, and Japan and was obligated to begin placing orders once the manufacturer had obtained approval of the extinguisher from the Underwriters Laboratories. Six years later the approval had still not been obtained. The consent requirement could have been, but was not, waived by the party for whose benefit the consent was to be obtained, the distributor. The consent required in the former two cases could not have been waived by the parties to the contract.

---

32 82 F. Supp.2d 434 (W.D. Pa. 2000).

33 6 Kan. App. 2d 656, 633 P.2d 1154 (Kan. App. 1981).

34 746 F.2d 936 (2d Cir. 1984).

A requirement that a consent be obtained to complete a task or enjoy a benefit is a hazard to the party that must complete the task or realize the benefit because it will be unable to do so without the consent. The risk that the consent will not be obtained is also the risk that the activity will not be completed or the benefit realized. The hazard can be avoided when a consent can be obtained prior to contract formation. If the consent must be obtained before contract formation, the absence of the consent goes to the formation of the contract; the contract may be void or voidable. The consent is one of the legal formalities that must be satisfied for the contract to be effective. Otherwise, the risk—the chance that the consent will be denied—exists from contract formation until the consent is obtained or the transaction terminated.

A third-party consent is analogous to supply in a supply transaction when the consent is required for an obligor to complete its performance. Like a supplier input that must be procured in a first transaction to complete a task in a second transaction, a third-party consent must be obtained in a process distinct from the transaction to enable the obligor to perform its obligation to the obligee. For example, in *Specialty Tires of America, Inc. v. CIT Group/Equipment Financing, Inc.*,[35] where the lessee denied the lessor access to the equipment when it sought to take possession, the seller was thus unable to deliver and failed to deliver the equipment to the buyer. The lessee, seller, and buyer were P1, P2, and P3, respectively; P2 required P1's consent to perform under the P2-P3 contract. If the lessee had been obligated under the P1-P2 contract to consent, its denial of access would have been a breach, just as a failure to supply can be a breach of a supply contract. In most instances, a consenting party will not be so obligated. In such a case, a third-party consent is analogous to a supply transaction when the supplier has no commitment to deliver under the P1-P2 contract.

A third-party consent is analogous to offtake in an offtake transaction when the consent is required for an obligee to realize the benefits of a transaction. Like offtake in a second transaction that yields the benefit of the first transaction to a party, a third-party consent must be obtained in a process distinct from the transaction to enable the party to realize that benefit. For example, in *Witchita Properties v. Lanterman*,[36] the tenant received possession of the premises but could not use them without a liquor license; it could not sell liquor and realize the benefit of the

[35] 82 F. Supp.2d 434 (W.D. Pa. 2000).

[36] 6 Kan. App. 2d 656, 633 P.2d 1154 (Kan. App. 1981).

lease. P1, P2, and P3 were the landlord, tenant, and licensing authority, respectively; the license, while not offtake, was essential for offtake to be permissible.

A consent mismatch exists when a party that needs a consent to complete a task has responsibility for obtaining that consent but does not have a commitment from the consenting party to consent. A mismatch would have existed in *Specialty Tires of America, Inc.*[37] had the equipment lessee no commitment to allow access to the equipment still on its premises and the lessor had a commitment to sell and deliver to the buyer. The finding that the lessee's denial of access in that case made the lessor's performance to its buyer impossible eliminated that mismatch.[38] A mismatch existed in *Witchita Properties*[39] because the tenant had a commitment to lease the premises while having no commitment from the liquor licensing authority to issue a liquor license. In both cases, the mismatches could have been avoided by obtaining the consent and license before contract formation or by conditioning the obligation upon the receipt of the consent.

Oversight, etc., of Supply, Offtake, and Consents

The supply, offtake, and third-party consent risks previously described may be compounded by the occurrence of one or more of the planning hazards described in chapters 3, 4, and 5: overlooking, recognizing but rejecting as unnecessary, or misunderstanding the importance of the process of obtaining a supply or offtake arrangement or a required consent. For example, in *McNamara Construction of Manitoba, Ltd.*,[40] the contractor contended the parties were "mutually ignorant of a material existing fact, namely the unavailability of responsible labor in the area of the project, as well as the exorbitant cost of such labor as was available."[41] The implication was that the contractor lacked sufficient

---

[37] 82 F. Supp.2d 434 (W.D. Pa. 2000).

[38] The buyer sued the lessor for breach of contract, and the lessor claimed the defense of impracticability. The court, after reviewing the lessee's earlier cooperation with the lessor's efforts to dispose of the equipment, concluded the lessee's cooperation was a basic assumption of the contract between the lessor and the buyer and the lessee's actions were sufficient grounds for the impracticability defense.

[39] 6 Kan. App. 2d 656, 633 P.2d 1154 (Kan. App. 1981).

[40] 509 F.2d 1166 (Ct. Cl. 1975).

[41] *Id.* at 1179.

information and made incorrect assumptions about its prospective labor costs and the match between its potential commitment to its labor and its commitment to the government. The process and the likelihood of obtaining a consent may be highly uncertain: the actions the parties are required to take and the criteria the consenting party must consider may be highly discretionary. For example, the manufacturer, in *Gerard*, claimed both parties misunderstood how long approval of the Underwriters Laboratories would take. It may have had incorrect information, incorrectly processed good information, or made an incorrect assumption, not based on information, about how long the process would take. The process was also highly uncertain: whether approval would eventually be forthcoming and how long the process would take could not be predicted.

SUPPLY, OFFTAKE, AND THIRD-PARTY CONSENT RISK MANAGEMENT

Supply, Offtake, and Consent Diligence

Diligence on suppliers and offtakers is similar to that on counterparties. The objective is to determine if at contract formation (1) they are willing and will thereafter remain willing to complete their tasks, and they will complete their tasks in the manner expected; (2) to the extent they must then be able, they are able and will otherwise obtain and retain that ability to complete their tasks, and they will complete their tasks in the manner expected; (3) their performance will be competent; (4) they have given the necessary commitments to supply and offtake; and (5) if they inexcusably fail to perform, they have the financial resources to pay compensation for such failures. Investigations of suppliers and offtakers that have minor but critical roles in supply or offtake chains can and, in some instances, should be conducted. *Evra Corp.*,[42] previously discussed in this chapter,[43] is illustrative: each bank that had to transfer the lessee's funds played a small, but indispensable part in helping the lessee perform and was thus part of its supply chain. It seems likely that the lessee assumed, without investigation, each bank in the payment chain would transfer the funds immediately following their receipt, an assumption that

[42] 673 F.2d 951 (7th Cir. 1982).

[43] See text accompanying notes 15–17.

proved in this instance to be incorrect. Had the lessee asked its bank how long each bank might take to effect its transfer and the bank's liability for transferring late, the lessee could have arranged for an earlier transfer of funds to ensure timely payment.

Diligence on third-party consents varies widely, depending on the third party, the scope of its discretion to refuse its consent, and its procedure for deciding whether or not to give it. The third party may be a private person or a governmental agency. The process may be highly predictable or uncertain. Such discretion may be absolute or circumscribed.

Supply and Offtake Risk Allocation

Contract law principles of interpretation, unilateral and mutual mistake, impossibility, impracticability, frustration, unconscionability, and good faith and fair dealing allocate supply and offtake mismatch and supplier or offtaker performance failure. For example, in *McNamara Construction of Manitoba, Ltd.*,[44] interpretation of the contract as one where the parties knew of the labor difficulties in the area would have resulted in the allocation of responsibility for the risk to the contractor, whereas interpretation of it as one where the parties were unaware of such difficulties would have resulted in allocation of responsibility for the risk to the government. The mismatch of responsibility for risk can be avoided altogether by matching a supply with an offtake commitment, and vice versa. Responsibility for each supplier and offtaker breach hazard can be allocated to the offtaker and supplier, respectively.

Supply Commitment Match. A commitment by a party to its offtaker in a second transaction to perform in circumstances when its supplier does not have a commitment to it to perform in a first transaction is a hazard in one or the other of the transactions. Elimination of that hazard entails either obligating the supplier to perform in the first transaction in all circumstances in which the party is committed to perform in the second or allowing the party to be excused from failing to perform in the second transaction when the supplier in the first transaction is not obligated to perform.

---

[44] 509 F.2d 1166 (Ct. Cl. 1975).

Following are cases that illustrate such commitment matches:

- *State Fuel Co.*[45]: The background to this case is previously summarized.[46] One month after the program was established, a seller and distributor, knowing of the regulations establishing the subsidy, agreed to the sale and purchase of kerosene shipped in boxcars. The seller's telegram, while not mentioning the new regulations, contemplated them when it stipulated, "Unloading and handling charges to be accumulated by you and to bill us and supported by proper evidence but not to exceed 2 cents per gallon." The distributor's subcontractor that unloaded the boxcars for the distributor charged the maximum. The distributor charged that amount to the seller; the seller invoiced the government-owned corporation for reimbursement; the government-owned corporation requested an audit of the subcontractor's books and records; and the subcontractor refused. The subcontractor had been incorporated by the distributor's treasurer and used the distributor's equipment and employees. The government-owned corporation paid only one-half cent per gallon for the excess unloading costs. Had the quoted language not obligated P1 to allow the audit, as the distributor claimed, there would have been a mismatch: the supplier would not have had the commitment from P1 it needed to satisfy the conditions required by the regulations to obligate P3 to pay. P2 would have assumed responsibility for the risk that P1 would not allow the audit and P3 would not pay. As P2 successfully claimed, however, the quoted language obligated P1 to allow an audit; P1's obligation to P2 under in the first transaction matched the conditions P2 had to satisfy to receive reimbursement from P3.[47] The case illustrates the first solution to mismatch risk: including terms in the P1-P2 contract that ensure P1 must perform in all circumstances in which P2 must perform under the P2-P3 contract.

[45] 179 F.2d 390 (1st Cir. 1950).

[46] See text accompanying note 5.

[47] The court advanced three theories on which the jury could find in favor of the seller: the seller was processing the distributor's claim for the subsidy; the seller was financing the distributor while the claim was being processed; and the seller did not assume the risk the government-owned corporation would deny or reduce the subsidy because the distributor failed to provide all necessary documentation and cooperation. 179 F.2d 390, 396–97 (1st Cir. 1950).

- *Chic Organization, Ltd.*[48]: This case is summarized in chapter 1.[49] Diana Ross, Motown, and Chic were P1, P2, and P3, respectively. P1 had no commitment to record with P2 once her contract expired. Had P2 a commitment to provide P1's collaboration, notwithstanding the expiration of her contract with Motown, as Chic claimed, P2 would have committed to perform in circumstances in which P1 had no corresponding obligation to perform. As Motown successfully claimed, P2 had no commitment to P3 if P1 had no commitment to P2. The case illustrates the second solution to mismatch risk: P2 impliedly limited its commitment to P2 to the circumstances under which P2 is entitled to a corresponding performance from P1 under a P1-P2 contract.
- *Cabriolet Porsche Audi, Inc.*[50]: This case is summarized in chapter 7.[51] The manufacturer, importer, and dealer were P1, P2, and P3, respectively. Had the importer committed to deliver to the dealer all the cars it ordered, notwithstanding the shortage to meet all dealers' orders, as the dealer claimed, P2's commitment to P3 would have been greater than P1's commitment to P2. As the importer successfully claimed, it reserved the right to allocate deliveries to dealers and to supply P3 with fewer than all the cars it ordered.[52] The case illustrates the second solution to supply mismatch risk when there are multiple offtakers or P3s. The case also illustrates how a party can, by reserving the discretion to adjust its commitment to its offtaker, whenever and for whatever reason its supplier fails to supply all its wants, avoid supply commitment mismatch.

Offtake Commitment Match. The mismatch hazard in an offtake transaction is an offtaker's commitment in a second transaction that does not require its performance in all circumstances in which the offtaker's counterparty (P2) must perform under its contract with its supplier in a first transaction. Elimination of that hazard entails increasing the offtaker's commitment in the second transaction so that its performance

---

48 582 F. Supp. 812 (S.D.N.Y. 1984).

49 See text accompanying ch. 1, notes 25–34.

50 773 F.2d 1193 (11th Cir. 1985).

51 See text accompanying ch. 7, notes 16 and 17.

52 The district court found in the dealer's favor. The appeal court reversed, holding that as a matter of law the continued use of the allocation system had been reasonable.

is required under all circumstances in which P2 must perform in the first transaction. Alternatively, P2's commitment to its supplier in the first transaction can be decreased to match P3's commitment in the second transaction.

U.S. v. Southwestern Elec. Coop., Inc.[53] illustrates the first solution to offtake mismatch. Southwestern and 14 other utilities acquired an interest in a nuclear electric generating plant to be built, borrowed the moneys to finance such acquisition, and agreed, as a condition to such loans, to purchase all their electricity requirements from the plant at a tariff that would repay the construction, construction financing, operating, and maintenance costs. The initial estimate of the construction cost of the plant of $361,195,000 in February 1976 rose to $666,654,000 in August 1976 and then to $3,250,000,000 in November 1985. The final cost exceeded $5,000,000,000. Southwestern filed an action to rescind the requirements contract. The contractor was P1, the plant owner and its lenders P2, and the utilities P3. Had the commitments of the utilities to pay the construction costs been limited to an amount below the actual costs, as the utilities claimed, P3's commitment to P2 would have been less than P2's commitment to P1. P2 would have assumed some or all of responsibility for the risk of cost overruns. As the plant's owner successfully claimed, the commitments of the utilities to pay the tariff matched the plant's commitment to pay the contractor; P3's commitment to P2 matched P2's commitment to P1. The utilities thus assumed the entire risk of cost overruns.[54]

Supplier Performance Risk Pass Through. Performance risk in supply transactions is the chance that a supplier in a supply transaction will fail to perform as committed. When a party has a commitment to its offtaker

---

[53] 869 F.2d 310 (7th Cir. 1989).

[54] The suit by the utilities claimed mutual mistake and frustration of purpose. The federal district court ruled against Southwestern and the appeal court affirmed. The court pointed out the construction contract acknowledged the uncertainty of costs: "The Participants are aware that the estimated costs of the Clinton Station (including cost of fuel) are subject to change by reason, among other matters, of inflation, compliance with additional governmental requirements, design and equipment changes, and delays in construction and commencement of operation." *Id.* at 314–5. The court also held mutual mistake was inapplicable to cost overruns: "[W]hile the parties to that contract may have been mistaken about the future costs of construction of the Clinton power plant, the doctrine of mutual mistake does not cover an erroneous 'prediction or judgment as to events to occur in the future.'" Citations omitted. *Id.* at 314.

in a second transaction that matches its supplier's commitment to it in the first transaction, the supplier's breach can result in a party's liability to its offtaker for breach when the supplier's breach in the first transaction causes its breach in the second. It may be able to avoid such breach by finding an alternative supplier. It may be prudent to assume it cannot find a ready, alternative supply source. It has recourse to the supplier, but it may still incur liability to the offtaker. The hazard is incurring the risk of that liability. That risk is eliminated by conditioning the party's obligation to perform in the second transaction upon performance by its supplier in the first transaction—what is referred to as "passing through" to the offtaker the risk the supplier will fail to perform. The party thereby avoids responsibility for its own breach that is the result of its supplier's failure to supply it with items it needs to perform.

Lewis v. Penthouse International, Ltd.[55] illustrates a successful pass through of supply risk. Lewis entered and won Penthouse magazine's Penthouse Pet of the Year contest, which, under the terms of the contract she signed, entitled her to an annual salary of $25,000 and the Pet of the Year prizes described in the magazine. The prizes were to be delivered directly by third-party suppliers. Penthouse agreed to use its best efforts to have the suppliers deliver and did, in fact, use such efforts, but a number of suppliers failed to deliver, including that of the primary prize, a new Heritage Legacy automobile. The prize suppliers, Penthouse, and the contestant were P1, P2, and P3, respectively. If the prize suppliers were legally bound to deliver the promised prizes, and the report of the case does not clearly indicate whether they were, they breached when they failed to deliver. Had Penthouse committed to Lewis to deliver or cause delivery of the prizes, notwithstanding the suppliers' failures to do so, as she claimed, it would have assumed as far as she was concerned responsibility for the risk of their breaches, though it would have had recourse to them. Had Penthouse committed only to pass along to the contestant those prizes delivered by the suppliers, it would have entirely passed through to her responsibility for the risk of their defaults. Their defaults would not have put Penthouse in breach of its commitment to the contestant. As Penthouse successfully claimed, Penthouse committed to do something to cause without guaranteeing delivery of the prizes; Penthouse assumed responsibility for the risk that it would fail to do what it committed to do, but nothing more.

[55] 825 F. Supp. 131 (S.D. Tex. 1992).

By agreeing to a standard of performance less than a commitment to deliver or cause the suppliers to deliver the prizes, it partially passed through to the contestant responsibility for the risk of breach by the suppliers.[56]

Offtaker Performance Risk Pass Through. Performance risk in an offtake transaction is the chance that an offtaker will fail to offtake as committed. When a party has a commitment to its supplier in a first transaction that matches its offtaker's commitment to it in the second transaction, the offtaker's breach can result in a party's having to choose to repudiate its supply contract or perform the supply contract without realizing the expected benefit. It has recourse to the offtaker but will still incur liability to the supplier. The hazard is incurring the risk of that choice. That risk is eliminated either by conditioning the party's obligation to perform in the first transaction upon performance by its offtaker in the second transaction or by the party "passing through" to the supplier responsibility for the risk the offtaker will fail to perform.

The following cases illustrate such risk allocations:

- *Howard v. Nicholson*[57]: A landlord hired a contractor to build a beauty salon that would be leased for 20 years to a beauty salon operator. The operator became bankrupt before construction started. The lessor terminated the construction contract (and the contractor sued). The construction contract nowhere expressly stated the landlord would be allowed to terminate in such circumstances. The contractor, landlord, and tenant were P1, P2, and P3, respectively. Had the landlord's obligation to the contractor been independent of the tenant's performance under the lease, as the contractor unsuccessfully implicitly claimed, the landlord would have had to choose between continuing to build a beauty salon for which it had no tenant and repudiating the construction contract. As the landlord successfully claimed, its obligation to the contractor depended or was conditioned upon the tenant's not repudiating the lease. The landlord successfully passed through to the

[56] Lewis sued Penthouse for breach of contract. The court ruled for Penthouse, which delivered what it promised: its best efforts to get the donors to deliver the advertised gifts.

[57] 556 S.W.2d 477 (Mo. App. 1977).

contractor responsibility for the risk of the tenant's repudiation.[58] This risk allocation would have become increasingly tenuous had the contractor started or finished construction.

- *Gilbane Building Co. v. Brisk Waterproofing Co.*[59] illustrates a "pay when paid" clause. Carly Capital Group hired Gilbane as the general contractor on a project to convert warehouses into condominium complexes. Gilbane hired Brisk as a subcontractor. The subcontract included a clear pay when paid clause.[60] Gilbane paid Brisk as the work progressed, except for the final payment. Carly had filed for liquidation in bankruptcy proceedings and had not paid Gilbane for the work by Brisk covered by the final payment. The appeal court found the pay when paid clause unambiguous and applicable. Since the owner was in bankruptcy and could not pay the general contractor, satisfaction of the condition was impossible. The subcontractor, contractor, and owner were P1, P2, and P3, respectively. Because the pay when paid clause conditioned the contractor's obligation to pay its subcontractor upon receipt of payment from the owner, as the contractor successfully claimed, the risk of nonpayment by the owner, as between the contractor and subcontractor, was allocated to the latter.[61] Had the pay when paid clause been a statement of when payment should be made and not a condition to payment, as the subcontractor unsuccessfully claimed, responsibility for the risk of the owner's nonpayment would, as between the contractor and subcontractor, remain with the contractor.

Force Majeure. Force majeure is defined as an event or effect that "can neither be anticipated nor controlled; esp. an unexpected event that prevents someone from doing something that he or she had agreed or officially planned to do."[62] Such events are associated with both natural

[58] The trial court found for the defense, and the contractor appealed. The appellate court upheld the trial court's ruling.

[59] 86 Md. App. 21, 585 A.2d 248 (Md. App. 1991).

[60] 86 Md. App. 21, 24, 585 A.2d 248, 250.

[61] Brisk sued for the unpaid final payment, and Gilbane claimed that because the condition precedent in the pay when paid clause had not been satisfied, it was not obligated to pay Brisk. The trial court granted summary judgment in favor of the subcontractor; the contractor appealed; and the appeal court reversed.

[62] BLACK'S LAW DICTIONARY, *supra* note 1, 761.

events and human acts.[63] A clause that excuses a failure to perform when caused by such an event can be expanded to include a supply failure that renders P2 unable to perform its obligation to P3. The effect of a force majeure clause in such a case is to pass through to the offtaker in the second transaction the risk that P2 will fail to perform due to P1's failure in the first transaction. Whether such a clause can be logically expanded to include an offtake failure seems doubtful: the offtaker's failure in the second transaction defeats the purpose of the first transaction but not P2's ability to perform its obligation to P1.

Following are two cases that illustrate the application of force majeure clauses to supply and offtake failures:

- *Facto v. Pantagis*[64]: A restaurant agreed to host a wedding reception. Shortly after the reception began, a power failure in the area of the restaurant occurred and continued for the duration of the reception. The customer claimed reimbursement of its costs from the restaurant. The contract between the restaurant and its customer included a force majeure clause that "excused . . . performance [by the restaurant] . . . if it is prevented from doing so by an act of God (e.g., flood, power failure, etc.), or other unforeseen events or circumstances." The utility, the restaurant, and the customer were P1, P2, and P3, respectively. P2's failure was directly attributable to the power failure caused by P1, whether or not that failure was excused. Had the clause not applied to power failures, as the customer claimed, because the restaurant might have used backup generators, the restaurant might, as between it and customer, have assumed responsibility for the risk of the utility failing to supply power during the reception. The restaurant might still have been excused by the impossibility doctrine. Because the clause specifically mentioned power failures, it did apply, as the restaurant claimed, and responsibility for the risk that the utility would fail to supply power during the reception had been passed through to the customer.[65] The case illustrates how the application

---

63 *Id.*

64 390 N.J. Super. 227, 915 A.2d 59 (N.J. Sup. Ct. 2007).

65 The customer sued for the amounts prepaid to the restaurant, the band, the photographer, and the videographer. The full force majeure clause read: "Snuffy's [the restaurant] will be excused from performance under this contract if it is prevented from doing so by an act of God (e.g., flood, power failure, etc.), or other unforeseen events or circumstances." The

of a force majeure clause to a supply failure passes through responsibility for the risk of such failure to the offtaker.

- *Specialty Foods of Indiana, Inc. v. City of South Bend*[66]: When, in 1993, the National Football League decided to locate the College Hall of Fame in South Bend, Indiana, it leased a facility from the city for 40 years. In 2000, the city agreed Specialty Foods would be the exclusive supplier of food for the facility for five years, with two options to renew for two further five-year terms. Specialty exercised both options. In 2012, with the city's agreement, the College Hall of Fame moved to Atlanta, Georgia. The city canceled its contract with Specialty Foods, which had three years remaining. The city invoked the force majeure clause, the relevant portion of which excused performances delayed, hindered or prevented by events, such as acts of God, or "any other reason not within the reasonable control" of the affected party.[67] Specialty Foods, the city, and the Hall of Fame were P1, P2, and P3, respectively. The relocation of the Hall of Fame defeated the purpose of the contract between P1 and P2, but the city could still perform. It would not realize the intended principal benefits from that performance. Had the application of the force majeure clause been limited to instances where the party claiming the benefit of the clause was unable or hindered in its performance, as Specialty Foods claimed, responsibility for the risk of P3's termination and relocation of the Hall of Fame would have, as between P1 and P2, been assumed by P2. The city successfully claimed that the force majeure clause extended to its situation, where the city was no longer able to

trial court dismissed the claim, holding the force majeure clause barred the claim. The appeals court affirmed, in part, holding the restaurant was not liable for damages incurred by the customer as the power outage, though not unforeseeable, "These are precisely the kind of circumstances under which the parties agreed, by inclusion of the force majeure clause, that the Pantagis Renaissance would be excused from performance." *Id.* at 62–63.

66 997 N.E.2d 23 (Ind. App. 2013).

67 The full clause stated, "In the event Century Center or [Specialty Foods] shall be delayed or hindered or prevented from the performance of any obligation required under this Agreement by reason of strikes[,] lockouts, inability to procure labor or materials, failure of power, fire or other casualty, acts of God, restrictive governmental laws or regulations, riots, insurrection, war or any other reason not within the reasonable control of Century Center or [Specialty Foods], as the case may be, then the performance of such obligation shall be excused for the period of such delay and the period for the performance of any such act shall be extended for a period equivalent to the period of such delay." *Id.* at 27.

realize the benefits of its performance. Such extension of the clause passed through to Specialty Foods responsibility for the risk of the offtaker's termination of its agreement with the city. Notwithstanding the previous comment, that force majeure clauses do not logically apply to offtake failures, the case illustrates the application of a force majeure clause to an offtake failure, where P3 terminates the P2-P3 contract, and not one in which P3 breached the P2-P3 contract at that.[68]

Direct Performance. Having a supplier supply directly to an offtaker or having the offtaker directly offtake from the supplier eliminates the middle party and reduces the scope of the performance required in both transactions. Two transactions and three parties still exist, but the first is no longer a supply transaction in the sense that the supplier supplies obligor P2 with an item of value it uses to perform its obligation to the offtaker in the second transaction. The offtaker has two contracts: one with the obligor P2 and the other with the supplier. By avoiding a contract with the supplier and a contract with the offtaker to supply such item of value to the offtaker, the obligor P2 avoids responsibility for the risk of the supplier's failing to supply. Similarly, by having an offtaker offtake directly from the supplier, the obligor P2 avoids any obligation to P1 concerning that performance and the risk of P3's failing to perform. Supply and offtake risk are avoided by structuring the transactions to redirect supply and offtake chains.

Windows, Inc. v. Jordan Panel Systems Corp.[69] illustrates such a supply structure. A window supplier delivered windows to a carrier, who improperly loaded the trucks for shipment from South Dakota to New York. The windows were extensively damaged en route. The buyer

[68] Specialty Foods argued the clause did not apply to the cancelation of the city's contract with the NFF since the city could still perform its contract with Specialty Foods. The court disagreed, holding, "[W]e conclude that the terms of the force majeure provision excusing performance for 'any other reason not within the reasonable control of Century Center' includes the closure and relocation of the Hall of Fame." *Id.* at 29. The court's rationale, however, speaks to frustration of purpose and does not explain how the city was prevented from performance: "The purpose was to use the services of Specialty Foods, the ancillary vendor, to enhance the products and services of the Hall of Fame, the primary business, in order to make the Hall of Fame a facility of the highest quality as stated in the UMO Agreement. Thus, when the Hall of Fame ceased to exist in South Bend, so too did the need for the services provided by Specialty Foods." *Id.*

[69] 177 F.3d 114 (2d Cir. 1999).

claimed compensation from the seller for such damages. If the carrier had contracted with the seller, the carrier, seller, and buyer were P1, P2, and P3, respectively, and P1 carried the goods under a P1-P2 contract, as the buyer claimed. P1 would have been liable to P2 and P2 liable to P3 for the damage caused by defective loading. As between P2 and P3, P2 would have assumed responsibility for the risk of P1's breach. As the carrier contracted with the buyer, because the seller delivered to the buyer when it delivered the windows to the carrier, as the seller successfully claimed, P3 had separate contracts with P1 and P2, and as between it and P2, P3 had assumed responsibility for the risk of P1's defective loading.[70]

Third-Party Consent Risk Allocation

The two solutions to supply risks—commitment match and pass through of the risk of the supplier's failure to perform—can be combined in a condition precedent that a required consent be given before an obligor must perform. The absence of a commitment by the consenting party to consent can be matched by a commitment by the obligor that becomes effective when the consent is given (P1 has no commitment to consent and P2 has no commitment to P3 to perform until the consent is given). The obligor bears no responsibility for the obligee's losses that result from the failure to obtain the consent. That commitment match can be qualified by terms that impose commitments to make efforts to obtain the consent or to pay compensation if the consent is not obtained.

Following are three illustrations of commitment matches and mismatches:

- *First National Bank of Chicago v. Atlantic Tele-Network Co.*[71]: A bank committed to make loans to a borrower to purchase a telephone network, subject to satisfaction of certain conditions precedent,

[70] In an action by the buyer against the seller for breach of contract, the seller's motion for summary judgment was granted by the federal district court and affirmed by the appeal court. Because the contract was a shipment contract, the seller's obligation was to "put the goods in the possession of such a carrier and make such a contract for their transportation as may be reasonable having regard to the nature of the goods and other circumstances of the case." Uniform Commercial Code § 2-504(a). The seller had no further obligation upon so doing, and the risk of loss passed to the buyer. Responsibility for the risk of the carrier's failure to perform was thus allocated to the buyer.

[71] 946 F.2d 516 (7th Cir. 1991).

one of which was obtaining a government approval of the pledge of the stock of the company that would own the telephone network. The condition matched the bank's commitment to loan with the agency's commitment to consent: it had no obligation to loan moneys until the consent was given and the government had no commitment to consent. But the borrower's commitment to pay the bank fees for the commitments was not matched with the agency's discretion to refuse the consent. The borrower had to pay the bank the agreed commitment fees even if the consent was not received. This mismatch resulted in the borrower alone assuming responsibility for the risk the consent would not be given.[72]

- *Brenner v. Little Red School House*[73]: A father agreed to pay a full year's tuition to a private school for his child, but his former wife refused to allow the child to attend the school. The contract stipulated that tuition was "payable in advance of the first day of school, no portion refundable." The ex-wife's lack of commitment to consent was matched by the school's conditional commitment to accept the child when the consent had been given. The school had no obligation to accept the child until the ex-wife consented. But the father's commitment was not similarly matched: he had to pay the tuition even if the ex-wife refused her consent. Because the father had to pay the full year's tuition without any right to a refund, he alone assumed responsibility for the consent risk.[74]

[72] The federal district court granted the bank's motion for summary judgment and the appeals court affirmed in part. Of the fees, the court held they were not conditional upon the bank making a loan. *Id.* at 520. Of the consent from the government agency, the court said, "The refusal of the Virgin Islands commission to allow the purchase of Vitelco did not prevent ATN from paying fees to the bank; it just prevented the loan from going through (at once anyway); the fees were (in part) to compensate the bank for setting money aside for a loan that might never close." *Id.* at 521.

[73] 302 N.C. 207, 274 S.E.2d 206 (N.C. 1981).

[74] The father sued for rescission of the contract with the school, claiming that his performance was excused by impossibility and frustration of purpose. The trial court granted him summary judgment. The appeal court reversed, remanding for summary judgment in favor of the school. The North Carolina Supreme Court affirmed the grant of summary judgment on the nonavailability of these defenses. The court cited a clause in the contract that states that tuition is "payable in advance of the first day of school, no portion refundable" and held, "This provision allocates to plaintiff the risk that the child will not attend, and prevents the application of the doctrine of frustration of purpose." *Id.* at 210.

- *T.S.I. Holdings, Inc. v. Jenkins*[75]: A shareholder in a company agreed to convert his common shares into preferred shares, which he would retain, and new common shares, which he would sell to an investor. The bank to which he had pledged the shares as security for a personal loan and of which he was a director had to consent to the reorganization and to release the shares from the pledge. The contract between the investor and shareholder obligated the latter to use his best efforts to obtain the bank's consent. The bank's regulator assumed control of the bank before a decision was made. The company terminated the contract. The shareholder assumed responsibility for obtaining the consent to the extent of the best efforts obligation. So long as it used its best efforts, it discharged its obligation. Beyond that effort the shareholder's commitment to the investor matched the bank's commitment to consent: the shareholder had no commitment to consummate the reorganization or compensate the investor. Both parties shared responsibility for the bank's failure to consent, as the contract could be terminated without either party having to compensate the other for loss of the anticipated benefits.[76]

The risk that the consenting party will not consent when it is obligated to do so or to follow certain procedures when deciding whether to give a consent is also passed through to the obligee by the condition since the consent must have been given before the obligor has a commitment to perform (P1 has a commitment to consent or to follow procedures, but P2 has no commitment to P3 to perform until the consent is given).

---

[75] 260 Kan. 703, 924 P.2d 1239 (Kan. 1996).

[76] The company sued for a declaration that the agreement with the investor had been terminated automatically on the scheduled closing date. The company argued, inter alia, its failure to consummate the conversion of the shares had been excused by the doctrine of impracticability. The district court ruled in favor of the company, and the Kansas Supreme Court affirmed. First, the contract included as a condition to the closing that the shareholder obtain and convert the common shares as agreed. Second, the sellers had a duty to use their best efforts to obtain the shares from the bank. "The sellers neither assumed the risk nor guaranteed the Bank's release of [the shareholder's] Paul's TSI stock. This is not an impracticability of performance case because under Section 4.1(a), sellers were required only to exert their best efforts to secure release of the stock." *Id.* at 719.

11

Uncontrollable Event Risks

HAZARDS

Events and acts beyond the control of parties can adversely affect their transaction. Such acts and events may be the work of natural forces or human agents. Such agents may be government agencies or private third parties, individuals, and entities. The actions of individuals and entities may be those of specific persons that directly affect parties to a transaction or those of many individuals and entities acting in the markets. Market changes are discussed in chapter 12.

Uncontrollable Events: Nature and Third Parties

Each incident, the occurrence or nonoccurrence of which is beyond the parties' control and affects their transaction, can be described using three variables:

- whether such incident was (1) the occurrence of an event that was not expected to or it was hoped would not occur, or (2) the nonoccurrence of an event that was expected to occur or it was hoped would occur,
- whether the incident affected (a) benefit realization or (b) task completion, and

- whether benefit realization or task completion was as a result of such incident partly or wholly (i) reduced, (ii) delayed, or (iii) made more expensive.

These variables can be combined to describe each uncontrollable incident. For example, a storm that delays a contractor's completion of a construction project beyond the scheduled date would be a (1)(b)(ii) scenario: an uncontrollable event that delays completion of a task. If additional cost is also the result, the scenario would be (1)(b)(ii) and (1)(b)(iii). Payment of a successor liability claim—a liability of the seller of a business that is automatically assumed by the buyer of that business—would be a (1)(a)(iii) scenario: realization of the value of the acquisition is made more expensive by the claim.

When task completion is impaired, partly or wholly, or delayed by an uncontrollable event, such incident can be further described using two additional variables:

- whether the task was intended to be completed for (A) the benefit of the party completing it or (B) the other party, and
- whether, in the case of (B), the effect of the event was to (I) constrain or otherwise impair performance or (II) to induce an obligor to choose between two adverse outcomes: performance and suffering or risking suffering a harm, on one hand, and not performing and avoiding that harm or risk, on the other.

These variables can be combined with the first three groups to describe each uncontrollable incident, with the result that 32 scenarios are possible. The storm example would be a (1)(b)(ii)(B)(I) scenario: the storm is an uncontrollable event that delays the contractor's performance (completion of a task for the other party's benefit is impaired). Understanding of all 32 scenarios will help to identify the different risk allocation devices needed to manage the different uncontrollable event hazards, though they are not all described in detail here.

Two other variables often stand out in the occurrence of uncontrollable events. These are

- whether the incident was the product of (1) natural forces or (2) human agency, and
- whether, if it was the product of human agency, the agency was (a) a private individual or (b) a governmental agency.

Where the different combinations of the first four variables may affect the choice of contractual device to manage the resulting risk, the last two variables do not. They help to understand the considerable range of uncontrollable events that can affect a transaction.

Events and Nonevents

An uncontrollable event is easily imagined. The words "act of God" conjure the image of a violent, natural event beyond the parties' control, such as an earthquake or an outbreak of thunder and lightning. What is less obvious is how nonoccurrence of an event can adversely affect a transaction. A transaction can be structured such that benefit realization or task completion can be achieved only if an uncontrollable event occurs. The passage of time without its occurrence results in such benefits not being realized or tasks not being completed as anticipated. An example is winning the lottery. Winning depends upon the occurrence of a highly improbable, uncontrolled event: drawing by the lottery of a sequence of numbers that match a participant's ticket. The risk to the lottery ticket buyer is that such event will not occur.

The following cases illustrate uncontrollable events that did not occur as expected, and as a result the transaction outcomes were also not as expected:

- *Chugach Electric Association v. Northern Corp.*[1]: A contractor agreed with a utility to repair the face of a dam using rock to be quarried from a specific source and stockpiled "for transport across Cooper Lake to the dam site when such lake is frozen to a sufficient depth to permit heavy vehicle traffic thereon."[2] When winter came, the contractor considered the ice too thin to traverse with heavy trucks, while the utility thought it sufficiently thick for work to continue. The contractor eventually attempted a crossing with two half-loaded trucks, but they broke through the ice and sank, resulting in the death of one driver. The utility then agreed the operation could not continue. The contractor terminated the contract.[3]

[1] 518 P.2d 76 (Alaska 1974), rehearing (rehg) over damages, 523 P.2d 1243 (Alaska 1974), *aff'd.* 562 P.2d 1053 (Alaska 1977).

[2] *Id.* at 78.

[3] Citing impossibility, the contractor also sued for costs incurred through the date of termination; the utility cross-claimed for damages. The trial court found the contract had been discharged by impossibility and dismissed both parties' claims. On appeal, the Alaska

The contractor's anticipated performance depended upon the occurrence of an event: the temperatures reaching their usual lows. The incident might also be recast as the occurrence of abnormally warm temperatures that prevented the formation of ice in its usual thickness.

- *Hensler v. Los Angeles*[4]: Paving work on runways at an airport operated by a city agency could not start until a state highway agency completed a new bypass road, enabling the state to stop using the old bypass road where the new runways would be located. When the new bypass had not been completed when expected, the city issued a change order deleting the work on the taxis, runways, and associated work. Eventually the bypass road was completed and the city let a new contract for the work to another contractor.[5] The contractor's performance depended upon the occurrence of an event: completion of the work on the bypass as anticipated. The incident might also be conceived as late completion by the state of the bypass road that prevented the city's work from starting when anticipated.
- *Wheelbrator Envirotech Operating Services Inc. v. Mass. Laborers Dist. Council Local 1144*[6]: A contractor contracted with a city to operate the city's water treatment plant and, at the same time, separately agreed with the labor union that represented the employees who worked at the plant that if the city agreed to let another contractor become the successor operator of the plant, that successor contractor would agree to the same terms to which the present contractor had agreed with the union. A successor contract was awarded to another operator,

Supreme Court held the quoted language "presupposed the existence of ice frozen to the requisite depth. Since this expectation of the parties was never fulfilled, and since the provisions relating to the means of performance was clearly material, [the contractor's] . . . duty to perform was discharged by reason of impossibility." *Id.* at 80.

4 124 Cal.App.2d 71, 268 P.2d 12 (Cal. App. 1954).

5 The contractor sued for breach of contract, claiming the items so deleted could not be removed under the terms of the contract. The city also claimed the state agency's delay made it impossible to perform. The trial court found for the contractor, the city appealed, and the appeal court affirmed. The contract limited changes to those the purpose of which was to implement the work, which was not the case. Because the city had an obligation to provide a site where the contemplated operations could be carried out, it could not claim impossibility.

6 88 F.3d 40 (1st Cir. 1996).

which refused to assume the contractor's union contract and negotiated a new contract with the union, with reduced benefits and wages. Performance by the contractor depended entirely upon the occurrence of an event: its successor's agreeing to the same terms with the union. The incident might also be viewed as the occurrence of an event: the union's agreeing to terms with the successor contractor that were less advantageous than those accepted by the contractor.

- *Wisconsin Electric Power Co. v. Union Pacific R.R. Co.*[7]: A railroad agreed to transport coal from a utility's mines in Colorado to its power plants in Wisconsin at two rates, one lower and the other higher. The latter was charged if the railroad could not reload its cars with iron ore in Minnesota for transportation to a steel plant in Utah on the return trip as a result of a force majeure event. The steel plant became bankrupt and stopped operating shortly after the contract was signed.[8] The incident might also be viewed as the occurrence of an event: the steel mill's bankruptcy, which prevented the carriage of the mill's ore from Minnesota to Utah.[9]

In the first two cases, performance could not begin until an event had occurred: the lake had frozen in *Chugach Electric Association*[10] and the bypass road had been completed in *Hensler.*[11] In *Wheelbrator Envirotech Operating Services Inc.*,[12] the contractor's performance could only be

[7] 557 F.3d 504 (7th Cir. 2009).

[8] The railroad invoked the force majeure clause and charged the higher rate. The application of the clause and higher rate was upheld by the federal district and appeal court.

[9] Judge Richard Posner questioned the choice of a force majeure clause to allocate the risk that the steel company might not load the railroad cars with iron ore on the back haul: "Why the parties used the term 'force majeure,' rather than simply providing that the railroad could charge the higher rate if the steel company stopped buying iron ore, has not been explained. More careful drafting might have averted this lawsuit."

[10] 518 P.2d 76 (Alaska 1974), rehg. over damages, 523 P.2d 1243 (Alaska 1974), *aff'd.* 562 P.2d 1053 (Alaska 1977).

[11] 124 Cal.App.2d 71, 268 P.2d 12 (Cal. App. 1954).

[12] The union claimed the present contractor had to pay as damages the difference between the wages and benefits the present contractor had agreed to pay under its contract and what the successor contractor actually paid the employees. The contractor claimed performance had been impossible all along because the successor alone decided whether to assume the existing contractor's union contract. This was true, Judge Norman Stahl acknowledged, but in upholding the arbitrator's award of damages as claimed, he said, "by agreeing to include

started and would then be completed when the successor contractor accepted the union's terms. In *Wisconsin Electric Power Co.*,[13] the steel mill's use of the railroad during the return journey triggered the lower rate. All five transactions were structured so that successful outcomes depended upon the occurrence of uncontrollable events. Those events did not occur, just as the numbers drawn in a lottery do not match those on the ticket purchased by the lottery participant.

The hazards in all five cases were transaction plans or structures that required for their successful outcomes the nonoccurrence of the events, upon the occurrence of which benefit realization or task completion depended. The cases illustrate the following hazards:

- nonoccurrence of an uncontrollable event (frozen lake in *Chugach Electric Association* and successor contractor's acceptance of union terms in *Wheelbrator Envirotech Operating Services Inc.*) prevents task completion (scenario (2)(b)(i)),
- nonoccurrence of an uncontrollable event (completion of the state bypass) delays task completion in *Hensler* (scenario (2)(b)(ii)), and
- nonoccurrence of an uncontrollable event makes the utility's task completion more expensive in *Wisconsin Electric Power Co.* (scenario (2)(b)(iii)).

Such hazards existed at contract formation and continued until they resulted in an unsuccessful outcome. They would have ceased had such events occurred. When the occurrence of an event causes the adverse outcome, the hazard does not exist at contract formation. They are only potential hazards in the transactions at that time.

Benefit Impairment

An uncontrollable event can reduce, delay, or destroy the value or utility a party expects to realize from a transaction or an item it expects to use to realize such value without directly affecting the obligor's performance

the successor clause, [the contractor] accepted and bargained for the risk that, if it lost the contract, it would effectively guarantee that its 'successor' would assume the terms and conditions of the [contract with the union]." 88 F.3d at 45 (1st Cir. 1996).

13 557 F.3d 504 (7th Cir. 2009).

that yields such value or utility (scenario (1)(a)(i)). It may also delay the realization of benefits (scenario (1)(a)(ii)) or make their realization more costly (scenario (1)(a)(iii)).

The following four cases illustrate scenario (1)(a)(i):

- *Warner-Lambert Pharmaceutical Co. v. John J. Reynolds, Inc.*[14]: A licensee made Listerine for 75 years using a secret formula licensed under agreements made in 1881 and 1885. The licensee paid royalties to the licensor in excess of $1.5 million annually. In 1949, the formula was published in the *United States Pharmacopoia*, the *National Formulary*, and the *Journal of the American Medical Association*. The disclosure directly impaired the value of the license to the licensee.[15] Because both the licensor and licensee could still perform their obligations—the licensor's continued permission to use the formula and the licensee's continued payment of royalties were unimpaired—the disclosure affected only the licensee's benefit. The case illustrates scenario (1)(a)(i) (uncontrollable event reduced value of formula to the licensee).
- *Felt v. McCarthy*[16]: A buyer purchased parcels of land with a note. He expected to develop the parcels because the area in which they were located had been designated for office and light industrial use. The county changed the zoning designation to wetlands.[17] The

[14] 178 F. Supp. 655 (S.D.N.Y. 1959).

[15] The licensee sued for a declaration that it was no longer liable to pay royalties for the use of the formula. Neither party was responsible for such publication. The court held the licensee remained liable for royalty payments. "The argument that there was failure of consideration in 1931 after the agreement had been in force for some forty-five years because of disclosure then, is wholly devoid of merit. The plaintiff does not question that the conveyance to it of the 'secret formula' furnished consideration for the contract. Once a contract is supported by consideration its terms are up to the parties. Whether the consideration is adequate or not is no concern of the court." *Id.* at 666.

[16] 78 Wn. App. 362, 898 P.2d 315 (Wash. App. 1995).

[17] The buyer repudiated the note, claiming supervening frustration. The trial court held for the seller, and the appeal court affirmed. "[The buyer] knew that the laws relating to land development were subject to change in the future. He drafted the option and sales contracts. He 'could have controlled the language of the contract to the extent of allocating the risk'. For example, he could have negotiated for a provision making the contract contingent upon obtaining all permits and approvals required for development." *Id.* at 366.

change impaired the value of the parcels to the buyer. The change did not affect the discharge of the parties' obligations: the seller had already completed the sale and the buyer could continue to pay the note. This case also illustrates scenario (1)(a)(i) (change in zoning reduced value of land to the buyer).

- *Uminous Neon, Inc. v. Parscale*[18]: A city began construction on the street on which a party's business was located, and as a result, her business declined. Separately, she had leased advertising signs located elsewhere and stopped paying rent because they served little immediate purpose while construction crimped her operations.[19] The street construction impaired the benefits of the billboard advertising contracts. The store operator could still pay rent for the signs and the sign owners could still allow her to use them for advertising. The value of that advertising diminished because the potential customers could not, or had to struggle to, reach her business. This case also illustrates scenario (1)(a)(i) (traffic detour on the street where the shop was located reduced value of billboard advertising elsewhere to the shop owner).
- *Wald v. Lenox Ave. & 140th St. Corp.*[20]: A landlord hired attorneys to apply for a government agency approval that would permit it to raise rents. The landlord agreed to pay the attorneys 50 percent of the increase in the rents for one year. At contract formation, the approval for which application was made was the only one required to increase rents. While the application was pending, a new ordinance was adopted that required the landlord to obtain an additional approval of another agency to increase rents. The change in law did not impair performance by either party: the attorney could continue with its efforts to obtain the first approval and the landlord could pay the agreed fee (when the second approval had been obtained). The nominal value of the benefit, the stated rent increase, remained the same. The case illustrates

[18] 17 Kan. App. 2d 241, 836 P.2d 1201 (Kan. App. 1992).

[19] The business owner claimed she was excused on the grounds her performance was impractical. The court dismissed the claim, holding, "The present case is one of subjective impracticability. Parscale [the lessee] could no longer afford to operate her business due to road construction or some other reason. It is not sufficient merely that the business suffered." *Id.* at 245.

[20] 197 Misc. 773, 94 N.Y.S.2d 793 (N.Y. Mun. Ct. 1950).

scenarios (1)(a)(ii) and (1)(a)(iii). The change in law added a task the landlord had to complete to realize those benefits, both delaying and increasing the costs of realizing the anticipated benefits.[21] The case does not illustrate scenario (1)(b)(ii)(A) or (1)(b)(iii)(A) because the second approval was an entirely new task the landlord had to complete, and not one modified by a change in law, to realize such benefits.

Task Impairment

A task that must be completed for a party to realize its benefits may be one the other party must complete, whether or not the other party is committed to completing it. It may also be one that the party itself must complete to realize its benefits, often but not always after the other party has completed its tasks. An uncontrollable event may make the completion of either such task as contemplated impossible, impractical, or infeasible (scenario (1)(b)(i)(B) or (1)(b)(i)(A)) or increase the time required (scenario (1)(b)(ii)(B) or (1)(b)(ii)(A)) or the costs to be incurred to complete it (scenario (1)(b)(iii)(B) or (1)(b)(iii)(A) (occurrence of an uncontrollable event prevents task completion)).

Following are two cases that illustrate scenario (1)(b)(i):

- *Taylor v. Taintor*[22]: An individual was arrested for grand larceny in Connecticut and was granted bail on condition that he appear in the Connecticut court. He returned to New York, where he was taken into custody and transferred to Maine, where he continued to be held in custody. As a result, he failed to appear before the Connecticut court and his bond was forfeited.[23] Neither he nor his

[21] The attorneys obtained the first approval and sued for their fees. The court dismissed analogies to cases that held the doctrine of frustration of purpose applied and the obligations were discharged.

[22] 16 Wall. 366, 83 U.S. 366, 21 L. Ed. 287 (1873).

[23] The sureties sued to recover the bond, contending the accused's appearance had been rendered impossible by his being held in custody in Maine. The trial court ruled against the sureties, and the appeal court affirmed. The U.S. Supreme Court affirmed, holding the sureties, having allowed the accused to go to New York, were responsible for his failure to appear and not entitled to be excused.

sureties who had ensured his appearance before the Connecticut court could perform. This case illustrates scenario (1)(b)(i)(B): the restraint on the suspect physically prevented the sureties from delivering him to the Connecticut court as promised.

- *J.M. Rodriguez & Co. v. Moore-MacCormack Lines, Inc.*[24]: A shipment of cloves, loaded on board in Madagascar, were missing when the vessel was unloaded following its arrival in New York and a two-month delay due to a strike at the port.[25] The theft of the goods prevented the vessel from completing its performance. This case also illustrates scenario (1)(b)(i)(B): the theft physically prevented the vessel from delivering the cloves as promised.

The distinction between frustration and impossibility helps our understanding of the difference between the hazards in scenarios (1)(a), (1)(b)(i)(A), (1)(b)(ii)(A), and (1)(b)(iii)(A), on one hand, and (1)(b)(i)(B), (1)(b)(ii)(B), and (1)(b)(iii)(B), on the other. Frustration may apply where the purpose of the contract has been defeated or destroyed by a supervening event not reasonably anticipated at contract formation. Harm to a benefit may occur from an uncontrollable event even if it or the facts of the case fall short of one where frustration discharges performance. In none of the previous three cases where the anticipated benefits were impaired (*Warner-Lambert Pharmaceutical Co., Inc.*, *Felt,* and *Uminous Neon, Inc.*) was performance discharged by reason of frustration, even though value was impaired, substantially in the first two cases. All three such cases were (1)(a)(i) scenarios: uncontrollable events diminished the anticipated benefits. Impossibility and impracticability may apply where a supervening event makes performance physically impossible or commercially impractical. The hazard (scenario (1)(b)) may occur even if it or the facts of the case fall short of one where impossibility or impracticability discharge performance. In *J.M. Rodriguez*

---

[24] 32 N.Y.2d 425 (N.Y. 1973).

[25] The carrier claimed it was not liable for the loss under a statutory limitation on its liability incorporated in the bill of lading, which exempted "the carrier from liability for loss or damage arising or resulting from . . . strikes or lockouts or stoppage or restraint of labor from whatever cause, whether partial or general." The New York Court of Appeal held that the strike had not caused the loss: "The total loss of the goods was due to the fault or allocable to the responsibility of the carrier or its servants, either on loading, in transit, or on unloading, and not to the strike. Consequently, the strike was not the proximate cause of the loss, but only of the delay in effecting delivery." *Id.* at 431.

& Co.,[26] the theft impaired performance by the vessel. The relevant distinction between the first (scenarios (1)(a), (1)(b)(i)(A), (1)(b)(ii)(A), and (1)(b)(iii)(A)) and second ((1)(b)(i)(B), (1)(b)(ii)(B), and (1)(b)(iii)(B)) groups of scenarios is between events that impair benefit realization and completion of performance.

Increased Costs

An uncontrollable event may increase the costs of benefit realization or task completion. Such events include traditional *force majeure* events that disrupt benefit realization and task completion and any claim that might be made by a third party against one of the parties in relation to the transaction or events that occur in connection with it.

The following cases illustrate how expansive is the range of uncontrollable events that can increase a party's costs of benefit realization and task completion.

- *Rainbow Navigation, Inc. v. United States*[27]: A vessel carried goods to Iceland where unloading was delayed until a strike at the port ended. The vessel incurred costs while waiting for the strike to end it would not otherwise have incurred. The case illustrates a scenario (1)(b)(iii)(B) (additional costs incurred by party completing task for the benefit of the other party). This case is further summarized later in this chapter.[28]
- *City of Vernon v. City of Los Angeles*[29]: Los Angeles agreed, in a series of contracts beginning in 1909, to dispose of Vernon's sewage, in return for a number of payments, all of which Vernon paid. The contracts did not provide for their termination. Decades later, a state agency obtained a court order prohibiting Los Angeles from continuing to dispose of sewage in Santa Monica Bay. To comply with the order, Los Angeles had to construct a $41 million sewage treatment plant and spend $500,000 in annual operating costs. Los Angeles claimed Vernon should share these costs. If Los Angeles could not terminate the contract and had to bear the entire increase in costs, an uncontrollable event, the court order,

[26] 32 N.Y.2d 425 (N.Y. 1973).

[27] 742 F. Supp. 171 (D.N.J. 1990).

[28] See text accompanying notes 117–119.

[29] 45 Cal.2d 710, 290 P.2d 841 (Cal. 1955).

would have considerably increased the costs of its performance of its contract with Vernon (scenario (1)(b)(iii)(B)(I)). For Vernon, which had to bear its share of the increased cost, notwithstanding that it paid Los Angeles in advance for the service, the court order increased its cost of performance, which it believed had been completed by previous payments (also scenario (1)(b)(iii)(B)(I)). The contract did not contemplate such additional costs.[30]

- *National Passenger Railway Corp. v. Atchison, Topeka & Santa Fe Railway Co.*[31]: Amtrak entered into contracts with various railroads to allow their employees and their employees' dependents who had received free or reduced-rate transportation on lines operated by Amtrak's predecessors before Amtrak began operation to continue to enjoy such benefits on the lines operated by Amtrak. Congress enacted a law that obligated the railroads to pay Amtrak for its costs in continuing to allow such railroad employees and dependents to enjoy such benefits.[32] For the railroads, the law imposed a new obligation to Amtrak and increased their cost of performance (scenario (1)(b)(iii)(B)(I)).
- *In re Grumman Olson Industries, Inc.*[33]: A truck parts manufacturer that was the subject of a bankruptcy proceeding obtained an order of the bankruptcy court approving the sale to an acquirer of substantially all its assets, free and clear of liens, encumbrances, "claims" and other "interests." The court's order specifically stated

---

[30] Los Angeles claimed its continued performance under the existing contracts had become economically and legally impracticable and that Vernon should share in these costs. The trial court held the court order had terminated the contracts, and Vernon appealed. The California Supreme Court partly agreed: "[T]he parties contemplated that there would be available for legal use disposal facilities, whether those in existence or to be constructed, the cost of which would not be completely disproportionate to the costs expressly referred to in those contracts." *Id.* at 720. The court held that the contracts had not been terminated as a result of the supervening events. Rather, certain terms and conditions in the contracts "can and should be salvaged, and although the case was not tried in such a way that all obligations between the parties could be precisely adjusted by the judgment herein, such judgment expressly contemplates an adjustment of those obligations." *Id.* at 721.

[31] 470 U.S. 451, 105 S. Ct. 1441, 84 L. Ed. 2d 432 (1985).

[32] The railroads unsuccessfully challenged the law as a violation of the contracts clause of the US Constitution. In effect Congress had inserted a new term into the contract between Amtrak and the railroads, adding a new task and increasing the costs of performance of the latter.

[33] 467 B.R. 694 (S.D.N.Y. 2012).

that the acquirer would not have any liability for claims against the manufacturer, including any successor liability claims. After the bankruptcy case was closed, an employee at another company, who was injured while driving a truck manufactured using a chassis supplied by the manufacturer before the bankruptcy case was filed, sued the manufacturer in state court. The employee amended the complaint to name the acquirer as an additional defendant. The acquirer was held to have assumed liability to the injured employee under successor liability principles. The combination of uncontrollable events was the employee accident and the court order holding the acquirer liable, and its liability to the employee was an additional cost incurred to realize the benefits of the acquisition (scenario (1)(a)(iii) (an uncontrollable event increases the costs incurred by an obligee to realize the anticipated benefits)).[34]

- *Brown v. Two Exchange Plaza Partners*[35]: An employee of a sub-subcontractor working on the atrium of a building was injured when the scaffold on which he was standing collapsed. The injured employee sued the building owner and general contractor; the general contractor filed a cross-claim against the scaffold subcontractor, the subcontractor hired to erect the walls and ceiling, and the sub-subcontractor of that subcontractor who was the employer of the injured worker. The trial court found that neither the scaffold contractor nor the injured worker's employer had been negligent or was liable to the general contractor but that the general contractor, who had not been negligent, was liable to the injured employee. The general contractor's liability to the injured employee added to the costs of its performance of its contract with the building owner. As such, the case illustrates a scenario (1)(b)(iii)(B)(I) (uncontrollable event causes an obligor's costs of performance to increase).

[34] The acquirer sued in the bankruptcy court for a declaration and an injunction barring the employee from proceeding in state court against it. The district court held the claims arising in the future had not been extinguished by the bankruptcy court's approval of the sale: "Because parties holding future claims cannot possibly be identified and, thus, cannot be provided notice of the bankruptcy, courts consistently hold that, for due process reasons, their claims cannot be discharged by the bankruptcy courts' orders." *Id.* at 707.

[35] 76 N.Y.2d 172, 556 NYS 2d 991 (N.Y. 1990).

Impairment and Inducements to Choose

As the previous examples illustrate, an uncontrollable event can impair the value or utility of a benefit or prevent or delay or increase the costs of benefit realization or task completion. An event can also create conditions in which a party must choose between actions with paired adverse outcomes: performing and suffering an adverse result or not performing and avoiding that adverse result. The source of such event may be nature or a third party. The third party might be a private third party or government agency. All such events create (1)(b)(ii)(B)(II) scenarios (uncontrollable event compels choice between completion of task for other party's benefit while suffering adverse consequence and not completing such task while breaching a commitment to that party).

The severity of the pressure or compulsion such events create will vary widely from immediate threats of serious harm to mild approbation and might be plotted on a metaphorical scale or continuum to reflect their immediacy, certainty, and seriousness of the harm that could or will result from choosing to perform an obligation: on one end is a threat of immediate, certain serious injury to person, damage to property, or other loss, and on the other end is strong approbation. The severity of the pressure does not change the nature of the hazard; it is still a (1)(b)(i)(B)(II) scenario. The question the scale helps to frame is not what might be cast as a factual one—when does coercion or pressure from such events overwhelm a party's ability or willingness to perform—but a risk allocation question: to what extent is a party willing to assume responsibility for losses that result from a choice between foregoing a benefit or not performing an obligation and avoiding an adverse outcome, on one hand, and realizing a benefit or performing and risking the occurrence of an adverse outcome, on the other. Understanding the degrees of immediacy, certainty, and gravity of coercion and pressure is essential to identifying and managing certain of the risks, what will be referred to as duress risks, created by potential uncontrollable events.

The following examples illustrate such threats in the order of the pressure to breach a commitment to complete a task for the other party's to avoid an adverse result:

- *Opera Co. of Boston, Inc. v. Wolf Trap Foundation for the Performing Arts*[36]: A foundation hired an opera company to give performances on four days at a center located in a national park. Shortly before

[36] 817 F.2d 1094 (4th Cir. 1987).

the performance was to begin on the second day, a thunderstorm caused an electrical outage in the park that could not be corrected in time and prompted the park service to recommend cancelation of the concert to enable patrons to leave the park safely and to prevent others from coming; the foundation canceled the performance. The foundation faced a choice: to go ahead with the concert, thus performing its obligation to the opera company but risking physical harm to its patrons, or canceling the concert and avoiding that risk.[37]

- *Kronprinzessin Cecile*[38]: The master of a German vessel carrying a shipment of gold to a port in England learned en route that Austria had declared war on Serbia and Germany and Britain had begun preparations for war. The master received orders from the ship's owners to return to New York, as he did. The only exception in the bill of lading was for "arrest and restraint of princes, rulers or people." The declaration of war by Austria on Germany and Serbia, and England's preparing for war, forced a choice between continuing to the port as obligated, with the risk of arrest once there, and returning to New York and not completing performance.[39] The threat was loss of property, whereas in *Opera Co. of Boston, Inc.*, the threat was physical harm.
- *Kolodin v. Valenti*[40]: A family court ordered two singers, who had collaborated professionally and had an intimate relationship

[37] The opera company sued for the balance of the payments under the contract. The district court held the "the existence of electric power was necessary for the satisfactory performance by the Opera Company on the night [of the performance] of June 15. The appeal court affirmed this finding but reversed the verdict, because the court had not decided "whether the possible foreseeability of the power failure in this case was of that degree of reasonable likelihood as to make improper the assertion by [the organizer] Wolf Trap of the defense of impossibility of performance." *Id.* at 1103.

[38] 244 U.S. 12, 37 S.Ct. 490, 61 L.Ed. 960 (1917).

[39] The vessel was sued for breach, for turning back from the voyage, as the vessel might have landed, the cargo unloaded and the vessel set back to sea before war was declared; the district court dismissed the action, as justified to avoid arrest upon entering into a British port. The Supreme Court affirmed, Justice Oliver Wendell Holmes, holding, "In this case the anticipation was correct, and the master is not to be put in the wrong by nice calculations that if all went well he might have delivered the gold and escaped capture by the margin of a few hours. In our opinion the event shows that he acted as a prudent man." *Id.* at 24.

[40] 115 A.D.3d 197, 979 N.Y.S.2d 587, 2014 NY Slip Op 745 (N.Y. Ap. Div. 2014).

that had badly soured, to have no contact with each other, other than through their counsel. Kolodin, the female singer, sued for rescission of her recording and management contracts with the company owned and controlled by the male singer, Valenti. The court order had not automatically voided Kolodin's contract. Rather, it forced her to choose between performing her contractual obligation to the company and breaching the court order or complying with the court order and breaching the contract.[41]

- *MG Marketing & Refining, Inc. v. Knight Enterprises, Inc.*[42]: A government agency challenged the legality of certain contracts to buy petroleum products. In response, the seller entered into a consent decree, agreeing to pay a fine and to advise its customers with whom it contracted that such contracts were illegal. The consent decree did not void such contracts, however. The consent decree forced the seller to choose between continuing such sales as already committed and violating the consent decree or complying with the consent decree and breaching commitments to its buyers. The threat or compulsion was arguably weaker here than in *Kolodin*,[43] where the order was by the court.[44]
- *Eastern Airlines, Inc. v. McDonnell Douglas Corp.*[45]: McDonnell contracted to deliver new aircraft to Eastern. McDonnell also contracted with the government to deliver military aircraft but lacked sufficient resources to meet both the delivery schedule requested by the government and the schedule agreed with Eastern. The government had authority under legislation to order McDonnell to give priority to its orders for military aircraft over production of civilian aircraft. Instead of so designating its orders, the government relied upon an understanding with McDonnell that

[41] The trial court granted her motion for summary judgment, and the appellate division affirmed, holding "It is of no moment that Jayarvee [the company] could hypothetically perform the contracts absent Valenti's involvement; to do so would require a sort of firewall, the very establishment of which would necessitate (direct or indirect) communication between Valenti and plaintiff [Kolodin]." *Id.* at 201.

[42] 25 F. Supp. 2d 175 (S.D.N.Y, 1998).

[43] 115 A.D.3d 197, 979 N.Y.S.2d 587, 2014 NY Slip Op 745 (N.Y. Ap. Div. 2014).

[44] The customers alleged breach of contract; the seller contended the contracts were illegal and, as a result, impossible to perform. The district court held that because the seller consented to the decree, the illegality of the contracts had not been established.

[45] 532 F.2d 957 (5th Cir. 1976).

such orders would be given priority. The aircraft manufactured for Eastern were delivered on average 80 days late. The government's request for priority had McDonnell choose between complying with that request and breaching its commitment to Eastern or not giving priority to the government's orders and performing its obligations to Eastern. Because no formal order was issued, the threat the government request created was seemingly weaker than the orders in *Kolodin*[46] and *MG Marketing & Refining, Inc.*,[47] though the government had the authority to issue orders if McDonnell had not cooperated.

- *Mishara Construction Co. v. Transmixed Concrete Corp.*[48]: A subcontractor who agreed to supply the concrete requirements of a construction project refused for a month to cross union picket lines to deliver the concrete. The union picket line forced the supplier to choose between fulfilling its commitment to the contractor and antagonizing the union and employees and accepting the union and employees' demands and breaching the contract with the contractor.[49] The report of the case does not indicate if the picket line threatened the use of physical force against or simply demanded moral support from those who had reason to cross it.
- *International Minerals and Chemical Corp. v. Llano, Inc.*[50]: A potash mine and processing facility operator agreed to purchase its gas requirements from a gas supplier. The contract also obligated the operator to pay for a minimum quantity of gas if not it did not purchase such minimum, subject to excused failures to perform due to events specified in the force majeure clause and provided the minimum purchase requirements would be adjusted if either

46 115 A.D.3d 197, 979 N.Y.S.2d 587, 2014 NY Slip Op 745 (N.Y. Ap. Div. 2014).

47 25 F. Supp.2d 175 (S.D.N.Y. 1998).

48 365 Mass. 122, 310 N.E.2d 363 (Mass. 1974).

49 The general contractor purchased its requirements elsewhere and sued the subcontractor for the additional costs. The subcontractor claimed the strike and picket line rendered its performance impossible. The general contractor asked the court to instruct the jury that the subcontractor had to deliver the concrete regardless of the strike; the court refused and the jury returned a verdict for the subcontractor. The Massachusetts Supreme Court affirmed, holding, "Much must depend on the facts known to the parties at the time of contracting with respect to the history of and prospects for labor difficulties during the period of performance of the contract, as well as the likely severity of the effect of such disputes on the ability to perform.

50 770 F.2d 879, 886 (10th Cir. 1985).

the seller was unable to deliver or the buyer unable to receive gas "for any reason beyond the reasonable control of the parties." The state adopted environmental regulations that would, two years after the ten-year contract term expired, require the operator to reduce its operations to a level below the minimum quantity of gas then being purchased under the contract. The operator negotiated a compliance schedule with the government agency that resulted in its reducing its operations and its gas requirements below the minimum for the final one and one-half years of the contract term (more than two years before compliance with the new law was required). The new law inspired, rather than compelled, a choice between compliance with the standards in the new law not yet effective and breaching the contract with the gas supplier or continuing compliance with the then effective standards and fulfilling its commitment to the supplier.[51]

- *Lyondell-CITGO Refining, LP. v. Petroleos de Venezuela, S.A.*[52]: Members of the Organization of Petroleum Exporting Countries agreed to voluntary reductions of their crude oil exports. Venezuela, one such member, directed the state-owned oil company to limit the export of Venezuelan product. As a result, that company did not deliver the agreed quantity of crude to its buyer.[53] A nonbinding decision by members of the OPEC to reduce their oil production, the decision by Venezuela to reduce its exports, and direction to the state-owned oil company compelled that company to choose between performing its commitment to its buyer, ignoring directions from the energy ministry, and dishonoring Venezuela's nonbinding commitment to OPEC, on one hand, and breaching its commitment to its buyer, complying with directions from the

[51] The operator sued for a declaration that it was excused from the obligation to pay for the minimum quantity. The district court found that because the operator had come into compliance earlier than the new regulations required, it could not claim impossibility. The appeal court held that while the "take-or-pay" obligation would not ordinarily be excused by the occurrence of a force majeure event—the buyer having agreed either to take or to pay for the minimum quantity—the adjustment provision entitled the buyer to a reduction of its minimum quantity obligation if it was "unable" to receive the gas.

[52] 2003 U.S. Dist. LEXIS 13809 (S.D.N.Y. 2003); 2003 WL 21878798.

[53] The contract allowed the seller, and the seller claimed it was in the circumstances entitled, to prorate its deliveries in response to the occurrence of a force majeure event, defined to include "acts, regulations, laws or restraints imposed by the government of any sovereign nation or state or any agency, branch, political subdivision or other similar body thereof."

oil ministry, and honoring Venezuela's nonbinding commitment to OPEC, on the other.[54] The compulsion here was moral, as the supplier was not subject to a threat of penalty for supplying as it committed to do so.

The first three cases illustrate strong pressure or compulsion on the obligors to deviate from their contractual commitments: the risk of immediate serious injury to patrons, the risk of high probability of immediate arrest of the vessel, and the high risk of violating a court order, in *Opera Co. of Boston, Inc.*,[55] *Kronprinzessin Cecile*[56] and *Kolodin*,[57] respectively. The pressure is less severe in the other cases. In *International Minerals and Chemical Corp.*[58] the pressure, if it can be called that, was the moral approbation that came with early compliance with the standards in a new law.

The hazards in these cases are the events that press or prompt a party to choose between performing and risking the occurrence of adverse results that will likely flow from performing, on one hand, and not performing and avoiding such adverse results, on the other. Unlike other uncontrollable events that impair benefit realization and task completion, uncontrollable events that affect choices leave an element of volitional decision-making, however severe the compulsion and unpalatable the choices. They do not impair a party's ability to enjoy benefits or complete a task, unlike the other hazards previously described.

---

54 The court held the clause inapplicable: "First, OPEC's directives are nonbinding on its member states. Therefore, Venezuela was not compelled to reduce its oil production by OPEC; it's (sic.) decision to do so was voluntary. Furthermore, Venezuela's oil minister is currently the President of OPEC, and so any OPEC related decisions are not beyond the reasonable control of PDVSA. Second, the instructions from the Ministry do not have the force and effect of an official government act under Venezuelan law. Third, defendants could have maintained their oil shipments to LCR even under the instructions issued by the Ministry, since those instructions did not specify exactly how to reduce oil production, only that it be reduced. They could have cut shipments to other customers and maintained LCR's. Finally, plaintiff asserts that Petroleo's ability to sell XHC [extra heavy crude] on the spot market indicates that the force majeure did not in fact prevent it from producing oil in sufficient quantities."

55 817 F.2d 1094 (4th Cir. 1987).

56 244 U.S. 12, 37 S.Ct. 490, 61 L.Ed. 960 (1917).

57 115 A.D.3d 197, 979 N.Y.S.2d 587, 2014 NY Slip Op 745 (N.Y. Ap. Div. 2014).

58 770 F.2d 879, 886 (10th Cir. 1985).

Natural Forces and Human Agency

The source of an uncontrollable event may be nature or human agency. Two of the cases previously summarized in this chapter illustrate the operation of natural forces: *Chugach Electric Association,*[59] where the temperatures failed to drop to their anticipated lows, and *Opera Co. of Boston, Inc.,*[60] where lightning shut down the use of electricity in the park where the concert was to be held. In all the other cases, human agents were the sources of the uncontrollable events.

Government Agencies and Private Agents

The human agents may be individuals, privately owned or controlled entities, or government departments, bureaus, ministries, organs, and other agencies (referred to as government agencies). The actions of private third parties are illustrated in four of the cases previously summarized: *Wisconsin Electric Power Co.,*[61] where the steel mill's bankruptcy resulted in the utility paying a higher rate; *J.M. Rodriguez & Co., Inc.,*[62] where a thief stole the cargo; and *Mishara Construction Co., Inc.,*[63] where the strikers deterred a supplier from crossing a picket line. The other cases illustrate actions by international, national, state, and local government agencies. *Wheelbrator Envirotech Operating Services Inc.*[64] illustrates combined private entity and government agency actions: the successor contractor and union were private entities, and the city that hired the successor contractor was a government agency.

A government agency that is a party to a transaction is not an uncontrollable third party as it otherwise would be. As a party, it controls all its acts and omissions and is capable of creating all the risks to the other party that any nongovernmental agency party may, as a counterparty, create: lack and loss of will and ability to perform. For example, when a government agency agreed with a foreign investor that it would not impair certain benefits of an investment, its enactment of a law that authorized certain government agencies to take actions inconsistent with that

59 518 P.2d 76 (Alaska 1974), rehg. over damages, 523 P.2d 1243 (Alaska 1974), aff'd. 562 P.2d 1053 (Alaska 1977).

60 817 F.2d 1094 (4th Cir. 1987).

61 557 F.3d 504 (7th Cir. 2009).

62 32 N.Y.2d 425 (N.Y. 1973).

63 365 Mass. 122, 310 N.E.2d 363 (Mass. 1974).

64 *Id.* at 45.

agreement repudiated that agreement, much as any counterparty might repudiate a contract.[65] A change in law or other action by a legislature may be outside the control of a government agency that is party to an agreement; to that extent the agency is like any other private party whose performance of its obligations may be impaired by governmental actions like any private party.[66] When a government agency is not a party to a contract, it is like any private third party who might legally or illegally interfere with a transaction, though by virtue of being cloaked with governmental authority it has a greater variety of superior rights that when invoked can impair a transaction. We are here concerned only with a government agency's role as such a third party to a transaction.

Political Risk

Political risk is sometimes broadly understood to refer to the risk that a government agency's acts or omissions will impair benefit realization or task completion. It thus encompasses all types of acts and omissions a government can take or not take and all conceivable adverse outcomes. It

[65] *E.g.*, Revere Copper and Brass, Inc. v. Overseas Private Investment Corp., 17 Int'l L. R. 1321 (1978), where legislation and other measures enacted by the Jamaican government violated its agreement with a foreign investor in a mining project in Jamaica.

[66] *E.g.*, U.S. v. Winstar Corp., 518 U.S. 839, 116 S.Ct. 2432, 135 L.Ed.2d 964 (1996), where the federal agency that insured savings and loan associations agreed, in three separate transactions over a period of six years, with acquirers of insolvent savings and loan institutions to allow the acquirers' favorable accounting treatment for the excess of the targets' liabilities over their assets, referred to as goodwill, and the cash contributed by the agency to the target. Several years later, Congress passed a law that prohibited the favorable accounting treatment of such items, and the acquirers sued for breach of contract. The Court of Claims granted partial summary judgment in favor of the acquirers, and the appeal and supreme courts affirmed. The court held the government agency assumed responsibility for the risk that the law might change and prohibit such accounting treatment, and when the law did change, "the Government was unable to perform its promise and, therefore, became liable for breach." *Id.* at 870. The court acknowledged that had the contract been between private parties, the defense of impossibility would have been available to the party whose promise could not be performed. It went on, however, to deny the government such defense, holding that the requirement that "the nonoccurrence of regulatory amendment was a basic assumption of these contracts" would be difficult to prove in cases where a regulatory agency has contracted with private parties: "Such an agreement reflects the inescapable recognition that regulated industries in the modern world do not live under the law of the Medes and the Persians, and the very fact that such a contract is made at all is at odds with any assumption of regulatory stasis." *Id.* at 905.

also has a narrower meaning, limited to four specific types of interference by a government with a foreign-owned business or investment: nationalization or expropriation by one country's government of the assets in that country belonging to an investor domiciled in another country, without due process or appropriate compensation; the imposition or increase in the restrictions on the conversion of a currency in a country into the currency of another country or on the transfer of a currency out of a country; disturbances that affect task completion and benefit realization, ranging from war to sabotage, including civil war and terrorism; and repudiation by a government of an investment contract with a foreign investor.

A party engaging in a transaction with a foreign-owned enterprise located in an area where the enterprise should evaluate political risks should consider such risks as relevant to the enterprise's willingness and ability to perform. Expropriation of the enterprise's assets may leave it unable to perform its obligations to the party. Assumption by a government of control of management or operations of the foreign-owned enterprise may increase a party's burdens and cost of performance. The imposition or increase in restrictions on the conversion of one country's currency into another's or on the transfer of a currency out of a country may interfere with payments by such enterprise to the party. Repudiation by a government of its investment contract with a foreign-owned enterprise may impair its financial condition or ability to perform its contract with the party. Political risks are relevant to a transaction to the extent they are risks to one of the parties.

Oversight, etc.

What was said previously about task and benefit oversight, rejection, and uncertainty, and about information and assumption risks (the use of bad information, the bad use of good information, and the making of bad assumptions), can be repeated for the uncontrollable events previously described. Just as it may overlook or reject a benefit or task, a party can overlook or reject as relevant to its transaction potential uncontrollable events; the oversight or rejection leaves open which party is responsible for the losses that result from such events. In the textbook English case *Taylor v. Caldwell*,[67] where a music hall to be used

[67] 3 Best & Smith 826, 2 New Rep. 198, 32 L.J. (Q. B.) 164, 8 L.T. 356, 27 J.P. 710, 11 R.R. 726, 12 Digest (Repl.) 419 (Q.B. 1863).

by a renter was destroyed by a fire after contract formation but before such use was to begin, Justice Colin Blackburn observed at the outset of his opinion that "[t]he parties, when framing their agreement, evidently had not present in their minds the possibility of such a disaster. . . ."[68] The case illustrates oversight of a possible contingency. Another example is *Chic Organization, Ltd.*,[69] where the record producer's attorney acknowledged he had not asked the counterparty, the record company, about Diana Ross's contract because "it didn't even occur to me. . . . She started as a child and like Stevie Wonder and all the other Motown people out of the original Motown and everyone assumed it was going on forever."[70] An example of contingency rejection, where at contract formation a party recognized a possible contingency but decided to proceed in the face of the risk of its occurrence, is *In re M&M Transportation Co.*,[71] where rights to operate as motor carriers granted by a government agency that bidders agreed to buy became worthless before the sale closed because legislation made such rights more freely available. The contingency, deregulation, was not a surprise, however, for the bidders. The bankruptcy court judge said of the bidders, "That defendants chose to disbelieve or to dismiss the possibility as a serious threat was a personal assessment. That defendants bid as they did with knowledge of a potential deregulation was a matter of their business judgment."[72] Another example of contingency rejection is *Alternative Thinking Systems, Inc. v. Simon & Schuster*,[73] where a publisher recognized the possibility that events might adversely affect the value of the work, proposed including in the contract a clause that provided the publisher's obligation to publish was discharged if "supervening events or circumstances since the date of this agreement have, in the sole judgment of the

---

[68] 32 L.J. (Q.B.) 164, 166. The music hall a landlord agreed to rent to a tenant for four days was destroyed by an accidental fire after contract formation but prior to the first day of performance. The tenants sued for damages, and received a verdict. The Queen's Bench Division held the landlord's obligation was subject to an implied condition that the music hall continued to exist until performance, and the destruction of the music hall discharged both parties' obligations.

[69] 582 F. Supp. 812 (S.D.N.Y. 1984). For a fuller summary of the case, see the text accompanying ch. 1, notes 25–34.

[70] *Id.*

[71] 13 B.R. 861 (Bankr. S.D.N.Y.1981).

[72] *Id.* at 872.

[73] 853 F. Supp. 791 (S.D.N.Y 1994).

Publisher, materially adversely changed the economic expectations of the Publisher in respect to the Literary Work at the time of the making of this agreement,"[74] but accepted the author's rejection of the clause, thus leaving open the allocation of responsibility for the losses that could flow from such events.[75] Uncertainty concerning a contingency will include not only the nature of such an event and the severity of its consequences on benefit realization and task completion but also, because it is always a future event, the probability of its occurrence. Such risks are referred to as contingency oversight, rejection, and uncertainty risks.

ACTS OF GOD AND THIRD PARTIES RISK MANAGEMENT

Diligence

Diligence on potential uncontrollable events has several objectives: to identify such events, to forecast the probability of their occurrence, to assess the likely damage to a transaction upon their occurrence, to list and evaluate the measures that might mitigate their occurrence and the losses that could result from their occurrence, to identify third parties willing to insure the parties against such losses, and to list and evaluate measures to allocate responsibility for the risk of their occurrence as between the parties to the transaction. It is beyond the scope of this book to explain the diligence that should be undertaken on uncontrollable events in any specific transaction or type of transaction.

Uncontrollable Event Risk Allocation

Parties do not have a blank slate when contracting for the allocation of responsibility for uncontrollable event risks. A commitment to complete a task includes an assumption of responsibility for the risk that uncontrollable events may interfere therewith. In certain conditions, the commitment is overridden by the legal principles of unilateral and mutual mistake, supervening impossibility and impracticability, and frustration of purpose; when applicable, performance is discharged. The

---

[74] *Id.* at 798.

[75] See text accompanying ch. 8, notes 37 and 38 for a summary of this case.

risk allocation implied by a commitment and such legal principles can be modified by express contractual terms that stipulate when uncontrollable events excuse performance.

The principal contractual terms that are used most often to expressly allocate responsibility for such risks are

- obligor covenants, representations, and warranties,
- limited scope of commitments,
- absolute obligations,
- conditions precedent and subsequent,
- force majeure clauses,
- indemnities,
- third-party covenants and indemnities, and
- "reopeners."

Obligor Covenants and Warranties

Commitments made in certain circumstances implicitly preclude discharge of performance by reason of the impossibility and impracticability defenses. A commitment to cause an uncontrollable event to occur by its terms will usually preclude any claim that failure to perform should be excused because the occurrence of the event was beyond its control. A commitment to cause a third party to act or not act in a certain manner likewise seemingly precludes any claim that causing the third party to so act was impossible. A commitment to complete a task that cannot be completed without the occurrence of an uncontrollable event or act of a third party not controlled by either party similarly should preclude any defense that the event or third party was uncontrollable. These are scenarios where an obligor lacks control over the completion of a task (or perform a covenant) for the benefit of the other party. *Wheelbrator Envirotech Operating Services Inc.*[76] is an example: the contractor covenanted that its successor would agree to the same terms with the union to which it had agreed, even though it had no control over its successor's decisions. It was precluded from claiming

[76] 88 F.3d 40 (1st Cir. 1996).

impossibility.[77] Because not all cases may be so clear that an obligor has committed to do the impossible, the implied exclusion of impossibility and impracticability may not be a foregone conclusion.

In principle, a representation or warranty could achieve the same result as a covenant: instead of covenanting to perform or cause the occurrence of an uncontrollable event or a third party to act or not act in a certain way, a warrantor could represent or warrant that such event will or will not occur or a third party will or will not act, as represented or warranted, and thereby assume responsibility for the occurrence of the event represented or warranted not to occur or the nonoccurrence of an event warranted to occur and thereby implicitly waive the supervening impossibility and impracticability defenses.

Chugach Electric Association[78] illustrates the strength and weakness of an allocation of responsibility for uncontrollable event risk through implied warranties. At contract formation, when the parties agreed to use the ice haul method, neither party warranted to the other the method was workable. Later, when the contractor insisted the ice haul method was impossible and the utility insisted that it be used, the utility impliedly warranted it was possible as if stated in a specification.[79] The utility thereby assumed responsibility for the risk the ice haul method was impossible. If, however, the contractor knew the ice haul method was impossible, it could not have relied upon the warranty and would have shared the risk with the utility. Whether the contractor had such knowledge was a question of fact, the answer to which was highly contested. While covenants to do the impossible and warranties that the impossible can be done allocate responsibility for the risk of the occurrence or nonoccurrence of an uncontrollable event, the effectiveness of such allocation may be challenged, depending upon the facts of the case. The use of express warranties more clearly states and affirms the implicit allocation of responsibility for a risk to a warrantor.

---

[77] "As long as EOS clearly foresaw and bargained with the knowledge that it could lose the contract—something we must assume if the arbitrator plausibly interpreted the successor clause—the fact that performance might be impossible if EOS indeed lost the contract is of no moment." *Id.* at 45.

[78] 518 P.2d 76 (Alaska 1974), rehg. over damages, 523 P.2d 1243 (Alaska 1974), *aff'd.* 562 P.2d 1053 (Alaska 1977).

[79] 523 P.2d 1243, 1246 (Alaska 1974).

Commitment Scope

If a task must be completed by one party for benefits to be realized, responsibility for completion of that task must be assumed by one or both parties. Responsibility can be assumed by the party who expects to realize the benefit or by the other party. Avoiding responsibility for completion of a task does not make either the task or responsibility disappear; it shifts responsibility for the resulting losses to the other side of the ledger, so to speak. Adding to the list of tasks an obligor is committed to complete (for the benefit of the other party) thus adds to its responsibility the losses that result from uncontrollable events that prevent the completion of such tasks (scenarios (1)(b)(i), (ii), and (iii) and (2)(b)(i), (ii), and (iii) (occurrence or nonoccurrence of an uncontrollable event impairs, delays, or increases the cost of task completion)), in the absence of agreement otherwise and subject to the doctrines of unilateral and mutual mistake and supervening impossibility and frustration. Conversely, omitting tasks from the obligor's list excludes from its responsibility the losses that result from such tasks not being completed due to such events. Responsibility for losses that result from uncontrollable events that affect task completion can thus be allocated by designating responsibility for completion of such tasks.

The following cases illustrate this use of commitments:

- *Badhwar v. Colorado Fuel and Iron Corp.*[80]: A seller sold a shipment of caustic soda to a buyer on terms that deemed the goods delivered when loaded on board the vessel once the bills of lading and other documents had been delivered to the buyer. The cargo was loaded on board the vessel. The documents were delivered to the buyer's bank five days later. In the meantime, the day after the cargo was loaded, the vessel's crew went on strike, as ordered by the union, with the result the shipment could not be unloaded or the vessel sailed. The vessel arrived at its destination three months late, during which time the price of caustic soda had dropped. If, in addition to loading the goods on board the vessel and delivering the bills of lading and other documents to the buyer, the seller had to choose a vessel whose crew would not join the strike, as the buyer claimed, responsibility for the risk of the strike remained with the seller. As the seller successfully claimed, its tasks were limited to

[80] 138 F. Supp. 595 (S.D.N.Y. 1955), *aff'd.* 245 F.2d 903 (2d Cir. 1957).

loading the goods on board a vessel whose crew had not declared they would strike and delivering the documents to the buyer; thus, responsibility for the risk of delay caused by the strike had been assumed by the buyer.[81] The case illustrates how defining a party's commitment to complete tasks limits its responsibility for losses caused by uncontrollable events that impair the completion of those and other relevant tasks (scenario (1)(b)(ii)(B)(I)).

- *Swift Canadian Co., Ltd. v. Banet*[82]: A seller located in Toronto agreed to sell lamb pelts to a buyer located in Philadelphia, free on board (FOB) Toronto. The contract included a note that shipment would be "Frankford Via: Buffalo-Penna. R. R. to Broad & Washington Ave. Freight Sta. Penna. R. R. Delivery." The contract also provided that neither party was to be liable for "orders or acts of any government or governmental agency." Another provision stated that "when pelts are sold FOB seller's plant title and risk of loss shall pass to buyer when product is loaded on cars at seller's plant." After the contract formation, the US government banned the importation of such pelts. The seller offered to load the pelts on board rail cars destined for Philadelphia; the buyer refused to accept the offer. The uncontrollable event was a change of law in the buyer's country after contract formation that made illegal its importation of the pelts it has committed to buy from a seller located in a country where the sale was legal. Responsibility for the risk of such a change in law would have been assumed by the seller or both parties if it had to deliver the goods at its facility on a rail car that could legally carry and deliver them to the buyer in Pennsylvania. The seller would have been unable to perform, and either party could have terminated. Such risk would also have been shared if the buyer could have terminated because the pelts lost value because they could not be imported into the United States. The buyer assumed responsibility for that risk because, as the seller successfully claimed, the seller had no obligation to deliver the goods in the United States and the buyer had no obligation to the seller to import them into the United States. If the seller's commitment to deliver the goods

[81] "In a CIF contract the 'property' right passes to the buyer upon delivery to the carrier. Hence the 'property right' to the caustic soda passed to the plaintiffs when the caustic soda was loaded aboard the [vessel] S.S. Hawaiian, which was prior to the walkout, and the risk of loss also passed to the plaintiffs." *Id.* at 606.

[82] 224 F.2d 36 (3d Cir. 1955).

at its facility was unaffected by the change of law, then the buyer had no commitment to import the goods. It had to do so to realize the benefits of the purchase, but the realization of that benefit had been blocked by the change of law.[83] The case illustrates how an obligor by limiting the tasks it must complete avoids responsibility for uncontrollable events that impair other tasks, which become tasks the obligee had to complete to realize its benefits (scenario (1)(b)(i)(A) (uncontrollable event impairs the completion of a task an obligee must complete to realize a benefit)).

Absolute Obligations

A party can expressly assume responsibility for all losses that result from impairment of its anticipated benefits and task completion by the occurrence of an uncontrollable event. Its obligation to complete a task is stated to be absolute and unconditional, whatever the uncontrollable events that occur. In such instances, an obligor is liable for its failure to perform even when an act of God or a third party makes performance impossible or impractical. This is the case even when performance is illegal due to a change in law, though the obligor is not expected to violate the law. Similarly, an obligee is liable for its failure to perform its obligations even when an uncontrollable event destroys the value or utility of its anticipated benefits. An obligor assumes responsibility for all risks and insures the obligee against losses incurred by the latter upon the happening of nearly all uncontrollable events that affect the former's performance and the latter's benefits.

Following are two cases that illustrate terms that successfully and unsuccessfully created absolute obligations:

- *Chase Manhattan Bank v. Traffic Stream (BVI) Infrastructure Ltd.*[84]: A Chinese joint venture constructed a toll road in China. It

[83] The seller sued for breach of contract and moved for summary judgment. The appeal court held summary judgment should be granted to the seller. The appeal court held the seller had performed its obligation by offering delivery of the pelts to the railroad. The note as to the shipping directions did not alter the FOB terms of sale. Because delivery of the pelts was entirely within Canada, the sale and delivery of the pelts was unaffected by the change in law in the United States.

[84] 86 F. Supp. 2d 244, 255 (S.D.N.Y 2000), *rev'd* on other grounds, 251 F.3d 334 (2d Cir. 2001), *rev'd* on other grounds, 536 US 88, 122 S. Ct. 2054, 153 L. Ed. 2d 95 (2002).

received the funds to pay its construction costs from its parent company, which received its funds from its parent, which issued bonds to raise the capital. The joint venture promised to pay its Hong Kong parent a minimum return on its investment, which promise assured the bond holders of repayment of the bonds. Later, a Chinese regulatory authority strengthened and increased its enforcement of the prohibition against such guarantees and the transfer of foreign currency out of the country to pay the same. The joint venture sought and was refused approval to remit foreign currency from China to pay the guaranteed return to its investor. The bond issuer claimed the regulatory change made payment of the bonds impossible. The indenture under which the bonds were issued stated a default occurred when any of the specified events of default occurred, "whether it shall be voluntary or involuntary or be effected by operation of law or pursuant to any judgment, decree or order of any court or any order, rule or regulation of any administrative or governmental body."[85] The clause was modeled on a provision in a model indenture intended to exclude the force majeure and impossibility defenses.[86] If the clause did not eliminate the defense of impossibility, as the issuer claimed, the bond holders had assumed responsibility for the risk that payments required to be made under the indenture could become illegal under Chinese law. As the indenture trustee successfully claimed, however, the clause eliminated the defense of impossibility; the issuer had assumed responsibility for the risk that any of the payments required to be made under the indenture would become illegal.[87]

---

[85] 86 F.Supp.2d at 255.

[86] "The preamble of section 501 quoted above is identical to section 501 of the Model Debenture Indenture Provision. See Model Debenture Indenture Provision § 501 (1965). According to the American Bar Foundation Commentaries on the Model Debenture Indenture Provisions ('Model Indenture Commentaries'), '[t]he parenthetical clause in the first sentence of Section 501 has the purpose of refuting any argument that events resulting from force majeure were not intended to be treated as defaults.' American Bar Foundation, Corporate Debt Financing Project, Commentaries on Model Debenture Indenture Provisions 205 (1971)." 86 F. Supp. 2d 244, 256. The court held accordingly the defense of impossibility was unavailable.

[87] "Under the plain language of section 501, the failure to tender a required payment constitutes an Event of Default, regardless of whether that failure was caused by a change

- *New York v. Long Island Airports Limousine Service Corp.*[88]: Long Island Airports Limousine Service (LIALS) entered into a franchise agreement with the city, pursuant to which LIALS was permitted to operate its omnibus route therein, and agreed to pay a franchise fee. The franchise agreement stated LIALS would pay all the amounts it was obligated to pay under a franchise agreement in the event such agreement was terminated. Changes in state law made the city's agreement to the operation of the limousine service in the city unnecessary. The city claimed LIALS was still obligated to pay the fee under the franchise agreement. If the clause was effective, as the city claimed, LIALS assumed responsibility for the risk that a change in law would destroy the value of the benefits of the franchise agreement. The clause was ineffective, however, as LIALS successfully claimed; it thus failed to allocate to LIALS responsibility for the risk that the license issued by the city would cease to have any benefit to LIALS.[89]

Conditions Precedent and Subsequent

A condition precedent or subsequent may be used to allocate to both parties any of the risks previously described in this chapter. A condition precedent can state that an obligor has no obligation to perform until an event that must occur has occurred or an event that must not occur has not occurred. Because the condition must be satisfied for the obligation to become effective, the failure of such a condition should allow the obligor to terminate the contract, in which event each party is responsible for its own losses, unless otherwise specified in the contract. The risk that the lake would not be sufficiently frozen in the winter in *Chugach Electric Association*[90] could have been allocated by expressly

---

in government policy. As plaintiff persuasively argues, the Indenture anticipates the risk of adverse government action, and it assigns that risk to defendant." *Id.* at 257.

88 62 NY2d 846, 477 NYS2d 613 (N.Y. 1984).

89 The Court of Appeal held the city was not entitled to the compensation stated in the contract. In effect, the court held unenforceable the attempt to have the limousine service waive the defense of failure of consideration of frustration of contract by stating it had an obligation to pay independent of the consideration given by the city.

90 518 P.2d 76 (Alaska 1974), rehg. over damages, 523 P.2d 1243 (Alaska 1974), *aff'd.* 562 P.2d 1053 (Alaska 1977).

conditioning the contractor's obligation to cross the lake upon the lake's being frozen to an agreed thickness or the average daily temperatures remaining at or below an agreed level for a certain period. Responsibility for the risk of delay and additional costs would not have thereby been allocated to the utility or the contractor. Additional terms would have been required, the absence of which would have left the parties sharing the risk: each would have been entitled to suspend or terminate, each bearing the extent of its losses. In *Hensler*,[91] responsibility for the risk the state bypass road would not be completed when anticipated could have been allocated by an express condition that such road be completed by a date certain after which each party would have been entitled to terminate the contract. In each case, the express condition would have had the parties share responsibility for the risk, as each would have had to bear its own losses without recourse against the other. A condition subsequent can state that an obligor may suspend, terminate, or reopen the negotiation of the terms of its obligation to perform upon the occurrence of an event that must not occur or upon the nonoccurrence of an event that must occur by a date certain. A condition subsequent could have allocated responsibility for the risk in the textbook case *Taylor v. Caldwell*,[92] had the risk been identified before contract formation, as both parties would have been relieved of their obligations as a result of destruction of the building; responsibility for the risk of the event would have been shared. The satisfaction of such condition discharges such obligation and leaves each party to be responsible for its own losses, unless specified otherwise in the contract. The contract can require that one party pay the other upon termination, whether the failed condition was precedent or subsequent, as compensation for the latter's cost and lost opportunity.[93]

Force Majeure Clauses

A force majeure clause is a specialized condition subsequent. Its application is triggered by the occurrence after contract formation of

[91] 124 Cal. App.2d 71, 268 P.2d 12 (Cal. App. 1954).

[92] 3 Best & Smith 826, 2 New Rep. 198, 32 L.J. (Q. B.) 164, 8 L.T. 356, 27 J.P. 710, 11 R.R. 726, 12 Digest (Repl.) 419 (Q.B. 1863).

[93] *E.g.*, *In re* Chateaugay, 186 B.R. 561 (S.D.N.Y. 1995), where the potential buyer of a target agreed to pay the target $25,000,000 if the required consents were not obtained.

one or more events specified in the clause, usually events beyond the reasonable control of the party affected thereby. The clause links such events to adverse outcomes, usually the failure by the affected party to perform its obligations under the contract. The clause permits the affected party to delay, suspend, or terminate further fulfillment of commitments, as stated in the clause. It may also entitle the affected party to compensation for its losses resulting from such event, again as stated in the clause. Such a clause may be as narrow or broad as the parties agree.

Nonoccurrences. A force majeure clause will not ordinarily be triggered by or apply to the nonoccurrence of an event that must occur by the anticipated time (scenarios (2)(b)(i), (ii), and (iii) (nonoccurrence of an event impairs, delays, or increases the cost of task completion)). A typical force majeure clause applies to events that actually occur and adversely affect performance. The nonoccurrence of an event has a different result: performance is not enabled because a circumstance that must exist never comes into existence. The appropriate risk allocation device for the nonoccurrence of an event that must occur is a condition precedent.

Still, the line between a nonoccurrence of an event and an event will not always be an obvious one, and as previously discussed, a nonoccurrence might be perceived of as an event. For example, unusually warm weather kept a lake from freezing instead of the lake failed to freeze. The nonoccurrence is thereby converted into an occurrence, with the result that a nonoccurrence and an occurrence are treated the same.

Hensler[94] illustrates a blurring of the distinction between occurrences and nonoccurrences of events. The contractor could not begin work under its contract with the city until the state's work near the site was completed, and the contract entitled the contractor to reimbursement for its extra costs if it was "ordered by the engineer, in writing, to suspend work for some unforeseen cause not provided for in the . . . contract . . . and over which the contractor has no control."[95] The court held the clause permitted the city to delay the contractor's beginning its work if the state's work was not completed by the agreed date. The city was obligated to reimburse the contractor for its costs and to permit it to

[94] 124 Cal.App.2d 712, 68 P. 2d 12 (Cal. App. 1954).

[95] *Id.* at 84.

begin work when the "when the obstacle to the progress of the work was removed."[96] That "obstacle" was noncompletion by the state of its bypass road project.

Impairment of Benefits. The application of a force majeure clause will not ordinarily be triggered by or apply to the impairment of benefits (scenario (1)(a)) or the completion of tasks that must be completed by a party for its own benefit (scenarios (1)(b)(i)(A), (1)(b)(ii)(A) and (1)(b)(iii)(A) (uncontrolled event impairs, delays, or increases the cost of completion by an obligee of a task that contributes to its realization of anticipated benefits)). First, as previously described, an uncontrollable event may directly impair the value or utility of a benefit. For example, cancelation of a parade destroys the value and utility of the use of a room that has been rented to view it, but the cancelation, the third-party act that directly interferes with benefit realization, does not affect the ability of the obligor or obligee to perform their respective obligations; such third-party interference changes a circumstance, the existence of which would contribute to yielding or yield value when the task (the landlord's letting of the room) was completed. Second, an uncontrollable event may impair an obligee's ability to complete a task that must be completed after the obligor completes all of its tasks, and when the obligee's task is completed, it will yield an anticipated benefit. In this instance the completion by the obligee of such a task may be delayed, prevented, or made more costly by an uncontrollable event, just as completion of a task by an obligor for the obligee's benefit might be. The difference between this benefit impairment and uncontrollable event task impairment is that the task to be completed by the obligee is for its, and not the other party's, benefit; it has no commitment to the obligor to complete the task and no obligation, the failure of which to perform is to be excused. Both parties remain capable of performing their obligations to each other, but the obligee is unable to complete the tasks that will yield value. This link—between the obligee's task completion and value creation—is what is impaired by the third-party act and distinguishes it from the link between third-party disruption and the obligor's task completion. A force majeure clause will usually be inapplicable to uncontrollable events that

[96] *Id.*

directly impair benefit realization or the completion by the obligee of a task that will yield an anticipated benefit.

The following are illustrative of the inapplicability of force majeure clauses to uncontrollable event benefit impairment risks:

- *North Indiana Public Service Co. v. Carbon County Coal Co.*[97]: An Indiana electric utility was able to buy electricity from other electricity generating plants at rates lower than its costs of producing its own electricity because it purchased coal at high prices under a long-term contract from a Wyoming coal mine operator. The state regulator prohibited the utility from charging its customers rates higher than those calculated based on purchasing electricity from other plants. The utility terminated the coal purchase contract. It invoked the force majeure clause and claimed it could stop buying coal "for any cause beyond [its] reasonable control . . . including but not limited to . . . orders or acts of civil . . . authority . . . which wholly or partly prevent . . . the utilizing . . . of the coal."[98] Had the order prohibited the purchase of coal, as the utility claimed, its performance would have been prevented and been subject to the force majeure clause. Instead, as the coal supplier successfully claimed, the utility was still able to buy and use the coal.[99] What it could not do, and what was a task it had to complete to realize the full benefits of its coal purchases, was to increase the rates it charged its customers to recoup those costs. The force majeure clause was not triggered by the order and thus did not allocate to the coal seller responsibility for the risk that an order would prohibit the utility from passing through its higher costs of coal to its customers.[100] The case was scenario (1) (b) (i) (A) (I): an uncontrollable event prevented the utility (obligee) from completing a task (raising its rates) that would help to realize its benefit (profits from sales of electricity).

---

97 799 F.2d 265 (7th Cir. 1986).

98 *Id.* at 274. The trial court rejected the claim and awarded damages to the coal supplier.

99 Judge Richard Posner, in the appeal court, which affirmed, explained, "Such an order does not 'prevent,' whether wholly or in part, NIPSCO [the utility] from using the coal; it just prevents NIPSCO from shifting the burden of its improvidence or bad luck in having incorrectly forecasted its fuel needs to the backs of the hapless ratepayers." *Id.* at 275.

100 *Id.* at 276.

- *National Association of Postmaster of the U.S. v. Grand Hyatt Washington*[101]: An arbitrator resolved a dispute under a collective bargaining agreement between postal workers and the United States Postal Service by ordering the rural mail count—an exercise that measures the volume of mail delivered on rural mail routes and affects compensation of rural mail carriers—to be done on certain dates. These were also the same as or close to or the dates scheduled for the annual leadership conferences of the National Association of Postmasters of the United States (NAPUS), which had already booked blocks of rooms and amenities at the Grand Hyatt for the three years after the first conference dates covered by the order. Because a substantial number of the postmasters would be unable to attend the conference, NAPUS terminated the contract with the Grand Hyatt.[102] The force majeure clause allowed either party to terminate if "acts of God, war, government regulation, terrorism, disaster, strikes, civil disorder, curtailment of transportation facilities, or any other emergency beyond the parties' control . . . materially affects a party's ability to perform its obligations under this Contract."[103] Had the order prevented NAPUS from continuing with organizing the conference, as NAPUS claimed, it would have "materially affected" NAPUS's "ability to perform its obligations under the [c]ontract." By making it inconvenient for the postmasters to attend the conference, the order drained away the conference attendees but did not affect NAPUS's ability to perform, as Hyatt claimed. NAPUS's benefits were impaired. The force majeure clause was not triggered by the order, and it did not allocate to Hyatt responsibility for the risk in question: that such an order would impair the value of the bookings to NAPUS.[104] The scenario was (1)(a)(i): the order reduced the potential number of postmasters who would likely attend the NAPUS conferences.

---

[101] 894 A.2d 471 (D.C. Ct. App. 2006).

[102] NAPUS terminated the contract with the Grand Hyatt and sought declaratory relief that the contract had been canceled; the hotel countersued for liquidated damages.

[103] 894 A.2d at 475.

[104] The appeal court, affirming the grant of summary judgment in favor of the Grand Hyatt, held, "The rescheduling of the Rural Mail Count may be an inconvenience or even make compliance with the contract inadvisable, but without an urgent need for prompt reaction, it cannot be considered an 'emergency' as that term is properly understood." *Id.* at 476.

Impaired Performance. A force majeure clause can allocate responsibility for the risks that an uncontrollable event will delay and impair an obligor's performance, that is, completion of a task intended to benefit the other party (scenarios (1)(b)(i)(B)(I) and (1)(b)(ii)(B)(I)). When a force majeure clause excuses delayed performance, the clause allocates to the obligee all or part of the responsibility for the risk performance will be delayed due to a force majeure event. Additional costs of performance are ignored for the moment. When a force majeure clause permits termination of the contract as a result of prolonged delayed performance or irreversibly impaired performance, the clause allocates responsibility for the risk of such delayed or impaired performance to both parties. The obligor is not liable to the obligee for its delayed or otherwise impaired performance but must cover its own losses, in the absence of terms to the contrary.

Force majeure clauses often vary the list of uncontrollable events that will excuse late or no performance. First, the more expansive the list of uncontrollable events included in the clause, the greater is the sharing of responsibility for uncontrollable event performance impairment risks; the narrower the list, the greater is the responsibility assumed by the obligor in the absence of other terms allocating such risks.[105] Such events may be described in detail: acts of God, mobs, public enemies, governmental agencies, and the like.[106] They may also be described in broad expansive terms that purport to cover all sources except those excluded: all events and actions "beyond the control" or "reasonable control" of the obligor.[107] The more detailed clause runs the risk of

---

105 "Force-majeure clauses are typically narrowly construed, such that the clause 'will generally only excuse a party's nonperformance if the event that caused the party's nonperformance is specifically identified.'" Kyrocera Corp. v. Hemlock Semiconductor, Inc., 313 Mich. App. 437, 451, 886 N.W.2d 445 (Mich. App. 2015).

106 *E.g.*, "Either party shall be excused for delay or failure to perform its agreements and undertakings, in whole or in part, when and to the extent that such failure or delay is occasioned by fire, flood, wind, lightning, or other acts of the elements, explosion, act of God, act of the public enemy, or interference of civil and/or military authorities, mobs, labor difficulties, vandalism, sabotage, malicious mischief, usurpation of power, depletion of wells, freezing or accidents to wells, pipelines, permanent closing of Buyer's operations at its Eddy County mine and refinery. . . ." Int'l Minerals and Chem. Corp. v. Llano, Inc., 770 F.2d 879, 882 (10th Cir. 1985), summarized in the text accompanying notes 50 and 51.

107 *E.g.*, "Snuffy's will be excused from performance under this contract if it is prevented from doing so by an act of God (e.g., flood, power failure, etc.), or other unforeseen events or circumstances." Facto v. Pantagis, 390 N.J. Super. 227, 915 A.2d 59, 62 (N.J. Sup. Ct. 2007), summarized in the text accompanying ch. 10, notes 64 and 65.

omitting one or more specific sources of disruption,[108] whereas the latter runs the risk of uncertainty about what it covers. The two approaches, however, may be combined.

Force majeure clauses vary little on the wording of the disruptive effects on the obligor's ability to perform that must occur for performance to be excused. The typical wording requires that the obligor be prevented or unable to perform as a result of the occurrence of the qualifying uncontrollable event. Yet such clauses are often expected to apply to two distinct types of disruptive events or hazards: first, interference or impairment of an obligor's ability to perform or performance (scenario (1)(b)(i)(B)(I)) and, second, events that compel an obligor to choose between performing and incurring adverse consequences, on one hand, and not performing and avoiding those consequences, on the other, and the obligor is pressured to make the latter choice (scenario (1)(b)(i)(B)(II)). *J.M. Rodriguez & Co.*,[109] where the cargo was stolen from the vessel, is an example of the former, an act that impairs performance. *Opera Company of Boston, Inc. v. Wolf Trap Foundation for the Performing Arts*,[110] *Eastern Airlines, Inc.*,[111] *International Minerals and Chemical Corp.*[112] and *Lyondell-CITGO Refining, LP*[113] illustrate the latter type: in each case, the obligor had to make a version of the choice previously described. The force majeure clause thus framed the question in each case artificially—whether the pressure on the obligor to choose not to perform overwhelmed its ability to perform. The answer is inevitably mixed with whether the choice was morally and socially the right one.[114] Such an

---

[108] *E.g.*, J.M. Rodriguez & Co. v. Moore-MacCormack Lines, Inc., 32 N.Y.2d 425 (N.Y. 1973), summarized in text accompanying notes 24 and 25. *See also* Sassower v. Blumenfeld, 24 Misc.3d 843, 878 N.Y.S.2d 602, 2009 N.Y. Slip Op. 29198 (N.Y. S. Ct. 2009), summarized in text accompanying ch. 8, notes 21–23 and ch. 10, notes 7–9.

[109] 32 N.Y.2d 425 (N.Y. 1973).

[110] 817 F.2d 1094 (4th Cir. 1987).

[111] 532 F.2d 957 (5th Cir. 1976).

[112] 770 F.2d 879, 886 (10th Cir. 1985).

[113] 2003 U.S. Dist. Lexis 1380; 2003 WL 218787989 (S.D.N.Y. 2003).

[114] *E.g.*, the court, in Int'l Minerals and Chem. Corp. v. Llano, Inc., 770 F.2d 879, 886 (10th Cir. 1985), held that "as a matter of policy, individuals and corporations who cooperate with local regulatory agencies and comply with the letter and spirit of legally proper regulations, environmental or otherwise, are to be encouraged. Stalling tactics are not regarded favorably. Second, as a matter of law, government policy need not be explicitly mandatory to cause impracticability." *Id.* at 886 (10th Cir. 1985). See also Eastern Airlines, Inc. v. McDonnell Douglas Corp., 532 F.2d 957 (5th Cir. 1976), summarized in the text accompanying note 45, where the appeal court held whether McDonnell's late deliveries

approach creates uncertainty about how the force majeure clause has allocated responsibility for uncontrollable event risk since the application of a clause may vary with specific choices and the circumstances in which they are made.

Additional Performance Costs. An uncontrollable event may increase an obligor's costs of performance (scenario (1)(b)(iii)(B)). Such event may or may not affect an obligor's ability to perform. The increase in a party's costs of benefit realization and task completion is separate and distinct from the impairment and delay of performance. A force majeure clause that excuses an obligor's failure to perform or delay in its performance does not thereby entitle an obligor to compensation from the obligee for its additional costs; such a clause only allocates responsibility for losses caused by such delay or failure to perform.

Contractual terms that allocate responsibility for such increased costs are similar to those that allocate responsibility for task and benefit oversight, rejection, uncertainty, and misconception. Compensation for performance that is based on the obligor's costs allows the obligor to pass through to the obligee the additional costs the obligor incurs as a result of interference by uncontrollable events. An example is a cost-plus construction contract, where the contractor charges the owner for all its costs plus a profit; the incremental costs due to force majeure events are charged to the owner as costs of performance. Fixed compensation for performance allocates to the obligor responsibility for the risk it will incur additional costs due to uncontrollable events in the absence of a clause that entitles it to compensation for such incremental costs. In an extreme case, an increase of costs due to an uncontrollable event may discharge the obligor of further performance as being impossible or impractical.[115] A force majeure or similar clause can be an exception to a fixed price and the risk allocation it implies, entitling the obligor to reimbursement or additional compensation for some or all of the costs it incurs as a result of or when responding to

were predicated upon the force majeure clause or the applicable section of the Uniform Commercial Code, "the military priorities policy . . . was in substance a governmental act beyond the control of McDonnell Douglas. The excusable delay clause cannot be made to turn on a distinction, which for so long has been held to be entirely artificial and unrealistic." *Id.* at 996.

[115] *E.g.*, Vernon v. Los Angeles, 45 Cal.2d 710 (Cal. 1955), summarized in the text accompanying notes 29 and 30.

such covered events; such provision allocates the risk of such additional costs to the obligee.[116]

The following cases illustrate how force majeure clauses can allocate the risk of additional performance costs resulting from an uncontrollable event:

- *Rainbow Navigation, Inc. v. United States*[117]: A vessel carried goods to Iceland where unloading was delayed until a strike at the port ended. Under the "liberty clause" in the bill of lading, the vessel was permitted to

  > decline to receive, keep or load the goods or . . . discharge the goods into any depot, craft or place or . . . proceed or return directly or indirectly to such other port or place as the Carrier may select and discharge the goods or any part thereof there, may retain the goods on board until the return trip or such time as the carrier thinks advisable or . . . forward or transship the goods by any means.[118]

  The clause further stated that "[f]or extra services rendered pursuant to this clause, the carrier shall be entitled to reasonable extra compensation." The first part of the clause quoted did not entitle the vessel to its extra costs, as the language nowhere mentioned them. The second clause turned on whether waiting to unload the vessel was an extra service, which the vessel claimed it was and the shipper successfully claimed it was not.[119] While the force majeure clause allocated responsibility for the losses resulting from delay due to a force majeure event to the shipper, neither it nor the liberty clause allocated responsibility for the risk that the vessel might incur additional costs in responding to such an event.

---

[116] *E.g.*, Iran v. Boeing Co., 771 F.2d 1279 (9th Cir. 1985), summarized in the text accompanying notes 120 and 121.

[117] 742 F. Supp. 171 (D.N.J. 1990). See text accompanying notes 27 and 28.

[118] 742 F. Supp. 171, 176 (D.N.J. 1990).

[119] The court held that the vessel owner's late delivery of the goods was excused under the first part of the clause, even though the strike had been announced before the vessel departed, because it was industry practice to set sail in the face of threatened strikes, and the wait at the port for more than three weeks was reasonable in light of the alternative destinations. The court further held that the waiting at the port for the strike to end was not an "extra service" within the meaning of the clause. *Id.* at 185.

- *Iran v. Boeing Co.*[120]: Iran agreed to reimburse a contractor for the costs of relocating its employees if the contract was not extended, subject to a maximum amount per employee. Conditions in Iran deteriorated while an extension of the contract was being negotiated. The contractor invoked a force majeure clause in the contract and temporarily relocated its employees to locations outside of Iran. Later, when the contract was not extended, the employees were relocated back to the United States. The contractor claimed the portion of the relocation costs up to the maximum under the relocation cost clause and the relocation costs exceeding such maximum under the force majeure clause, which provided, "[t]he price . . . shall be increased to reflect any increases in cost of performance due to Excusable Delays." Excusable Delays included "one or more of a series of normal forces majeures, including wars, strikes, acts of God, failures or acts of the government, etc., provided that these were not due to . . . [the contractor's] fault or negligence." To the extent the additional relocation costs were attributable to the deteriorating conditions in Iran, as the contractor successfully claimed, the clause allocated responsibility therefor to Iran.[121]

"Reopener" Clause

A party may be willing to concede at contract formation that certain uncontrollable events, while not automatically entitling the other party to any specific relief from performance or to compensation or indemnification, may be grounds for a request from the other party to discuss or negotiate an amendment to the contract that grants the other party appropriate relief. Such uncontrollable events can include those that affect benefit realization, affect tasks a party completes for its own benefit, and compel choices that yield undesirable outcomes, as well as events that directly impair, delay, or increase the cost of performing obligations. A clause that allows one party to request reconsideration of the bargain combines a condition subsequent and an agreement to negotiate or agree: the condition identifies the event that allows one party to initiate negotiation and the agreement to negotiate prescribes

---

[120] 771 F.2d 1279 (9th Cir. 1985).

[121] The court held the temporary relocation to locations outside of Iran was reasonable, since Iran and the contractor were negotiating an extension at the time. *Id.* at 128–29.

the extent to which the parties are committed to finding relief for the party adversely affected by the uncontrollable event. While the party unaffected by the event may be under little (an obligation to negotiate in good faith in some circumstances) or no legal obligation to accommodate the affected party's concerns, it may have good financial and other business reasons for doing so. The failure to reach agreement on such relief may leave the affected party in the same position as if the reopener clause had not been included in the contract, however.

In principle, the procedure for amending a contract so as to entitle a party adversely affected by an uncontrollable event to relief or compensation for such an event might be determined by one party, exercising absolute discretion, be proposed by one and accepted by the other, or agreed by both parties. Amendment procedures useful for allocating oversight and rejection risks, discussed in chapter 3, apply here. The amendment procedure included in a reopener clause will usually be the product of the parties' negotiation, rather than custom or practice in an industry. Because such an amendment will usually strike at the fundamental elements of the transaction, parties will ordinarily be reluctant to agree at contract formation to allow other parties to unilaterally dictate such an amendment.

Autry v. Republic Productions, Inc.[122] illustrates a reopener clause that covered an uncontrollable event. Gene Autry, a well-known singer and actor, agreed to act in ten photoplays during the first year of his contract (1938) with Republic Productions (RP), which had options to extend the contract for four successive years, during each of which he would act in eight photoplays. His compensation was $6,000 for the first two photoplays and $10,000 for each of the others during the first year; and his compensation for each photoplay would be increased by $1,000 each year. His compensation during 1939, for example, was $11,000 per photoplay. In 1942, he was ordered to report for a physical examination for conscription into the armed services during the war. He and RP agreed an amendment to their contract. RP received a further one year option for eight photoplays at $15,000 each. The parties also agreed:

> In the event that the Artist shall be required to serve in the armed forces of the United States pursuant to the Selective Service Act,

[122] 30 Cal.2d 144, 180 P. 2d 888 (Cal. 1947).

> or shall volunteer for such service, the parties hereto will agree upon their mutual rights and obligations hereunder in view of such military service.[123]

Sixteen months later, he voluntarily enlisted and served for three years. When discharged, he claimed the contract had terminated, its purpose having been frustrated or his performance made impossible. The uncontrollable event was the government's mobilization of eligible individuals for service in the armed forces during the war. His decision to enlist, however, was not beyond his control. It was scenario (1)(b)(ii)(B)(II) (uncontrollable event creates a choice between performing as committed while forbearing from volunteering for military service and volunteering for service while delaying completion of a task to be completed for the benefit of the other party). Had he been conscripted, the scenario would have been (1)(b)(ii)(B)(I) (an uncontrollable event delayed his completion of tasks for RP's benefit). The clause, however, allowed Autry to be excused either way without breaching his contract or having to agree, before voluntarily enlisting, when or even if he would perform. The clause left for a later day the full consequences to the parties of Autry's volunteering. To the extent the clause excused his failure to perform his contract with RP because he chose to serve or was conscripted, it allocated the risk of his so choosing or being conscripted to RP. It assumed responsibility for the risk his performance would be delayed during the period he served in the armed forces. To the extent Autry had a commitment to RP to perform if it exercised the option after he finished his service and what remained to be agreed was his compensation, Autry assumed responsibility for the uncertainty about the losses he might incur because he had to perform later for compensation agreed to at an earlier time. Since RP had an option, it could choose not to exercise the option if it decided Autry's value would no longer be worth what had been agreed he would be paid; it did not assume responsibility for the risk it would have to pay Autry more than he could then command for his performances. To the extent, however, Autry's commitment to perform at all under the RP contract was open to negotiation, RP assumed responsibility for the uncertainty risk created by the agreement to agree.[124]

---

123 *Id.* at 147.

124 Autry claimed the clause was an agreement to agree and had no effect. The trial court held for the production company, finding that the clause continued the contract, and

Indemnification

Indemnification is one of the most common devices used to allocate responsibility for losses in a transaction, especially losses incurred in resolving third-party claims. It is defined as "[t]he action of compensating for loss or damage sustained."[125] A party that agrees to indemnify another thereby agrees to compensate the other for the losses covered by the indemnity that are reduced to a monetary amount. Though the courts interpret the insurance and indemnity agreements quite differently because insurers and indemnitors play quite different roles in drafting and negotiating such contracts, insurance contracts are an economic subset of indemnification agreements: an insurer agrees to compensate an insured against specific losses, above a minimum amount or deductible and up to a maximum amount, that result from specific or covered events, subject to exceptions or exclusions.[126]

A party may agree to indemnify any and all losses another incurs as a result of acts and omissions of the indemnifying party, the indemnified party, acts of God, and acts and omissions of third parties, subject to laws that limit indemnification. First, one or each party may agree to indemnify the other for certain losses the latter incurs in the transaction as a result of the former's acts and omissions. To the extent that the covered acts and omissions are breaches of the contract, the indemnity restates as indemnification claims that may be prosecuted as breaches of

---

his rights under the contract had not been prejudiced by the three years' service. The California Supreme Court reversed. Although agreeing the quoted clause continued their agreement in effect while he was serving and would further continue the agreement if the parties agreed to appropriate modifications, it held that requiring his performance on the agreed terms would be inequitable, as the value of his compensation had been eroded by inflation during the three-year period, with the result it was less than that paid artists of similar stature. The court's ruling meant that the agreement to agree to modified terms did not trump the parties' respective rights under the frustration doctrine, in effect putting the artist in the same position as if the clause had not been included.

[125] Black's Law Dictionary 886 (10th ed. 2014).

[126] "Though indemnity agreements resemble liability insurance policies, rules for interpreting the two classes of contracts do differ significantly. Ambiguities in a policy of insurance are construed against the insurer, who generally drafted the policy, and who has received premiums to provide the agreed protection. . . . In noninsurance contexts, however, it is the indemnitee who may often have the superior bargaining power, and who may use this power unfairly to shift to another a disproportionate share of the financial consequences of its own legal fault." Crawford v. Weather Shield Mfg., Inc., 44 Cal.4th 541, 552, 79 Cal. Rptr.3d 721, 187 P.3d 424 (Cal. 2008).

contract. Unless such an indemnity expands or contracts the indemnified party's entitlement to damages for breach, the indemnity does not augment the indemnified party's rights under a contract. To the extent that the covered acts and omissions are not breaches of the contract, the indemnifying party insures the indemnified party against such acts and omissions and supplements the right to damages for breach. Second, one or each party may agree to indemnify the other for certain losses that result from acts and omissions by the indemnified party, in effect insuring the indemnified party against certain of its own acts and omissions. Third, a party may agree to indemnify another for certain losses that result from certain uncontrollable events, in effect insuring the indemnified party against such losses. Life insurance indemnifies a beneficiary against losses assumed to result from the death of an insured, howsoever caused, subject to exceptions; casualty or property insurance indemnifies an insured against certain losses caused by certain acts of the insured, God, and third parties; business interruption insurance indemnifies an insured against lost revenue caused by covered events; and liability insurance indemnifies an insured against claims by third parties for covered acts, omissions, and events. Such an indemnity can be expanded to include a duty to defend the indemnified party against claims that, if proved, are covered by the indemnity.

Except for an indemnity by a party that covers its existing liabilities to third parties and the indemnified party and liability for breach of contract, an indemnity allocates to the indemnitor responsibility for the covered losses sustained by the indemnified party, which can include the costs of defending the indemnified party against the claims, even if they prove to be unmeritorious. Such losses may include the value of anticipated benefits not realized and unanticipated costs incurred to realize benefits, to perform obligations, and incurred to resolve claims by the other party and third parties resulting from participation in the transaction.

An indemnity may cover costs incurred in response to an act of God or a third party beyond the control of the parties. Such costs may include those incurred while the affected party was prevented from performing its obligations by an uncontrollable event. An example is the costs of the vessel, in *Rainbow Navigation, Inc.*,[127] incurred while waiting for the strike that prevented its delivery of the cargo to end. But an indemnity need

[127] 742 F. Supp. 171 (D.N.J. 1990).

not be linked to costs incurred while unable to perform. An indemnity can cover some or all of the additional costs a party incurs as a result of an uncontrollable event to complete a task it must complete for its own benefit (scenario (1)(b)(iii)(A)), a task it must complete for the other party (scenario (1)(b)(iii)(B)), and realization of benefits (scenario 1(a)(iii)). An indemnity that protects benefit realization or the completion by a party of tasks for its own benefit is a version of a yield indemnity. In all such instances, the indemnitor thereby assumes responsibility for the extra costs so incurred by the indemnitee.

The following cases illustrate such indemnification:

- *Kruzits v. Okuma Machine Tool, Inc.*[128]: An equipment lessee agreed to indemnify its lessor for

  > any and all liabilities, losses . . . imposed on, incurred by, or asserted against [the lessor] . . . in any way relating to or arising out of this Lease or the manufacture, purchase, ownership, delivery, lease, possession, use, operation, condition, return or other disposition of the equipment by [the lessor] . . . or . . . [the lessee], . . . any claim arising out of strict liability in tort, and any taxes for which [the lessee] is responsible hereunder.[129]

  An employee of the lessee, who was injured while using the equipment, sued the lessor, who, in turn, claimed indemnification from the lessee. If the lessor had no further obligations to perform, having delivered the equipment and giving no continuing warranties, the liability was an additional cost it incurred to realize the benefits of the lease (scenario (1)(a)(iii)). The employee was a third party over whom the lessor had no control. The indemnity allocated responsibility for the risk of such third-party claims to the lessee, who unsuccessfully argued the clause did not apply because it did not specify claims based on strict product liability, as claimed by the employee.[130]

---

[128] 40 F.3d 52 (3d Cir. 1994).

[129] *Id.* at 56–57.

[130] "The indemnity clause . . . contains a direct reference to strict products liability claims and Vistek must therefore indemnify Heller in the underlying action." 40 F.3d 52, 57

- *Brown v. Two Exchange Plaza Partners*[131]: This case is previously described in this chapter.[132] An employee of a sub-subcontractor working on the atrium of a building was injured when the scaffold on which he was standing collapsed. He sued the general contractor. The subcontractor agreed to indemnify the general contractor for "any other claim arising out of, in connection with or as a consequence of the performance of the Work and/or any acts or omission of the Subcontractor or any of its . . . subcontractors."[133] As previously noted, the sub-subcontractor's claim against the contractor added to the latter's liability and cost of performing its obligations to the building owner (scenario (1)(b)(iii)(B)). As the indemnity was enforceable, as the general contractor successfully claimed, as between the subcontractor and the contractor, the indemnity allocated responsibility for the risk of such additional liability and costs to the subcontractor.

Third-Party Agreements

The chance that a third party might interfere with performance or benefit realization can be mitigated by having such third party agree to forbear from interfering with the transaction. Such an agreement is practical when the third party can be identified and brought into the transaction by a contract with one or both parties. The contract between the obligor and obligee can stipulate that, as a condition to the obligee's covenants or as a covenant of the obligor, the third party must agree to forbear from disruptive actions. In many transactions this will be infeasible because the third party will not be identifiable at contract formation or even when

(3d Cir. 1994). The lessee also unsuccessfully argued Pennsylvania, and not Illinois, law should apply to the indemnity, and the indemnity was not enforceable under Pennsylvania law.

131 76 N.Y.2d 172 (N.Y. 1990).

132 See text accompanying note 35.

133 The trial court found that neither the scaffold subcontractor nor the subcontractor who employed the injured worker were liable to indemnify the general contractor under the contractual indemnity agreements because neither had been negligent; it also held that the indemnities were unenforceable because the general contractor was liable under New York Labor Law §240(1). The appellate division reversed, holding the indemnity was enforceable and applicable, even though the subcontractor had not been negligent. The New York Court of Appeals affirmed. Because there was no evidence the general contractor had been negligent, the prohibition against indemnifying a party for its negligence in a construction contract did not apply.

the transaction closes. For example, the successor liability claimant in *In re Grumman Olson Industries, Inc.*[134] could not have been identified at contract formation or later when the sale of the business closed. He was an unknown potential creditor at the time. Nor could the injured employee in *Kruzits*[135] have been identified at contract formation, as he was not then a creditor (not having been injured). Existing creditors can be identified, however. The third-party agreement with such creditors could be delivered at contract formation or later in satisfaction of a condition, before the obligee must perform any of its obligations.

In re Three Strokes Ltd. Partnership[136] illustrates an agreement between two creditors and the limits of the agreement's effectiveness. A debtor owed $29 million to one creditor and $2 million to another. Both debts were secured by separate liens on a real estate development the value of which was estimated at $25 million. The second creditor agreed with the first creditor that its right to payment was subordinated to the payment of the entirety of the debt to the first creditor. It also agreed that its lien was subordinate to that of the first creditor and any distribution of assets that the debtor might receive in the event of its insolvency or bankruptcy should be remitted to the first creditor until the obligations owing to the first were paid in full. When the first creditor sought to foreclose, the second creditor filed for bankruptcy, successfully claiming that its lien on the collateral could not be extinguished without relief from the bankruptcy court. Had the agreement with the second creditor been enforceable without permission of the bankruptcy court, the first creditor would have avoided the risk of the second creditor's asserting its claims in the debtor's bankruptcy proceeding.

For the first creditor in *In re Three Strokes Ltd. Partnership*, the uncontrollable disruptive event to its transaction with the debtor was the assertion by the second creditor of its claims against the debtor, and the hazard to the first creditor was the second creditor's right to assert its claims. The first creditor mitigated this risk by entering into a second transaction with the second creditor. The intercreditor agreement allocated to the second creditor responsibility for the risk the debtor's assets, when liquidated, would be insufficient to pay both creditors. The intercreditor agreement did not eliminate the risk that the first creditor would not be paid in the priority agreed with the second creditor as

---

[134] 467 B.R. 694 (S.D.N.Y. 2012); see text accompanying notes 33 and 34.

[135] 40 F.3d 52 (3d Cir. 1994).

[136] 397 B.R. 804, 50 Bankr. Ct. Dec. 272 (N.D. Tex. 2008).

the debtor might pay the other creditor out of the agreed order, and that creditor might accept payment. A separate risk was that the second creditor might repudiate the intercreditor agreement, as it effectively did in *In re Three Strokes Ltd. Partnership,* by filing for bankruptcy.

Uncontrollable Event Risk Mitigation

A contract can include terms the purpose of which is to reduce the occurrence of uncontrollable events that could impair or increase the costs of performance or benefit realization. Against each hazard previously described, affirmative and negative covenants that have such purpose could be listed. Such terms would be a version of private regulations that have as their objective the preservation of an obligor's willingness and ability to perform and pay compensation.

The varying terms and arrangements that are effected by a creditor to protect its claims against a debtor from competing claims by other creditors are illustrative. First, the contract between debtor and creditor can include negative covenants that restrict actions by the debtor likely to create liabilities to competing creditors: limits on incurrence of debt, guaranties, and indemnities; purchases of businesses; and investments in joint ventures and other enterprises. Second, the debtor may be required to identify potential competing creditors and cause them to agree on the priority of their claims with, or otherwise to accommodate the realization of benefits by, the creditor. Third, the portion of the debtor's business the creditor most wants to shield from competing creditors' claims can be placed in a single purpose entity so that it transacts business and otherwise deals with only those third parties with whom dealings are essential and can be managed, as previously described in this chapter.

This strategy can be used when a business has specific assets that can be dedicated to the performance of obligations under a contract with the creditor; those assets can be vested in a company whose sole business is the ownership of those assets and the performance of those obligations. The structure is common in accounts receivable financings, where the obligor's business is limited to the purchase from affiliates and the sale to a single buyer of accounts receivable; the special purpose entity insulates such assets, the accounts receivable purchased from affiliates, from the claims of the affiliates' creditors. Such arrangements are also common in real estate and infrastructure projects, where a single building, road, plant, or other facility is vested in a special purpose company. The arrangement is also used in supply chains, where the key assets the vendor uses to fabricate the goods it supplies to an important customer are placed in a single purpose entity so that the operation of a business using those assets can continue and the customer will receive an uninterrupted supply of the products, even if disruptions caused by other third-party claims affect other lines of a vendor's business.

In re Doctors Hospital of Hyde Park, Inc.[137] illustrates the use of a special purpose entity to mitigate the risk of claims by competing creditors. A hospital sold its receivables to a special purpose subsidiary, for which the sole assets were the receivables, and received financing from a lender, whose loans were calculated based on and secured by those receivables. The subsidiary's business appeared in some respects like a division or arm of the hospital's operations. It was conducted from the same office as the hospital; it also used the same stationary, checks, business forms, post office box, telephone number, books of account, financial records, computer and operating systems, and limited liability company records, and its board held no meetings. It did make separate corporate filings, adopt annual resolutions ratifying the actions of its manager, and had a separate bank account, which had activity, and separate certificates delivered to the lender. The hospital filed for bankruptcy, and the bankruptcy trustee claimed the assets of the hospital included those of the special purpose subsidiary.[138] The purpose of the special purpose entity was to shield the lender's collateral from the claims of the hospital's other creditors and thus to mitigate the disruptive effects of such third-party claimants. Had the trustee successfully proved the subsidiary was not separate from the hospital's business, the receivables would have been subject to the hospital's other creditors' claims. As it was, sufficient separateness was maintained, and the arrangements mitigated the lender's risk of competing claims against its collateral.

It is outside the scope of this text to list measures appropriate for all the hazards described in this chapter.

---

137 507 B.R. 558, 2013 WL 5524696 (Bankr. Ill. E.D. 2013).

138 The evidence cited by the trustee was alone insufficient to destroy the separateness of the entity. The court noted the lender had failed to require the special purpose entity to deliver separate financial statements as required by the loan agreement, a fact that the trustee argued demonstrated the separateness had not been maintained. "That choice was its [the lender's] to make dependent on the information it needed in extending credit. Daiwa's [the lender's] failure to enforce that requirement should not, by itself, destroy the separateness of a validly composed corporate entity." 507 B.R. 558, 717.

12

Market Change Risks

MARKET CHANGE HAZARDS

A market is a location where "goods or services are bought and sold."[1] It is also a "geographic area or demographic segment considered as a place of demand for particular goods or services" and "the demand there is for any particular article."[2] In this latter sense, a market is an activity of individuals, demanding goods, services, and other items of value and supplying such items to satisfy that demand.

A change in supply or demand is a change in the market for the good, service, or other item of value so demanded and supplied. Such a change may be comparable to the uncontrollable events described in chapter 11 when no party to the transaction controls its occurrence, and it may or may not be foreseeable. Market changes are the cumulative effects or aggregation of the results of individuals' buying and selling goods, services, and other items of value; usually no specific individual controls such effects or aggregation. The exception is a "thin" market, which is defined as a market "in which the number of offerings is relatively low." Such a market may be controlled or influenced by a few individuals in a way uncontrollable events are not. Still, the market changes even in a

---

1 Black's Law Dictionary 970 (10th ed. 2014).

2 *Id.*

thin market may be beyond the control of both parties to a transaction. The reference to "market forces" enhances the comparison to other uncontrollable events: like earthquakes, lightning, and the like, changes in supply and demand seemingly deny a party affected thereby the ability to perform or realize a benefit or compel or pressure it to make a choice between two adverse outcomes. The analogy is far from perfect, however, as explained as follows.

Adverse Outcomes of Market Changes

Each market change whose occurrence or nonoccurrence is beyond the parties' control and affects their transaction can be described using the three variables used for other uncontrollable events:

- whether such change was (1) the occurrence of an event that was not expected to or was hoped would not occur or (2) the failure to occur of an event that was expected to occur or was hoped would occur;
- whether the change affected (a) benefit realization or (b) task completion; and
- whether benefit realization or task completion was as a result of such change partly or wholly (i) reduced, (ii) delayed, or (iii) made more expensive.

The market changes discussed in this chapter are assumed to be beyond the control of the parties. The previous variables can be combined to describe each market change. For example, an increase in a contractor's labor and material costs purchased in the open market would be a (1)(b)(iii) scenario: a market change that increases costs at the time of performance. If additional delay is also the result, because labor and materials take longer than anticipated to procure, the scenario would be (1)(b)(ii), as well.

The impact of uncontrollable events on task completion may also be repeated for market changes. The impact on task completion may be that (A) task completion is impossible, impractical, or difficult or (B) a choice is created between completing the task and suffering adverse consequences, on one hand, and breaching and avoiding the adverse consequences, on the other. When task completion is impaired, partly or wholly, or delayed by a market change, it can be further described by whether, if task completion is affected, the task is intended to be completed for (I) the benefit of the party completing it or (II) the other party. These previous variables can be combined with the first three groups to describe each uncontrollable incident. If the contractor was unable to procure an item needed for construction, it would be unable to perform its obligation to the owner. Such scenario is (1)(b)(i)(A)(II).

Contingencies and Nonoccurrences

A nonoccurrence of a market change is comparable to the nonoccurrence of an uncontrollable event and can adversely affect a transaction. In both instances, a transaction is structured such that benefit realization or task completion can be achieved only if an anticipated event or market change occurs. The passage of time without its occurrence results in such benefit not being realized or task not being completed. The hazard is proceeding with a transaction assuming or hoping such event or change will occur.

Columbian National Title Insurance Co.,[3] summarized in chapter 10,[4] may illustrate such a structure. Either the demand for title insurance in the county title insurance market had changed after contract formation, precluding the entry of new insurers in that market, or the demand for the new insurer's insurance policies did not develop after contract formation, as hoped. Viewed as the latter, which seems a more accurate description of events, the agent's realization of the benefits of the contract depended upon the occurrence of a market change. Accordingly, the agent's claim implied that he had not assumed responsibility for the risk of such nonoccurrence. Rather, both parties had jointly assumed responsibility for the risk of such nonoccurrence, and he could terminate the contract. Each party would have had to bear its losses. The title insurer's successful claim that the agent could not terminate the contract implied that the agent had assumed responsibility for the risk the market would not develop as anticipated.[5] So viewed, the case illustrates a (2)(a)(i) scenario (nonoccurrence of event precludes benefit realization).

---

[3] 659 F. Supp. 796 (D. Kan. 1987).

[4] See text accompanying ch. 10, note 27.

[5] The agent claimed termination was permissible because performance was commercially impracticable and frustration of purpose. The court agreed that the purpose of the exclusive agency contract had been frustrated: "When the insurance policies became unmarketable, defendant [the agent] was totally deprived of the benefits of the contract. Although the

Benefit Impairment

Several market changes are frequent hazards to benefit realization: first, a decrease in the demand or offtake for or the price of the goods, services, or other items of value, the sale of which is expected to yield an anticipated benefit; second, an increase in supply of such items, depressing their price in the market; and third, inflation that diminishes the relative value of the prices realized from such sales.

Demand and Offtake. Chapter 10 describes the risk to a party in a supply chain transaction that can occur when an offtaker does not perform as expected. The offtaker's repudiation or breach in a second transaction diminishes or destroys the value of the benefit the party hoped to realize in a first transaction, wherein it would receive a good, service, or other item of value to be used to perform in the second. Chapter 10 assumes an offtaker has or could have been identified. This chapter assumes no offtaker has been identified and explains the risk to a party (P2) where no offtaker can be identified because demand for an item, if it previously existed, has collapsed. This is an extreme case, when demand for goods, services, or other items have vanished. In other instances, discussed later in this chapter, demand may be weak, reducing the price of such items. When demand has collapsed, the result is the same for P2 as breach or repudiation by the offtaker: the value of the benefit of the first transaction correspondingly decreases with the loss of value in the second transaction. But the hazard described in this chapter is a change in the market, a drop in demand, not a failure of the offtaker to perform.

The following illustrate such a hazard:

- *OWBR LLC v. Clear Channel Communications, Inc.*[6]: In November 2000, conference organizers booked 2,270 hotel rooms for conference scheduled for February 2002. They also agreed to pay, as liquidated damages, the full rates for such rooms if the conference was canceled 30 or fewer days before the event. The organizers canceled the event within a 30-day period, citing the

unmarketability of the policies did not make performance by either party impracticable, it did make performance useless." *Id.* at 804. The court held that the frustration doctrine did not apply because the agent had superior knowledge of local conditions and could have foreseen the change in market conditions. By failing to provide for such change, it had assumed the risk. *Id.*

[6] 266 F. Supp.2d 1214 (D. Ha. 2003).

"events of September 11th coupled with the fragile condition of the U.S. and international consumer economies," which had "resulted in the withdrawal of commitments to this event from many of our sponsors and participants."[7] Whatever demand for the conference that existed at contract formation had dried up by January 2002 due to the combined effects of the 9/11 events and the subsequent downturn in the economy, which were the hazards to the transaction. (The hotel, the conference organizers, and attendees were P1, P2, and P3 respectively; the value of the P1-P2 contract was destroyed by the drop in demand by potential P3s.) If responsibility for the risk of such a drop was not assumed by the conference organizers, as they implied in their claim, it was borne by both parties, and the organizers could terminate. Each party would be left to bear its losses. The hotel's successful claim that the organizers could not terminate implied that responsibility for the risk had been assumed by them. This case also illustrates a (1)(a)(i) scenario, where the market change is a drop in demand.

- *Karl Wendt Farm Equipment Co., Inc. v. International Harvester Co.*[8]: Because of a sharp downturn in the demand for farm equipment, a manufacturer sold its farm equipment division through an asset sale, assigning most of its contracts with its distributors to the buyer. It did not assign the contract with Karl Wendt (KW) because the buyer already had a distributor in the area in which KW sold farm equipment. The drop in demand did not prevent the manufacturer from selling equipment to KW; it made continued operation unprofitable. The drop in demand, together with the buyer's existing contract with another distributor, reduced the value or benefits of the KW contract to the manufacturer because he could not assign it to the buyer. If responsibility for the risk of such a drop in demand was not assumed by the manufacturer, as the manufacturer's claim implied, it was borne by both parties and the manufacturer could terminate. Each party would be left to bear its losses. KW's successful claim implied that responsibility for such risk had been assumed by the manufacturer, who could not terminate and who

[7] *Id.* at 1216.
[8] 931 F.2d 1112 (6th Cir. 1991).

breached the contract by selling the division without assigning the contract.[9] (The manufacturer, distributor, and customers were P1, P2, and P3, respectively. Because P2's commitment to buy from P1 did not have to exceed the demand from P3, P1 bore responsibility for the risk of demand for farm machinery declining. The decline in demand by P3 decreased the value of the P1-P2 contract to P1.) This case illustrates a (1)(a)(i) scenario, where the market change is a drop in demand.

Quantity and Price Changes. Demand for a good, service, or other item may decrease without entirely disappearing, or the supply may increase dramatically. If a party can pass through to its supplier to whom it has committed to buy items the reduced demand by taking less or fewer of the supplied items, responsibility for the risk of a drop in demand is also passed through to, and assumed by, the supplier. Another result of a decrease in demand may be a drop in the price in the market for the goods, services, or other items a party expects to sell. A similar result may occur because the supply is increased more quickly than a corresponding increase in demand. If a party can pass through to its supplier the reduced price by paying less for the supplied item, responsibility for the risk of a drop in demand is also passed through to, and assumed by, the supplier. If such party cannot pass through to its supplier the reduced demand or price for items because it has agreed to take a fixed or minimum quantity or pay a fixed price, then it bears responsibility for the risk of such drop in demand or price, unless it is otherwise excused. In either case, the value of the supply contract to the supplied party is diminished by the reduction of demand or price, resulting in a lower quantity or prices being desirable.

[9] KW sued for breach of contract; the manufacturer claimed performance was commercially impractical because of the sharp change in market conditions, citing the fact that the division had been losing $2 million per day. The trial court allowed the jury to consider the defense, and the jury found for the manufacturer. The appeal court reversed, holding that "application of the impracticability defense in this case would allow IH [the manufacturer] to avoid its liability under franchise agreements, allow [the buyer] Case/Tenneco to pick up only those dealerships it sees fit, and leave the remaining dealers bankrupt. In such circumstance, application of the doctrine of impracticability would not only be a misapplication of law, but a windfall for IH at the expense of the dealers." *Id.* at 1118.

The following illustrate such hazards:

- *Great Lakes Gas Transmission Ltd. Partnership v. Essar Steel Minnesota, LLC*[10]: In September 2006, a pipeline company agreed to transport a quantity of gas each day from a receiving point to a delivery point for a steel producer. The contract term was to begin July 1, 2009. In 2008, a global financial crisis began, and steel prices dropped to a six-year low. The steel producer claimed its duty to pay the tariff was excused because the demand for steel had dropped, steel prices were low, and financing for the construction of the steel plant was unavailable due to the shortage of credit in the financial market. The drop in demand for steel did not make the steel producer's performance impossible: it could still pay the agreed tariff even if it did not transport any gas; the value or benefit of the contract had been diminished by the drop in demand for steel. The risk allocation implied in the steel producer's claim was that responsibility for the risk of decreased demand and steel prices was shared with the pipeline. It was entitled to reduce or delay (or both) its demand for the transportation services to reflect its own delay and reduction in production.[11] (The pipeline, the steel producer and its customers were P1, P2, and P3, respectively. The value of the P1-P2 contract was reduced by the reduction in demand and prices prospective P3s were willing to pay.) This case is also a (1)(a)(i) scenario, where the market change is a drop in demand and price that affects the value of the anticipated benefit.
- *Kyrocera Corp. v. Hemlock Semiconductor, Inc.*:[12] Between 2005 and 2008, a manufacturer of solar panels agreed in four contracts to buy a certain quantity of polysilicon annually at a fixed price over a period of ten years. Beginning in 2010, Chinese companies flooded the international market with solar panels at reduced prices. Chinese companies gained 75 percent of the global solar panel market, causing more than 20 US and European manufacturers to go out of business and solar panel prices to decline precipitously. The continued purchase by the manufacturer of components used in its manufacture of solar panels became uneconomic. The supplier agreed to lower prices for 2011 and 2012, but not beyond.

---

10 871 F. Supp. 2d 843, 104 A.L.R.6th 675 (D. Minn. 2012).

11 This case is further discussed in *infra* note 64.

12 313 Mich. App. 437, 886 N.W.2d 445 (Mich. App. 2015).

The manufacturer sued for a declaration that it was no longer bound to buy polysilicon pursuant to the contracts because of the lower market prices for solar panels attributable to the actions of Chinese suppliers and government. The lower prices did not prevent the manufacturer from performing its contract with its supplier: it could still take delivery of polysilicon in the agreed quantities and pay the agreed price or pay the agreed minimum without taking delivery of any amount. The depressed prices diminished the value of the supply contract to the manufacturer. (The supplier, the manufacturer, and its customers were P1, P2, and P3, respectively. The value of the P1-P2 contract was diminished by the drop in solar panel prices.) The P1-P2 contract effected a risk allocation usually effected by a fixed price take-or-pay contract for an item like polysilicon: first, the manufacturer or buyer assumes responsibility for the risk the contract price of the item will be higher than the market price as and when the item is required, and second, the manufacturer assumes responsibility for the risk that its need for polysilicon will be less than the minimum quantity it agreed to buy.[13] The case is another illustration of scenario (1)(a)(i): a drop in demand for a party's products reduced the value to that party of the contract with its supplier for the components used in making the products.

Inflation. Inflation, defined as "[a] general increase in prices coinciding with a fall in the real value of money,"[14] erodes the value of benefits when amounts received are fixed over a period of time. Inflation could create risks in a supply chain transaction comparable to the effect of price decreases due to drops in demand or increases in supply. For example, if a party buys goods, services, or other items and pays market price, over time that price could increase consistent with inflation and those

[13] "Specifically, even taking plaintiff's factual allegations as true and construing them in plaintiff's favor, the allegations of the complaint only indicate that the deflation of the market price for polysilicon has rendered plaintiff's contract with defendant unprofitable. The risk of such a deflation of market prices—no matter the cause—was expressly assumed by plaintiff in its take-or-pay contract with defendant. Plaintiff opted not to protect itself with a contractual limitation on the degree of market price risk that it would assume. It cannot now, by judicial action, manufacture a contractual limitation that it may in hindsight desire by broadly interpreting the force-majeure clause to say something that it does not." *Id.* at 452–53.

[14] Black's Law Dictionary, *supra* note 1, 898.

increases could not be passed through to offtakers because the party had agreed to sell its products at a fixed price; the value of the offtake contract would diminish over time, as inflation erodes its benefits. This is also true when the transaction is not one in a supply chain. For any party who anticipates realizing value over a period of time, inflation will reduce that value unless it is increased consistently with inflation or the contract can be terminated.

The following illustrate inflation hazards:

- *Shell Oil Co. v. Kapler*[15]: In 1939, a landlord leased property for five years. The lease was later renewed for another five years. The lease granted the tenant an option to purchase the leased property for a fixed price of $25,000 and a right of first refusal. Before the expiration of the second five-year term, the tenant exercised the option. The landlord responded, stating it had another offer for $35,000 and insisted that the tenant meet this price or relinquish its right to buy. The tenant sued for specific performance. The owner contended that relief should be denied because of "the increase in the value of the property and the depreciation in value of money since the lease agreement was entered into by the parties."[16] The landlord remained capable of performing, selling the property. Neither the increase in the value of the property nor the decline of the purchasing power of the fixed price prevented the landlord from selling. The benefit of the fixed price had eroded. The landlord's claim that the tenant should match the higher price or lose the option implied that responsibility for the risk of inflation rested with the tenant. If both parties shared responsibility for the risk of inflation eroding the value of the fixed price, the option would have no longer been effective. The tenant's successful claim that the option was enforceable notwithstanding the reduced value of the fixed price implied that the landlord had assumed responsibility for that risk.[17] This case also illustrates a

---

[15] 235 Minn. 292, 50 NW2d 707 (Minn. 1951).

[16] *Id.* at 302.

[17] The court disagreed, holding, "It is the general rule that ordinarily the fairness of a contract is to be determined in the light of the circumstances that existed at the time of its making rather than by the effect of subsequent events which intervene before specific performance is sought. Adequacy or inadequacy of consideration for the property sold is

(1) (a) (i) scenario, but the market change was the erosion of the value realized due to inflation.

- *Cumberland Trust v. Maritime Electric Co. Ltd.*[18]: In 1853, a landlord leased to a gas light company four parcels of land in Charlottetown, Queens County, Prince Edward Island, for 999 years at a fixed annual rent of £18 local currency (which amounted to C$58.40 in Canada's 2000 currency). In 1999, the landlord applied to the court to increase the rent and limit the term to 20 years, claiming that inflation has eroded the value of the rent to the owner, which was used for charitable purposes. Had the tenant alone bore responsibility for inflation, as the landlord's position implied, the landlord would have been entitled to increase the rent to its value adjusted for inflation. If both shared responsibility for the risk of inflation, the landlord could have terminated the lease when the value of the rent had been substantially reduced, as it was. The landlord could not increase the rent or terminate the lease, however, if it alone assumed responsibility for inflation, as the tenant's successful claim implied.[19]

Task Completion

The unwillingness of even a single supplier to supply a good, service, or other item of value that is needed to complete the task and was previously available is a market change that can prevent or impair task completion. We ignore an increase in prices due to short supply because price increases are discussed later in this chapter. Supply of a necessary item may become temporarily or permanently unavailable because its suppliers discontinue supplying it altogether. Procurement of an item may become

to be determined as of the inception of the contract rather than according to the increased or decreased value of the property at the time of trial." *Id.*

18 2000 PEISCTD 1 (2000).

19 Justice Armand DesRoches refused the request, rejecting application of the frustration doctrine to the case, though expressing some reluctance about the result. "The respondent's payment of an annual rental of $58.40 for four prime city waterfront lots appears clearly to result in it enjoying a hugh (sic) economic advantage under the lease for which it pays virtually nothing. This economic advantage is especially striking when measured against the fact that the annual rental is used by the Cumberland Trust for the awarding of educational scholarships and prizes." *Id.* at 17.

more difficult. The difficulty or unavailability cannot be attributable to the party's inability to procure the item. Procurement has to be infeasible, i.e., no one can procure the item in the market. The disruption in the supply of an item cannot be due to an uncontrollable event, such as a storm destroying a crop in a region, because the unavailability or increased price of the item would be the result of such event and not market changes. Such a market change—change in supply availability—is a hazard only in a supply chain transaction: task completion in one transaction depends upon identifying, contracting with, and the performance by a supplier in a separate, concurrent, or earlier transaction.

The following illustrate such hazards:

- *Gander Mountain Co. v. Islip U-Slip LLC*[20]: A tenant rented premises for 15 years, aware of the history of flooding in an area. It agreed to obtain an all-risk policy of insurance covering its merchandise, trade fixtures, furnishings, equipment, and all other items of its personal property and all buildings and improvements on the premises. Two years later, the premises were severely flooded by the nearby stream, and again by a tropical storm six years later. The tenant was unable to obtain all-risk insurance because of these incidents and the history of flooding before it rented the premises and sued for a declaration that the lease was terminated as a result, claiming impossibility or frustration of purpose. (The insurer, tenant, and landlord were P1, P2, and P3, respectively. Obtaining the insurance under the P1-P2 contract would satisfy P2's obligation to P3 under the lease.) The tenant's position was comparable to a loan applicant who could not qualify for a loan. The required insurance was available in the market but not to the rented premises because they did not qualify, given the history of flooding. Put another way, satisfying the insurance company's requirements was feasible in appropriate circumstances, but the rented premises did not qualify. The tenant's claim implied both landlord and tenant shared responsibility for the risk the tenant would lose its ability to obtain the insurance. Each could terminate without liability for breach when the tenant could not obtain insurance. The landlord successfully claimed the tenant assumed

[20] 923 F. Supp. 2d 351 (N.D.N.Y. 2013).

responsibility for the risk it would be unable to obtain the required insurance.[21]

- *Kel Kim Corp. v. Central Markets, Inc.*[22]: A tenant leased premises to operate a roller skating rink open to the public and agreed to maintain public liability insurance with aggregate liability of $1,000,000 for the ten-year term of the lease. After five years it was unable to obtain renewal or replacement of such insurance because the reinsurer of its insurer had become insolvent. The best replacement insurance the tenant could obtain limited coverage to $500,000. The tenant claimed its failure to obtain the policy was excused by impossibility and the force majeure clause. Whether procuring the required insurance was infeasible because the insurance market had changed—reinsurers were no longer willing to reinsure liability insurance for roller skating rinks—is unclear. If not, this was another case of inability. Assuming the case was one where the market had changed, the tenant's claim implied that the landlord bore the risk of an adverse change in the insurance market that prevented the tenant from complying with the insurance requirement; the tenant could continue to rent the premises while not having to comply with that requirement. The landlord's successful claim implied the tenant had assumed responsibility for the risk it would be unable to obtain the required insurance.[23]

---

[21] The court dismissed the tenant's claims, holding that however the defense was characterized, the inability to obtain insurance was foreseeable, and as such, neither defense was available. The market in all-risk insurance did not materially change after contract formation; rather, the insurers' willingness to insure the specific property declined because of the flooding, together with the prior history of flooding.

[22] 70 N.Y.2d 900, 524 N.Y.S.2d 384, 519 N.E.2d 295 (N.Y. 1987).

[23] The landlord notified the tenant of the default, and the tenant responded that obtaining the replacement insurance was impossible and sued for a declaration that its performance was excused. The trial court awarded summary judgment to the landlord. The New York Court of Appeal affirmed, holding the tenant's "inability to procure and maintain requisite coverage could have been foreseen and guarded against when it specifically undertook that obligation in the lease, and therefore the obligation cannot be excused on this basis." *Id.* at 902. The court also held the force majeure clause did not apply to the tenant's inability to procure the required insurance, stating, "[T]he events listed in the force majeure clause here are different in-kind and nature from *Kel Kim's* [the tenant's] inability to procure and maintain public liability insurance." *Id.* at 903.

- *Hoosier Energy Rural Elec. Coop., Inc. v. John Hancock Life Ins. Co.*[24]: A power plant lease obligated the lessee to maintain a credit default swap with a qualified counterparty for the benefit of the lessor and to replace such swap within 60 days if the swap provider ceased to be qualified. The lessor could demand payment under the swaps if they were not replaced within that period. During the 2008 financial crisis, the swap provider's credit rating dropped below the required level. The lessee sought a replacement swap provider but could not find a qualified counterparty because of the crisis. The lessee sued for an injunction to prevent the lessor from demanding payment under the swaps when the swap provider was not replaced within the 60-day period, claiming temporary impossibility. The change in the market was that some of the potential previously qualified counterparties ceased to be so; the supply in the market had shrunk to a point where such counterparties were not readily available. It was the clearest case where compliance with the requirement had become infeasible because of a shortage of suppliers.[25] The lessee's claim implied the lessor bore responsibility for the risk qualified counterparties would not be available, at least temporarily; the lessee could continue to lease the power plant without having to comply with the credit default swap requirement so long as qualified counterparties were in short supply. The landlord's unsuccessful claim implied the tenant had assumed responsibility for the risk it would be unable to obtain the credit default swap.[26] This and the previous case illustrate (1)(b)(i)(A)(II) scenarios: a change in the insurance and credit default swap markets prevented an obligor from completing a task for the benefit of the other party.[27]

---

24 582 F.3d 721 (7th Cir. 2009).

25 "[I]f no one could have foreseen the extent of the credit crunch in 2008—and if it really made performance impossible, a subject on which the parties profoundly disagree—then the sort of argument that Hoosier Energy [the lessee] makes could satisfy the requirements of *Kel Kim*." *Id.* at 729.

26 The district court found in favor of the lessee. Affirming the decision, Chief Judge Frank Easterbrook added an important qualification: "So although we affirm the district court's preliminary injunction, we conclude that, if Hoosier Energy [the lessee] has not produced a replacement for Ambac [the credit swap provider] by the end of 2009, the time will have arrived when the court must let John Hancock realize on its security." *Id.* at 730.

27 *See also* Ner Tamid Congregation of North Town v. Krivoruchko, 638 F. Supp.2d 913 (N.D. Ill. 2009), where a contract for the sale of property did not include a condition that the buyer obtain the financing it required to complete the purchase, the buyer being confident

- *CERAbio LLC v. Wright Medical Technology, Inc.*[28]: This case is summarized in chapter 4.[29] CERAbio (C) sold its business, which made a bone replacement product, to a buyer for two payments of $1.5 million each and royalties, the first at closing and the second when the buyer verified the product could be made following the protocol agreed by the parties. After closing, the parties learned the sole supplier of a key ingredient used to make the product no longer supplied it. C believed that with a change to the protocol the product could be produced using a new ingredient. The buyer was unwilling to make the change and claimed fraud.[30] The market in the key ingredient was indeed very thin. The loss of the supplier of that ingredient was a change in that market. C's claim implied that responsibility for the supply risk was shared by the buyer, which had to use a substitute for the key ingredient if one was available. The buyer's unsuccessful claim implied that C assumed responsibility for the risk. (Any supplier of the ingredient, C, and the buyer would have been P1, P2, and P3, respectively. The absence of a supplier precluded a P1-P2 contract and P2's ability to supply P3 with the ingredient required to run the test protocol.) This case illustrates a (1)(b)(i)(A)(I) scenario: C was not obligated to have the buyer run the test protocol. Doing so was a condition to its receiving the second payment, a benefit of the sale. A change in the supply of the key ingredient would have prevented it from completing a task for its benefit as much as for that of the other party but for the availability of the substitute.

---

it would be able to obtain such loans. When he failed to close the purchase, the seller sued and moved for summary judgment, which was granted. The buyer's argument that the recession in 2007 to 2009 had made it impossible for him to obtain the loans was dismissed. The court held the risk of the recession was irrelevant: "It is precisely because inability to obtain financing is a foreseeable (and significant) risk that can be readily guarded against in the parties' agreement that financing contingency provisions are common in both commercial and residential real estate contracts." *Id.* at 928.

[28] 410 F.3d 981 (7th Cir. 2005).

[29] See text accompanying ch. 4, notes 23 and 24.

[30] The seller sued for the second payment and royalties, and the buyer counterclaimed for fraud. The trial court dismissed the buyer's claim, and the jury awarded a verdict in favor of the seller.

Increased Costs

An increase in the price of goods, services, and items of value procured in the open market for use by a party can be a hazard to benefit realization and task completion. If the additional costs are paid directly by the ultimate offtaker who consumes such items when realizing the benefits of a transaction, it cannot recoup such costs by raising its own prices. The hazard to the offtaker is that the market price of such inputs will increase beyond its expectations. Such instances are scenario (1)(a)(iii). If the additional costs are paid by a supplier who uses such items to perform obligations, it may be able to recoup the additional costs by charging higher prices for the items it supplies. Price increases are a hazard to such a supplier to the extent it cannot match its increased costs with increased prices to its offtaker. Such instances are scenario (1)(b)(iii)(B)(II).

The following are cases that illustrate such mismatch hazards:

- *Maple Farms, Inc. v. City School District of Elmira*[31]: A milk supplier agreed to supply milk to a school district for $.0759 per half pint, at which time the mandated price of raw milk was $8.03 per hundredweight (cwt). Subsequently, the price of raw milk increased 23 percent to $9.89 cwt. In the prior three years, the price of raw milk ranged from $6.73 cwt to a high of $7.58 cwt, or 12 percent. The supplier sued for a declaration that its performance had been rendered commercially impracticable by the price increase, citing as the unforeseen causes the "agreement of the United States to sell huge amounts of grain to Russia and to a lesser extent to unanticipated crop failures."[32] The price mismatch was between the market price at which the supplier bought and the fixed price at which the supplier sold milk. The supplier's claim implied that both parties shared responsibility for the risk that the market price of milk would increase beyond the level the supplier anticipated, and as a result the supplier would be able to terminate its contract with the school district.

[31] 76 Misc.2d 1080, 352 NYS2d 784 (N.Y. Sup. Ct. 1974).

[32] *Id.* at 1082.

The school district's successful claim implied that responsibility for the risk had been assumed by the supplier.[33]

- *Staffordshire Area Health Authority v. South Staffordshire Waterworks Co.*[34]: In 1929, a water company agreed to supply a hospital authority with the first 5,000 gallons per day of water for free and additional water at a fixed price per 1,000 gallons "at all times hereafter." The water company's costs rose eighteen times over the next forty-five years. In 1975, the water company terminated the contract and offered to supply the first 5,000 gallons of water per day free and additional amounts at its normal rates. The mismatch was between the market prices the water company paid for labor and materials and the fixed price it charged the hospital authority. The water company's successful claim implied that both parties shared responsibility for the risk the water company's prices might increase over time, allowing the water company to terminate when they dwarfed the payments from the authority. The authority's unsuccessful claim implied the water company assumed responsibility for the risk of such price increases.[35]
- *Bernina Distributors Inc. v. Bernina Sewing Machine Co., Inc.*[36]: A sewing machine importer agreed to pay its Swiss supplier prices denominated in Swiss francs but agreed to sell the machines to its US distributor at prices denominated in US dollars. Those prices were subject to change to the extent the invoice price to the importer or duty charges were increased or decreased and to the extent the importer's insurance, freight, handling, broker, and port fees, and similar charges, were increased 20 percent or more over such charges at contract formation. When the value of the US dollar decreased relative to the Swiss franc, the importer treated its increased cost in US dollars (to buy the additional francs) as an increase in the invoice price. When challenged by the distributor, it also claimed it could terminate the contract, as the drop in the

---

[33] The court disagreed, finding the price increase of 10 percent during the year running up to contract formation should have made the supplier "aware of the general inflation in this country during the previous years and of the chance of crop failures." *Id.* at 1085.

[34] [1978] 3 All ER 769, [1978] 1 WLR 138.

[35] The hospital authority took out an originating summons to have the contract declared enforceable, and the trial court found in its favor. The appeal court allowed the water company to terminate the contract.

[36] 646 F.2d 434 (10th Cir. 1981).

value of the dollar frustrated the contract. The mismatch was buying at prices in Swiss francs and selling at prices in dollars. The importer's first claim, that it could pass through to the distributor its higher costs resulting from unfavorable swings in the exchange rate, implied the distributor bore the risk of the dollar's decline in value relative to the Swiss franc (but not the benefit of declines in the value of the Swiss franc).[37] The second claim implied the parties shared responsibility for that risk, allowing the importer to terminate. The distributor's successful claim that the importer could not charge for the higher cost of Swiss francs or terminate implied responsibility for the risk had been assumed by the importer.

- *Eastern Air Lines, Inc. v. Gulf Oil Corp.*[38]: In June 1972, Gulf agreed to sell jet fuel to Eastern for four and one-half years at prices calculated using the posted prices for West Texas sour crude oil, as published in *Platt's Oilgram Crude Oil Supplement.* In 1973, the price of crude oil produced outside the United States increased, such that the unregulated price of foreign crude exceeded that for domestic crude. The government adopted a tiered pricing regulation for crude oil produced in the United States. One result was that the posted price continued to reflect the regulated, and not the higher foreign or unregulated, domestic market prices of crude oil. Gulf demanded a price increase, threatening to cut off supplies to Eastern, which sought an injunction to compel performance. Gulf claimed it was not bound by the contract because the posted price was lower than the foreign and unregulated domestic prices; its performance had become commercially impracticable. The mismatch was between the prices of unregulated foreign and domestic crude, on one hand, and regulated domestic crude, on

[37] The trial court determined that the contract did not allow the importer to increase the price for exchange rate fluctuations and the appeal court affirmed. The importer claimed the exchange rate fluctuations rendered its performance under the contract impractical under the Utah version of Uniform Commercial Code section 2-615. The appeal court disagreed, citing a letter from the importer before contract formation: "Importer's letter to Distributor concerning a 7% devaluation of the dollar in relation to the franc, sent three weeks prior to the contract execution, shows clear foreknowledge of the possibility of currency fluctuations (Ex. 41) and, thus, supports the finding that section 2-615 is inapplicable." *Id.* at 439. The court added, "Finally, cost increases alone, though great in extent, do not render a contract impracticable." *Id.*

[38] 415 F. Supp. 429 (S.D. Fla. 1975).

the other. One view of Gulf's claim was that its costs of the crude oil used to produce jet fuel soared with the increase in the price of foreign crude, rendering the contract with Eastern less profitable or unprofitable. Implicit in Gulf's claim was that responsibility for the risk of such price mismatch was shared, allowing Gulf to terminate. Another view of Gulf's claim was that sale of jet fuel to Eastern at the posted price for West Texas sour crude was less profitable than sales at a price that reflected the market price of crude. In effect, Gulf was comparing the benefit it agreed to accept at contract formation with a more valuable benefit created by the increase in the price of foreign crude. That implied a different risk allocation: the risk that a change in the market price of crude would make the agreed price less profitable than another price, a risk responsibility for which Gulf's claim implied was shared by the parties. Responsibility for the risk remained with Gulf, as Eastern successfully claimed.[39]

Impairment and Choice

As explained in chapter 11, an uncontrollable event can create a predicament for an obligor where it must choose between performing a contractual obligation and thus suffering an adverse consequence and avoiding such consequence by not performing and thus incurring potential liability for breach of contract. Performance is not prevented or necessarily more difficult as a result of such an event. A supply shortage does not create such a predicament because it eliminates the choice of compliance and with it the ability to perform. An increase in the prices of inputs does create such a choice: between continuing with performance and incurring the higher costs, on one hand, and avoiding the higher costs and breaching, on the other. A drop in demand by offtakers or

[39] After hearing the evidence, District Judge James Lawrence King held in favor of Eastern. He found that the parties "intended to be bound by the specified entries in Platt's, which has been published at all times material here, which is published today, and which prints the contract reference prices. Prices under the contract can be and still are calculated by reference to Platt's publication." *Id.* at 439. Some 60 percent of Gulf's production was still subject to price regulation. The judge found that Gulf had not met its burden of proof on the commercial impracticability defense because he could not determine Gulf's cost of production of crude outside the United States. Gulf's domestic subsidiaries bought crude oil from its foreign subsidiaries at prices determined by Gulf. *Id.* at 441.

the value of benefits also creates a choice: between performing and realizing less or no value, thus avoiding such realization, and breaching the contract. In *Karl Wendt Farm Equipment Co., Inc.*,[40] for example, the manufacturer had to choose between honoring its contract with the dealer and incurring financial losses and avoiding those losses and breaching that contract. This is true of all cases in which benefits are impaired, whether as a result of an act of God or a third party or a drop in demand or value. The pressure created by a change in the price of an input or the demand or value is financial or economic: the obligor must give or invest more value to perform than it than anticipated or realize less value or incur more losses than anticipated from performance.

Oversight, Etc.

Like uncontrollable events, the potential for market changes may be overlooked, recognized but rejected as unimportant to transaction planning, misunderstood because of bad information or incorrect processing of good information, and be highly uncertain as to both their nature and probability of occurrence. Oversight of market changes is evident in cases where it is claimed such changes were unforeseeable, notwithstanding that they frequently occur, though perhaps due to different and unusual events. Unforseeability admits ignorance of the potential event at contract formation. In *Northern Illinois Gas Co. v. Energy Coop., Inc.*,[41] a naptha buyer claimed naptha price increases and natural gas price decreases (it used the naptha to produce the gas) could not have been foreseen, and these circumstances made its purchase of naptha so financially burdensome that the contract should be terminated. Holding the supplier was entitled to summary judgment on this claim, Justice James Heiple unsympathetically commented, "Changing and shifting markets and prices from multitudinous causes is endemic to the economy in which we live. Market forecasts by supposed experts are sometimes right, often wrong, and usually mixed."[42] The buyer had either overlooked or recognized and rejected as significant such potential price fluctuations. In *Bernina Distributors Inc.*,[43] the importer claimed it should not be bound by the mismatch between the prices to be paid and received because it

[40] 931 F.2d 1112 (6th Cir. 1991).
[41] 122 Ill. App.3d 940, 461 N.E.2d 1049 (Ill. App. 1984).
[42] 122 Ill. App.3d 940, 952.
[43] 646 F.2d 434 (10th Cir. 1981).

was "unaware of the risk of an exchange rate fluctuation" and "ignorant of the term of the contract (as construed by the trial court)."[44] Because the importer was aware of currency fluctuations, it had not overlooked their potential; rather, it did not appreciate or appreciated and rejected their importance to the transaction. The importer seemingly incorrectly processed correct information about exchange rate fluctuations to reach the wrong conclusion about the significance of their risks.

MARKET CHANGE RISK MANAGEMENT

Diligence

Diligence on market changes has the same objectives as that on uncontrollable events: to identify, assess, and determine the potential changes that should be considered as hazards for purposes of the transaction; which, if any, such changes have already occurred at contract formation; and which, if any such changes might occur after contract formation. Because courts are nearly always hostile to claims that failures to perform should be excused because market changes made performance or benefit realization more onerous, expensive, or impossible, identifying and allocating responsibility for the risk of such a change is all the more important to a transaction participant who would expect to be excused or compensated. Just as it is outside the scope of this text to explain what diligence on such events should be undertaken in any specific or specific type of transaction, it is beyond the scope of this book to explain the diligence that should be undertaken on market changes in any transaction or type of transaction.

Firm Commitments

Like risks of an uncontrollable event, responsibility for the risk of an adverse market change is allocated, first, by a commitment to perform or complete a task, notwithstanding such a change; second, when applicable, one or more of the legal doctrines of unilateral and mutual mistake, supervening impossibility and impracticability, and frustration of purpose; and third, by an express term included in a contract that is intended to allocate responsibility for such risk. A commitment to complete a task includes an assumption of responsibility for the risk that

[44] 646 F.2d 434, 439.

a market change may adversely affect completion. The commitment is overridden by the legal principles of unilateral and mutual mistake, supervening impossibility and impracticability, and frustration of purpose; when applicable, performance is discharged. The commitment and such legal principles may be further overridden by an express contractual term that stipulates when a market change excuses performance.

In principle, arrangements and terms similar to those used to manage uncontrollable events risks can be used to manage market change risks; the principal devices that allocate market change risks are conditions precedent and subsequent, obligor and third-party covenants, representations and warranties, and force majeure clauses.

Fixed or Minimum Offtake and Supply. Responsibility for the risk that the market demand for or the offtake of an item might be less at the time of sale than the level anticipated at contract formation can be allocated to one or more offtakers by having it or them commit in advance of their procurement to buy such items instead of a seller disposing of them on the open market as and when it decides to sell them. By covenanting to buy an item at some time after contract formation, the buyer who expects to resell it assumes responsibility for the risk that the demand in the market for it may at the time of purchase be less than was anticipated at contract formation. A take-or-pay contract is an example of such an offtake contract: an offtaker agrees to pay for a fixed or minimum amount when it elects to accept delivery of less than an agreed or minimum quantity of such items. The take-or-pay or other contract to buy a fixed or minimum quantity allocates only responsibility for offtake risk; it does not allocate or mitigate responsibility for the risk prices that might fluctuate.

Resources Investment Co. v. Enron Corp.[45] illustrates such an arrangement: sellers and buyers entered into 32 contracts over 18 years for the sale and purchase of natural gas. Each contract included typical take-or-pay obligations, by providing that if in any year the buyers did not accept delivery of the amount specified to be purchased during that year, the deficiency in purchases would nonetheless be paid for. Provision was made for gas paid for but not used to be carried forward to subsequent years. In response to a sharp downturn in demand for natural gas, the buyers stopped taking delivery of the minimum quantities and failed to make the payments for those quantities under the contracts, claiming the take-or-pay obligations violated public policy (burdening consumers contrary

[45] 669 F. Supp. 1038 (Colo. 1987).

to certain statutes), were unconscionable (imposing oppressive terms), constituted penalties, were based on a mistake of fact (unexpected changes in demand), and were discharged by the impossibility and frustration principles and the force majeure clause (due to changes in demand for natural gas). The buyers' claims implied that the take-or-pay clause was ineffective to allocate responsibility for the risk of a drop in demand for natural gas; responsibility for that risk was shared by buyers and sellers, and the former could terminate when demand dropped. The sellers' successful claim that termination was not permitted implied the buyers had assumed responsibility for the risk of changes in demand for natural gas.[46]

The mirror image of the offtake risk allocation effected by a take-or-pay contract is the supply risk allocation effected by a deliver-or-pay contract. The risk that the available supply in the market of an item might be less at the time of purchase than the level of supply anticipated at contract formation can be allocated to one or more suppliers by having them commit in advance of their delivery to sell and deliver such items instead of buying them on the open market. By covenanting to sell an item at some time after contract formation, the seller who expects to buy it beforehand assumes responsibility for the risk that the available supply in the market for it may at the time of sale be less than was anticipated at contract formation. A deliver-or-pay contract is an example of such a supply contract: a seller agrees to pay a fixed or minimum amount when it fails to deliver an agreed or minimum quantity of such items over an agreed period of time. As with the take-or-pay contract, the deliver-or-pay or other contract to sell a fixed or minimum quantity allocates only supply risk; it does not allocate or mitigate the risk that prices to be paid might fluctuate.

A contract can combine take-or-pay and deliver-or-pay arrangements, and a contract that commits a seller to sell and a buyer to buy a fixed quantity is a foundation for such arrangements. The buyer commits to buy a minimum quantity of an item over a period of time or pay a fixed amount, thereby assuming responsibility for the risk that demand for such item will be less than at the time of sale. The seller commits

[46] "The purpose of the take-or-pay clauses is to apportion the risks of natural gas production and sales between the buyer and seller. The seller bears the risk of production. To compensate seller for that risk, buyer agrees to take, or pay for if not taken, a minimum quantity of gas. The buyer bears the risk of market demand. The take-or-pay clause insures that if the demand for gas goes down, seller will still receive the price for the Contract Quantity delivered each year." Universal Resources Corporation v. Panhandle Eastern Pipe Line Company, 813 F.2d 77, 80 (5th Cir. 1987); *quoted at* 669 F. Supp. 1038, 1041.

to sell a minimum quantity of such item over the same period of time or pay a fixed amount, thereby assuming responsibility for the risk the available supply will be less at the time of sale. Either risk allocation can be unilateral, rather than reciprocal, by using an option: a contract can grant a seller a right without an obligation, or an option, to sell a minimum quantity of items to a buyer, in which event the buyer assumes responsibility for the offtake risk as described in the take-or-pay arrangement, but until the option is exercised, the seller does not assume responsibility for the supply risk as described in the deliver-or-pay arrangement. A contract can grant a buyer a right without an obligation, or an option, to buy a minimum quantity of items from a seller, in which event the seller assumes responsibility for the supply risk as described in the deliver-or-pay arrangement; but until the option is exercised, the buyer does not assume responsibility for the offtake risk as described in the take-or-pay arrangement.

Fixed Offtake and Supply Prices. Responsibility for the risk that the price that a seller can obtain from its offtaker in the market at the time it sells an item will be less than the price that at contract formation was expected for such sale is allocated by having an offtaker agree to buy at a fixed price. The offtaker by covenanting to buy at a fixed price assumes responsibility for the risk that the market value of the item it buys will be lower at the time of purchase than the market price. It assumes responsibility for the risk of such adverse changes in the market price of the item. Without such commitment from its offtaker, the seller bears responsibility for the risk the price it will receive for its product in the market will be lower than anticipated.

Health-Chem Corp. v. Baker[47] illustrates how a fixed price protects one party against and exposes another party to market changes in price. To settle a shareholder dispute, a principal shareholder of a publicly traded company resigned as director and agreed to sell his shares to the company over a period of time for $13.50 per share. The company wanted to avoid a single sale or even a series of sales of the stock over a short period, as these might have precipitated a drop in the share price. Shortly after contract formation, in October 1987, the stock market crashed. The company's share price dropped to $3.875. The company sued the shareholder to amend the contract, claiming mutual mistake of fact, commercial impracticability, and frustration of purpose. The chance share prices would drop after contract formation was a risk to one or both

[47] 915 F.2d 805 (2d Cir. 1990).

parties. To the shareholder the risk was that it would receive less over time if the price dropped and it was paid the market price for his shares; to the company the risk was that it would overpay if the price dropped and it paid a fixed price for the shares. If the shareholder bore responsibility for the risk that share prices would drop, as the company's claim implied, the shareholder would have remained obligated to sell its shares but at the lower market price; the fixed price would have been effectively overridden by the frustration doctrine. The shareholder's successful claim that the commitment to pay the fixed price was unaffected by the change in the share price in the market and not subject to the frustration doctrine implied that the company assumed responsibility for the risk of a price drop.[48] The case illustrates how a fixed price contract allocates responsibility for the risk in scenario (1)(a)(i) and the zero-sum game implicit in such risk allocation.

The mirror image of the offtake price risk allocation effected by a fixed price offtake contract is the supply price risk allocation effected by a fixed price supply contract. The risk that the price that a buyer must pay in the market at the time an item is bought for use or resale will be higher than the price at contract formation is allocated by having a supplier agree to sell at a fixed price. The supplier by covenanting to sell at a fixed price assumes responsibility for the risk that the market value of the item it sells will be higher at the time of sale than the market price. It assumes responsibility for the risk of adverse changes in the market price of the item. Without such commitment from its supplier, the buyer bears responsibility for the risk the price it will pay for an input in the market will be higher than anticipated.

The following illustrate supply arrangements that allocate supply price risk as previously described:

- *Louisiana Power & Light Co. v. Allegheny Ludlum Industries, Inc.*[49]: A supplier agreed to supply tubes for a fixed price, subject to increases of three percent if shipment was ordered between 30 and 36 months after contract formation and 10 percent if shipment was delayed beyond that time. Fifteen months after contract formation, the supplier asked for a price increase because its costs had increased: for example, electrolytic nickel, low carbon ferrochrome, and labor had increased 24 percent, 185 percent, and 21 percent, respectively. The buyer responded, demanding

[48] The district court granted the shareholder summary judgment on these issues.
[49] 517 F. Supp. 1319 (E.D. Lou. 1981).

assurances the supplier would perform. The supplier claimed its performance was excused by mutual mistake and commercial impracticability. The increase in the prices of raw materials and labor was a risk to both parties. If the buyer bore responsibility for the risk of extraordinary price increases, as implied in the supplier's claim, the buyer would have had to buy the tubes at the higher prices; the mutual mistake doctrine, about the extent to which prices would rise, would have trumped the risk allocation in the fixed price and adjustment clauses. As the buyer successfully claimed, the supplier had to sell at the agreed prices, implying that responsibility for the risk of price increases beyond those contemplated in the contract had been assumed by the seller.[50] The case illustrates how a fixed price contract allocates responsibility for the risk in scenario (1)(b)(iii)(B)(II) and the zero-sum game in such price risk allocation.

- *Aluminum Corporation of America v. Essex Group, Inc.*[51]: Alcoa agreed to smelt alumina for Essex for twenty years, beginning in 1968. Essex agreed to pay Alcoa initially fifteen cents per pound, a fee that consisted of two components: a demand component of five cents per pound, which would increase in proportion to changes in the Engineering News Record Construction Cost-20 Cities Average Index published in the *Engineering News Record*, and a production component of ten cents per pound, which itself consisted of three components—a fixed component of four cents per pound, a nonlabor production cost component of three cents per pound, which was to be varied in proportion to periodic changes in the Wholesale Price Index-Industrial Commodities (WPI-IC) published by the Bureau of Labor Statistics of the United States Department of Labor, and a labor production cost component of three cents per pound, which was to be varied in proportion to periodic changes in Alcoa's average hourly labor cost at the Warrick, Indiana, works. The adjusted price was also subject to an overall "cap" price of 65 percent of the price of a specified type of aluminum sold on specified terms, as published in a trade journal, *American Metal Market*. Alcoa's purpose was to ensure that the price paid by Essex

[50] The alleged mutual mistake was that the clauses providing for escalation of the price would be sufficient to cover the supplier's cost increases, and the commercial impracticability was the assumption that labor and material would not rise so sharply. The district court, granted the buyer's motion for summary judgment on both issues. *Id.* at 1326.

[51] 499 F. Supp. 53 (W.D. Pa. 1980).

covered increases in its production costs, while preserving its net income covered in the fixed component of four cents per pound. Beginning in 1973, Alcoa's electricity costs rose much faster than allowed for in the WPI-IC because increased oil costs forced utilities to raise electricity rates. Alcoa estimated that instead of making an annual profit of $6,000,000, it would lose $60,000,000 over the remaining term of the contract. Each price component allocated to Alcoa responsibility for the risk that the price it would pay for labor, materials, and services included in such component in the market would exceed the amount by which it could increase its price to Essex. The overall cap further allocated responsibility for the risk to Alcoa that the aggregate of its cost increases might exceed that cap. Alcoa, Essex unsuccessfully argued, had superior knowledge of its costs in operating the Warwick facility and knew the inherent risks in proposing the WPI-IC as the index for adjusting for nonlabor costs. It chose to protect itself against the fluctuations in nonlabor costs measured by the WPI-IC and to leave itself exposed to the risk of fluctuations that were not measured by that index. According to Essex, "[T]he parties made a calculated gamble with full awareness that the future was uncertain, so the contract should be enforced despite the mutual mistake."[52] Alcoa argued that the contract should be reformed, as it was based on a mutually mistaken assumption: the variation in nonlabor costs would not vary from the WPI-IC by more than five percent. This cap was nowhere stated in the contract. Implicit in this claim was that the limitations on price adjustments in the component formula and overall cap was subject to the mutual mistake doctrine, and as it bore that risk, Essex bore responsibility for the risk of the increase in nonlabor costs above five percent. The case illustrates how the limitations in a formula-based price may be functionally equivalent to a fixed price in allocating responsibility for supply price risk in scenario (1)(b)(iii)(B)(III) and also how such risk allocation can be trumped by the mutual mistake doctrine.[53]

---

[52] *Id.* at 68.

[53] Alcoa and Essex had acknowledged the risk that nonlabor costs could deviate significantly from the WPI-IC, assessed the probability of the risk occurring to be low, and chose not to address it. The judge concluded that "the absence of an express floor limitation can only be understood to imply that the parties deemed the risk too remote and their meaning too clear to trifle with additional negotiation and drafting." *Id.* at 69.

Either price risk allocation can be unilateral, rather than reciprocal, by using an option: A contract can grant a seller an option or a "put" to sell items to a buyer at a fixed price, in which event the buyer assumes responsibility for the risk that the price it pays will be higher than the market price at the time of sale, but the seller does not assume responsibility for the risk that market prices at the time of sale will be higher than the contract price because it has no commitment to sell until it exercises the option to sell. A contract can grant a buyer an option to buy items from a seller at a fixed price, in which event the seller assumes responsibility for the risk the price at which it sells will be lower than the market price at the time of sale, but the buyer does not assume responsibility for the risk that market prices at the time of sale will be higher than the contract price because it has no commitment to buy until it exercises the option to buy.

Inflation Adjustment. The risk that inflation will reduce the value or relative purchasing power of a partly or wholly fixed price that a seller can obtain over the period it sells to the offtaker is allocated by adjusting that price to reflect inflation. The choice of an index to measure inflation is itself a risk: the index may understate or not be a measure of the true extent of the inflation that affects the seller, and the offtaker assumes responsibility for the risk that such adjustment overstates inflation. As with any fixed price, the offtaker by covenanting to buy at price adjusted for inflation also assumes the risk that the inflation adjusted price will exceed the market value of the item.

The following cases illustrate how clauses adjust for inflation and how they are themselves subject to risks:

- *Printing Industries of Northern Ohio, Inc. v. International Printing and Graphics Communications Union, Local No. 56*[54]: Collective bargaining contracts between employers and the unions provided for a two cent per hour cost of living adjustment to the employees' wages for each one-point increase in the Consumer Price Index for Urban Wage Earners and Clerical Workers, new series, for Cleveland, Ohio (Cleveland CPI-W). In 1982, the U.S. Bureau of Labor Standards expanded the geographic reach of its sample beyond the Greater Cleveland area because too few home sales

[54] 584 F. Supp. 990 (N.D. Ohio 1984).

were recorded in the Greater Cleveland area over the relevant period. The result was that the variance between National CPI-W and the Cleveland CPI-W increased from 3.7 points to 17.9 points in 1982 and 21.5 points in 1983. The adjustment clause protected the union members against inflation eroding their wages. What the clause did not expressly cover were changes to the data used to calculate the index stipulated to be used in that clause, which changes were distinct uncontrollable events, creating still another risk that a governmental agency would modify calculation of Cleveland CPI-W, thereby reducing or increasing the annual adjustment. The employers' organization sued to reform the contract, claiming mutual mistake of fact and frustration of purpose: that the Cleveland CPI-W no longer represented a cost of living adjustment but effected a wage increase the employers would not have accepted. The employers' claim implied that they had not assumed responsibility for the risk that changes in the calculation of index could increase wage increases above those that would have been made in the absence of such change. They were entitled to continue paying wage increases as if no change had been made. The union's successful claim implied that each party by agreeing to the clause assumed responsibility for the risk of adverse changes and were not subject to the mutual mistake doctrine. In this instance, the employers suffered the loss.[55]

- *Waegemann v. Montgomery Ward & Co.*[56]: A commercial lease for ten years, followed by two additional five-year terms at the tenant's option, provided that the rent would be increased annually by the percentage by which the real estate taxes on the property were increased. Because property values were annually appraised by assessors to calculate real property taxes, the adjustment clause reflected the increase in property values, which were likely higher than inflation. During the initial 10-year term, Proposition 13 passed by referendum in California, limiting increases in real estate valuations to two percent per year. Accordingly, rent increases under the lease were also limited. The landlord sued for a declaration that the lease was no longer binding, its purpose having been frustrated by

[55] The court found that the employers' organization had not proved that it was an assumption of the contract that the Cleveland CPI-W would not deviate from the National CPI-W or the parties intended that the union members enjoy a cost of living adjustment that would accurately and closely reflect the inflation rate in Cleveland.

[56] 713 F.2d 452 (9th Cir. 1983).

the limitation on rent increases that was an unintended consequence of Proposition 13. The landlord's claim implied that the adjustment clause, while allocating inflation risk, did not allocate responsibility for the risk that a change in law would modify how property value increases would be measured for the purpose of calculating real estate taxes; responsibility for that risk was shared by the parties, and the landlord was entitled to terminate the lease. The tenant's response, accepted by the court, implied that the risk allocation effected by the clause had not been trumped by the frustration doctrine. In this instance the landlord suffered the losses.[57]

Conditions Precedent and Subsequent

Conditions precedent and subsequent can allocate market change risks. A condition precedent can state an obligor has no obligation to perform until a market change that must occur has occurred or a market change that must not occur has not occurred; the failure of such a condition allows the obligor to terminate the contract, in which event each party is responsible for its own losses unless otherwise specified in the contract. A condition subsequent can state that an obligor may suspend, terminate, or reopen the negotiation of the terms of its obligation to perform upon the occurrence of a market change that must not occur or upon the nonoccurrence of a market change that must occur by a date certain. Conditions precedent and subsequent can thus be used to allocate responsibility for all market change risks, usually, but not always, to both parties, because termination will ordinarily result in both parties losing their investment in the transaction without further liability to each other.

Pan Am Corp. v. Delta Air Lines, Inc.[58] illustrates how a condition can allocate responsibility for risks of market changes. Delta agreed to purchase certain of Pan Am's routes and assets and to extend credit to Pan Am, subject to certain conditions, one of which was that since the date of the agreement "there shall have been no material adverse change in the business, financial position, results of operations or prospects of . . . [Pan Am's business remaining after the acquisition]."[59] Between the contract formation and scheduled sale dates, Pan Am's revenues and projected

[57] The court denied relief to the landlord, holding frustration was available only when "the difference [between what had been and what was now required] be so excessive as to make performance extremely impracticable." *Id.* at 454.

[58] 175 B.R. 438 (Bankr. S.D.N.Y. 1994).

[59] *Id.* at 492.

revenues declined materially more than forecast: for example, in November 1991 Pan Am reduced its revenue forecast prepared only two months earlier by $19.5 million or 17.1 percent. Passenger demand for Pan Am's flights declined dramatically during these and the following months. Delta successfully claimed a material adverse change in Pan Am's business and financial condition had occurred, and it was not obligated to close the sale. The condition allocated to both Delta and Pan Am responsibility for the risk that the demand for its flights would decrease between the dates of contract formation and sale. Delta was not obligated to complete the sale or compensate the other for the failed transaction.[60] Nor was Delta entitled to compensation from Pan Am. The case illustrates how a condition precedent allocates a scenario (1)(a)(i) risk for the occurrence of a change that was not to occur: a drop in demand for a Pan Am's products reduced its value to Delta, the buyer of a portion its business.

Force Majeure Clauses

Force majeure clauses have been invoked by parties to excuse their failure to perform when market changes have adversely affected their realization of the anticipated benefits or their completion of tasks. Such parties usually confront difficult challenges in doing so: First, the litany of trigger events in a force majeure clause—earthquakes, hurricanes, strikes, and the like—do not usually include any of the adverse market changes previously described. In principle, a force majeure clause could be, and on occasion has been, expanded to include them. Second, with the exception of unavailability of supply in the market and financial distress, none of the hazards previously described render the obligor unable to perform or otherwise prevent it from performing. Any pressure on an obligor not to perform is financial or economic. Third, almost none of the market changes previously described is truly unforeseeable. The usual requirement that an uncontrollable event must be unforeseeable would have to be omitted from and not otherwise implied in the force majeure clause.

Drop in Demand or Offtake. A drop in demand for an item an obligor expects to sell in the market to realize the benefit of a procurement contract will present a difficult choice but not necessarily impair its ability to perform the procurement contract. Because the value of the

[60] The bankruptcy court found this condition was not satisfied because after contract formation Pan Am's revenues and projected revenues had declined materially more than forecast.

procurement contract to the obligor depends upon its realizing in sales to offtakers in the market the value of what it procures, it will have to choose between procuring items it cannot resell (and realize value therefrom) and thus performing and avoiding losses on such procurement but breaching. Since it remains able to perform, it is not disabled by the drop in offtake.

Sabine Corp. v. ONG Western, Inc.[61] illustrates the difficulty of using a force majeure clause to allocate responsibility for a drop in demand risk. A buyer agreed to take or pay for a minimum quantity of gas to be supplied by the supplier each year. When demand from the buyer's customers dropped, partly due to energy conservation and partly due to the availability of gas at lower prices from other suppliers, the buyer claimed its obligation to take or pay for the minimum was excused under the force majeure clause, which listed the usual events but did not specifically mention changes in demand or price for gas.[62] For the buyer's claim to succeed, the force majeure clause had to be interpreted to include such market changes as force majeure events and to apply when those changes did not impair its ability to perform but presented it with a costly choice between performing and losing on purchases of gas that could not be resold at a price that would yield a profit and breaching and avoiding those losses. Both conclusions would have been a far stretch to reach in the facts of the case.[63] In addition, the force majeure clause had to trump the take-or-pay clause. The buyer's claim implied the parties shared the risk that demand for the buyer's gas would drop, allowing the buyer to terminate the contract, whereas the seller's claim, accepted by the court, implied that the buyer had expressly assumed responsibility for that risk when it agreed to the take-or-pay clause.[64]

---

[61] 725 F. Supp. 1157 (W.D. Okl. 1989).

[62] *Id.* at 1166.

[63] The court, while acknowledging demand for the buyer's gas had shrunk, concluded demand was still sufficient to keep the contract effective. "While Defendant has submitted evidence that it has lost some of its customers and that its customer base is smaller, it is implicit in affidavits submitted by Defendant and in Defendant's arguments that Defendant has customers who still need a supply of gas and that its parent's division, as a public utility, is still obligated to supply customers with gas." *Id.* at 1179.

[64] The court held that neither a decline in demand nor price was a force majeure event within the meaning of the clause. "[T]he Court must reject an interpretation of the force majeure clause which would render the take-or-pay and price redetermination provisions, pursuant to which Defendant ONG clearly assumed the risk of a decline in market demand and market price." *Id.* at 1171. *See also* Great Lakes Transmission Ltd. Partnership v. Essar Steel Minnesota, LLC, *supra* note 10. The force majeure clause in the contract read, "Neither Shipper nor Transporter shall be liable in damages to the other for any act, omission or circumstances occasioned by or in consequence of: any acts of God, strikes, lockouts, acts

However, a drop in offtake can be devastating to an obligor's financial ability, as when it is nearly total or total, and the obligor is entirely or nearly entirely dependent upon that offtake to survive financially; the obligor will likely become insolvent and unable to pay its supplier (or for that matter any other party). It is unable to perform financial obligations, and that inability is the result of market change in demand for its products. A force majeure clause constructed to apply to such scenario would have to include insolvency as equivalent to an inability to perform.

Compare the following cases in which efforts were made to shoehorn financial distress into the list of events excused under force majeure clauses:

- *Urban Archaeology Ltd. v. 207 East 57th Street LLC*[65]: The tenant agreed to lease premises for 10 years, intending to operate an upscale store for the sale of luxury goods. A year later, the 2008 financial crisis occurred, demand for its products severely dropped, and the tenant became financially unable to pay the rent and claimed its delay in doing so was excused under the force majeure clause. The force majeure clause in the lease provided:

  > The obligation of each party hereunder to perform all of the covenants and agreements hereunder on the part of such party to be performed shall be excused by the period of

of the public enemy, wars, blockages, insurrections, riots, epidemics, landslides, lightning, earthquakes, fires, storms, floods, washouts, arrests and restraints of rulers and peoples, civil disturbances, explosions, breakage or accident to machinery or lines of pipe, line freeze ups, . . . or the binding order of any court or governmental authority which has been resisted in good faith by all reasonable legal means, and any other cause, whether the kind herein enumerated or otherwise. . . ." *Id.* at 851–52. The shipper sued for a declaration that the contract was no longer enforceable because the facility could not be built, financing being unavailable because of the financial crisis. The supplier moved to dismiss for failure to state a cause of action. The court granted the motion. Judge Susan Richard Nelson held the force majeure clause inapplicable because financial crisis was not included in the list of force majeure events, the contract expressly stated that payment obligations were not excused, and the contract was for the transportation of gas and did not state it was conditioned upon the construction of the facility. She similarly dismissed the shipper's commercial impracticability defense. "It was completely foreseeable that ESML [the shipper] might not secure the necessary financing for the Nashwauk facility. Given that possibility, MSI/ESML could have conditioned its performance on obtaining such financing. It failed to do so." *Id.* at 858.

65 34 Misc.3d 1222(A), 951 N.Y.S.2d 84 (Table), 2009 WL 8572326 (N.Y. Sup.), 2009 NY Slip Op 52825(U) (N.Y. Sup. Ct. 2009), *aff'd.* 68 A.D.3d 562, 891 N.Y.S.2d 63. (N.Y. App. 2009).

> Unavoidable Delay, as it relates to the particular obligation affected by such Unavoidable Delay and such party's inability to perform shall not relieve the other party of its obligations to perform under this Lease.[66]

The lease defined an "Unavoidable Delay" as

> a delay resulting from strikes or labor troubles or accident, or from any cause whatsoever beyond Landlord or Tenant's reasonable control (other than Landlord or Tenant's financial hardship), including, but not limited to, acts of foreign and/or domestic terrorism, laws, governmental preemption in connection with national emergency or by reason of any requirements of any governmental authority, or by reason of the conditions of supply and demand which have been or are affected by war or other emergency.[67]

While the definition specifically included "supply and demand," it also specifically included the words "other than Landlord or Tenant's financial hardship." The parties contemplated events such as a downturn in the economy resulting in hardship could occur but excluded it from the clause. This implied that responsibility for the risk of a downturn so reducing demand for the tenant's products that it could not pay rent was thus allocated to the tenant.

- *In re Old Carco (f/k/a Chrysler LLC)*[68]: In 2000, Chrysler agreed with a city and a county in Ohio to invest in and to exercise reasonable efforts to retain a number of full-time positions at a plant located there. The city and county each agreed to grant a 50 percent tax exemption for eligible new tangible personal property acquired in conjunction with the project. Following the bankruptcy and reorganization of Chrysler during the 2008–2009 financial crisis, in 2010 Chrysler decided the plant was too financially burdensome to keep open. The drop in demand for its cars resulted in the benefits of operating the Ohio plant and the corresponding contracts with

---

[66] 2009 NY Slip Op 52825(U), at 3.
[67] 2009 NY Slip Op 52825(U) at 3–4.
[68] 452 B.R. 100, 55 Bankr. Ct. Dec. 72 (S.D.N.Y. 2011).

the city and county having little or no value to Chrysler. However, the force majeure clauses in the contract with the city and county required that Chrysler be unable to perform to be excused:

> [Chrysler] shall not be considered . . . in default in the performance of its obligations under this agreement as a result of any cause beyond its reasonable control, including but not limited to severe and unusual weather, acts of God, or explosion, riot, acts of civil disobedience or sabotage, *change to economic conditions and productivity* and technological changes, power failures or shortages, restraint by court order or order of public authority, action or omission by any government agency, labor strikes or other labor disturbances[69] (emphasis added).

For the clause to excuse the plant closure and repudiation of the agreements with the city and county, as Chrysler successfully claimed it did, first, the drop in demand for Chrysler's cars had to be a "change to economic conditions and productivity." That claim seemed superficially plausible: a drop in demand for cars is a change in the economic conditions for a car manufacturer. Nowhere is there any comment about how much the drop must be for it to qualify under the clause. Second, Chrysler's default had to be "as a result" of such conditions. That implied a causal link. One interpretation would be that the change in conditions either disabled or rendered Chrysler unable to perform. The logic of such a claim would be that Chrysler had insufficient funds to continue its operations at the Ohio plant and elsewhere; as a result, it had to choose which operations to continue. That economic compulsion had to satisfy the causal requirement. Chrysler's successful claim implied that the force majeure clause allocated responsibility for the risk of Chrysler having to make such a choice to the city and county.[70] While the case illustrates a successful application of a

---

[69] *Id.* at 107.

[70] The court held that while economic considerations would not normally excuse a failure to perform, in this case, where the clause expressly mentions "change to economic conditions," such considerations would excuse where they caused the plant's closure. *Id.* at 119–20. The court found the financial crisis of 2008–2009 qualified as "change to economic conditions." It also found that such events were beyond Chrysler's control.

force majeure clause to a downturn in demand for products, it also illustrates how far the logic of the clause must be stretched to achieve that result.

Short Supply. A supply shortage can more directly preclude an obligor from performing an obligation. Such an obligor cannot procure an item that it must have to perform; as a result, it cannot perform. Its inability may be due to a change in the market: suppliers previously willing are no longer willing to supply, and other potential suppliers have not stepped in to cover the gap. Its inability may be due to suppliers no longer willing to supply the obligor. Where they once judged the obligor as eligible or qualified to buy, they no longer do so. A force majeure clause constructed to apply to the former scenario would have to include a short supply that results in the unavailability in the market of the required item. It would allow an obligor to be excused only where no one can procure the required item. A force majeure clause constructed to apply to the latter scenario would have to include changes in suppliers' attitudes toward the obligor. It could more liberally allow an obligor to be excused even though other buyers can procure the item in the market. It is disabled by a market change when other firms would not. The distinction between the two clauses is also analogous to objective and subjective impossibility and infeasibility and inability. Force majeure clauses can thus be used to allocate supply shortages.

Kel Kim Corp.[71] illustrates the challenge of using a force majeure clause to allocate a supply shortage risk. The case is previously summarized.[72] A tenant who operated a roller skating rink could not procure public liability insurance consistent with the lease terms. The force majeure clause in the lease excused either party's failure to perform if such performance was "delayed or prevented . . . by reason of labor disputes,

---

The court forged the causal link between such events, and the plant closure by finding Chrysler had "little or no choice" but to close the plant: "Further, the determination by New Chrysler not to continue operations at the Plant was simply a business decision of New Chrysler based on its anticipated production needs. The substantial carrying costs associated with the Plant would have rendered Old Carco's retention of the Plant impossible, or at the least, unreasonably expensive. . . . Absent a continuation of the license agreement with New Chrysler or some other similar arrangement, Old Carco, having no business to conduct at the Plant, and in the process of liquidating all its remaining assets, was left without any alternative except to close the Plant." *Id.* at 124–25.

[71] 70 N.Y.2d 900, 524 N.Y.S.2d 384, 519 N.E.2d 295 (N.Y. 1987).

[72] See text accompanying notes 22 and 23.

inability to procure materials, . . . Acts of God, or other similar causes beyond the control of such party."[73] The clause did not specifically mention an inability to procure insurance. For the clause to have applied to the tenant's failure to procure the required insurance, as the tenant claimed, either "inability to procure materials" or "other similar causes" had to include such inability or the unwillingness of insurers to insure the tenant even if insurers were willing to insure operations similar to the tenant's.[74] The tenant's claim that the force majeure clause excused the insurance requirement so long as it could not procure the required insurance implied that responsibility for the risk of a supply shortage was borne by the landlord, as the tenant could continue to enjoy the benefits of the lease without having to perform the excused obligation.

Price Changes. Similar to a drop in demand, a drop in price for an item, the sale of which is anticipated to yield the buyer the benefit of its procurement contract with its supplier, presents that party with a difficult choice but does not impair its ability to perform the procurement contract. This predicament exists only where the price received for its item is less than the price it pays for that item or the input to make the item. The buyer must choose between procuring items it cannot resell at the anticipated price (and thus realize anticipated value therefrom) and performing and avoiding losses on such procurement but breaching. Because it remains able to perform, it is not disabled by the drop in offtake. A force majeure clause constructed to apply to the former scenario would have to include a reduced price from offtakers as a force majeure event. It might allow a buyer to be excused only when the drop in price subjects the buyer to financial pressure or severe financial pressure to make such choice. Such a clause would acknowledge the buyer is

---

[73] The complete force majeure clause read, "If either party to this Lease shall be delayed or prevented from the performance of any obligation through no fault of their own by reason of labor disputes, inability to procure materials, failure of utility service, restrictive governmental laws or regulations, riots, insurrection, war, adverse weather, Acts of God, or other similar causes beyond the control of such party, the performance of such obligation shall be excused for the period of the delay." 70 N.Y.2d at 902, footnote.

[74] "Here, of course, the contractual provision does not specifically include plaintiff's inability to procure and maintain insurance. Nor does this inability fall within the catchall 'or other similar causes beyond the control of such party.' The principle of interpretation applicable to such clauses is that the general words are not to be given expansive meaning; they are confined to things of the same kind or nature as the particular matters mentioned." *Id.* at 903.

not disabled from performing by the drop in offtake prices and being confronted with such difficult choice is sufficient to excuse a decision not to perform. Such a clause might omit the requirement of financial pressure on the obligor and excuse its decision not to perform because doing so would be unprofitable or highly unprofitable. The difficulty of obtaining agreement to such a clause may be a reason why the wording in the force majeure clause *In re Old Carco (f/k/a Chrysler LLC)*[75] referred to an inability to perform.

Seaboard Lumber Co. v. United States[76] illustrates an effort to apply a force majeure clause to such a drop in prices. A contractor agreed to cut, remove, and pay a fixed price for a quantity of timber on US Forest Service lands. Prices for lumber dropped after contract formation due to depressed demand for lumber in the housing market. Deregulation of savings and loan institutions and the imposition of monetary controls may have contributed to the drop in demand for lumber. The contractor refused to perform, claiming force majeure, impossibility, commercial impracticability, and frustration of contract. The force majeure clause excused delays in performance due to one or more of events listed in the clause.[77] For the force majeure clause to apply, the trigger events would have had to include the changes in government policy affecting the economy generally and lumber prices specifically. The clause would also have had to apply when the contractor had to choose between performing and thus suffering a loss and breaching and avoiding that loss. The lower price did not actually prevent the contractor from cutting and selling timber. The contractor's unsuccessful claim that its contract should have been extended under the force majeure clause implied that the government bore responsibility for the risk of price decreases, as it could neither terminate nor hold the contractor in breach so long as such condition existed.[78]

---

75 452 B.R. 100 (S.D.N.Y. 2011).

76 308 F.3d 1283 (Fed. Cir. 2002).

77 The contract entitled the contractor to an adjustment if it "experiences delay in starting scheduled operations or interruption in active operations either of which stops removal of Included Timber from Sale Area through curtailment in felling and buckling, yarding, skidding and loading, hauling or road construction, as scheduled under B6.31, for 10 or more consecutive calendar days during a Normal Operating Season due to causes beyond Purchaser's control, including but not limited to acts of God, acts of the public enemy, acts of Government, labor disputes, fires, insurrections or floods." *Id.* at 1292.

78 The court's comment on the force majeure defense is illustrative: "Seaboard entered into a fixed-price contract with the Forest Service. The contract allowed for term adjustment if acts of government prevented removal of timber. At most, the government's acts indirectly

An increase in the price a buyer pays its supplier is the mirror image of a decrease in the price the buyer receives from its offtaker. An increase in the price a buyer pays for an item, the sale of which at a fixed price is anticipated to yield the buyer the benefit of its procurement contract with its supplier, presents the buyer with a difficult choice but does not impair its ability to perform the procurement or the offtake contract. This predicament exists where the price received does not at least match the price paid for an item. It may have to choose between procuring items it cannot resell at the anticipated price (and thus realize anticipated value therefrom) and thus performing and avoiding losses on such procurement and thus breaching. Alternatively, it may have to choose between selling items it cannot buy at the anticipated price and thus performing and avoiding losses on such sale but breaching. Since it remains able to perform, it is not disabled by the increase in procurement prices. A force majeure clause constructed to apply to the former scenario would have to include an increased price from suppliers as a force majeure event. It could allow a buyer to be excused when the increase in price subjects it to financial pressure or severe financial pressure to make such choice. Such a clause would acknowledge the buyer is not disabled by the increase in procurement prices and being confronted with the difficult choice is sufficient to excuse a decision not to perform. As in the case of a drop in price for the products a party sells in the market, a force majeure clause might omit the requirement of financial pressure on the obligor and excuse its decision not to perform because doing so would be unprofitable or highly unprofitable. Again, the difficulty of obtaining agreement to such a clause may be a reason why examples of such clause cannot be found.

Hudson v. D & V Mason Contractors, Inc.[79] illustrates an effort to use a force majeure clause to cover the increases in a contractor's labor and material costs. A contractor agreed to build a house for a fixed price. Between the contract formation and scheduled completion dates, construction costs increased 10 to 15 percent. The contractor notified

made performance of the . . . contract unprofitable. The timber was of sufficient quality, and Seaboard simply made a business decision not to harvest. Timber prices fell and Seaboard must bear this market risk in the absence of contractual language that directs otherwise. For these reasons, the Court of Federal Claims did not err in holding that Seaboard's force majeure defense fails as a matter of law." *Id.* at 1294.

[79] 252 A.2d 166 (Del. Sup. Ct. 1969).

the owner that the work could not be completed at the agreed price but could be at a higher price. Two clauses were relevant. The first read:

> If for any reason Seller's title is not good and marketable and Seller shall be unable to perfect such title, or if for any other reason Seller is unable to construct or complete said premises or make title as herein provided, Seller shall return to the Purchaser the sum or sums paid on account of the purchase price, without interest, and this agreement shall thereupon become cancelled, null and void, and the Seller shall have no further liability whatsoever to Purchaser.[80]

The other clause provided:

> This agreement is conditioned upon the ability of Seller to complete the above described property under conditions similar to those presently existing in the home building industry. If Seller is unable to procure promptly, as and when needed, labor and material required for construction as aforesaid, or if Seller for any reason cannot complete these premises due to any present or future rules, regulations or restrictions (particularly those involving priorities or material allocation) by the federal, state or municipal governments, or their agencies, then, and in any such event, Seller is hereby given the option to cancel this contract upon written notice to Purchaser, in which event the full deposit money shall be returned to Purchaser without interest, and this agreement shall thereupon become cancelled, null and void, and Seller shall have no further liability whatsoever to Purchaser.[81]

For the first clause to apply to the seller's increased labor and materials costs, "any other reason" would have to have included an increase in such costs, and "unable to construct or complete" would have to have included the choice the contractor was compelled to make, between performing and suffering a loss, on one hand, and breaching and avoiding the loss, on the other. For the second clause to apply, "conditions similar to those presently existing in the home building industry" would have to include the labor and material costs at contract formation, and the

---

[80] *Id.* at 168.

[81] *Id.*

second sentence would have to have been inapplicable. No additional requirement would have to be satisfied for the contractor to be excused under the first sentence of the second clause. The report of the case is unclear on whether the contractor simply demanded an increase in price to cover its higher costs or confronted the buyer with a choice: to pay more or suffer termination of the contract. The former implied that the buyer bore the risk of increase labor and material costs, while the latter implied that the parties shared the risk, allowing the contractor to terminate when such costs increased. In either event, the force majeure clause, as the buyer successfully claimed, did not allocate responsibility for the risk.[82]

"Reopener" Clause

As observed in chapter 11, a party may be willing to concede at contract formation that certain uncontrollable events, while not automatically entitling the other party to any specific relief from performance or to compensation or indemnification, may be grounds for a request from the other party to discuss or negotiate an amendment to the contract that grants the other party appropriate relief. Such uncontrollable events can include all market changes: loss or a material deterioration of the benefits, an increase in the costs of performing obligations for the benefit of the other party or completing a task that enables a party to realize its benefits, and delays in such performance, completion, or benefit realization. Such a clause that allows the affected party to request reconsideration of the bargain combines a condition subsequent, the occurrence of an adverse market change, with an agreement to negotiate or agree modified terms. As noted in chapter 11, the party unaffected by the event may be under little or no legal obligation to accommodate the affected party's concerns, but nonetheless it may have good financial and other business reasons for doing so. As with a reopener clause for uncontrollable events, the failure to reach agreement on such relief may leave the affected party in the same position as if the reopener clause had not been included in the contract.

[82] Judge Robert O'Hora applied the rule that the court would construe these clauses against the contractor. He said, "Unavailability of labor and materials and existence of rules and regulations making completion impossible are the only factors which will excuse performance under paragraphs 13 and 26 [quoted above] of the contract. Nowhere does the contract say that increased cost to the Seller will excuse performance." *Id.* at 169.

The alternative procedures for amending a contract so as to entitle a party adversely affected by a market change to relief or compensation for such an event are also comparable to those for a reopener clause for an uncontrollable event: the amendment might be determined by one party, exercising absolute discretion, be proposed by one and accepted by the other, or agreed by both parties. *Novelis Corp. v. Anheuser-Busch, Inc.*[83] illustrates a reopener clause expressly applicable to market changes. Under contracts dating to 1987, Novelis sold Anheuser-Busch, Inc. (A-B) aluminum can sheets at a price calculated using two components: a metal component and a conversion component. The metal component could not be increased above an agreed maximum amount. Another clause stated:

> If during the Term of this Agreement, either party believes that market conditions have changed structurally up or down, in such a manner that causes the current pricing mechanisms to no longer be appropriate, A-B and [Novelis] . . . will meet to discuss a new pricing mechanism with the continued intent to provide competitive pricing to A-B, including without limitation, providing B the Contract Discount set forth above. It is the intent of the parties, however, that if the parties, in each party's sole discretion, are unable to reach a mutually acceptable modification to this Agreement, this Agreement as amended shall remain in full force and effect until the expiration or earlier termination hereof.[84]

In 2008, Novelis invoked this clause, claiming a "rise in energy prices, speculation by hedge funds and other investors, and dramatically increased demand for aluminum from China and other developing countries" had changed the structural price conditions. The parties failed to agree on a new price, and Novelis sued A-B for breach of the obligation to negotiate the new price. The parties clearly identified the risk that Novelis's procurement prices might be higher than could be passed through under the metal component of the price formula. The clause created a condition subsequent that was triggered when a

[83] 559 F. Supp. 2d 877 (N.D. Ohio 2008).

[84] 559 F. Supp. 2d 877, 880.

"party believes that market conditions have changed structurally up or down."[85] Novelis's claim that A-B had to negotiate a change in price implied that A-B bore responsibility for the risk of price increases above the cap on the metal component. In effect, that cap would have been trumped by the mistake of fact, frustration, and impossibility doctrines. A-B's successful motion for summary judgment implied responsibility for the risk of procurement price increases was allocated by the cap to Novelis, notwithstanding the clause for renegotiating the terms. Had the clause allowed either party to terminate upon failure to agree new terms, responsibility for the risk would have been shared; each party would have had to bear the loss of its investment in the transaction to the extent not recovered prior to termination and the loss of anticipated benefits that could not otherwise be earned elsewhere. Had the clause stated how new terms were to be determined, responsibility for the risk would have been allocated to the party disadvantaged by the new terms. The case illustrates how a reopener clause applies to a (1) (b) (iii) (B) (II) market change risk: an increase in the market price a supplier must pay for raw materials to perform its obligations to its buyer can trigger a price reopener in the contract with its buyer, but responsibility for the risk remains as allocated by the price formula unless an alternative price can be formulated. Finally, the case illustrates the value of an express disclaimer, in this instance a clear disclaimer of any commitment by A-B to agree to any changes in the compensation payable to Novelis notwithstanding one or more significant market changes. The disclaimer narrowed the scope of the reopener to discussions, with no commitment to negotiate, let alone to agree to an amendment.

---

[85] The buyer moved for summary judgment. The court granted the motion, finding the buyer had met and discussed changing the price as it was obligated. "Ultimately, these two international corporations negotiated and renegotiated at arm's length a detailed and complex contract governing hundreds of millions of dollars in sales. If they intended the price to automatically change along with market conditions, they would have omitted the price ceiling and explicitly provided in the contract for an adjustment to the price in accordance with the market conditions." Footnotes omitted. 559 F. Supp. 2d 877.

Table of Cases

Index

O

P